WITHDRAWN

THE NATURE OF THEORY AND RESEARCH IN SOCIAL PSYCHOLOGY

THE NATURE OF THEORY AND RESEARCH

IN SOCIAL PSYCHOLOGY

CLYDE HENDRICK and RUSSELL A. JONES
Kent State University *University of Kentucky Medical Center*

ACADEMIC PRESS New York and London

COPYRIGHT © 1972, BY ACADEMIC PRESS, INC.
ALL RIGHTS RESERVED
NO PART OF THIS BOOK MAY BE REPRODUCED IN ANY FORM, BY PHOTOSTAT, MICROFILM, RETRIEVAL SYSTEM, OR ANY OTHER MEANS, WITHOUT WRITTEN PERMISSION FROM THE PUBLISHERS.

ACADEMIC PRESS, INC.
111 Fifth Avenue, New York, New York 10003

United Kingdom Edition published by
ACADEMIC PRESS, INC. (LONDON) LTD.
24/28 Oval Road, London NW1 7DD

LIBRARY OF CONGRESS CATALOG CARD NUMBER: 79-182651

PRINTED IN THE UNITED STATES OF AMERICA

301.107
H384n

CONTENTS

Part II Case Studies in Social Research

PREFACE

The purpose of this book is twofold: to provide advanced undergraduate and graduate students with a solid foundation in the logic of theory construction and the experimental method and to teach students how to read, critically evaluate, and appreciate professional literature in the behavioral sciences. We believe the book is unique in this latter respect and that it will serve a vital need in several different courses.

Basically, the book grew out of our personal experiences during the course of our own education. Most undergraduates are exceedingly naive concerning research reports, tending to accept them literally and uncritically. In the process of becoming a professional, some difficult learning experiences are encountered. Somehow the student has to become a skilled reader and evaluator of the relevant literature. Our observations have been that the acquisition of these skills is largely hit-or-miss. Readings may be assigned and discussed for methodological purposes, but the skill in handling such assignments varies widely. More commonly, the student is simply expected to "pick up" the necessary critical abilities. This book should help take the "hit-or-miss" out of such learning, and put it on a systematic basis.

In writing the book we had psychology students primarily in mind. Our own discipline is social psychology, and all the examples and case studies are drawn from research in this area. However, we have tried to keep the book general enough so that behavioral scientists from other disciplines who have an experimental orientation might also find value in it. It should be suitable for a variety of courses concerned with the nature of research and theory construction in the behavioral sciences. Because of the specific illustrations and examples, the book should, of course, be relevant to most social psychology courses.

The book is organized into two major parts. Part I contains a detailed exposition of the nature of theory and research. We discuss the nature of formal theory, derivation of hypotheses, and the testing of hypotheses. We explicate in great detail the experimental approach to hypothesis testing. Both formal and informal aspects of a psychological experiment are discussed. Throughout this discussion we make our points by examples, including many references to the experiments that follow in Part II. What we try to do in Part I is to provide the student with a basic understanding of the nature of theory and experimental methodology which can then be applied in some detail to the chapters in Part II.

In each of the five chapters in Part II the student is provided with an opportunity to put his analytical skills to use. We have selected five substantive areas from social psychology. Each chapter includes three reprinted journal articles, and the chapter may be considered a "case study" in the analysis of experimental research in a given problem area. Initially in each chapter we give a detailed overview of the problem area or the relevant theoretical positions. We believe that theory and research go hand-in-hand. Thus we present the theoretical concerns in some detail. Following this introduction we present a specific implication of the theoretical area. We then reprint an experimental report relevant to the test of that implication.

The initial experiment is an important one, often generating considerable interest and controversy. Typically there are conflicting or alternative interpretations of the results. For our purposes, such possibilities offer excellent opportunities for pointing out the flaws in the experiment, discussing alternatives, and making various other methodological points. Our discussion leads into the second experiment which tries to solve these problems. We show why and how it fails to do the job completely, thus leading to the third experiment. At the end of each chapter we provide a final summing-up of the research area and evaluate its general progress.

Within each chapter of Part II our editorial comment precedes and follows each article very closely. We believe that having the student read the actual articles plus our editorial comments will result in a rapid sharpening of the student's critical abilities. One value of each of these chapters is that all the experiments are based on a common experimental paradigm. In this way the student can literally see and appreciate the continuity and progress of empirical research. We have not reprinted all the relevant articles in a given area. Indeed, we have carefully selected each article to make various methodological points as well as to provide a sense of continuity in the research area. Thus we hope the book will be a convenient and valuable tool in teaching students how to evaluate professional literature.

The articles reprinted in the case studies generally use an analysis of variance to analyze the data. For those students who have not yet had a statistics course that includes this technique, we have included a brief section on the analysis of variance in Chapter 2. This should be sufficient to provide the student with an intuitive understanding of the reasons for statistical analyses and to enable him to comprehend the summary tables of an analysis of variance so that the Results Sections of the case study reports may be meaningfully read and interpreted.

The final manuscript is a joint product of mutual suggestion and criticism. However, the primary responsibility for writing the various chapters is as follows: Hendrick wrote the five chapters in Part I and Chapters 6 and 7 in Part II. Jones wrote Chapters 8, 9, 10, and 11.

We are indebted to many people who contributed to our efforts in writing this book. Primarily we are indebted to some of our former professors who made us sensitive to the issues involved in the articulation of theory and to the values of the experimental method. We are also grateful to our students for constructive comment and criticism of various portions of the manuscript. A special note of thanks goes to the many authors who allowed us to reprint and criticize their work. Finally, thanks are due to Academic Press, The American Psychological Association, Duke University Press, Rand McNally & Company, The American Educational Research Association, Addison-Wesley Publishing Company, Holt, Rinehart and Winston, Inc., for permission to use material included in this book.

CLYDE HENDRICK

RUSSELL A. JONES

PROLOGUE

The advance of any science depends upon the quality of its research. For those in a specific scientific discipline, learning to read, to evaluate, and to contribute to the literature of that discipline constitutes a major part of their training. These two aspects of scientific training are not independent, and both must be learned. Highly complex skills, not to say some measure of creativity, is involved. Learning to review research critically requires considerable practice. Development of this skill might be compared to learning to evaluate critically a work of art such as a painting. When an individual is naive regarding art, he is likely to give only an overall global evaluation. With training, his perception of a painting gradually becomes more sophisticated and differentiated. He notices the symmetry of the figures, the balance, the use of shades and tints, the perspective, and other techniques. In a similar fashion a student gradually becomes more discriminating in his evaluation of research. We can remember from our own undergraduate and early graduate days our relatively unsophisticated appreciation of research. There was a strong tendency to accept literally everything an author said simply because it was in print. Gradually the realization dawned that some works of research are better than others and that, in fact, some published research is terrible.

It is difficult to point out the specific learning steps involved in becoming a connoisseur of research. One thing that is certain, however, is that a lot of hard work is involved along with a substantial amount of trial-and-error learning. It is our hope that the introduction to the methodology of social research in Part I and the critical evaluation of several areas of research in Part II will provide some insights into how we can reduce the amount of trial-and-error labor involved in becoming proficient in evaluating research.

There are a tremendous number of details one must be concerned with when evaluating a research study. For example, one must ask whether the research really provides a sensitive test of the hypothesis or theory that it purports to test. Indeed, one has to ask the more general question of whether the hypothesis or theory is actually testable. Asking these questions presupposes that one has a good idea of what a hypothesis and a theory are and that one knows the criteria for adequately testing them. These are some of the problems discussed in Part I.

There are many other problems to be considered in evaluating a research study. What kind of subjects were used? How were they used? What specific procedures did the investigator employ? What effects other than those intended might these procedures have had on the subjects? What did the researcher do while he was collecting his data? How might his behavior have influenced the subject in ways, perhaps, that he did not foresee?

Still other considerations are involved. One must always be concerned with the adequacy of a research design. There are usually many ways in which answers to a specific research question can be obtained. The reader will note that all the studies reported in this book are laboratory experiments. Why experiments rather than some other kind of research is certainly a legitimate question. As will be seen, the majority of scientists feel that the experimental method is the most reliable and efficient one for obtaining knowledge. At the same time, the method has its limitations, and these must be borne in mind when evaluating an experiment. One of its major problems is the applicability of its results to everyday life. Also, many important and interesting aspects of social life cannot be studied in the laboratory. It would be difficult to create a carefully controlled mob in the laboratory, and no ethical researcher would attempt to manipulate laboratory variables that might lead to an increase or decrease in suicide attempts. Thus the social relationships created in a laboratory experiment and the ethical considerations stemming from those relationships must be considered when evaluating a research study.

Most of these considerations become second nature to the experienced researcher. He may not consciously think of each and every possibility, but the evaluation is made nevertheless. In the chapters in Part I we try to make explicit as many considerations in evaluating research as we can. In Chapter 1 we consider several aspects of theory and hypothesis testing. These considerations are rather formal although we do not deal with the statistical aspect of experimental designs in any depth because such design problems are thoroughly discussed in most statistics textbooks. Rather, we are concerned with basic problems in science such as the nature of theory and the deduction of hypotheses and how these hypotheses are tested. Chapter 2 is concerned with the interpretation of experimental results. We discuss topics such as alternative interpretations of a hypothesis, null hypothesis results, multiple independent variables, and interactions between variables. Some consideration is given to statistical analysis, primarily the analysis of variance. Most of the experiments reprinted in Part II use this technique for data analysis.

In Chapter 3 we explicitly consider the social nature of a social psychology experiment. Topics such as experimenter–subject role relations, demand characteristics, and experimenter bias are discussed in detail. Chapter 4 is concerned with a variety of practical problems involved in conducting an actual experiment. Problems involved in pretesting, selecting the specific operations and measures to be used, and alternative experimental techniques are discussed. Chapter 5 is concerned with some limitations of the experimental method, particularly the problem of generalizing the experimental results. Sampling problems, internal and external validity, chronic versus acute manipulations of variables, and nonrandom assignment of subjects are some of the problems discussed.

We have not discussed every conceivable issue of theory construction and research in Part I, but we have discussed a great many of them. Clearly our own values determined the positions taken on specific issues. Perhaps our most basic assumption is that the experimental method is preferable to other research strategies and should be used wherever it can be applied. Not everyone would agree with us, and would pursue other viewpoints of the nature of theory and research. As one example, the general research method of participant observation differs considerably from the approach presented in this book. The difference is in terms of the philosophy of scientific procedure as well as of specific research methods (see Bruyn, 1966). Whether the value orientation toward science developed in this book is ultimately accepted, if a better understanding of the experimental approach is gained and can be used in evaluating experimental research, our purpose in writing this book will be well served.

Part I

BASIC ISSUES IN THEORY CONSTRUCTION AND RESEARCH METHODS

Chapter **1**

FORMAL ASPECTS OF THEORY AND HYPOTHESIS TESTING

Our discussion begins with a few remarks concerning the nature of science. Scientific objectives or goals have been variously described, but there are three themes that recur repeatedly: *prediction, understanding,* and *control* of phenomena. We will look at each of these important concepts in turn. In explaining them we will, in fact, examine the basic nature of theory and hypothesis testing.

Prediction

Intuitively, everyone has a notion of the meaning of prediction; psychologically, it is the anticipation of an event before it occurs. Being able to predict events in advance is, of course, quite useful in daily life, and is very important in science. However, the accurate prediction of events is only a first step toward scientific understanding. People have made correct predictions about some phenomenon for, perhaps, centuries, and yet remained totally ignorant in terms of a scientific understanding of what was occurring. For example, the highly accurate prediction of "sunrise" each day was not incongruent with the notion that the earth was flat. Astronomical predictions of the movement of stars could be made with considerable accuracy before the time of Newton. The poisonous and therapeutic effects of many drugs were known long before the chemical bases for their effects were understood. In our own interpersonal relations we make accurate predictions about other people continuously. We learn a whole set of assumptions about the nature of man and his behavior during our formative years. This naive psychology (Heider, 1958) enables us to survive in our interpersonal environment. If we consider a person to be cold and cruel rather than warm and kind we make considerably different predictions for his behavior in various situations. In this way, naive common sense psychology helps us predict behavior. At the same time, however, we do not necessarily feel that we understand people satisfactorily just because we can predict their behavior. Many married people can predict their spouse's behavior quite accurately and still be totally puzzled by it.

So, our viewpoint is that prediction is an indispensable aspect of science as well as everyday life. However, it is only the beginning of what we will call scientific understanding.

Understanding

The notion of understanding is a nebulous concept. In daily living we tend to feel that we understand a phenomenon when we come to the point at which our curiosity rests, when we think we know the reason for something existing or working the way it does. Thus, understanding is knowing the reasons (Kaplan, 1964, p. 332).

Another way of stating the matter is that we feel we understand a phenomenon when we know or can give an explanation for it. For example, an adult who has not previously encountered an electric door is very puzzled the first time he encounters one. In all of his experience it has required physical human effort to open a door. Most of us ultimately obtain a crude explanation for the electric door that satisfies our curiosity. We learn that the door has a mechanical arm attached to it. We also learn that when we approach the door we step on an electrical switch that closes a contact. We had already learned that when contacts are closed, electrical gismos are activated. We then learn that such an electrical gismo is connected to the arm of the door. Presto—we have a rough but serviceable explanation of how the electric door works.

Our point is that understanding involves a process of explanation. It is the nature of scientific explanation that we want to examine in some detail. As might be expected, it is considerably more involved than the everyday example just given. Essentially, our set of crude, half-formed notions constituted a theory by which we explained the operation of the door. So it is with science as well. Explanation (and the psychological understanding that it provides) in science is generally considered to reside in theories. To understand the nature of explanation therefore requires that we understand the nature of theories.

Theories

There are at least four different general types of theories (Nagel, 1961). Each type is indicated briefly and then the first type, deductive theory, is focused on more fully.

Deductive Theory

A deductive theory is a formal system that contains a set of assumptions or premises from which consequences can be deduced. Geometry is the classical example of this type of theory. The theorems (consequences) of geometry are logically implied by the axioms and postulates (assumptions).

Probabilistic Theory

This type is a variant of deductive theory. When the assumptions of a theory are statistical in character, the consequences can be logically implied only with a certain stated probability. The consequences do not follow inexorably, but only probabilistically. The basic procedures for deducing consequences are similar in the two cases, however, so that a probabilistic theory may be considered as a subclass of deductive theories.

Functional (Teleological) Theory

This type of theory explains a phenomenon by showing the functions or uses that the phenomenon serves. Such phrases as "in order that," "for the sake of," etc., will often be found in sentences giving this type of explanation. For example, the question of why humans have lungs might be given the answer, "In order to supply oxygen to the body." This explanation shows the function or use of the lungs with respect to the rest of the body. Darwin's theory of evolution is the best known theory of this type. Very often, a functional explanation of a given phenomenon is compatible with a deductive explanation for the same phenomenon (Braithwaite, 1953, p. 343). The theoretical language and the way it is used differs, rather than the basic nature of the explanation involved.

Genetic Theory

A theory of this type is historical in nature. An explanation for the present state of a given object or event is provided by describing how the object evolved from earlier states. Knowledge of how the object was transformed over time is presumed to satisfy the need to know why it is as it is now. Genetic explanations may or may not be couched in the framework of a deductive system.

Most philosophers of science have devoted the bulk of their attention to the deductive type of theory. We shall do likewise. The reader should be warned in advance that few scientific theories (and no social psychological theory) fit the deductive model very well. Rather, the deductive model constitutes an ideal toward which actual theories might strive. By understanding how a formal theory works, how implications are derived from it, and how these implications are tested hopefully will yield a fuller critical appreciation of actual theories. We will not discuss all the possible topics that could be discussed because an entire volume would be required to do so. There are several excellent books that serve this function, including Beveridge (1950), Braithwaite (1953), Campbell (1952), Conant (1951), Hempel (1966), Kaplan (1964), Kuhn (1962), Nagel (1961), McCain and Segal (1969), Marx (1963), Rudner (1966), and Turner (1967).

Formal Deductive Theory

A well-developed, formal deductive theory has several properties.

1. It has a set of basic concepts with which the theory is concerned.

2. The concepts are related to each other, usually in sentences or mathematical notation, in such a way as to form a set of propositions. A proposition is simply a statement linking at least two concepts together. For example, the statement "Redheads are high tempered" is a proposition relating the concepts *redhead* and *high tempered.* The propositions are assumed to be true without proof. They are in a sense the "heart" of the theory. The basic propositions may be open to empirical proof or disproof in some theories but they are often quite abstract. The main

point is that since they are assumed as basic, it is not necessary that they be proved true. Of course some sets of propositions are better than others. In fact, coming up with a "good" set of basic propositions demands a very high level of creativity.

There are no rules for how many basic concepts one should have in a theory, or how many propositions one should construct from them. Usually, it is desirable to have as few as possible. Essentially, this is what is meant by the simplicity or parsimony of a theory. There is something elegant and powerful about a theory which contains a few basic assumptions, but which has implications for a wide range of empirical phenomena. These basic sentences at the heart of the theory have several names. In mathematics they are called *postulates.* In logic they are often called *premises* or *assumptions.*

3. The third property of a formal theory is that, given the basic assumptions, the laws of logic are applied to those assumptions to obtain new propositions. This procedure is sometimes called "deducing consequences of the theory." The basic point is that these new sentences or propositions necessarily follow from the basic assumptions as a consequence of following certain logical rules. These new sentences are known by a variety of names. In logic or mathematics the new propositions are variously called *deductions, inferences,* or *conclusions.* When we are concerned with scientific theories, however, the new propositions are generally called *hypotheses.* As we shall see later, testing hypotheses is one important reason why we do experiments.

Until this point we may think of our theory as a purely formal system. It is a kind of word game in which we have a set of symbols (that we have called concepts). We use a set of (logical) rules for forming propositions out of the concepts, and for suggesting manipulations of the propositions to obtain new propositions. The theory is purely abstract or formal. It has no necessary contact with empirical reality. Symbolic logic systems and formal mathematics are theories of this type. Scientists are not usually interested in formalism for its own sake, however. They want to apply the theory to the real world to extend their knowledge of that world. This leads us to a fourth important property of formal theories when we translate them into empirical theories.

4. At least some of the concepts must be given an *operational* definition. This statement simply means that we must specify real examples of the concept. We must be able to point to instances in the real world and say "That is what I mean by concept X." Without such operational specification the theory is meaningless. For example, the phrase "Grabulunkas lead to brookalookas" may be a perfectly good deduction drawn from some set of premises. However, unless I can point to instances

of what I mean by grabulunkas and brookalookas, this proposition has no scientific value. So, basically, to define a concept operationally means to specify instances of that concept in the empirical world. In scientific work "pointing to instances" typically involves measurement procedures. An operational definition of a concept is often considered to be the set of procedures or measuring operations by which the concept is identified (Underwood, 1966). This approach will be developed more fully later, when we introduce the notion of a variable. An example will suffice for the present. *Intelligence* is one important psychological concept. If we want to say what intelligence is, we need some way of specifying how it is manifested. Stated differently, we need a set of operations that will allow an exact specification of the concept of intelligence in the real world. One very common set of such operations is the intelligence or IQ test. Such tests include a battery of items which may be scored to yield an "intelligence score." The meaning of intelligence in this instance is the score obtained on the IQ test.

There has been considerable controversy and misunderstanding over the nature of operational definitions (Marx, 1963). One problem lies in the statement that the meaning of a concept is the set of operations used to measure the concept, and nothing more. Taken literally, such an approach to operationism seems too restrictive. Every time we change an operation even slightly we would have a new concept. For example, suppose there were twenty questions on the intelligence test. If a new version of the test were created which contained nineteen of the old questions and one new question, would we want to say that we are measuring some new concept? Probably not, but the situation becomes more realistic if two experimenters develop two very different tests both purporting to measure intelligence but which are unrelated to each other in terms of the results they yield. Do we have two different concepts (such as intelligence 1 and intelligence 2) in this case? The answer cannot be prejudged. Much more analytic work and research would be needed. With further work researchers might decide that one test is measuring intelligence, but that the second test is really measuring something else. On the other hand, researchers might eventually conclude that both tests are measuring different kinds of intellectual abilities which are independent of each other. The latter conclusion would constitute essentially a redefinition of the general meaning of intelligence.

The position of many philosophers at the present time is that important concepts shared by a scientific community always mean more than the specific set of measurement operations used in a specific instance. Intelligence certainly means more to researchers than the score people obtain on John Doe's IQ Test. The general meaning of the concept of intelligence is therefore something more than a specific set of measurement operations. In fact, important concepts will usually have several different sets of operations which may be used to give the concept a concrete form or meaning. However, these various sets of operations should be more or less convergent in the sense that when they are applied they lead to nearly the same results or conclusions.

Thus the meaning of most concepts will be something more than a specific set of operations. However, it should be emphasized that if the concept is to be useful scientifically, there must be at least one set of operations which identifies the concept in the real world. In an actual research project, this identification is necessarily always specific. Unless one can point to and measure specific features of the world, a meaningful scientific theory cannot be developed.

An Example of a Theory

At this point it may be helpful to illustrate the properties of a formal theory with an example. It should be noted that the example is extremely simple, and that no actual theory would be this simple.

1. For our concepts we will use the symbols F, E, H, and A. These symbols are the basic concepts of our theory. At this point the symbols have no empirical meaning.

2. We must now relate the symbols to each other to form propositions. We will relate the symbols by use of the logical implication sign $\rightarrow$. The $\rightarrow$ sign is to be read "implies" or "leads to." For simplicity this will be the only type of relationship that we use. We will further specify that our symbols are related to each other in the following way:

$$
\begin{gathered}
F \rightarrow E \\
E \rightarrow H \\
H \rightarrow A
\end{gathered}
$$

We have three basic statements, F implies E, E implies H, and H implies A. These three statements are the basic propositions (postulates, premises, or assumptions) of our formal theory.

3. We now use formal logic to deduce another proposition from the theory. That proposition is $F \rightarrow A$. This deduction is very simple. We have applied what is called the law of the syllogism (see Dinkines, 1964, for a more extended analysis of formal logic). This basic logical principle says that if X implies Y, and Y implies Z, then X implies Z. For our little formal theory, the law of the syllogism was applied twice, and the statement $F \rightarrow A$ was the consequence. The application is as follows: if F implies E, and E implies H, then it follows that F implies H. We then

use the conclusion F implies H as a premise for the second application of the law of the syllogism. If F implies H, and H implies A, then F implies A. These statements may be listed schematically as follows:

$$\begin{array}{c} F \rightarrow E \\ E \rightarrow H \\ H \rightarrow A \\ \hline F \rightarrow A \end{array}$$

The statement $F \rightarrow A$ is our deduction from the three premises.

4. Our theory is at this point purely a formal creature devoid of empirical meaning. However, let us transform it into an empirical theory by specifying a meaning for each of the concepts. Let each of the symbols be identified as follows:

F = Frustration
E = Loss of Self-Esteem
H = Hostility
A = Aggression

For the moment we will assume that our common-sense notions of the meaning of each concept suffices as an operational definition of that concept (such casual use of operational definitions would of course be disastrous in an actual experiment). Let us also use the verbalism "leads to" instead of the $\rightarrow$ symbol to indicate a relationship. We see that our previously purely formal symbols now translate into the following set of theoretical assumptions with the consequent deduction:

1. Frustration leads to lowered Self-Esteem
2. Lowered Self-Esteem leads to Hostility
3. Hostility leads to Aggression

Frustration leads to Aggression

Given the particular definitions of the formal symbols, we see that the set of assumptions formally implies a time-honored hypothesis in psychology (Dollard *et al.,* 1939). Our hypothesis "frustration leads to aggression" is on the one hand a purely formal *deduction* from our premises. On the other hand, the hypothesis is also a *prediction* about the real world. The hypothesis implies that if we subject a living organism to something called frustration, we should, as a consequence, observe something else about that organism that we can call aggression. We would of course have to specify much more carefully in operational terms just what it is that we mean by instances of frustration and aggression.

Although the example is contrived, it does illustrate the connection between a formal, abstract system and an actual empirical theory. By coordinating our abstract concepts to real-world entities, we are able to use the mechanics of formal logic to obtain hypotheses about the real world. This is a very convenient procedure. A well-developed formal theory should, with the proper definitions of concepts, imply a great many hypotheses. Unfortunately there are no such formal theories in social psychology. In most of the chapters in this book, the investigator seems to start with the hypothesis. On the basis of plausible hunch, intuition, etc., he comes up with a testable hypothesis. Given that the investigator can intuitively generate many creative hypotheses, one may wonder why he should bother with a set of assumptions that imply the hypothesis. One may argue of course that such a set of (hopefully, non-trivial) assumptions is already implicit in the investigator's thinking. The value of making these assumptions explicit is that they would possibly lead to the deduction of several other different hypotheses that would not otherwise have been considered. In this way the theory generates a whole set of interconnected hypotheses, rather than single isolated hypotheses. Such an interrelated set greatly increases our knowledge of the phenomena in question. This is the primary value in the explicit formulation of formal theory.

Let us return to consideration of our example. We were able to deduce the hypothesis "frustration leads to aggression." The next major step is to ask whether this is a true hypothesis. The hypothesis is certainly true in the formal sense that it logically follows from the premises. However, there is no assurance that the hypothesis is true in a factual, empirical sense. It is perfectly conceivable that in the real world one might induce a state of frustration in an organism and not get a state of aggression as a consequence. In short, the hypothesis could be factually false. Therefore, we must test the hypothesis in some way to determine whether it is true or false. We might note that one criterion for a "good" scientific theory is that it can generate hypotheses which can be proved true or false when they are tested.

Testing the hypothesis usually requires that we do some kind of research. Very often this research will be an experiment. We will discuss the nature of an experiment in more detail in a later section. For the moment, however, we will assume that we have conducted the necessary research and have decided that the hypothesis is indeed true. Given that the hypothesis is true, we feel that we have some *understanding* of the concepts of frustration and aggression. Finding that the hypothesis is true helps corroborate the assumptions of our theory—we infer that they are good assumptions. We never really prove or disprove the theory, but we do confirm or disconfirm implications of the theory. It is sometimes said that a theory is neither true nor false, only useful. The theory or, more precisely, the basic propositions of the theory are neither true nor false because we assume them without proof. However, the theory is useful if it generates numerous hypotheses which can be proved or disproved. If the hypotheses cannot be tested in some way, the theory is not even useful.

In summary, we would say that having a scientific *understanding* of a phenomenon involves having (a) a coherent theory about the phenomenon, (b) hypotheses derived from the theory which are in fact predictions about the real world, and (c) some way of testing those hypotheses. A large part of the remainder of Part I of this book will be concerned with testing hypotheses. Before we turn to that topic, however, we first need to consider the third major goal of science—*control* of events.

Control

Often a psychologist is said to be interested in controlling behavior. This statement is not quite precise. The psychologist is more properly concerned with the variables that influence behavior. The notion of control (or stimulus control) is usually meant in this sense—control of *variables*. The notion of a variable is important. Variables are sometimes called *factors* and occasionally *parameters*. Essentially, a variable is a concept that has a measurement dimension; that is, the concept can be scaled or measured. It can contain various degrees of magnitude. The concept of temperature is a variable. This concept refers to the varying amount of heat energy that an object can possess. The concept "strength of grip" is another variable. This concept refers to the varying force with which individuals can squeeze a hand dynamometer.

Practically all concepts can be assigned properties of magnitude. In that sense most concepts are also variables. Sometimes a distinction is made between "qualitative" and "quantitative" concepts, but the distinction is not very clear. Properties of objects that exist on an all or none basis seem to be what is referred to by the notion of a quality. The quality is either present or absent in an object. An organism is either dead or it is alive. A women is either pregnant or she is not pregnant. However, even such rudimentary qualitative distinctions may be considered as defining a variable if one wants to consider the matter in that way. In fact such distinctions form an "either-or" basis for classifying objects and events. In measurement theory, this type of classification constitutes a type of measurement scale: a nominal scale. In addition, most dichotomous variables can usually be conceived as more finely graded.

This notion of variable magnitude of a concept has important consequences. The most basic consequence involves the notion of *change*. If a concept is something that can exhibit varying magnitude, the possibility of change in objects or events is introduced. As we shall see, the notion of a changing variable, and relating one changing variable to another changing variable, is basic in hypothesis testing. It will be recalled that the hypothesis derived from our theory stated that "frustration leads to aggression." Actually, it turns out that the hypothesis is most imprecise in that form. The hypothesis is really in crude qualitative form. The concepts of frustration and aggression are not explicitly defined as variables. The nebulous phrase "leads to" tends to conjure up an image of each concept as an all or nothing affair. An organism is frustrated or it is not frustrated. The organism either aggresses or it does not aggress.

We certainly want our concepts to be variables—not crude qualitative concepts. Frustration can exist in many different degrees. Similarly, aggression can exist in many different degrees. We actually would have built these quantitative properties into our assumptions and consequently into our hypothesis if the statement had been intended as a serious hypothesis. We would have selected our assumptions in such a way that our hypothesis would at least read "changes in frustration lead to changes in aggression." This statement implies that each of our concepts is a variable. The statement also implies that the two variables are related to each other in terms of changes. A change in one variable leads to a change in the second variable. Only by relating changes in variables is it possible to specify relationships in a precise way. Of course the hypothesis is still quite crude. Changes can usually occur in several ways. The hypothesis does not say what kind or how much change in one variable leads to what kind of change in the other variable. The phrase "leads to" is very ambiguous. There are many ways something can lead to something else. One thing may lead to another in a simple positive fashion, in a simple negative fashion, or in some more complicated way. As we shall see shortly, the most precise way we can state how one thing leads to another is in terms of a mathematical rule or function. We should keep in mind, however, that in many sciences, it is not yet possible to state such precise rules of relationship. In fact, we may often have to be satisfied with the gross verbal rule "leads to."

One final point should be made concerning variables. A variable may be either simple or complex. A simple variable is one which has only a single measurement dimension. A complex variable has more than one measurement dimension. Whether a concept will be considered as simple or complex is often arbitrary, depending on the purposes of the investigator. For example, consider the concept of *pleasure*. If we wish, we may think of pleasure as a simple variable of experience that can vary continuously from very high to very low amounts. However, Bentham, an early English philosopher, considered pleasure as a complex concept. Pleasures can have differing degrees of *duration, intensity, purity, certainty,* and *extent,* among other measurements (Allport, 1968). Conceptually, each of these terms denotes a different dimension of pleasure. If these various dimensions are independent of each other, the notion of pleasure is indeed a complex variable. As another example, the concept of attitude in social psychology is usually considered as a variable. A typical definition of an attitude is a tendency to evaluate an object positively or negatively. Essentially, an attitude is a simple variable in this definition, since a basic evaluative dimension is specified which can range from positive to negative. Other dimensions of an attitude could have been specified, creating a complex concept. Dimensions such as *importance, clarity, connectedness* to other attitudes, and *resistance* to change have at one time or another been proposed as important attitudinal dimensions. Ideally, variables should be simple because of the greater precision in meaning and measurement. Stated differently, simple variables can be operationally defined in a more rigorous way. In actual fact, however, most important psychological concepts are probably multidimensional. Important notions seem to acquire a multitude of measurement dimensions. Usually only one or two measurement dimensions will be explicitly used, while other dimensions remain implicit in the background. The phrase "surplus meaning of a concept" is sometimes used to denote these implicit measurement properties of a concept.

At the beginning of this section we said that the concern was with control over variables. We examined the nature of variables and saw that our hypothesis was best viewed as a change in one variable leading to a change in a second variable. To develop precisely what we mean by control we first need to make some distinctions concerning the two variables contained in our hypothesis. The phrase "leads to" in the hypothesis is often translated as "causes." Thus, "frustration *causes* aggression." The notion of cause is a complicated one and we defer full discussion of it until later. At this point we note that the way the hypothesis is stated seems to indicate that frustration is *a priori,* and in some sense responsible for aggression. The occurrence of frustration antedates the occurrence of aggression. In logical terminology, the first part of the hypothesis is referred to as the *antecedant* variable, and the second part as the *consequent* variable. At the level of finding out if the hypothesis is true, of actually testing it, we refer to the variables somewhat differently. We refer to the first variable (frustration) as the *independent* variable, and the second variable (aggression) as the *dependent* variable. The second variable in some sense "depends" upon the conditions of the first variable.

When we are concerned with the study of behavior, there is still a third way of referring to the two variables in the hypothesis. Frustration, of course, is literally a process occurring within the organism. It is a fundamental assumption that frustration does not intrinsically occur in and of itself. It has to be produced by something. That "something" is a set of environmental conditions either external or internal to the organism. We have to hit the organism, shock him, block his path to a goal, etc., before he experiences what we have called frustration. These various procedures or operations may be summarized by saying that we have created a stimulus situation which we have brought to bear on the organism. Of course whether these various operations really induce a varying state of frustration is another matter—one which we will consider in more detail presently.

The fundamental notion of a *stimulus* or *stimulus variable* is that of a set of conditions in the environment of the organism. The environment may be either "outside" or literally "inside" the organism, but the basic notion is of a set of conditions *conceptually* distinct from the essence of the organism. In actual practice of research, these conditions are created by doing something, by manipulating or changing some aspect of the real world. These manipulations constitute the stimulus with respect to the organism.

As a consequence of bringing the stimulus to bear on the organism, we expect something to occur—in short, a *response* or a change in behavior. In our hypothesis, that response is some aspect of ongoing behavior that we have called aggression. Fundamentally, then, we associate the second variable of the hypothesis with the organism and the responses he produces. The first variable is associated with the environment and its impact on the organism. These notions of stimulus and response variables are perhaps the most basic notions in psychology. In summary, our hypothesis "frustration leads to aggression" may be considered at three different levels. As a purely formal, logical statement frustration is the antecedent variable and aggression is the consequent variable. At the level of a testable empirical hypothesis, frustration is the independent variable and aggression is the dependent variable. At the level of what might be called the substantive psychological relationship, frustration is the stimulus variable and aggression is the response variable.

We are finally in a position to state exactly what we mean by control over variables. We have control over variables in the following sense: if we can set in advance the amount of our independent (or stimulus) variable and predict precisely the amount of the dependent (response) variable that will occur, we may say that we have control over behavior. Thus, we see that we do not control behavior in a direct sense, but, rather, indirectly, by controlling or setting the independent variables to which behavior is responsive. Of course there is usually a great deal of slippage in our control. For one thing, when we speak of setting the amount of our independent variable, we are speaking of setting the amount of a process that actually occurs within the organism. In our hypothesis, we are trying to set the level of frustration within the organism. Frustration in this sense is what Aronson and Carlsmith (1968) have called a "conceptual independent variable." We can achieve this setting only by doing something or manipulating conditions external to the organism. This is our operational attempt to create or set the desired level of frustration. It is important that we distinguish between the conceptual independent variable of frustration, and the external frustration operations by which we hope to induce a specified amount of conceptual frustration. In actual practice the fit between our physical operations and the actual amount of the conceptual independent variable that is induced will be extremely loose. At the present time we do not know how to create a precise, specified amount of frustration within the organism.

In a similar fashion a distinction should be made between the conceptual dependent variable and the actual behavioral measurements. Conceptual aggression has many forms and is exhibited in many ways. In a given case there may be considerable looseness in the fit between our concept of aggression and the instrument by which we purport to measure it.

There may also be slippage in specifying the exact relation between the stimulus variable and the response variable. To the extent that we cannot specify the relation exactly, we cannot say that we have control over behavior because we do not know exactly how the independent variable will affect the dependent variable.

The distinctions between conceptual variables and operational variables are shown in Fig. 1. The organism is shown as a box with the conceptual independent variable located inside the organism. Conceptually, frustration is a process occurring within the organism. Likewise, the tendency to aggress is a property of the organism. The dotted line between the two concepts shows the assumed relationship between them. In contrast with the unitary conceptual variables, there is a variety of operational procedures that may induce frustration, and a variety of

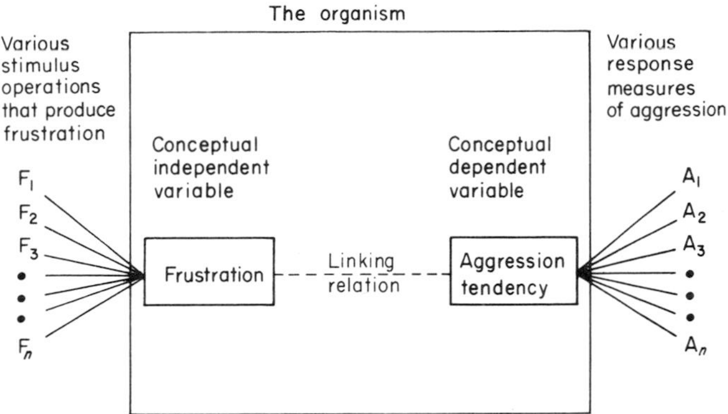

Fig. 1. The relationships between operational variables and conceptual variables with frustration and aggression as examples.

behavioral indices that may reflect the tendency toward aggression. It is at the interface between the physical operations and the conceptual variables where most of our slippage occurs. In social psychology, particularly, we usually have no way of making accurate translations from operations to concepts. These slippages may be considered in part as practical, technological problems.

In principle, control can always be refined. Concepts may be refined, operations purified, and relations specified exactly. To the extent that these things occur, our control over behavior increases. At the same time, most of us would feel that we have an increased understanding of behavior.

As a final point in this section we will illustrate what we mean by specifying a precise relation between two variables. Essentially this means translating the nebulous phrase "leads to" into some other statement. The most precise relationship that we can specify between two variables is what, in mathematics, is called a *functional* relationship. Functions have many forms. The most familiar example is a simple algebraic expression such as $y = 2x^2$. The symbols y and x stand for variables. They are in a sense place-holders because actual magnitudes may be substituted in place of the symbols. The entire expression is a rule that tells exactly how the two variables are related. For example, if we know that variable x has a value of 5, we know that variable y has a value of 50. In terms of notation it is conventional when speaking of empirical hypotheses to let x represent the independent variable and y the dependent variable.

Let us assume that we have such a function rule relating frustration to aggression. Let the rule be:

$$A = 2F + 1$$

The expression says that if we start with some given amount of frustration, the amount of aggression that we will observe is twice that level of frustration plus one unit. The relation might be more complex, such as $A = F^2 + F + 1$. Each of these possibilities is shown in Fig. 2. We see that with a functional relationship between two variables, we have exact prediction of our dependent variable, given a specified amount of our independent variable. Such ultimate predictability and control is the goal of most sciences, although only a few, such as certain areas of physics, have achieved it. In social psychology we are stymied at a very basic level. We usually cannot scale our independent variable in the even steps implied by the intervals on the abscissa in Fig. 2. In fact, we will often have to be satisfied with only two points on the continuum, and sometimes those two points will be designated simply as presence or absence of the independent variable. Even if we could scale the independent variable, we still have a problem in making the measurement units commensurate with the measurement units of our dependent variable. At present there is no way of measuring a unit of frustration and determining its equivalence to a unit of aggression. In this respect social psychology still has a long way to go in terms of measurement of its concepts. We begin to appreciate the great importance of advances in ability to measure for advances in science.

We also begin to realize just how naive our little theory of aggression really is. There is a world of difference between "Frustration leads to aggression" and "$A = 2F + 1$." In terms of the rate of advances of the sciences at present, that difference may be something on the order of a century or more.

We have now examined in some detail the notions of *prediction, understanding,* and *control* in science. As we have seen, these three concepts are interrelated. As an abstract ideal, understanding resides in theories from which we deduce testable hypotheses. The hypotheses are propositions which predict relationships between variables in the real world. To the extent that we can specify such relationships, we have achieved control over variables. In this sense all three goals of science come as an interconnected bundle.

We have advanced to the stage of having a hypothesis. We are concerned with going out into the real world to discover if the hypothesis holds true. We have alluded to hypothesis testing several times, but we still need to examine the process in some detail. In the next section we will consider several rather formal aspects of testing hypotheses and some of the conceptual problems involved.

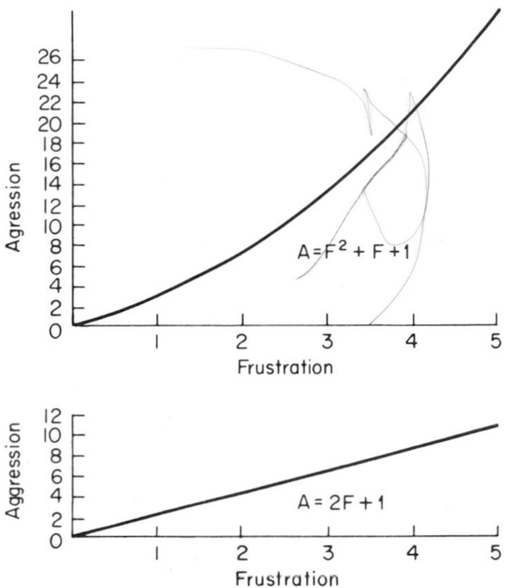

Fig. 2. Two examples of aggression as a mathematical function of frustration.

Hypothesis Testing

We now want to test our hypothesis that changes in frustration lead to changes in aggression. More specifically, we want to test the hypothesis that *increases* in frustration lead to *increases* in aggression. First we will illustrate two examples of how the hypothesis might be tested. One example is superior to the other, as we shall see.

Example 1

Suppose that a researcher developed a test that is a measure of general frustration. The instrument is called "Frustration with Life's Conditions." The test contains a number of verbal agree-disagree statements which can be scored, and the total test score can range from 1–10; the higher the score, the greater the frustration the person experiences in his life. The researcher also needs a measure of aggression. After due consideration he decided that one of the main ways people exhibit aggression in modern society is by verbal attacks on other people. He decided to set up a structured interview situation in which subjects were given the chance to make snide, derogatory comments about other people. A frequency count of the number of derogatory comments during the interview served as the operational measure of the subjects' level of aggression.

The researcher selected a large sample of subjects (e.g., college students) and administered the frustration test to them. He then interviewed each subject individually. Thus, he obtained two scores for each subject. The relation between the two measures may be shown graphically. Suppose that the results obtained were like those shown in the top panel of Fig. 3. Each dot represents one subject, and the placement of a dot is determined by the particular combination of frustration and aggression scores that the subject received. A graph of this type is called a scatter plot. The plot shows a very strong positive relationship between frustration and aggression. The higher a subject scored on the frustration test, the higher he tended to score on aggression. The researcher was elated. He claimed to have proven his hypothesis.

Example 2

Suppose that a second researcher decided to test the hypothesis in a different way. Instead of trying to measure frustration as it naturally existed in subjects, he decided to try to create different amounts of frustration in different subjects. After careful thought, he devised a series of four reasoning puzzles. The puzzles varied in the difficulty of their solution. The researcher believed that working on the puzzles would create differing degrees of frustration. The puzzles were designated as Easy, Difficult, Very Difficult, and Impossible. These four degrees of difficulty were considered as four levels of the frustration variable. Thus, frustration was operationalized in terms of puzzle difficulty.

The researcher assigned subjects to one of the four levels and had them work on the puzzles at that level for one hour. After working for one hour, each subject was then interviewed in the same way as the first researcher in Example 1 interviewed his subjects. The researcher believed that as the difficulty level of the puzzles increased, the resulting frustration should also increase. As a result of the increasing frustration, the subjects should make more derogatory comments. In this way the researcher hoped to test the frustration-aggression hypothesis.

There is one very important consideration that must be mentioned at this point. One hundred students were available to participate in the research. The researcher assigned 25 students to each of the four difficulty levels of the puzzle. It is a very crucial point that allocation of a particular difficulty level to a particular student was randomly determined. In other words, the researcher followed the principle of random assignment of

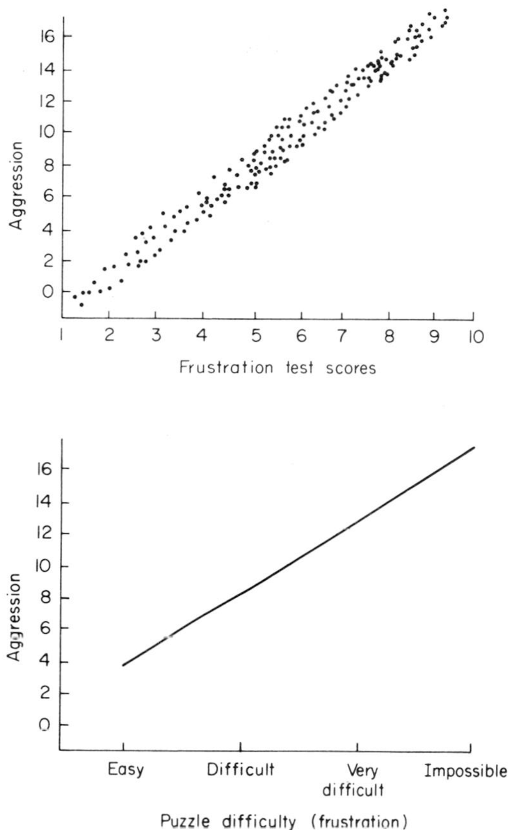

Fig. 3. Hypothetical sets of results from the two examples of the test of the frustration-aggression hypothesis.

subjects to levels of his independent variable. Each of the 100 subjects was just as likely to be assigned to one difficulty level as to another. The subjects differed in many ways. Only by random assignment could the researcher be sure that these differences between subjects were balanced out across the difficulty levels of the puzzles. With the differences between subjects controlled in this way, any differences in aggression between the difficulty levels of the puzzles must presumably have been due to differences in frustration. In this way a relatively pure test of the relation between changes in frustration and changes in aggression was provided. If the subjects had not been randomly assigned, then any differences between conditions in aggressiveness could have been due to (1) frustration differences, plus (2) personality differences, plus (3) differences due to other unknown variables. Clearly this would provide a very muddy test of the hypothesis. Therefore the researcher made quite sure that subjects were randomly assigned to difficulty levels.

The researcher obtained the results shown in the bottom panel of Fig. 3. The average number of derogatory comments (aggression) has been plotted for each of the four difficulty levels (frustration), and the means have been connected by a line. The results were very clear. As the level of frustration increased, the number of aggressive comments increased dramatically. The second researcher was elated. He claimed to have proven his hypothesis.

Each example illustrates an approach to doing research. Both studies seem to have demonstrated the hypothesized positive relation between frustration and aggression. However, the certainty that we can have in the demonstrated relation differs greatly in the two cases. The first example illustrates a *correlational study.* The second example illustrates an *experiment.* The basic difference between a correlational study and an experiment is that in a correlational study measures of both variables as they naturally occur are taken, but in an experiment the researcher actively manipulates one variable and observes how it affects the second variable. In fact, in a correlational study the terminology of independent and dependent variables is not really applicable. In the first example frustration was not independently manipulated among different subjects; rather, it was simply measured as it naturally occurred. Therefore it is difficult to say in what sense the aggression scores are dependent upon the frustration scores. We can say that the two sets of scores covary, but that is about all we can say.

Most researchers consider the experiment as vastly superior to a correlational study. Why should this be so? Why is an experiment superior to a correlational study when both apparently lead to positive evidence of the relation between frustration and aggression? The usual answer that is given is that an experiment allows the demonstration of *causal* relationships, while a correlational study does not allow such a demonstration. "The major value of experiments is that they are better able to test hypotheses about causal relationships than non-experimental studies" (Mills, 1969, p. 412). "When an experiment is possible, it is the most effective method of testing a hypothesis that one variable, *X*, causally influences another variable, *Y*" (Selltiz *et al.*, 1959, p. 90). "In sum, the major advantage of the laboratory experiment is its ability to provide us with unambiguous evidence about causation" (Aronson & Carlsmith, 1968, p. 10).

There is a high degree of consensus among various writers that an experiment allows the demonstration of a causal relation between the independent and the dependent variables. Our own position is that the experimental approach is certainly superior to other approaches. However, we do not believe that discovery of causal relations is the most important reason for the superiority of the experimental approach.

An explanation of our position requires an analysis of the concept of causality. When one examines the writings of philosophers of science on the concept of causality, it turns out that the notion of cause is a very ambiguous notion. Nagel (1961, p. 73) has an excellent discussion of the criteria for a causal relationship or causal law. Nagel indicates that a relationship can be called causal if it satisfies four conditions:

(a) The relation is invariable and uniform. When the alleged cause is present, the effect invariably appears.

(b) The relation holds between events that are contiguous in space.

(c) The cause precedes the effect in time and is temporally contiguous with it.

(d) The relation is asymmetrical. It works only one way. If A causes B, then B cannot in turn cause A.

These are a rather restrictive set of criteria, and, as Nagel indicated, the notion of cause is often superfluous, particularly in advanced sciences such as mathematical physics. A causal relationship is only one of several kinds of relationships, and, depending on the science, the search for "causal" laws may be of minor significance. The functional relationship (in the mathematical sense) that was discussed earlier in the section on control of variables is a more general approach to relations than the notion of causality. The functional relation is completely neutral with respect to whether or not the relation is causal. Yet the true function gives perfect predictability between variables as was illustrated earlier.

As an example from physics (Nagel, 1961, p. 77), the Boyle-Charles' law for ideal gases states that $pV = aT$, where p is gas pressure, V its volume, T its absolute temperature, and a is a constant. This functional relation is not a causal relation. The relation asserts that a change in temperature is concurrent with changes in pressure or volume. The product of pressure and volume does not "cause" a certain temperature in the sense specified by the four criteria for a causal relation. Functional relations of this type are very common in many sciences. Therefore, if causal relations are only one type of relation, and if general functional relations are generally superior, we are left with the problem of justifying why an experiment is superior to a correlational study. Actually, a perfect positive (or negative) correlation is a mathematical function, and as such affords perfect predictability. So why is an experiment better?

We suspect that the answer is that an experiment provides greater certainty about the nature of the relationship between the two specific variables in which we are interested. In the real world, innumerable variables are always intertwined with each other. However, we are interested in the relationship between just two of these variables, in our example, frustration and aggression. The experiment helps us to untangle variables in a way that is not possible with a correlational study. Random assignment of subjects and other experimental techniques that we shall discuss breaks the linkage between our independent variable and other potential extraneous variables with which it might be related. Our independent variable is then operating "independently" of the other variables. When this is the case, we can then have considerable confidence in our hypothesis if we obtain the expected relation between our independent and dependent variables.

Our confidence is considerably lower when we have a correlational relation. In our first example, frustration was not manipulated independently of other variables. Rather it was measured by a verbal test as it appeared naturally in different subjects. The odds are high that the test was impure, that it measured other variables as well. For example, the test items might simply be measuring a person's tendency to give extreme responses on a test. If true, our actual relation is a correlation between the tendency to make derogatory statements and the tendency to make extreme test responses. This is a very different relation from the one we set out to examine. As an extreme, a critic might examine the frustration test and decide that it was in fact a measure of aggression. In this case we would simply have a correlation between two different measures of aggression. Thus, in a correlational study, the exact nature of the variables being measured is usually quite ambiguous. In our second example, the experimental manipulation of frustration was rather clearcut, and because subjects were randomly assigned to different levels of the frustration operations, we were relatively certain that the different degrees of manipulated frustration were not contaminated by the effects of unknown variables. Therefore, we had relatively much greater certainty of the nature of the relationship obtained.

So our argument is that experiments are superior to other approaches to research. Experiments allow relatively greater certainty in the obtained relationships between variables. A given relation may or may not be causal in nature. The ultimate goal of research is to be able to isolate variables clearly and repeatedly, and to show the relationship to other variables in as precise a manner as possible. At present the experiment is the best empirical vehicle we have for this task. This is not to say that the experimental approach is perfect for the required task. In fact, experiments fail rather often. Very often, when we do an experiment our confidence in the obtained relation will be quite low. We may obtain a relationship different from what we expected or, worse yet, no apparent relationship at all. Critics may accuse us of a sloppy job of manipulating our independent variable and propose an alternative hypothesis to account for the empirical relationship that we obtained. It may turn out that our dependent variable is sensitive to many independent variables, each related to it in a different way. So, in interpreting actual experimental results there are a variety of problems that can occur. We will discuss several of these problems in the next chapter, including (a) a null hypothesis outcome, (b) alternative hypotheses, (c) multiple independent variables, and (d) interactions among variables.

Chapter **2**

INTERPRETING EXPERIMENTAL RESULTS

A Null Hypothesis Outcome

Suppose that we performed the experiment described in the previous chapter and obtained the results shown in Fig. 4. These results show that the same mean number of aggressive responses was obtained for each of the four frustration conditions. Apparently, increases in frustration do not lead to increases in aggression. From these results can we conclude that the hypothesis is false? The answer is that the situation is ambiguous. We cannot conclude anything with any certainty. We have obtained a null hypothesis outcome—no differences between the experimental conditions on the dependent variable measure. There are several possibilities which must be considered. First, we may not have really varied the independent variable of frustration. Varying the difficulty of the puzzle task seemed intuitively reasonable as a manipulation of frustration. However, we may have been wrong. Creating experimental operations that

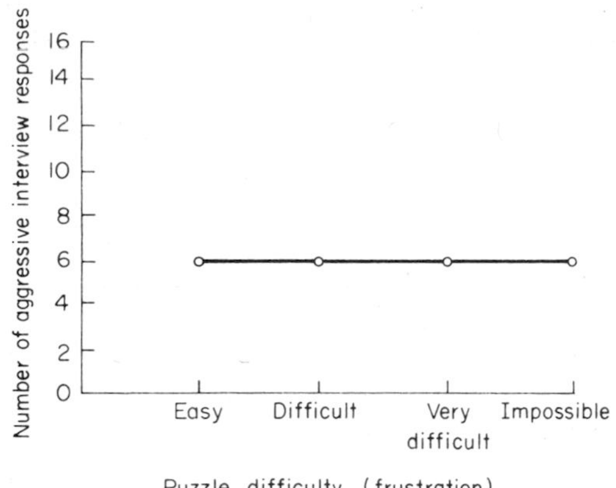

Fig. 4. Hypothetical results of the frustration-aggression experiment.

vary the conceptual independent variable is always an empirical bootstrap operation. For most variables of interest in social psychology, there are no rules specifying how the variable should be manipulated. Since standardized operations seldom exist, the researcher must rely on his own ingenuity and creativity to come up with a reasonable set of operations. However, there is no a priori way of assuring that the manipulation will be successful. Most researchers develop a sense of what will work and what will not work after they have some experience in a given area of research. Unfortunately, each experiment must be evaluated on its own merits, and the sense of what will work remains largely intuitive with each investigator.

Most experimenters usually design some way of checking on the manipulation of their independent variable. For example, in the experiment discussed above we might have had the subjects rate how frustrated they felt after they worked on the puzzle. We would examine the mean ratings of frustration across experimental conditions for evidence of the success of the manipulation. If these ratings showed no differences between conditions we would be tempted to conclude that we had not varied frustration. Suppose, however, the check ratings showed that we had varied frustration in the expected direction, but we still obtained a null hypothesis outcome on the dependent variable. Such an outcome would not necessarily disprove our hypothesis. There are still other possibilities, as we shall see.

The check on the manipulation is usually a secondary measure, not as carefully designed or measured as the main dependent variable. Experimenters are usually quite cautious in interpreting these checks. So, although the second outcome mentioned above is embarrassing, it is not necessarily fatal. The reluctance to give full credence to the check on the manipulation is occasionally seen in research reports. The experimenter obtained the predicted results on the dependent variable measure, but the check on the manipulation did not show that he had successfully varied the independent variable. The fact that the research was published indicates that the experimenter (and the journal editor) had considerably more confidence in his dependent variable measure than in the check on the manipulation. Such practices indicate the secondary nature of the manipulation check.

Failure to manipulate the independent variable is only one possible reason for a null hypothesis outcome. Frustration may have been manipulated slightly, but the strength of the manipulation was too weak to show a relationship. We mentioned earlier that in most social sciences it is impossible to scale our independent variables precisely. The levels of frustration shown in Fig. 4 are given only verbal labels. The graph shows nice even spacing between the four levels, but there is no assurance that the manipulations were in actual fact evenly spaced in this way. Also, there is no assurance that the total distance between "Easy" and "Impossible" implied by the graph did, in fact, occur. For example, all four levels of conceptual frustration might actually have been squeezed into the distance between "Easy" and "Difficult" shown on the graph. Even though we manipulated frustration, the manipulation was extremely weak. Given the slippage in linking most dependent variables to independent variables, it is not surprising that with such a weak manipulation we obtained a null hypothesis outcome.

Usually we have no way of knowing how strong our manipulation was. This is another reason for caution in interpreting the check on the manipulation. We may have manipulated our variable, although very weakly. However, in a given case our check question might have been extremely sensitive. The check question would show large differences between conditions when the actual differences in frustration were quite small. There is usually no way of making questionnaire scale responses exactly equivalent to actual physical operations.

So far, we have focussed on the independent variable. We might obtain a null hypothesis outcome because of a defective dependent variable measure. We may have chosen a poor measure of aggression, or perhaps a very insensitive measure. If the measure is so insensitive that a subject must be practically paralyzed with frustration before he shows more aggressive responses than a nonfrustrated subject, then a null hypothesis outcome is virtually certain.

Constructing good dependent variable measures is a creative bootstrap operation. In that respect, measuring the dependent variable is similar to constructing the independent variable. There is usually no way of scaling the conceptual dependent variable precisely. We are trying to assign numbers to an underlying psychological process, and there is no foolproof way in which it can be done. There is still a further problem in measuring the dependent variable. The ordinate of the graph in Fig. 4 shows the number of aggressive interview responses. Suppose that a given subject scored zero. We cannot say that the actual amount of conceptual aggression the subject experienced was zero. The true amount of aggression might have been quite high. On our particular measure it simply happened that the subject gave no verbal responses of the type that we had defined as aggressive. The point is that the *absolute* level of our dependent variable scores cannot usually be interpreted. The fact that the average score in Fig. 4 was six for all groups has no particular meaning. We do not know if six means an absolute low level of aggression, a moderate level, or a high level.

Most measures in social psychology are ordinal in nature. They cannot be given an absolute interpretation. Only directional differences are interpretable. It is usually safe to assume that a subject with a higher score is manifesting more of a given attribute than a subject with a lower score. But we cannot say how much more because we do not know whether each unit on our measuring scale represents a unit of the underlying variable. For this reason, only changes in the dependent variable across levels of the independent variable can be meaningfully interpreted. This is the major reason why it is important to obtain differences between experimental conditions—only by showing differences or changes can we show the hypothesized relationship. Thus, the relative difference in scores between experimental conditions can be very informative, but the absolute level of response for a specific condition is not very meaningful for many measures.

There are still other reasons why the null hypothesis outcome is ambiguous. We may have actually varied frustration and have a good measure of aggression. However, some uncontrolled third variable may be working differentially across experimental conditions. For example, suppose that subjects in the Easy condition participated in the experiment at 1:00 PM, subjects in the Difficult condition at 2:00 PM, and the other two conditions at 3:00 PM and 4:00 PM, respectively. Let us assume that people tend to become less and less aggressive during the day due to fatigue. This tendency is working against the manipulation of our independent variable. If the natural decrease in aggressiveness exactly offsets the increase we get from the manipulation of frustration, we would obtain a null hypothesis outcome. Of course no good experimenter would actually conduct his experiment in the way we have described. He would try to collect data from all the conditions at the same time and preferably in the same place, or possibly run all the conditions once at each of several different time periods. In this way any third variable due to time and place that might affect the results would be held constant across levels of the independent variable. However, no matter how carefully the conditions are controlled there is always the possibility that some third variable was operating differentially to influence the results. Such a possibility always requires careful interpretation of an experimental report.

We see now why a null hypothesis outcome is ambiguous. A false hypothesis is only one of several reasons why such an outcome is obtained. Usually an experimenter has a lot of effort, not to mention faith invested in his hypothesis. He wants it to be true. Therefore, accepting the null hypothesis is usually done only as a last resort. The experimenter will explore all the other possibilities first. If the hypothesis is an important one, he will usually try to test it again in a different way perhaps. Thus we conclude that experiments that do not show differences between conditions have little value. There is too much ambiguity in interpreting such an outcome. We also see how difficult it is at the empirical level to demonstrate the lack of a relationship. Only if several competent investigators have tested a hypothesis in several different ways and all of them obtained a null hypothesis outcome do we finally accept the falsity of the hypothesis. On the other hand, one good demonstration of a predicted relationship is usually convincing. There may be a problem here occasionally. Because of their ambiguity, experiments with null outcomes are seldom reported in the journals. If there are 20 such unreported studies and one reported positive instance, there is some difficulty in interpretation. By chance we might get one positive instance out of 20 trials when in fact the hypothesis is false. The answer to this problem would seem to be replication of reported experiments. In some sciences replication of important experiments is done routinely. Unfortunately, this is less true in social psychology. We have selected sets of readings for this book in which experiments were replicated. Usually the replications were not done merely for the sake of replication. Rather the replications were done to test an alternative interpretation for the original results. We examine now in some detail the problem of alternative interpretations of a hypothesis.

Alternative Interpretations of the Hypothesis

When we say that we have an alternative interpretation for an experiment, we usually mean something like the following.

> The experimental operations that you chose to manipulate your conceptual independent variable, *A*, may not have manipulated that variable. It seems reasonable to me that your operations actually manipulated some other independent variable, *B*. Further, *B* is related to the dependent variable in the same way as your hypothesized independent variable *A*. Therefore your results actually show a relation between *B* and the dependent variable.

We will illustrate the nature of alternative interpretations by an example. A classic study by Aronson and Mills is reprinted in Chapter 7. In that experiment the investigators tested the general hypothesis that the more severe the initiation into a group, the more attractive that group would be to the new member. The general hypothesis was given a specific test, namely that increases in unpleasant effort in the initiation resulted in increased attraction to the group.

The conceptual independent variable was *unpleasant* effort. The conceptual dependent variable was *attraction to a group*. The independent variable was operationalized in the following way. The researchers tried to create two levels of effort (mild and severe). [There was also a third (control) condition, but we will ignore it for simplicity of the discussion.] Subjects were female college students, randomly assigned to the two conditions. In the mild condition subjects were asked to recite some innocuous words as their initiation into the group. Subjects in the severe condition were asked to recite obscene words as their initiation. The difference between reciting mild and obscene words was the operational manipulation of unpleasant effort. After the initiation, subjects listened to a tape recording of a purported group discussion which was in fact excruciatingly dull and boring, and then rated how attractive the group was to them. The attraction rating was the operational measure of the conceptual dependent variable. The results came out as predicted—subjects in the severe initiation condition rated the group as more attractive than subjects in the mild initiation condition.

The results supported the hypothesis. The main question with regard to an alternative interpretation is whether the differences in attraction were in fact due to differences in unpleasant effort or to some other unidentified variable. When we examine the actual operations, it appears that there are several reasonable alternatives. A schematic representation of the experiment is shown in Fig. 5. In examining Fig. 5 we see that the difficulty arises primarily with the operationalization of high unpleasant effort, although subjects in the mild condition may have been bored, an unwanted effect. Having the subjects recite obscene words may have created high unpleasant effort, but it may have had several other consequences as well (Chapanis & Chapanis, 1964). These consequences are what Aronson and Carlsmith (1968, p. 13) have called multiple

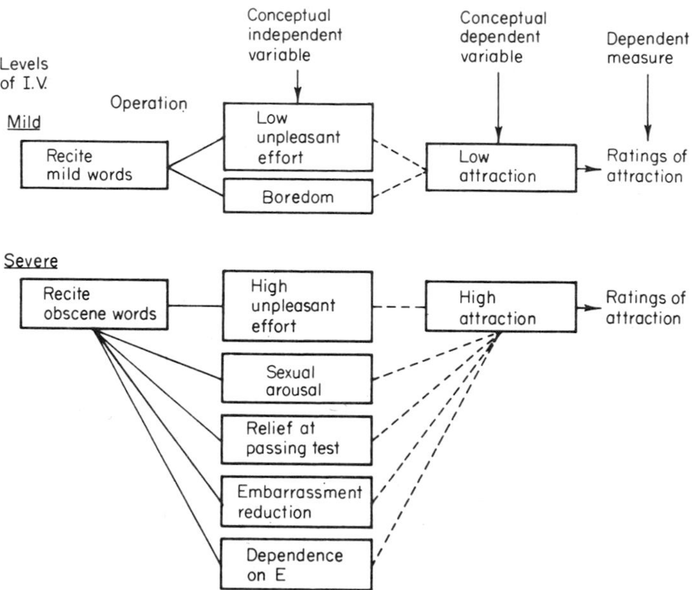

Fig. 5. Schematic representation of the Aronson-Mills experiment.

meanings of a set of experimental operations. Essentially, this notion means that the operations may have varied one or more conceptual independent variables other than the intended one. Some of these consequences are listed in the bottom panel of the figure. As Aronson and Carlsmith (1968, p. 14) have indicated, having subjects in the severe initiation condition recite obscene words may have created greater embarrassment. The reduction of embarrassment at the end of the recitation may have enhanced attraction toward the group. Or it may have been that relief at passing a difficult test created greater attraction. Another possibility is that reciting the obscene words created sexual arousal in the subjects, again leading to more favorable attraction ratings. Each of these possibilities is an alternative explanation for the obtained results. Instead of increased effort leading to increased attraction, it may have been increased sexual arousal, or increased relief at test passing, or increased embarrassment reduction. Still another interpretation is that the severe initiation made the subject more dependent upon the power of the experimenter. As a result, the subject conformed more closely to what she thought was the experimenter's opinion, i.e., that the group was attractive.

This latter alternative interpretation was suggested by Schopler and Bateson in the second article reprinted in Chapter 7. They found mixed support for their alternative interpretation, as will be seen. One important point to note is that Schopler and Bateson replicated the original experiment as part of their total experiment. They included the crucial mild and severe conditions and obtained results similar to those obtained by Aronson and Mills. They also included two further conditions which, for theoretical reasons, were expected to yield results different from the results of the severe condition. If they had not included the original conditions, there would have been no basis for evaluating the results of their new conditions. It was important that they were able to replicate the original results. Without such replication, a new experiment proposed to test an alternative hypothesis does not have much value. Not infrequently an experimenter will propose an alternative explanation for a previously reported experiment. He will then proceed to test his alternative with different experimental arrangements, neglecting to reproduce the original conditions and results as well. Such partial replications are usually worthless if results different from the original results are obtained. The two experiments undoubtedly differed in many details, the presumed crucial difference in procedure being only one difference. The difference in results may be due to any one of the several changes. If the second experimenter can replicate the original results, however, he has a solid baseline against which he can compare his different results from the changed conditions.

It is sometimes possible to rule out alternative interpretations by changing the procedures considerably and still obtain results comparable to those found in the original experiment. Such a strategy was used in an experiment by Gerard and Mathewson which is reprinted as the third article in Chapter 7. Gerard and Mathewson changed the nature of the initiation. Instead of having subjects recite mild or obscene words, they had them experience either mild or painful electric shock as the initiation into a group. This change in procedure automatically ruled out all sex relevant alternative explanations. Since the original results were replicated even with the very different procedures, Gerard and Mathewson provided powerful support for the original hypothesis. Of course, an element of risk was involved in changing the procedures that much. If the results had been different from the original results, not much could have been concluded. There would have been too many possibilities because of changed procedures for obtaining such divergent results.

Generally, if a hypothesis can be tested in six different ways, and each test supports the hypothesis, we would have more confidence in the hypothesis than if it were confirmed by six identical replications. Obtaining the same results with divergent operations shows that the hypothesis is robust. It is susceptible to several empirical manifestations, and because it is, we have greater confidence that it is a true hypothesis. In the example, Gerard and Mathewson enhanced our confidence in the original hypothesis much more conclusively than if they had simply replicated the original experiment.

In summary, then, an alternative interpretation of a hypothesis means we can specify some other plausible independent variable rather than the assumed one that led to the obtained results. Testing the alternative requires varying the experimental conditions in such a way that both the original results and some new results can be produced. All experiments are susceptible to alternative interpretations. The very nature of empirical operations almost ensures that this will be the case. Concrete operations vary many things, only one of which will be the crucial independent variable. The main consideration is whether or not these other potential variables are important, whether they could have accounted for the obtained results. The skill of the experimentalist lies in minimizing the potential impact of other (presumably irrelevant) aspects of the situation rather than ruling them out completely. One possibility is that if some (supposedly irrelevant) aspect of the procedure might make a difference, this aspect should be varied independently of the main independent variable. In a sense, the experiment is then concerned with the effects of two independent variables on one dependent variable. In fact, we may vary not two, but several independent variables. We turn now to consideration of multiple independent variables in an experiment.

Multiple Independent Variables

Let us assume that our hypothesis "frustration leads to aggression" has received strong experimental confirmation. If, then, in everyday life we observe an act of aggression, can we infer that the person was frustrated? Not at all. The hypothesis merely stated that frustration leads to aggression. It did not deny that other independent variables may lead to aggression as well. There may be a whole host of other such variables. If we can identify other variables that also lead to aggression, we can design a much more powerful experiment if we vary these other variables as well. In our experiment we had four levels of frustration. At a minimum we must have two levels. These will be designated "low" and "high" or, perhaps, "absent" and "present." A second independent variable will also require at least two levels. We want to arrange the experiment so that we vary levels of one variable independently across levels of the second variable. Such an arrangement is shown in Fig. 6. One reasonable second independent variable is the perceived intent of another person to aggress against us. The person may not have frustrated us in any way, but if we think that he is about to hurt us in some way, we may aggress against him. Perception of aggressive intent in another person could be very high or very low, as shown in Fig. 6.

Experiments of this type are very common. They are usually called *factorial* experiments. We see that we have all possible combinations of the two levels of our two independent variables. In this case, four different experimental groups of subjects are required. Subjects are assigned randomly to the four cells. One group gets the joint operations for a high level of frustration and a high level of aggressive intent by another person. Another group gets the joint operations for a low level of frustration and a high level of aggressive intent, and so on. The entries in the four cells usually are means for the dependent variable measure.

This kind of experimental arrangement allows us to assess the effect of frustration on aggression, and the effect of the variable of perceived intent on aggression. In addition, we can assess another effect we have not mentioned previously. We can assess *interaction* of the two independent variables in determining the dependent variable scores. We shall have more to say about interactions shortly. This kind of experimental arrangement can be continued indefinitely. We may use three instead of two independent variables. The use of more than three independent variables is relatively uncommon, however, because interpretation of all the effects, particularly higher order interactions, is very difficult. Various kinds of experimental designs and their analyses are given detailed consideration in most statistics textbooks.

Assume that we have conducted our experiment and obtained results

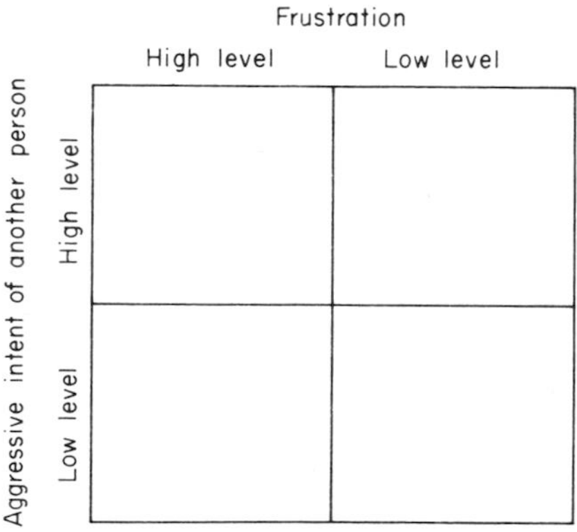

Fig. 6. Representation of a 2×2 factorial experiment with frustration and aggressive intent as the independent variables.

like those in Fig. 7. We see that both frustration and perceived intent affected the amount of obtained aggression. At the low level of perceived intent, the hypothesized relation between frustration and aggression holds true. At the high level of perceived intent, the frustration-aggression relation still holds. However, the graph is displaced upward for high levels of perceived intent. High levels of perceived intent generate more aggression than low levels. Thus, increases in both frustration and perceived intent lead to increases in aggression. We might revise our hypothesis to read "increases in frustration and increases in perceived intent to aggress against us both lead to increases in aggression in the same positive, additive fashion." The word *additive* is used in the revised hypothesis because increasing the level of one independent variable simply seems to "add" an increment of aggression beyond that which is obtained when only one independent variable is considered. In the experimental literature, it is conventional to refer to such results by stating that "both effects made a difference" or that "both effects were significant."

There is one other possibility that we must consider. The two independent variables may not lead to increases in the dependent variable in the same fashion. They may *interact.* The discovery of interacting variables is important, and sometimes such interactions are more interesting and informative than the discovery of additive effects. We turn now to a consideration of interactions.

Interactions Between Independent Variables

Let us suppose that instead of the results shown in Fig. 7, we had obtained the results shown in Fig. 8. We observe a very different pattern of results. Increases in frustration lead to increases in aggression at a low level of perceived intent, but at a high level of perceived intent the relationship is completely reversed—increases in frustration lead to decreases in aggression. These results illustrate an interaction between frustration and perceived intent in determining aggression. We cannot make a simple statement about the relation between frustration and aggression. We must qualify our statement with some reference to the level of perceived intent at which the relation holds.

Knowledge of interactions is valuable because interactions help specify the limits of our hypothesized relationship. In a sense they specify boundary conditions under which the relation holds. Probably no relationship has unrestricted generality. It is always limited to some par-

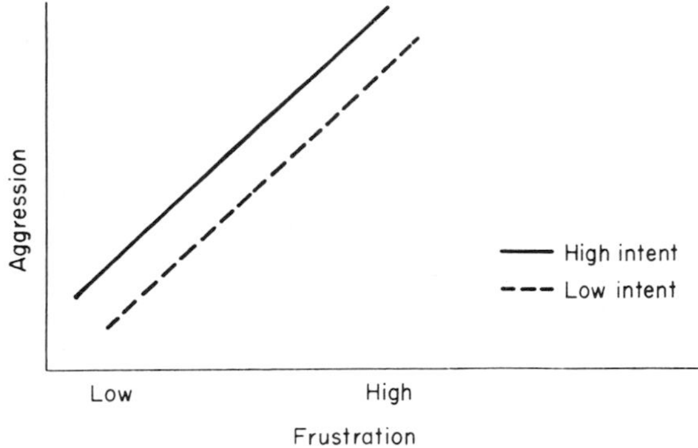

Fig. 7. The effects of frustration and perceived intent on aggression.

ticular combinations of other variables. As noted earlier, one value of an experiment is that it helps untangle the variable of interest from some of those other variables. However, every experiment has definite limitations. It is performed in a specific setting at a specific time with a specific sample of subjects. There may be unknown variables connected with time, setting, or subjects that limit the relationship. If we can determine some of those limiting conditions, we have increased the precision of our knowledge.

Ideally, the interacting variables are important conceptual variables rather than the more trivial variables associated with time or place of the experiment. If we can build these variables into our theory in advance so that we can deduce specific interaction predictions, we generally have a more powerful theory. Not only can we predict a relationship, but we can also specify the conditions under which the relationship holds.

At the same time, manipulating additional variables to observe inter-

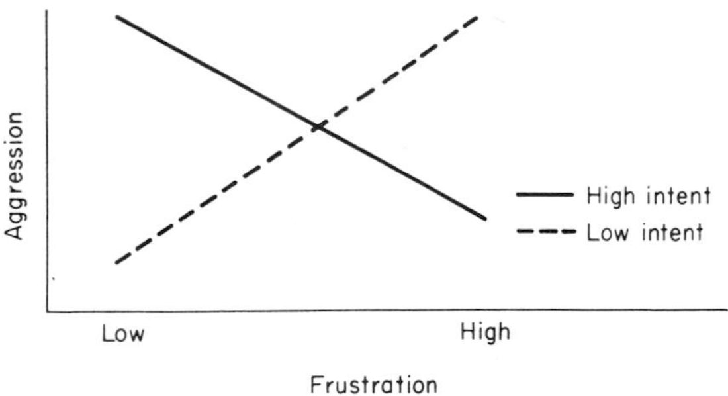

Fig. 8. Interaction between frustration and perceived intent in determining aggression.

action effects provides information about whether the results are specific to our specific experimental conditions. For example, if, for some reason, we think that we shall get the positive frustration-aggression relation only when we test subjects in the afternoon, the obvious thing to do is vary time of testing. Half the data are collected in the morning and half in the afternoon. Time of day becomes an independent variable. We would hope that time of day would not interact with frustration. The limitation imposed by such a trivial variable would largely vitiate the importance of our main relation. We want to say that frustration leads to aggression all the time, not merely in the afternoon. On the other hand, if such a restriction were indeed true, it would be important that we know about it. Otherwise we would continue to deceive ourselves and claim unwarranted generality for our hypothesis as long as we continued to test subjects only in the afternoon. Also, what at first glance appears to be a trivial variable may turn out to have fascinating conceptual properties. The researcher may be able to deduce important psychological reasons why subjects behave so differently in the afternoon than in the morning. His theory would be further elaborated in a way that would not have been possible had he not explicitly varied time of testing as a variable.

We see, then, that interactions between variables provide valuable information. They may help us in further theoretical development and refinement. They help us determine boundary conditions under which our relationship holds. Finally, by explicitly varying specific procedural variables, interactions tell us to what extent our results are limited to our specific experimental operations. For these reasons it has become very popular to design social psychological experiments in which interactions are explicitly predicted. We shall see several examples of such interactions in the readings in Part II.

Statistical Analysis of Research Data[1]

In this last section we will consider certain aspects of the analysis of the data obtained from an experiment. Our main purpose is to provide the student with sufficient understanding of data analysis so that the Results Sections of the experiments reported in Part II will be meaning-

[1] This section is primarily for the novice in statistics. It may be skipped if the student has had an introductory statistics course which includes basic analysis of variance. For students with such a background but in need of a review, the section may be read rapidly.

ful. Most of those experiments used an *analysis of variance* as the method of analyzing the dependent variable scores. Therefore, our attention will be devoted primarily to this particular technique. Two points should be stressed. First, computational competence in the use of statistics is not one of the purposes of this book. There are many excellent texts that serve that purpose (e.g., Hays, 1963; Winer, 1962). Second, the material presented in this section omits many important topics. The basic purpose is to provide the student with an intuitive understanding of the analysis of variance so that the results of an experiment may be understood at an elementary level. Statistical understanding may proceed to increasingly more sophisticated levels. The average social scientist has had perhaps three or four courses in statistics, and has obtained enough proficiency to use routinely many standard techniques of data analysis and to understand, in some depth, the data analyses reported in the literature by his colleagues. The intent of the present section might best be described as directed toward a "minimum depth" understanding of the analyses of variance reported in the case study chapters.

A reasonable way to begin the discussion is to ask why statistical analyses are necessary. One may legitimately wonder why the data do not "speak for themselves." It seems odd that complex statistical manipulations must be performed on the scores before one can decide whether or not the results supported the research hypothesis (e.g., frustration leads to aggression). If life in general (and experimental results in particular) were very simple and completely orderly, the criticism implied in the above statement would be warranted. Unfortunately, neither life nor experimental results are that orderly. The necessity for statistical analyses of data can be illustrated best with an example.

Assume that we have conducted a simplified version of the frustration-aggression experiment introduced in Chapter 1. In that example the experimenter attempted to manipulate frustration by varying the level of difficulty of a puzzle on which subjects worked. After working on the puzzle for an hour, subjects were interviewed and the number of derogatory remarks made during the interview was the operational measure of aggression. For our present example assume that the experimenter used only two levels of puzzle difficulty, Easy and Impossible. Two hypothetical sets of results from this simplified experiment are shown in Fig. 9. There was a total of twelve subjects in the experiment; six were randomly assigned to the Easy condition and the remaining six to the Impossible condition. The scores given in the tables were the number of aggressive interview responses emitted by each of the subjects.

Inspection of the tables indicates that for both Example 1 and Example 2 the mean number of aggressive responses was 5.0 in the Easy

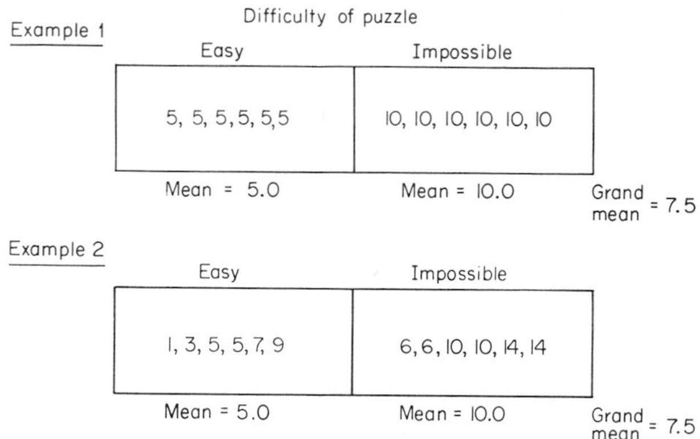

Fig. 9. Two hypothetical sets of data for the simplified frustration-aggression experiment.

condition and 10.0 in the Impossible condition. The mean for all subjects in both conditions combined (referred to as the grand mean) was 7.5 in each example. Although the means were identical for both examples, the individual scores listed in the cells were very different. In Example 1 all the scores in the Easy condition were the same (5.0), and all scores in the Impossible condition were 10.0. This fact means that there was no *variability* of scores within each of the experimental conditions. Example 1 is completely unrealistic in terms of data obtained in an actual experiment. If such results were typically obtained in experiments, there would be little need to perform statistical analyses on scores. In fact, if such a set of scores were obtained, it would not be possible to perform an analysis of variance on them. This technique depends upon variation within a set of scores, and if there is no variability it cannot be applied.

The scores obtained in Example 2 are much more realistic. These scores exhibit considerable variability. In the Easy condition a subject scored as low as one, but another subject scored as high as nine aggressive interview responses. In the Impossible condition two subjects scored as low as six (only one unit above the mean of the Easy condition), and the two most aggressive subjects scored fourteen aggressive responses. This kind of variability in sets of scores is quite common. The variability also poses a problem with regard to easy interpretability of the results. The average or mean scores of 5.0 and 10.0 for the two conditions seem to indicate that subjects were more aggressive in the high (Impossible) than in the low (Easy) frustration condition. Thus the direction of the difference between the means tends to support the hypothesis that increases in frustration lead to increases in aggression. However, two subjects in the Impossible condition actually made fewer aggressive responses than two other subjects in the Easy condition. If increased frustration leads to increased aggression, the two low scorers in the Impossible condition were (relative to the two higher scorers in the Easy condition) behaving contrary to the hypothesis. This kind of overlap in scores leads one to wonder whether subjects in the Impossible condition were "really" more aggressive than subjects in the Easy condition. What one needs is a method of deciding how much contrariness against the hypothesis is permissible in a set of scores. As an extreme instance, if five of the subjects in the Impossible condition had scores of zero, but the sixth subject had a score of 60, the mean would still be 10.0. The difference between the two means would still be in the direction supporting the hypothesis. However, intuitively we would not feel very confident about the results because five of the six people in the high frustration condition actually had lower aggression scores than any of the subjects in the low frustration condition. In this case it would be difficult to conclude that highly frustrated subjects really are more aggressive than nonfrustrated subjects.

This last example is quite unrealistic also, and such a pattern of scores would almost never occur. The pattern of dispersion of scores in Example 2 is much more common, and much more difficult to interpret. It is hard to tell if the two sets of scores are separated from each other enough so that we can say with confidence that the highly frustrated subjects were truly more aggressive. This difficulty illustrates one of the values of statistical analysis. A statistical technique, such as the analysis of variance, may be used as a guide or decision rule to make inferences from the data. As will be illustrated below, application of analysis of variance to the scores in Example 2 will enable us to decide whether the two sets of scores were sufficiently separated to claim support for the frustration-aggression hypothesis.

Before we see how the analysis is applied, there are several preliminary points which must be made. Statistics may be used to describe a set of scores, as well as to make decisions or inferences about hypotheses. Statistics used to summarize a set of scores are called *descriptive statistics.* There are two commonly used types of descriptive statistics: measures of central tendency and measures of variability. The *arithmetic mean* is the most common measure of central tendency. It is simply the sum of the scores divided by the number of scores which were summed. The mean may be thought of as a kind of center of gravity for a set of scores. One interesting property of the mean is that if the mean score is subtracted from all the individual scores in a sample, the sum of the resulting difference scores is always zero. These difference scores are usually called deviation scores.

The mean communicates some descriptive information about a set of scores, namely the typical score or central tendency of the scores. This information tells us nothing, however, about how scores vary around the central tendency. Both examples in Fig. 9 have the same means but differ widely in variability or dispersion of the scores. The *standard deviation* is the most common descriptive statistic used to denote the variability of a set of scores. The standard deviation is itself a kind of average score. Suppose that X represents an individual score, and M represents the mean of a group of scores. The expression $\Sigma_1^n\ (X - M)$ then represents the sum of the differences between all the scores and the mean. The Σ_1^n expression says sum all the difference scores, i.e., add the $(X - M)$ difference scores for all n cases. As noted above this sum will always be zero. For example, in the Easy condition of Example 2 the computation would be:

$$(1 - 5) + (3 - 5) + (5 - 5) + (5 - 5) + (7 - 5) + (9 - 5) = 0$$

The deviations around the mean have useful properties in the analysis of variability. One ploy is to square the difference scores—in this way they will not sum to zero. Thus

$$(1 - 5)^2 + (3 - 5)^2 + (5 - 5)^2 + (5 - 5)^2 + (7 - 5)^2 + (9 - 5)^2 = 40$$

We have six such squared difference scores which sum to forty. The sum of these squared difference scores is often called the *sum of squares*. We may divide the sum of squares by the number of cases and obtain an average score.[2] This average measure of dispersion of the scores around the mean is called the *variance*. A formula for the variance may be written as:

$$\text{Variance} = \frac{\Sigma_1^n\ (X - M)^2}{n} = \frac{40}{6} = 6.67$$

Recall that we squared each deviation score before summing to avoid the problem of a sum of zero. As a descriptive statistic, the variance is a number in squared score terms. It is often convenient to have this statistic translated back into the original score units. This translation can be accomplished by taking the square root of the variance. This new measure is called the *standard deviation*, and a formula for it may be written as:

[2] The sum of squares is usually divided by $n - 1$ instead of n, the number of cases. The expression $n - 1$ is referred to as degrees of freedom, and will be discussed briefly in the following pages.

$$\text{Standard deviation} = \sqrt{\frac{\Sigma_1^n (X - M)^2}{n}} = \sqrt{6.67} = 2.58$$

In words, this statistic describing the variability of a set of scores is the square root of the average of the squared deviation scores.

These two statistics, the arithmetic mean and the standard deviation, are frequently used to summarize the information contained in a set of scores. Such summary devices are very useful, particularly if there are a large number of subjects in a sample. Just looking at all the individual scores may not be at all informative, and may even be confusing. Condensing the data so that we have the essential information about central tendency and dispersion of the scores is therefore a useful, time-saving device. Such condensation is the primary function of summary descriptive statistics.

Analysis of Variance of Example 2

The basic question we want to answer in our analysis is whether the two sets of scores are different enough so that we may be fairly confident in claiming support for the hypothesis that increases in frustration lead to increases in aggression. Some preliminary considerations are necessary. We selected 12 people and assigned them randomly to our two experimental conditions. These people were a *sample* from a much larger *population* of people that might have been used. If we could have obtained an aggression score from every member of that large population, we would have a grand mean of the aggression scores for the entire population. We might even in some sense consider this mean as the *true* mean of all the aggression scores that could be obtained if the experiment were run indefinitely.

Assume that the large total population was randomly divided into two subpopulations. Since the division into subpopulations was made on a random basis, the initial level of natural aggressiveness should be the same in both subpopulations. Level of "natural aggressiveness" refers to the aggression scores that would occur before any experimental manipulations were introduced. One subpopulation is then assigned to experience the Easy frustration condition and the other to experience the Difficult frustration condition. As a result of the frustration manipulation, each of the subpopulations would have a new mean aggression score (presumably at some level higher than the "natural" aggression score). Each of these means could be considered as a true aggression mean for each of the two experimental conditions. Another way of stating the matter is that the two subpopulation means that existed after the frustration manipulation reflect the true effect of the two frustration manipulations. If the hypothesis that increases in frustration lead to increases in aggression is true, then the subpopulation mean for the Impossible condition should be higher than the subpopulation mean for the Easy condition. If this hypothesis is false, however, then either (a) the two means should be the same, indicating that the null hypothesis is true, or (b) the Impossible mean is actually smaller than the Easy mean, indicating that the exact opposite of the original hypothesis is really the true state of affairs.

In actual fact we usually never know the true population means. All we have to rely on are our sample means. The issue is whether our sample means differ enough from each other so that we may make an *inference* that the actual subpopulation means would probably differ from each other as a result of the experimental treatments. Since the sample means are all that we have, we take our sample means as the best estimate of our population means. The sample mean of 5.0 for the Easy condition is the best estimate of the subpopulation mean of all possible subjects in the Easy condition. The sample mean of 10.0 for the Impossible condition is the best estimate of the subpopulation mean of all possible subjects in the Impossible condition. If we drew different samples of subjects, the means of the two experimental conditions would probably vary. The obtained difference of 5 between the two means might be 4 in another sample, 6 in a third sample, etc. Nevertheless, given our present sample, the difference of 5 between the two means is our best estimate of the difference between the true population means.

If the two sample means are our best estimates of the two true subpopulation means, then the variability of scores within a sample around its mean is problematic. This variability may be due to a variety of factors. The initial level of natural aggressiveness may vary widely among members of the sample. The experimental manipulation may not have had precisely the same effect on different members of the sample. Score variability may have been due to inadequacy of the experimenter's measurement technique, etc. This variability in scores around the sample mean is treated conceptually as error in the sense that the variability is a deviation from the best estimate (the mean) of the true subpopulation mean. Experiments always contain such error variability, and it is in this sense that the "errorless" scores given in Example 1 of Figure 9 were unrealistic. At the same time, it is precisely this variability within a sample which makes inferences concerning differences between means so difficult. What is needed is some mechanism or decision rule which allows inferences about differences between means for different experimental conditions, at the same time taking into account the variability within a sample.

In the analysis of variance, the decision rule for making such an inference may be stated as follows: if the ratio of variability *between* the means of the experimental conditions to the pooled error variability *within* the experimental conditions is sufficiently large, then we make the inference that the subpopulation means are really different from each other. The meaning of "sufficiently large" is defined by the type of statistical technique we are using. In the analysis of variance the meaning of "sufficiently large" is defined by what is called the F-test, which will be discussed in more detail shortly.

The variability of the two sample means around the grand mean may be found from the formula: $n\Sigma_1^2\ (M - M_g)^2$, where M is a sample mean and M_g is the grand mean of 7.5. The squared deviations of the two means are summed and then multiplied by n, the number of subjects in a condition, in order to express the variability between means at the level of the individual scores. The expression given above is called *the sum of squares between experimental conditions.* It is usually abbreviated SS. In Example 2, calculation of this term is as follows:

$$\text{SS between Conditions} = 6\,\Sigma\,[(5 - 7.5)^2 + (10 - 7.5)^2] = 75$$

We now need to calculate the error variability within each condition. First we proceed to calculate the sum of squares within each condition separately:

$$\text{SS Easy} = (1 - 5)^2 + (3 - 5)^2 + (5 - 5)^2 + (5 - 5)^2 + (7 - 5)^2 + (9 - 5)^2 = 40$$

$$\text{SS Impossible} = (6 - 10)^2 + (6 - 10)^2 + (10 - 10)^2 + (10 - 10)^2 + (14 - 10)^2 + (14 - 10)^2 = 64$$

Sums of squares are said to be additive, meaning that we may add the two error sum of squares to obtain a total error sum of squares: $40 + 64 = 104$.

In order to construct a ratio of the two variabilities, we do not compare the sum of squares between conditions directly with the error sum of squares. Instead we compare their variances. In analysis of variance terminology these variances are called *mean squares,* and are usually abbreviated MS. Technically, we do not divide the respective sum of squares by the number of cases as we did to compute a sample variance. The total number of "cases" *between* conditions is two because we are dealing in this instance with condition means, and there are two such means. The total number of cases *within* the conditions is 12, which is the number of subjects in the two conditions. The sums of squares are divided by a modified version of the total number of cases called *degrees of freedom,* usually abbreviated *df*. The number of degrees of freedom between conditions is $K - 1$, where K is the number of experimental conditions. In the example $K = 2$, hence *df* between conditions $= 2 - 1 = 1$. The *df* within a condition is $n - 1$, where n is the number of subjects in a condition. In the example $n = 6$, and, therefore, *df* within a condition is $6 - 1 = 5$. We added or pooled the two error sum of squares to obtain a total error sum of squares. We can also pool the *df* within a condition for both conditions to obtain a total *df* within conditions: $5 + 5 = 10$ *df* within conditions. Each of the two sums of squares may now be divided by its respective *df* to obtain the mean square (or MS):

$$\text{MS between Conditions} = \frac{75}{1} = 75$$

$$\text{MS Error (Pooled within Conditions)} = \frac{104}{10} = 10.4$$

We will not discuss why these two variances (or mean squares) are calculated by using *df* instead of the respective number of total cases. Extensive discussion of this issue may be found in any elementary statistics textbook.

We can now compare our two mean squares as a ratio. As noted earlier, this comparison is called an F-test or F-ratio. Thus,

$$F = \frac{\text{MS between Conditions}}{\text{MS Error}} = \frac{75}{10.4} = 7.21$$

Full interpretation of F-ratios and the concept of *sampling distributions* on which they are based are beyond the scope of this book. It is sufficient to state that once the F value has been calculated, a table of F values may be consulted to interpret the obtained F-ratio (such tables are included in the appendix of most statistics textbooks). If the obtained F-ratio equals or exceeds the value of F in a table for the appropriate *df*, then the results of the experiment are said to be *significant*. In the example, an F-ratio of 4.96 is required (Winer, 1962, p. 642) for the results to be called "significant at the .05 level." The usual interpretation of the latter statement is that if there were really no difference between the two subpopulation means, a difference between the sample means as large as the obtained one would occur by chance only five times in a hundred. Since the probability of such a chance occurrence is small (only .05), we would infer that the obtained difference was not a chance difference, and accept the hypothesis that the population means represented by the two sample means were truly different as predicted. Since our obtained F value of 7.21 was considerably larger than the critical tabled value of 4.96, we do in fact accept the hypothesis.

In journal reports only a summary statement of the analysis of variance is usually given. The summary is often presented in a table which has the following form.

Source of variation	SS	*df*	*MS*	*F*
Between conditions	75	1	75	7.21[a]
Error	104	10	10.4	

[a] Significant at the .05 level of confidence.

If the analyses are rather simple, the author may just discuss the *F* values and associated probabilities within the text of the results without bothering to present a formal summary table like the one above.

Factorial Experiments

The example given above was extremely simple, so simple in fact that the designs of all of the experiments reported in this book were considerably more complicated. Likewise, the statistical analyses were more complicated, although the basic principles detailed above are the same. One common experimental design is the 2 × 2 factorial shown in Fig. 6. In such designs there are two independent variables. In the simple example above we assessed only one experimental effect—the between conditions variation for two levels of frustration. In the 2 × 2 factorial shown in Fig. 6, there is the variable of frustration at two levels, but there is also a second variable: perceived aggressive intent of another person. In addition, these two variables in combination create the possibility of an interaction effect. An interaction may or may not be important in a given experiment. (See Fig. 7 and Fig. 8 for explication of the meaning of an interaction.)

In a 2 × 2 factorial experiment there is not one but three sources of variation that may be tested for significance. These sources are: (a) effect of first independent variable, (b) effect of second independent variable, and (c) the interaction between the first and second independent variables. The effects of (a) and (b) are usually referred to as *main* effects, while (c) is simply called the interaction effect. A schematic summary table for a 2 × 2 factorial follows for the two independent variables noted above.

The factorial experiment is very efficient in terms of information yield. Just by adding a second independent variable, one obtains an extra increment of information (the interaction effect) that is not available when only a single independent variable is manipulated. There is no end to

Source of variation	SS	*df*	*MS*	*F*
A. Frustration		1		
B. Perceived aggressive intent		1		
Interaction		1		
Error		$4(n - 1)$		

the number of variables that may be included in a design. For example, a $2 \times 2 \times 2$ factorial includes three independent variables, which may be designated A, B, and C. With these three variables, information is available concerning four interaction effects: AB, AC, BC, and ABC. The last term is sometimes called a "triple interaction," and it is a measure of the degree of interaction of all three independent variables with each other. With four or more independent variables the number of interaction terms increases rapidly. Higher order interactions are difficult to interpret, as noted earlier; therefore, three, or at most four independent variables will usually be the upper limit on the number of variables manipulated in the great majority of experiments.

In some experiments, subjects may serve in more than one experimental condition. For instance, in the frustration-aggression example the experimenter might have first exposed all subjects to the Easy condition, obtained aggression scores from them, and then later exposed the subjects to the Impossible condition and obtained aggression scores from them in this condition. Experimental arrangements in which subjects participate in more than one experimental condition are called *repeated measures* experiments. The circumstances in which such an experiment may be conducted are discussed in some detail in Chapter 5. Suffice it to state here that if such an experiment is feasible it has the advantage of reducing the size of the error variance, consequently making it easier to obtain significant effects due to the experimental manipulations. This advantage is due to the fact that in a repeated measures experiment, the variability due to individual differences between subjects may be separated or partialed out as an effect separate from the experimental effects and error variance. In the analyses discussed earlier the variance due to individual differences is part of the error variance. If such individual differences can be extracted from the error variance, it follows that the error term should be smaller, thus making it easier to obtain significant *F*-ratios as noted above.

The basic logic behind a repeated measures analysis of variance is quite similar to that of the analyses discussed earlier. The computational procedures differ somewhat, and the format of the summary tables differs slightly, as well. For example, there may be not one but several error terms in a repeated measures analysis. However, this should not cause any particular problem. The logic remains the same: the significance of a main effect or interaction is tested by comparing the mean squares for those effects against the correct mean square for error. In each such comparison the resulting F-ratio and its significance is interpreted in exactly the same manner as previously indicated.

It should perhaps be reiterated that the brief introduction to the analysis of variance presented in this section was extremely elementary. Many important issues were not discussed. The calculational procedures used were for demonstration purposes only. Much more efficient formulas exist to aid calculation, but they tend to obscure the logic behind the analysis of variance. Hopefully, this introduction will enable the reader completely unfamiliar with inferential statistics to gain some intuitive understanding of the Results Sections of the articles reprinted in Part II. Beyond basic intuitive understanding, however, becoming a skilled consumer and user of statistical analyses will require several courses in basic statistical techniques.

Chapter 3

THE SOCIAL NATURE OF SOCIAL PSYCHOLOGICAL RESEARCH

The Experiment as a Social Contract

So far, we have been largely concerned with formal aspects of theory and research. The comments about hypothesis testing, alternative interpretations, etc., would be valid regardless of the type of experiment conducted. Whether amoeba, rats, or men serve as subjects, for example, a null hypothesis outcome is still ambiguous for all the reasons specified earlier.

In social psychology, we are usually concerned with the behavior of humans, although there are some important exceptions (see Zajonc, 1969). In a social experiment with humans, the experimenter cannot relate to the subject in a completely impersonal way as he can with a lower organism such as the white rat. He must interact with the subject on a human-to-human basis. This interaction often introduces considerations into the experiment beyond the purely formal manipulation of variables and the collection of data in which the experimenter is interested. As a consequence, Orne (1962) has argued for a social psychology of the psychological experiment. The experiment is another type of social situation in the same sense that "going to the store" or "tending the baby" are social situations. Each situation has its own rules for appropriate behavior. The experimental situation is no exception, and therefore deserves to be studied as a type of social behavior with its own special rules and obligations.

Part of the difficulty arises because much of social behavior is conducted within the context of role relations. People orient to each other in terms of reciprocal roles. Teacher-students, clerk-customer, and husband-wife are examples of such role relations. Each reciprocal role relation is governed by sets of mutual expectations held by both role players. The expectancies define how the persons should behave, think, and feel when they are engaging in appropriate role behavior.

The social experiment may also be considered as a role situation. There are two major roles, that of *experimenter* and that of *subject*. When an individual agrees to participate in an experiment, he makes an implicit contract to play the role of a subject. As part of this contract, he is agreeing to participate in a special form of social interaction known as "taking part in an experiment." Orne believes that within our culture the roles of subject and experimenter are well understood, and that mutual expectations governing the two roles are well defined.

One important aspect of the role relationship is the extent to which individuals take the role of subject seriously. People often want to be "good subjects." This strong motivation to perform well is, as we shall see, a hindrance to the experimenter in providing a valid test for his hypothesis. A second aspect of the role relationship is that it is one of differential power. The subject places himself under the control of the experimenter, and consequently does almost anything he is asked to do. This differential power relation is usually extraneous to the variables under investigation. However, the possibility exists that the power relation distorts the obtained relationship in a way that would not have occurred if the power differential had not existed. We see, then, that the role aspect of the social experiment forces us to be cautious in generalizing our results beyond the experimental situation. As long as an individual is "playing the role of subject" we do not know if any obtained relationships between variables will still hold when he is playing some other role, such as husband. The existence of the power relationship is well illustrated by an experiment by Orne and Evans (1965). Six subjects were hypnotized and, under hypnosis, performed a variety of tasks such as picking up a snake. Six other subjects were not hypnotized. They were told that their role as subject was to fool the hypnotist. They were to simulate a hypnotic state. The results showed that the simulating subjects obeyed the experimenter more closely than the truly hypnotized subjects.

A third important aspect of the experimenter-subject role relationship is that once the subject agrees to participate, he implicitly agrees to perform a wide range of acts on request without inquiring as to their purpose. Orne (1962) illustrated this phenomenon with an informal experiment. He asked five acquaintances if they would do him a favor. When they agreed, he asked them to do five pushups. The typical reaction was amazement and the question "why?" Similar people were asked if they would take part in a brief experiment. When they agreed to do so, they were then asked to do five pushups. The typical response in this case was "where?" It seems that just about any request the experimenter makes is legitimized as long as the subject thinks he is participating in an experiment.

Thus, when individuals participate as subjects in an experiment they are strongly motivated to perform well, they place themselves under the power of the experimenter, and they will perform a variety of tasks they probably would not do in other social situations. Because of his motivation to do well, the subject has a stake in the outcome of the experiment. He wants to feel that he made a useful contribution and did not ruin the experiment. This leads directly into the problem of what Orne (1962) has called the *demand characteristics* of the experimental situation.

Demand Characteristics

We have discussed the subject's desire to do well and be a good subject in the experiment. In an earlier section we alluded to the investment the experimenter has in his experiment, particularly in confirming his hypothesis. Therefore, the best possible way a subject can behave is in a manner that confirms the hypothesis. Now, of course, the experimenter does not want the subject to confirm the hypothesis simply by being a nice guy and conforming. He wants the hypothesis confirmed because of the hypothesized variable relationships. For this reason, experimenters seldom tell subjects what the hypothesis is before they engage in the experiment. In fact, elaborate strategies may be used to hide the hypothesis from the subject. The strategy of deception will be discussed more fully below.

Most subjects do have the idea that the experimenter is trying to prove something, and they very often view their task in terms of "helping" the experimenter find what he is looking for. In a sense, then, the experiment becomes a project in problem-solving for the subject. He views his task as trying to determine the true purpose of the experiment, and to respond in a manner which will support the hypothesis. Therefore, all the cues which convey an experimental hypothesis to a subject become significant determinants of his behavior. Orne (1962) has called the sum total of such cues the *demand characteristics of the experimental situation.* Demand characteristics include such things as campus scuttlebutt about the experiment, the nature of the experimental setting, the experimenter and his behavior, and the explicit and implicit communications between experimenter and subject during the experiment. Each aspect of the situation may provide a source of cues which convey the hypothesis in whole or in part to the subject. Therefore, in any experimental situation the subject's behavior is jointly determined by some combination of the experimental variables and demand characteristics.

Orne suggests that demand characteristics always exist because people always ascribe purpose and meaning to what they are doing. Therefore the experimenter's job is not to rule out demand characteristics completely, because that is not possible. Rather, his job is to try to minimize them as much as possible, and to ascertain to what extent they existed in a given experiment. Discovering to what extent the subject has deduced the hypothesis is not always easy. One common procedure is to interview the subject at the end of the experiment. An interview is not foolproof, however, because both experimenter and subject have a vested interest in the subject's ignorance of the hypothesis. Both may, therefore, implicitly and unconsciously make a pact of ignorance so that the true depth of the subject's awareness will not be discovered. It follows that the nature and extent of hypothesis communication may be very difficult to determine in a social experiment.

Orne (1962) has a particularly rosy view of the subject's motivation. The subject is viewed as an altruistic, cooperative creature who is only too happy to do the experimenter's bidding. Other experimenters are more pessimistic about subjects' motivation. In some experiments the subjects seem unconcerned about what the experimenter is trying to accomplish. Worse yet, the subjects' motivations may be antithetical to the experimenter's purposes. "General contrariness, a desire to be the exception to the rule, or a motivation to reduce the status between the experimenter and subject by refuting the experimenter's hypothesis would also lead the subject to ferret out the solution and to produce its opposite" (Kiesler, Collins, & Miller, 1969, p. 52). Differences in such motivations probably depend upon the specific type of experimental situation. Some experiments are just much more fun to participate in from the subject's point of view than others. There may also be differences between experimenters. Some experimenters may "bring out the best" in subjects while other experimenters generate antagonism for one reason or another. We will discuss experimenter effects more fully below. The fact remains that whether the subject's motivation is positive, neutral, or negative, the problem of demand characteristics must be dealt with in the social experiment.

An important consideration in the literature on demand characteristics is the nature of the subject population from which samples are drawn. The issue of population sampling will be considered in more detail later when the problem of generalizing beyond the experiment is discussed. For present purposes it should be noted that many experiments use subjects who are volunteers. There is a growing literature which indicates that volunteer subjects differ in certain characteristics from nonvolunteers. Volunteers tend to have higher intelligence and a higher need for social approval, among other things. Thus volunteers' motivation and ability to deduce and confirm the experimenter's hypothesis should be greater than for nonvolunteers. Therefore, volunteers should be more susceptible to demand characteristics, and the fact that Orne has typically used volunteers may be responsible for his rosy view of subjects' motivation. Rosenthal and Rosnow (1969) have done an excellent job in summarizing the literature on volunteer subjects.

In addition to the problem of volunteers noted above, experiments probably differ in their susceptibility to demand characteristics. As a general rule, the more complex and elaborate an experiment is, the more possibilities which exist for conveying an hypothesis (either correct or incorrect) to a subject. This statement should not be taken as a mandate that only simple experiments should be performed. Even in the simplest experiment, the hypothesis may be inadvertantly communicated to the subject. For example, the article by Hendrick and Costantini in Chapter 8 describes two relatively simple experiments. Both experiments were concerned with the primacy effect in impression formation. Subjects were read sets of trait adjectives that purportedly described individuals, and then rated how much they would like each individual. Sets of traits were read in either a desirable-undesirable or an undesirable-desirable sequence. Typically, more favorable ratings were obtained with the desirable-undesirable sequence than with the reverse sequence. This difference in ratings is called a primacy effect.

When subjects participate in such a study, the general nature of impression formation is usually explained to them before they do the ratings. However, the primacy effect is not explained. If the subject knew that the experimenter expected more favorable ratings for the desirable-undesirable sequences, it would be very easy for him to comply and produce them. Several strategies may be employed. A large number of sets may be used. The experimenter is careful to see that a given set and its reverse order do not follow each other consecutively. Additionally, several filler sets may be used in which the trait words are arranged in a random order. In this way the subject does not develop an expectancy that the traits are always arranged in desirable and undesirable blocks.

Thus, even in simple experiments, such as the primacy studies, demand characteristics must be taken into account. Just how this may be accomplished will vary from one experiment to another. However, a number of general approaches have been used in many social experiments. We discuss some of these strategies in the next section.

Overcoming Demand Characteristics

There are several techniques that may be used to minimize demand characteristics. We will discuss three of them: the use of deception, including a cover story; the use of deliberate role-playing, and the experiment disguised as a nonexperiment.

Deception

Deception is very common in social psychological experiments. In fact, Mills (1969, p. 419) says that ". . . it is almost always necessary to conceal the true purpose of the investigation from the subjects until the experiment is completed." Actually, deception includes a variety of practices ranging from a minor deceit to an elaborate staging game in which the true purpose is actually very different from what the subject is told. In the experiment by Hendrick and Costantini discussed earlier, the deceptions were relatively simple. Basically, they involved omissions rather than outright lies. The subject was told the truth about the general purpose of the experiment—that it was concerned with personality impression formation. However, he was not told of the specific concerns of the experimenter. He was not told the hypothesis, and in fact several ploys, as previously described, were used so that the subject would not discover the specific variable under investigation.

In contrast, the experiment by Aronson and Mills discussed earlier was much more elaborate and carried deception to high degrees of refinement.

A cover story was used which gave the subjects a (pseudo) reason for the experiment. Subjects thought that they were going to join a group discussing the topic of sex. The manipulation of unpleasant effort was consistent with the cover story. Due to the nature of the topic, it was reasonable that some individuals would be embarrassed and could not participate fully. Therefore it was reasonable to institute an "embarrassment test" to screen out unsatisfactory discussants. The embarrassment test, of course, constituted the manipulation of the independent variable. After the subject "passed the test" a further deception was used. Subjects listened in on what was ostensibly an ongoing group discussion. The discussion was in fact a tape recording, and making it credible required considerable finesse on the part of the experimenter.

In the Aronson-Mills study, the entire experiment was, in a sense, a staged deception, beginning with the cover story and continuing throughout the experiment. The cover story provided an important rationale which helped to maintain the credibility of the experiment. Most experiments which involve much deception usually have a rather elaborate initial cover story. Constructing the cover story often seems to be a work of art in social experiments. If done well, the cover story leads nicely into the manipulation of the independent variable. Also, the cover story provides the subject with a substitute hypothesis for the actual hypothesis. It is not usually satisfactory to fail to give the subject some kind of initial explanation for the experiment. The subject will not maintain a blank state of mind just because he has not been told anything about the experiment. He will play the guessing game of trying to figure out what the experiment is all about. These attempts to deduce the hypothesis may have unwanted effects. Variability of subjects' behavior is increased. Some subjects may discover the correct hypothesis, others may "discover" an incorrect hypothesis, etc. It is better, then, to give the subjects an initial standardized rationale for the study. The cover story serves this function.

One may genuinely question whether such elaborate deceptions are necessary. The issue of deception is quite controversial at present in social psychology. Recently, Kelman (1967) has criticized deception in social experiments. He points out a number of problems with deception as a technique. Ethical considerations are relevant since the use of deception may constitute an unwarranted invasion of the subject's privacy. Also, in deceiving the subject the experimenter is taking advantage of an unequal power relationship. He may be abusing his power advantage. In addition, the systematic use of deception involves a certain degradation of human relationships, which may ultimately create a group of dishonest cynics, otherwise known as social psychologists. Finally, there is the practical consideration that subjects become "gun-shy" from repeated deceptions. The consequence is that social psychologists may put themselves out of business within a couple of generations.

One's position on the problem of deception is a value question. Our own position is that, given the nature of social research, some deception is probably necessary. The kinds of questions which social psychologists are interested in investigating just cannot be investigated adequately if subjects knew all the details of the hypothesis in advance. People are too self-conscious and sensitive to their own behavior. For example, one area of social research is attitudes and attitude change (see Kiesler, Collins, & Miller, 1969 for a review). The determinants of attitude change are studied in numerous experiments. One relevant variable is communicator credibility. Does a highly credible communicator effect more attitude change than a low credible communicator? The typical approach to the problem is to attribute a constant communication to two different communicators, expose a group of subjects to one of the communications, and then measure acceptance of the communication on a rating scale. The usual result is that the more credible the communicator, the greater is the acceptance of his message.

It seems relatively clear that the usual results would not be obtained if the experimenter explained his hypothesis and manipulations to subjects before presenting the communication. For one thing, it seems to be a cultural norm that people should make up their minds on the basis of the "evidence." Their attitudes should not be influenced by factors that are not part of the rational arguments. In actual fact, of course, attitudes are influenced by a variety of nonrational variables. The actual facts are discrepant with the cultural norms. If people were aware that they were in an attitude experiment, the odds are high that they would behave according to the (assumed) cultural norm. But then the results of the study would be results about cultural norms rather than results about variables which change attitudes.

Of course, the effects of such knowledge can be made an empirical question. One can ask just what would be the effects if people thought their attitudes were going to come under persuasive attack. One novel answer is that there would be an anticipatory belief lowering following the warning of the impending attack. This type of research is dealt with in Chapter 9. Several articles are reprinted that deal explicitly with the effects of warning of persuasion on actual persuasion. Thus, in this area of research the question of the effects of deception versus no deception has become an empirical question.

There are other areas of research where deception seems necessary to study the variables of interest. Dissonance research, discussed in Chapters 6 and 7, seems to be such an area. The study of conformity is another example. The cultural norms against being a conformist are very strong. If an experimenter set up a conformity experiment and told subjects he was interested in how much they conformed, it is unlikely that he would observe much conforming behavior.

Thus, some use of deception seems inevitable. Of course there is no point in using deception simply for the sake of deception. In trying to test an hypothesis an experimenter should make certain the hypothesis cannot be tested without deception. If deception is necessary, a good general rule would be to use as little deception as possible. In a given case more deception may be used than is absolutely necessary. For example, in the Aronson-Mills study discussed earlier, the experiment could undoubtedly have been simplified and less deception used. However, given the hypothesis that severity of initiation leads to greater attraction for a group, it seems clear that a considerable amount of deception was necessary to give the hypothesis an adequate test. Also, deception may sometimes be used to create a more powerful manipulation of the independent variable, a possibility that Aronson and Carlsmith (1968) have noted. We shall have more to say about this use of deception in the next section.

Therefore, our position is that some use of deception is inevitable, given the pervasiveness of demand characteristics and the present nature of social psychological research. The nature of social psychology may change drastically in the future so that this statement may no longer be valid. The ethical issue in the use of deception should not be overlooked. As Aronson and Carlsmith (1968) have noted, social psychological research involves a clash between two values: a belief in the value of free and unfettered scientific inquiry, and a belief in the dignity of man and his right to privacy. People differ in the relative importance they assign to the two values. The majority of social psychologists probably emphasize the scientific value, at the same time recognizing the importance of the second value. Since one's choice is itself a value question, we are obligated to respect those who feel that the value of dignity and privacy must be given overriding concern. One solution that has been proposed for the problems of deception is the use of role-playing as an experimental technique.

Role-Playing

The essence of a role-playing experiment is that the subject is asked to take the role of a particular person in a particular situation, and behave "as if" he were that person. No problems of deception are involved. Also, the problem of demand characteristics is attenuated because there is no need for the subject to engage in elaborate guessing games concerning the experimenter's hypothesis. For some types of experiments, role-playing may be an effective technique. However, as a general strategy for social research we cannot recommend it. The role-playing strategy may be effective when the usual social behavior is consistent with the cultural norms for that behavior, but there are discrepancies between norms and actual practice in a great many social situations. The norm that one should not be gullible to a persuasion attempt has already been mentioned. Norms concerning "bravery" and conformity are also likely to diverge from actual behavior. In an excellent example, Aronson and Carlsmith (1968, p. 27) pointed out that if we want to select marine officers, it is unlikely that we would do so on the basis of a "brave" response to a hypothetical role-playing situation. We would be more confident in our selection procedure if we placed the recruit in an actual situation that required some actual behavior. So, we see that although the problem of demand characteristics is reduced with role-playing, other problems are introduced. The major problem is the subject's distortion of his verbal responses so that they fall into line with the approved cultural norms for that behavior. Thus, role-playing may be a good technique for gathering data on cultural norms, but probably not very good for data about actual behavior in actual situations. The question is ultimately empirical. It would be valuable to see several research problems investigated with both role-playing and with the conventional approaches. In this way we could discover to just what extent role-playing does give results comparable to those of a deception experiment.

Orne (1969) has proposed a variant of role-playing as a device for uncovering whether or not demand characteristics exist in a given experiment. This version of role-playing is one of several quasi-controls (Orne 1969, p. 153) that may be used to assess whether demand characteristics potentially exist. Orne called this type of role-playing "pre-inquiry" (also a "non-experiment"). A better term might have been a phenomenological pretest, because subjects are shown the experimental room and equipment, the procedures are explained to them, and they are asked to produce data as if they were real subjects. If the preinquiry subjects produce data similar to that of actual subjects, then it is possible that actual subjects may have guessed the hypothesis and confirmed it. This is only a possibility, however, as Orne indicated, because the phenomenology of preinquiry subjects and actual subjects may have been very different. Actual subjects may have produced their results because of the manipulations, while preinquiry subjects produced identical results because they deduced what the results should be. This use of role-playing may be of minor usefulness at times, particularly if the pattern of results the experimenter expects seems contrary to common sense expectations, and if he has some reason to suspect that subjects may deduce his hypothesis.

The Disguised Experiment

This final technique for controlling demand characteristics involves conducting an experiment without the subjects realizing that they are participating in an experiment. An example of this type is a study reported by Insko (1965). The experiment was a verbal conditioning study. The paradigm for this type of study involves an experimenter or interviewer giving subjects verbal reinforcement (such as uh-huh, good, etc.) for certain types of verbal responses by the subject. The question of interest is whether the rate of verbal output (of the reinforced responses) increases as a result of the reinforcement. Insko's experiment was concerned with the verbal reinforcement of an attitude. Undergraduates at the University of Hawaii were called on the telephone and asked to strongly agree, agree, disagree, or strongly disagree with a series of 14 statements. The issue was concocted—the creation of a Springtime Aloha Week. Half the subjects were reinforced for giving a pro response and half were reinforced for a con response. A week later the students were asked to complete a questionnaire in class that contained a crucial question on the issue. The results showed that subjects who were positively reinforced were more favorable on the issue than subjects who were reinforced for holding a negative attitude.

The subjects in Insko's study were not aware that they were participating in an experiment, at least not until the final attitude measure was taken. Therefore it is unlikely that demand characteristics were operating on them. As another and, perhaps, more extreme example, Abelson and Miller (1967) conducted a disguised experiment in which an experimenter approached an individual sitting on a park bench. Ostensibly, the experimenter was conducting a man-on-the-street interview. The individual was questioned on his views concerning an issue. The "interviewer" then questioned a person sitting next to the subject. In reality the second person was an experimental confederate who proceeded to express an opposite viewpoint, and to derogate the subject's position. The experimenter then questioned the actual subject once more to observe the effect of the stooge's insult. As expected, the subject became even more extreme in his initial viewpoint.

The technique of the disguised experiment may be very effective in some cases. However, it is no panacea to the problems of demand characteristics. For one thing, probably not all (or perhaps very many) hypotheses may be tested with this technique. Many social experiments require complex cooperative behaviors on the part of the subject. It may literally be impossible to conduct the experiment unless the subject explicitly knows that he is participating in the experiment. Another problem is control of extraneous variables. In the disguised experiment, the experimenter cannot usually bring the subject into the laboratory. He must go into the subject's behavioral settings. These settings may contain a great many unwanted factors that vary in an unpredictable way from subject to subject. Thus the disguised experiment will contain much variability due to uncontrolled factors, and the experimenter increases the risk of a null hypothesis outcome.

A final problem with the disguised experiment is an ethical one. In the disguised experiment the subject has not made a social contract with the experimenter to engage in his experiment. In this sense, the deception involved is more blatant than in the most deceptive of explicit laboratory studies.

As a technique for minimizing demand characteristics, selective use of the disguised experiment has much to recommend it—assuming the experimenter can overcome his qualms about the type of deception involved. One great value of this approach is that it allows assessment of the generality of a relationship outside the context of the experimenter-subject role relationship. Earlier we indicated that the power difference between the two roles is a contaminating variable. Because of this variable we usually do not know whether relationships obtained in an experiment will hold in nonexperimental settings. It would be valuable if more hypotheses were tested with both the traditional experiment and with the technique of the disguised experiment. If similar results were obtained in both cases, we could have considerably more confidence in the generalizability of our experimental results.

Thus, the problem of demand characteristics must always be dealt with in social research. Hopefully, the preceding discussion has shown that the experimenter can use a variety of strategies to minimize their effects. We would reiterate that the problem of demand characteristics must be handled individually in each specific experiment. Deception, or role-playing, or the disguised experiment are general approaches. They cannot be mechanically applied with any assurance of success in a specific case. Each experiment will require its own additional strategies that are unique to that experiment. With experience, the researcher becomes more sophisticated in the problem of hypothesis communication to the subject, and more or less automatically builds in procedures to prevent it. Actually, as Mills (1969, p. 419) has indicated, experimenters were aware of these problems long before the term demand characteristic was coined. Nevertheless, we feel that Orne (1962) has provided a valuable service in explicitly coining and discussing this concept. It is our impression that in the intervening years (since 1962) social psychologists have become more careful and rigorous in the conduct of their experiments.

One important variable in the total experimental situation is the experimenter himself. In some respects he may be the most important variable. He provides a directive focus for the subject's behavior. He engages in complex role behaviors and transmits complex communications to subjects. Thus, the experimenter can have many effects, both intentional and unintentional, wanted and unwanted, and conscious and unconscious. The experimenter can be a prime source of demand characteristics. In short, the experimenter is a variable in the social psychological experiment and his behavior requires close scrutiny. We turn now to a consideration of the experimenter as a variable. We will focus largely on those unintended, unwanted, and unconscious effects that the experimenter can have when engaging in his role as experimenter.

The Experimenter as a Variable

Robert Rosenthal (1966) has studied experimenter effects in great detail. In his 1966 book, Rosenthal reviewed a number of his own as well as other investigators' studies on this topic. The evidence indicates that experimenter effects do exist. There are a variety of such effects ranging from recording errors to subtle communication of the hypothesis to the subject. Experimenters do make unconscious recording and computational errors. They are a minor source of bias, but they tend to be in the direction of supporting the hypothesis. The sex of the experimenter may make a difference in the results obtained. Rosenthal cited a number of studies showing sex effects. In some cases there are complex interactions between the sex of the experimenter and the experimental conditions. In other cases the sex of the experimenter may interact with the sex of the subjects. Other experimenter attributes that have affected the outcome of a study include the experimenter's age, his race, religion, anxiety level, birth order, intelligence, socioeconomic status, and length of experience as an experimenter. The list is discouragingly long.

The bulk of Rosenthal's work has been concerned with one specific experimenter effect—the experimenter's expectancy about the experiment and the effect of this expectancy on the subject's behavior. Experimenter expectancies include a variety of things, but the most important is his expectancy (and desire) that the hypothesis be confirmed. If the expectancy is communicated to the subject in either obvious or nonobvious ways, the odds are increased that the experiment will come out as predicted because of the subject's desire to be a good subject. We see, then, that experimenter expectancies and their communication are a special case of Orne's (1962) demand characteristics.

Rosenthal designed a standard task to study experimenter expectancies. A set of 20 photographs was selected from a large initial collection. The photographs had been rated by judges on how successful the individuals appeared to be. In the critical set of 20 photos used in the many experiments, the mean rating of "successful" was neutral, around zero on a scale ranging from —10 to +10. In a typical experiment, several advanced undergraduate majors were used as experimenters. Their task was to conduct the experiment with college freshman. The basic task was to have each subject rate all the photos in the set. The experimenters were divided into two different groups. One group was told that the mean rating of the photos would be around +5. The other group was told that the mean rating would be around —5. In this way differential expectancies about the outcome of the experiment were created. The results showed that experimenters expecting positive ratings from their subjects obtained higher ratings than experimenters expecting negative ratings.

The inference to be drawn is that somehow the experimenter communicated his expectancy to the subject which in turn affected the subject's behavior. Rosenthal has systematically replicated the basic experiment many times. In many of the replications, communication of experimenter expectancy does seem to occur. However, it is unclear how it occurs, that is, whether by subtle voice cues, postural and gestural cues, etc.

Some caution is required in interpreting these studies. For one thing, such subtle communication of expectancies seems counter to much of our everyday experience. It is difficult enough to get your meaning across to the other fellow when you are talking to him directly. The communication of subtle covert meanings would seem even more difficult. Most teachers have had the experience of making a clear factual statement to a class, and then discover that there are at least 15 different interpretations of what was said. At a more substantive level, Barber and Silver (1968) recently published a penetrating critique of Rosenthal's work. Much of their criticism concerned the statistical analysis Rosenthal performed on his data. Their general conclusion was that the evidence for the effects of experimenter expectancies was much weaker than had previously been thought. More importantly, other investigators (Barber *et al.,* 1969) have failed repeatedly to replicate Rosenthal's earlier results. On the other hand, Rosenthal (1969) has more recently offered extensive documentation for the experimenter expectancy effect.

Rosenberg (1969) offered some possible insights into why some researchers obtain expectancy effects while others do not. Rosenberg coined the term *evaluation apprehension* to designate the subject's concern that when he participates in an experiment his emotional adequacy and mental health will be evaluated by the psychologist. Fear of evaluation will often stimulate subjects to "put their best foot forward." This conception is roughly similar to Orne's concept of the helpful, faithful subject. In several experiments Rosenberg (1969) manipulated both experimenter expectancy and degree of the subjects' evaluation apprehension. Results typically showed that strong expectancy effects were obtained only under conditions of high evaluation apprehension. Apparently subjects are more attuned to slight voice and postural cues when they are highly apprehensive, and therefore more likely to deduce and confirm the hypothesis. Rosenberg's data suggest that the failure of some laboratories (e.g., Barber *et al.,* 1969) to replicate the experimenter expectancy effect may be attributed to a failure of their procedures to arouse evaluation apprehension in subjects. Implicit in Rosenberg's work is the notion that experimenter expectancy effects are obtained because: (a) the experimenter (or some aspect of his procedures) arouses apprehension about evaluation in subjects, and (b) the experimenter in some subtle way communicates his expectancy to subjects. Rosenberg (1969) offered some evidence that expectancies are communicated via intonations of the experimenter's speech, such as variations in volume, pitch, and rhythm. However, more research is required to pin down such effects with any certainty.

Despite our uncertainty about the communication of experimenter expectancies, there is abundant evidence that the experimenter is an important variable. Even if expectancies are not subtly communicated, the facts of the experimenter's race, sex, etc., may interact differentially with experimental conditions. Such interactions limit the generality of the results. One of us (Hendrick) has recently been severely plagued with the problem of experimenter effects. To make matters worse, these effects were obtained in a very simple experimental situation. The experimental situation was modeled after the primacy experiments by Hendrick and Costantini discussed earlier and reprinted in Chapter 8. However, instead of trait words, numbers were used as stimuli. The basic reasoning was that the trait task was one instance of a more general problem area concerned with how people analyze and process serially presented information. If this were so, then comparable results should be obtained for a variety of different stimuli. Consistent with this reasoning, several number sets were constructed that contained a block of three large numbers and three small numbers. The number sets were each read to the subject at a rate of one number about every two seconds. The subject's task at the end of each set was to give a "psychological average" for the entire set. Unknown to the subject, each set was read twice to him, once in a large number-small number sequence, and once in the reverse sequence. It was expected that a primacy effect would be obtained in the guesses—the guess for the large-small sequence should be consistently larger than the guess for the small-large sequence.

This hypothesis was strongly confirmed in two different experiments (Hendrick & Costantini, 1970). In the experimental situation, the subject sat facing the experimenter. When the subject arrived, he was seated, and the experimenter gave a five minute oral explanation of human information processing and explained how the task was to be performed. He then read the sets to the subject and recorded his guesses. Given the simplicity of the experiment, there was little reason to suspect that any experimenter effects might be operating in the situation.

The first two experiments described above were conducted by Experimenter A, an advanced graduate student with considerable research experience. The following quarter a more elaborate experiment was planned which incorporated one of the previous experiments as a replication. A new experimenter (J), a new graduate student, was used. One further change was that the initial instructions were tape recorded. Over a series of 50 or so subjects, there are undoubtedly practice effects from repeating the instructions so many times. The delivery to the 50th subject may be very different from the delivery to the 10th subject. A nicety of experimental control would be to repeat exactly the same instructions to every subject. For this reason the instructions were tape recorded. However, the experimenter still read the number sets orally.

Much to our surprise, there were no significant effects in the experiment. None of the conditions showed a significant primacy effect. There were two major possibilities. First, the taped instructions may have seemed too cold and impersonal, so that the subject had a very different cognitive set for the number averaging than in the first two experiments. Another possibility was the näiveté of Experimenter J. This was the first experiment he had conducted, and as Aronson and Carlsmith (1968, p. 21) have noted, failures to replicate are sometimes due to incompetence. Learning to be a good experimenter takes practice, and since this was J's first experiment, näiveté was a reasonable explanation.

At this point, another experiment was conducted. There were two independent variables. One variable was the experimenters. Three experimenters were used: A, J, and K. Experimenter K was an advanced undergraduate psychology major. The second variable was the delivery of the instructions. Half the subjects received their instructions from the tape recorder. For the remaining subjects the instructions were orally delivered by the experimenter. This experiment illustrates well something that was discussed earlier. If a procedural variable is suspected of having an unwanted effect, it should be incorporated into the experimental design and explicitly varied. In the present experiment two such variables were manipulated in a 2×3 factorial design. Both independent variables were, therefore, concerned with procedural problems. Experiments of this type are called *methodological* studies—they are concerned solely with problems of method and procedure, rather than with conceptual independent variables.

One final procedure was that after the experiment, the subject completed an extensive questionnaire evaluating the experimenter and the experimental situation. The results for the guessed averages were disappointing. Experimenter A obtained strong primacy effects for both the taped and oral instructions. Experimenters J and K obtained no effect in either condition. Also, the questionnaire responses were unenlightening. There were no differences in the ratings of the three experimenters.

At this point a certain consistency in experimenters was evident. Experimenter A could obtain a primacy effect under almost any conditions, while J could not obtain a primacy effect at all. There were still further possibilities. We began to consider seriously the possibility of differential communication of expectancies. All three experimenters knew the nature of the primacy research and the results that the senior investigator hoped to obtain. Experimenter A may have unconsciously behaved so that the subjects would confirm the hypothesis, while J and K "leaned over backwards" not to be positively biased, and consequently were negatively biased. Another possibility not completely ruled out was differential experimenter näiveté. Experimenter K had not conducted an experiment before, and J, although he had now run about 100 subjects, was still näive relative to A.

Given these possibilities, still another experiment was conducted. Two students, one male and one female, were recruited from an introductory psychology course to serve as experimenters. They were trained only in the mechanics of gathering data. They were not told anything about the hypothesis, impression formation, or anything else. We think they were exceedingly näive. As a further control, A trained one of these experimenters, and K trained the other one. Both of these näive experimenters obtained huge primacy effects from their subjects. In fact, the results were even better than any that A had ever obtained, and with fewer subjects as well!

Thus, in one swoop, communication of experimenter expectancies and näiveté were eliminated as explanations for the previous experimenter effects. Of course, the problem remained of explaining why those experimenter effects occurred. Frankly, we are still not sure at this point. The explanation may lie not in the experimenter per se, but in the more interesting conceptual variable of rate of information processing. We suspect that the experimenters varied ever so slightly in the rates at which they read the stimulus sets to subjects. If so, the possibility exists that the occurrence of a primacy effect depends very critically upon the rate at which information is presented. The effects of rate of presentation have not yet been explored in the primacy research. We selected the two-second interstimulus interval because this interval had been used in several previous experiments. There was no reason to believe that slight variations in rate of presentation was a critical variable. The next step of course is to explicitly vary rate in a carefully controlled and precise manner. There are still other possibilities for stimulus presentation that will be discussed more fully in the next section.

We hope that the preceding discussion shows clearly that the experimenter is an exceedingly important variable in the social experiment. The example should also illustrate just how difficult it can be to pin down the nature of experimenter effects. Even in simple experiments, the possibility for experimenter bias always exists. The control of bias should, therefore, be a major consideration when planning an experiment. We turn now to consideration of some general tactics experimenters have used for controlling bias in social experiments.

Controlling Experimenter Effects

There are a number of techniques for controlling experimenter bias, or at least minimizing its effect. We will discuss four of them, automating the experiment, the ignorant experimenter, the blind experimenter, and performing the experiment in two stages.

Automating the Experiment

When experimenter bias seems likely to occur in an experiment, it is sometimes possible to minimize it by reducing the experimenter's presence or getting rid of him entirely. Our previous discussion of the number averaging experiments provides a good example. We indicated that the experimenter effects may have been due to slight differences in the rate of pronunciation of the numbers. Automation of the experiment provides an ideal way for checking this hypothesis. One way is to use an adapted slide projector and present the stimuli visually. Rate of presentation can be exactly varied. For some subjects, the numbers may be presented at one second intervals, for other subjects, at two second intervals, etc. In fact, the experimenter can leave the room entirely after he seats the subject and explains the initial instructions. The subject is provided with a score sheet and asked to record his guesses after each number set. Another possibility is to use taped oral presentation of the numbers. Recording technology is such that the time interval between stimuli can be controlled precisely. Comparison of oral versus visual presentation might reveal some fascinating differences in information processing by different sensory modalities. At any rate, experimenter effects would be well controlled because the experimenter would not directly present the stimuli.

In the example above, automation seems an excellent strategy for overcoming experimenter effects. One should not conclude, however, that automation is always (or even often) the answer to the problem. In most social experiments it is usually not possible to dispense with the experimenter. For example, in the experiment by Aronson and Carlsmith reprinted in Chapter 6, it is difficult to imagine how the experimenter might have been dispensed with entirely. One part of his job was to provide "success" or "failure" feedback to subjects after a block of trials. The social situation of having the experimenter provide the feedback constituted a powerful manipulation of the independent variable. If it were possible to automate the feedback, it is doubtful whether the subject would have been affected very strongly by the manipulation.

Thus, the experimenter is often an important motivating force for the subject to take the experiment seriously. The physical presence of the experimenter provides a social inducement to perform well. This inducement is independent of whether or not the experimenter provides a specific source of bias. In fact, the absence of the experimenter may induce its own peculiar form of bias. For example, in the number averaging experiments discussed above, it was most important that the subjects take their task seriously. On the one hand, we did not want subjects to guess the exact average because we were concerned with a particular kind of error in the guesses—the primacy effect. On the other hand, it was necessary that the subject try to "handle" or process all six members in a set. If he was so unmotivated that he started daydreaming, he might respond randomly or use only two or three numbers as a basis for his guess. The results would probably be worthless. Therefore, even if the presentation of the stimuli were automated, it would probably still be necessary to have the experimenter unobtrusively present in the room. Of course the question is an empirical one and could easily be investigated. Experimenter present versus experimenter absent could be manipulated as an independent variable.

We conclude that some minimal presence of the experimenter is necessary in most social experiments. Given this requirement, however, there are still several ways to handle the problem of bias.

The Ignorant Experimenter

One possibility is for the senior investigator on a research project to have his assistants conduct the experiment in ignorance of the hypothesis. The assumption is that if the experimenter is ignorant of the hypothesis there is no way he can communicate it to the subjects. On the face of it, this strategy seems very reasonable. There are some problems, however. There is no assurance that the senior investigator will not subtly communicate the hypothesis to his assistants, who in turn will communicate it to the subjects (Rosenthal, Persinger, Vikan-Kline, & Mulry, 1963). Also, experimental assistants are usually graduate assistants who are in a doctoral training program. They would not be content to run subjects in perfect ignorance, and, indeed, would probably deduce the hypothesis in short order.

Rosenthal (1966, p. 364) has an interesting suggestion that we need a new professional discipline—that of the professional experimenter. The training and qualifications for this professional would be in terms of craftsmanship and skill in doing the actual job, rather than in abstract considerations of theory and hypothesis testing. His position would be somewhat analogous to that of professional interviewer, or in medical research, the laboratory technician. His training and orientation would involve collecting accurate data. He probably should be unconcerned with hypothesis testing or publishing in journals. His skills would be in the craftsman aspect of the trade, and his rewards would derive from excellence in plying that trade.

We do not know if the proposal is feasible, but it is an interesting possibility. In a sense, experimenters are often involved in a conflict of interest. They want their hypothesis to be confirmed, but they also want their data to be accurate. Rosenthal's (1966) work indicates that the desire for confirmation sometimes wins out in subtle ways over the desire for accuracy. The suggestion for a professional researcher potentially reduces that conflict. The creative Ph.D. comes up with the great hypothesis, but the testing of it is taken out of his hands and turned over to a skilled, sensitive, but disinterested professional researcher. The idea may have some merit.

The Blind Experimenter

Given that the experimenter is not usually ignorant of the hypothesis, it is still possible to make him strategically ignorant during certain parts of the experiment. The real problem arises in experiments where each subject must be run individually. It is always possible that the experimenter can behave in subtly different (but inappropriate) ways in the different conditions. There are several possibilities for overcoming this problem.

First, it is sometimes possible to design an experiment so that more than one (or possibly all) conditions can be run at once. There are several subjects, but different subjects receive the different treatment combinations. Attitude experiments provide a good example. Suppose one wants to vary communicator credibility and strength of the arguments in a 2×2 factorial design. All the manipulations and the communications are constructed in booklet form, and the booklets are randomly distributed to a large group of subjects. Since all conditions are run simultaneously, the experimenter cannot usually have a differential biasing effect. He explains the nature of the experiment and the instructions only once, and thus his behavior is a constant for all subjects.

There are many social experiments in which it is necessary to run subjects individually. For example, in the Aronson and Mills experiment it might have been possible to run two or three subjects at once, although it would have been very complicated. Also, the strength of the "embarrassment test" would have been attenuated because the subjects would have had each other's social support in getting through the test.

The ideal for the experiment where subjects are run individually would be the *double-blind* experiment. This technique is used in medical research. Half the subjects are given the experimental drug, and half are given a placebo, but neither the subjects nor the experimenter know who gets which. This ideal is not possible in most social research because the manipulations necessarily differ for different experimental conditions. Partial use of the technique is possible, however. The experiment may be arranged so that the experimenter does not know which condition the subject is in until a certain stage in the procedure. For example, the experimenter might explain the initial rationale for the study, and then check some cue which tells him which condition the subject is in. He might consult a slip of paper, glance at his wristwatch, etc. If still an additional manipulation is to be introduced at a later point, the experimenter can remain ignorant of that condition also until the appropriate time. In the experiment by Aronson and Carlsmith these possibilities could have been used. The experimenter could have presented the introductory statements in ignorance of the condition to which the subject was assigned. After the instructions he could have consulted a slip of paper to see whether the subject was to "succeed" or "fail" on the first four trials. The second manipulation was introduced on the fifth and final trial. Before the beginning of the fifth trial, the experimenter could have consulted a second slip of paper to see whether the subject succeeded or failed on that trial. The possibility of biasing differences in the experimenter's behavior would not have been eliminated, but such blinding would have reduced that possibility considerably. The blind experimenter is, therefore, a useful strategy to reduce bias. It should be incorporated into the experimental design whenever feasible.

The Two-stage Experiment

This last strategy for reducing bias basically involves a separation of the manipulation of the independent variable from the measurement of the dependent variable. The use of this strategy is not possible in some experiments. When it is possible, there are several ways in which it can be employed. One ploy is to have the subject think he is in two different experiments when in fact there is only one. In one attitude experiment, Rosenberg (1965) had subjects write essays opposed to their own position for different amounts of money. The dependent variable of attitude change was measured in a following "second experiment." The staging was elaborate enough so there was little doubt the subject actually thought he was participating in two experiments. The beauty of this strategy is that the first experimenter could not have communicated a subtle expectancy of how the subject should respond on the attitude scale because the first experimenter did not administer the scale. Also, the second experimenter was ignorant of which money condition the subject was in, so that it is unlikely that he could have influenced his behavior.

Another possibility is that the subject is aware that he is participating in only one experiment, but two different experimenters are used. The first experimenter introduces the manipulation, and the second one collects the relevant dependent data. Both experimenters, of course, remain blind to what the other one has done. There are probably numerous other variations on the two-stage experiment.

Thus, there are many possibilities for minimizing experimenter bias. The most appropriate techniques depend upon the specific requirements of each experiment. One certain generalization is that the possibility of experimenter bias always exists, and it must be taken into account in every experiment.

The techniques discussed above may be used to minimize experimenter bias or eliminate it entirely. Such techniques may not always be possible. If not, then some check on the magnitude of expectancy effects may be profitably incorporated into the experimental design. Rosenthal (1966, 1969) has called such checks *expectancy control groups*. The nature of these controls may be illustrated with an example. Suppose that in a certain community there exists a group of very poor families and a group of very well to do families. Following sociological convention we may designate the former group as "lower" or "working" class families, and the latter as "upper" class families. Based on many years of previous testing, the average score on an intelligence test is 115 for children from upper class families, but only 85 for children from lower class families.

Each year children from both types of families serve as experimental subjects for graduate students at a nearby university who are learning to administer IQ tests. These graduate students know both the average IQ score of the two social class groups and the particular social class membership of each child tested. This knowledge automatically creates differential expectancies of test performance which may bias the behavior of the graduate students during the administration of the test so that they do in fact obtain the expected IQ scores.

Certainly it is a reasonable experimental hypothesis that children from the upper class have higher IQ scores than children from the lower class. But there is also the possibility that all men are indeed created equal, leading to the null hypothesis prediction of no difference in IQ between the two social classes. It is entirely possible that the difference in IQ found between classes over the years was due to the testers' expectancies that such differences should occur. Expectancy is an additional, potentially contaminating variable which could be assessed by explicitly varying expectancy in some way independent of actual social class membership.

Let us suppose that the professor teaching the testing course decided to assess expectancy effects. He proceeded in the following manner. First, he went to a great deal of trouble to ensure that in the test situation lower class children did not overtly appear to be very different from upper class children (e.g., type of clothing worn by the two groups was controlled). Second, the professor lied a little to his graduate students who gave the tests. To be precise he lied half the time. He told one group of students that they would test only upper class children. In fact, half of the children tested were upper class, but the other half were lower class. The remaining group of graduate students were told that they would test only lower class children. Half of these children were indeed lower class, but the other half were upper class. With this bit of deception the professor was able to create two different levels of expectancy for test performance (an "upper expectancy" and a "lower expectancy"), and this expectancy was independent of the actual social class membership of the children that were tested. The nature of the experimental design is shown in Fig. 10. The columns in each matrix show the actual social class of the children, while the rows show the expectancy of type of children the graduate students thought they were testing. The numbers in the cells of the two matrices are hypothetical mean IQ scores illustrating two possible outcomes of the experiment.

First, let us assume that the pattern of means shown in the left matrix of Fig. 10 were the results the professor obtained from his experiment. It is quite clear that the only variable that made a difference was actual social class of the children. Upper class children had an average IQ of 115 and lower class children had an average IQ of 85, regardless of the expectancy graduate students had for the type of children they were testing. Clearly expectancy of how the results should come out did not influence how they actually came out.

A very different conclusion would be drawn, however, if the results shown in the right matrix of Fig. 10 had been obtained. Those results show that when graduate students thought they were testing upper class children, they obtained average IQ scores of 115, regardless of the actual social class membership of the children. Similarly, when students thought they were testing lower class children, they obtained average IQ scores

Social class graduate students expected to test	Actual social class of children: Lower	Upper
Upper	85	115
Lower	85	115

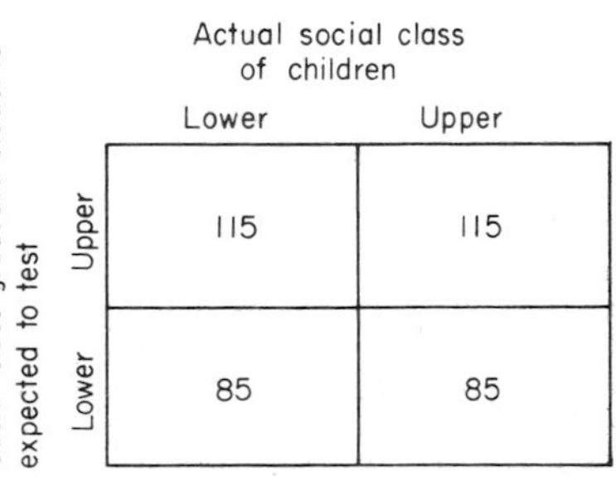

Fig. 10. Illustration of the use of expectancy control groups.

of 85, regardless of actual social class membership. The set of results shown in the right matrix indicate that (had they actually occurred) the expectancy of the tester is indeed a powerful variable. These results suggest that the hypothesis of an actual difference in IQ between the two social classes is untenable. The difference actually found over the years was probably due to tester expectancy. However, until expectancy control groups were created, this fact could not be discovered.

Although expectancy control groups do nothing to eliminate experimenter effects, such groups do provide a way for assessing such effects. In so doing, they help prevent false inferences concerning the relationship between independent and dependent variables. Therefore, whenever feasible, such expectancy controls are highly desirable and should be incorporated into the experimental design.

Chapter **4**

CONDUCTING THE EXPERIMENT

In this chapter we will deal with some topics that have been mentioned earlier, but which require more explicit discussion. We include a discussion of (a) the types of social experiments, (b) pretesting, and (c) the nature of experimental operations—particularly the issue of *behavioral* versus *cognitive* operations.

The Types of Social Experiments

Social psychology more than most areas of psychology varies in the types of experiments which go under the banner of "social psychological." The articles reprinted in this book illustrate this variety. These experiments range from the relatively simple impression studies to the fairly complex dissonance studies. One reason for this variety is the lack of standardized manipulations of independent variables. In contrast, areas such as verbal learning and operant conditioning have fairly well standardized research paradigms which include an elaborate technology.

Another reason for the variety of different experiments is that social psychologists are interested in a wide range of behavior—from small group processes to the study of cognition within the individual head. Such diverse interests necessarily require variation in techniques and procedures. However, even within a specific research area, diversity of procedures is endemic. One investigator may manipulate a variable in one way, a second in a very different way. Consequently, it is difficult to compare the two experiments in any meaningful manner. Some people have become discouraged with the seemingly endless production of independent research studies. On the other hand, the series of articles in this book indicate that continuity of research does exist. Nevertheless, the criticism does have some merit. The independent, single studies probably still outnumber the cumulative research series. This is due only in part to the variation in methodology. It is also due to lack of systematic, wide-ranging theory. The result is that the creative social psychologist comes up with an interesting (but rather specific) hypothesis, tests it, and then moves on to another hypothesis. Theoretical traditions are beginning to develop, however. One immediate example is the several consistency theories. Also, fairly elaborate theories of attitude change have been proposed during the last decade (e.g., Insko, 1967; Kiesler, Collins, & Miller, 1969). As a consequence, we may see a number of fairly standard research paradigms emerge during the next several years.

One crude way of classifying social experiments is according to a simplicity-complexity dimension. This classification may be applied both to the staging of the experiment (primarily to the manipulaton of the independent variable), and to the method of data collection. The impression formation studies are quite simple in both manipulations and data collection. The elaborate performance expectancy studies in Chapter 6 are perhaps of average complexity for a social experiment. Another way of classifying experiments is in terms of whether behavioral manipulations and behavioral measures are used, or whether more cognitive procedures are used. We will have more to say about this issue later.

Actually, the complexity of social experiments has received considerable criticism. For example, Ring (1967) has suggested that the complex experimentation derives not so much from necessity, but from the particular values that social psychologists hold. Ring feels that experimental social psychology is dominated by an ethic of having fun. Clever experimentation on exotic (implication unimportant) topics with a zany manipulation is the sure path to professional success. Ring even suggests that the fun-and-games approach has its own set of rules. First your experiment should be as flashy and flamboyant as possible. An effective manipulation is good, but an effective, *amusing* manipulation is even better. If you have selected a topic for study which is ordinary, you should reconsider. Finally, you should never make an obvious prediction. If one detects a note of cynicism about social psychological experiments, he has interpreted Ring correctly.

Our own answer to the problem of overly complex experiments is more muted. We are somewhat skeptical that social psychologists deliberately set out to complicate their experiments—it is just too much work. What happens is that once you get a problem or hypothesis, you come up with an initial general strategy for testing it. The more you think about it, the more problems you think of, and the more procedural refinements you add to overcome those problems. When you pretest (discussed below), still more problems arise, and more refinements are required. The end result is an elaborate, complex experiment. The social nature of the social experiment, the problems of bias, the need for deception, and the complex nature of the variables manipulated—all of these things work together to produce a complex experiment.

We do have some concerns with complex experiments that are more mundane than Ring's concerns. Obviously an experiment should be no more complex than is required for an adequate test of the hypothesis. But it should be no less complex either. The principle of Occam's Razor has had a moderating effect on the development of complicated theories. The principle says that a theory should be no more complex than is absolutely necessary to explain the phenomenon in question. Similarly, a principle of the procedural paring knife may be proposed which states that experiments should be no more complex than is absolutely necessary to test the hypothesis adequately.

One problem with complex experiments is that the experimenter often does not know what is going on. Of course this can happen in simple experiments as well—the number averaging studies discussed earlier provide a good example. However, in general, the more complex the manipulation, the more likely it is that extraneous variables, as well as the variable of interest, will be manipulated; thus, the results may be due to the extraneous variable rather than the proposed independent variable. Additionally, the more complex the experiment, the more difficult it is for the experimenter to explain exactly what he did. Journal space is at a premium. The experimenter will describe only what he considers to be the important aspects of the procedure. If some small procedure was actually important but he did not know it, the journal article becomes the experimenter's myth rather than a factual report. This means that if someone else attempts to replicate the study, he will probably fail in the attempt. Replications may fail for many reasons as Aronson and Carlsmith (1968, p. 21) have noted. However, if very many replications fail very many times, confidence in the original results is severely eroded. If such lack of replicability occurs in many areas of research, confidence in social psychology as a substantive discipline will also erode. Experimenter incompetence is certainly one reason why replications fail. But "incompetence" probably increases in direct proportion to the complexity of the experiment. If the net result is that social experiments can only be performed by the talented few, the question of generalizing (or using in a practical way) the obtained knowledge becomes quite acute.

We are not saying that complex experiments should not be done. We are saying that the norm of doing the job as simply as possible is a good one. Complexity of the manipulations does pose its own special problems as indicated above but very often experimental complexity will be required. The would-be researcher should develop the best design he can to test his hypothesis. If the design and associated procedures must be complex, then so be it. We do feel that it would be a good idea if the experimenter would keep our paring knife principle in mind. Once the general strategy for the experiment is relatively firm, it would not be a bad idea for the experimenter to ask himself if a simpler procedure would work as well.

We have finally arrived at the stage of actually doing the experiment. The researcher has a hypothesis, and has decided on a general strategy—either simple or complex—for testing it. It is now time to iron out the details. Usually that requires pretesting.

Pretesting and Pilot Studies

Pretesting may be thought of as a partial run of the experiment to see how well some of the procedures work (Aronson & Carlsmith, 1968, p. 49). A pilot study is a run through the entire experiment, usually with a small number of subjects. Complex experiments usually require considerable pretesting. The experimenter may think that certain procedures will work, but he cannot know for sure until he gives them an actual test. For example, if deception is used, the experimenter invents what he believes to be a credible cover story. However, in the actual situation, subjects may find it quite incredible. Pretesting (or a pilot study) is, then, quite valuable for ironing out rough spots in the procedures.

There are both positive and negative aspects of pretesting. One positive aspect was discussed above. Another use of pretesting is to help define more precisely the nature of the manipulation of the independent variable. Suppose the experimenter starts an experiment and continues it through to the point of manipulating the independent variable. At this point, the experimenter discontinues the formal experiment and assesses the effect of the manipulation without collecting the dependent variable data. Some behavioral manifestations of the subject may be noted, he may be asked to complete a questionnaire, and he may be interviewed intensively. In the actual experiment, the check on the manipulation must usually be performed near the end when the dependent variable is measured. The effects of the manipulation may be obscured at this point. Therefore, a check on the manipulation just after it is introduced can be more informative about how well it worked. An interview with the subject can be especially useful. His personal reactions to the manipulation (e.g., fear, surprise, anger, etc.) can be detected more easily. If the subject is likely to get suspicious, introduction of the manipulation is usually the crucial point for arousal of such suspicion. The immediate pretest interview is more likely to ferret out such suspicion than the casual postexperimental interview during the actual experiment.

The intensive checks just after the manipulation can help to purify the manipulation. For example, suppose an experimenter wants to manipulate fear at low and high levels in different subjects. The pretest interview may reveal that the high fear manipulation not only aroused fear, but also hostility, an unwanted reaction. If the check were not performed until the end of the experiment, the subject might be so relieved that he forgot that he was angry earlier. As a result of the interview, the experimenter could refine his procedures until the high fear manipulation produced just fear, uncontaminated by anger arousal. In this way, pretesting the manipulation enables the researcher to zero in on the conceptual independent variable with his empirical operations.

Pretesting is also helpful in assessing the strength of the manipulation. In the example above, the experimenter may intuitively feel that his high fear manipulation induces more fear than the low fear manipulation. However, he may discover in pretesting that his intuition was wrong. If the entire experiment had been conducted without this check, a great deal of time and effort would have been wasted. The pretest allows the researcher to change his procedures at minimal expense so that a stronger manipulation can be designed.

Pretesting is also useful in refining the dependent variable measure. The particular quantitative index initially selected may be too crude to reflect accurately the manipulation. Pretesting the measure may suggest possible refinements. The quantitative nature of the dependent measure is a problem at times. The particular measure used will tap only a small segment of what is a total behavioral complex. The particular measure may miss the most important behavior, or it may constrain behavior in inappropriate ways. For example, if one is interested in the emotional effects of a manipulation, a convenient measure is a mood rating form. Such forms typically contain a number of mood words (e.g., worried, angry, tense, etc.). The subject rates himself on a numerical scale on each of the words. In actual fact, the subject's emotional state may be quite different from anything that might be inferred from the ratings. Discovery of this difference would not be possible, however, because the dependent measure constrained the subject's responses to a predefined set of categories.

The problems of constraint by the dependent measure, and the increased likelihood of measuring the wrong behavior are important ones. As Aronson and Carlsmith (1968, p. 58) have noted, "Any experimenter who has seen many subjects close at hand has experienced the feeling that a given subject is 'really' showing lots of interesting effects, but that the measures are too constrained to be sensitive to them." One possible solution that Aronson and Carlsmith (1968) have noted is to run a fairly large number of pretest subjects with the dependent variable as unconstrained as possible. Introduce the manipulations of the independent variable, and then see what the subject says or does.

> By this means we may get some ideas as to exactly what behaviors we can look at which are likely to reflect the processes we believe are taking place. As one observes what the subjects do and say in response to the manipulations, it becomes possible to select dependent measures which may assess accurately the responses of the subjects, and to rule out certain alternative behaviors so as to maximize the likelihood of change on an important variable (Aronson & Carlsmith, 1968, p. 58).

These recommendations have the merit of ensuring that the experimenter selects and measures an important dependent behavior. However, there is a serious danger, we believe, which must be guarded against. Let us pose the danger by an illustration. Suppose we have an experimenter who does not have a hypothesis in mind, but he thinks of an interesting independent variable manipulation. He performs the manipulation and observes the behavioral consequences. He notices that one particular behavior is very responsive to the manipulation. He then decides that this behavior is an instance of some conceptual dependent variable. Presto—he now has a hypothesis which is a sure bet for confirmation in the formal experiment.

The basic danger is a conceptual smearing together of the independent and dependent variables. Even if the experimenter does have a hypothesis in advance, it is all too easy to choose opportunistically any behavior that is sensitive to the manipulation, and then rationalize it as an adequate instance of the conceptual dependent variable. The major difficulty is that a beautiful empirical relationship may be obtained without much clarification of the underlying relationship between the conceptual variables.

We are not saying this procedure is indefensible. On the contrary, it may be very valuable when a new hypothesis is proposed for which there are no guidelines for appropriate operations. We feel that the derivation of such a dependent measure should be carefully explained in the journal report (something almost never done). Also, follow-up studies should carefully explore the limits of the particular behavior to determine if it is indeed an appropriate measure of the conceptual dependent variable.

The biggest problem in letting the manipulations dictate the dependent measure is that the hypothesis may be falsely confirmed. The particular measure chosen may in fact be better suited as an instance of some very different conceptual dependent variable. Given the looseness of fit between our concepts and our operations, a facile writer can make almost any bit of behavior seem like a reasonable example of the general dependent variable. The net result is a retardation in the development of social psychological theory. We recommend, therefore, that when testing hypotheses, the conceptual nature of the independent and dependent variables be carefully defined and distinguished. A set of operations (or perhaps multiple sets) for manipulating the independent variable, and proposed measures for the dependent variable, should be specified in advance of any pretesting. It would be desirable to pretest the independent variable and dependent variable separately, if at all possible. The manipulations and measures could be revised and tested again if necessary. In this way, the independent variable remains empirically separated from the dependent variable. At the same time, the two variables also remain conceptually distinct from each other. In those cases where the experimenter is too uncertain about the behavior to propose tentative measures in advance, Aronson and Carlsmith's (1968) recommendations have considerable merit. In this case, however, we feel that the written report should describe the pretesting in as much detail as the description of the main experiment.

One other problem with pretesting is that it can capitalize on chance. Suppose we have a hypothesis which is really false. Suppose we perform 20 different experiments to test it. By chance we will get positive results once or twice in the 20 trials. Pretesting and pilot studies may similarly capitalize on chance in a more insidious way. A procedure may be continually pretested and revised until the experimenter discovers one that gives positive results. However, by fortuitous combinations of (irrelevant) variables, some procedure is bound to show positive results sooner or later. The result is apparent confirmation of a false hypothesis.

> This statistical problem is particularly aggravated if the experimenter runs a few subjects and then analyzes the data to see if they conform with his hypothesis. If they do not, he makes a revision in the procedure and starts over again. If they do, he continues to run subjects and includes the data from the "pretest" subjects who confirmed his hypothesis. This procedure capitalizes on chance even more blatantly than the successful pilot study procedure. It is as though the experimenter ran successive groups of twenty subjects in the same procedure, stopping and starting over again every time the first twenty subjects fail to confirm the hypothesis and continuing with the experiment only in the event that the first half of his subjects confirmed the hypothesis. He has waited until chance favors the hypothesis for the first half of his subjects (Kiesler, Collins, & Miller, 1969, p. 77).

There is no pat solution to this problem. Kiesler, *et al.*, (1969) recommend that the researcher report the number of previous unsuccessful pilot studies. We think this is a good idea. In this way the consumer can make up his own mind about whether the reported relation is genuine.

Pretesting, as we have seen, has problems as well as positive features. This is not surprising since there are problems involved in all stages of research. We would not want the reader to get the impression that pretesting is undesirable. On the contrary, it is both desirable and necessary. By being aware of the problems, the would-be experimenter can guard against them. We can then feel more confident that the obtained relationships are genuine rather than artifacts of chance.

We turn now to a fuller consideration of the nature of experimental operations. It is at the level of actual operations that success or failure as an experimenter (at least in social psychology) is most likely to be determined.

Experimental Operations—Behavior Versus Cognitions

There are two basically different ways of constructing operations and measures for social experiments. With respect to manipulating the independent variable, "The basic decision for the experimenter is whether his independent variable will be produced by some set of instructions to the subject, or whether it will be some event which happens to the subject" (Aronson & Carlsmith, 1968, p. 42). Similarly, a decision must be made about the dependent variable. The experimenter has an option of measuring some aspect of actual, overt behavior, or measuring a verbal response either on a questionnaire or in an interview.

The events-versus-instructions approach to research corresponds to a general behavior-versus-cognition approach to the study of social behavior. The researcher may have a relative preference for "events," or "happenings" as manipulations of variables, and some measure of overt behavior on the dependent variable. Other researchers prefer to rely on verbal instructions to the subject to manipulate the independent variable, and to collect verbal responses from the subject on the dependent measure.

The distinction between the behavioral approach and the cognitive approach to research is not completely clear-cut. As an example of an event manipulation, consider the performance expectancy experiment by Aronson and Carlsmith in Chapter 6. In that experiment subjects either successively "succeeded" or "failed" on a social sensitivity test. The success-failure manipulation was a powerful one. Things happened to the subject, he was involved in the experiment, and it had a strong impact on him. In that particular experiment, the measure of the dependent variable was also behavioral in nature—the number of changes the subject made in a repeat of the last test trial.

As another example, consider the experiment by Aronson and Mills in Chapter 7. The independent variable was manipulated by the event of having subjects recite either mild or obscene words. However, the measure of the dependent variable was cognitive—the subjects rated the degree to which they were attracted to the group. In contrast, consider the personality impression experiments in Chapter 8. They are almost entirely cognitive in nature, involving the subject largely at a verbal level. The attitude experiments on forewarning in Chapter 9 are also examples of "cognition" experiments. They achieved their effects almost completely through verbal instructions to the subjects.

The distinction between the behavioral and cognitive approaches to research is relative. Even the strongest "event" experiment usually requires some minimum of instruction. Nevertheless, the distinction is a useful one. The evaluative question of whether one approach is better than the other requires consideration. Our answer is that both approaches can be useful. Some areas of research seem more amenable to the behavioral approach; other areas make sense only when conceptualized in terms of the cognitive approach. For example, the impression research is a viable, active area of interest at present. It is difficult to visualize how that area could be translated into a series of event experiments. So, the particular problem area or hypothesis will usually dictate which approach is best.

Sometimes an experimenter has an option of going either the behavioral or cognitive route in executing an experiment. In that case preferences will show. Some social psychologists, either by training or temperament, prefer behavioral experiments. Others are more comfortable with cognitive experiments. Aronson and Carlsmith (1968) recommend a behavioral experiment when at all possible, and there are several good reasons for their recommendations. An event manipulation has a stronger personal impact on the subject—usually creating a more powerful manipulation of the independent variable. Powerful manipulations are at best difficult to achieve in social experiments, but without strong manipulations we run the risk of a null hypothesis outcome. Using event manipulations may, therefore, help ensure a successful outcome to the experiment. Event manipulations may also have some negative effects. Strong manipulations may, on occasion, vary an unintended variable, such as the subject's emotionality. When such effects occur, the precision of the manipulation of the intended conceptual independent variable is attenuated.

Another advantage of the event manipulation is that when the subject is highly involved, he is likely to forget that he is "playing the role of a subject." He is too busy coping with some problem situation to be overly sensitive to experimenter-subject role relationships, or to play the guessing game of trying to deduce the hypothesis. The net outcome is that the results are more likely to be generalizable to nonexperimental situations.

Another alleged advantage of the event manipulation (which we think is debatable) is that by successively refining the event, the subjects are likely to place the same interpretation on the event that the experimenter does. To the extent that such consensus occurs, the experimenter can have more confidence in the operational realization of his conceptual independent variable. An empirical question is involved here. The issue is whether meaning may be more uniformly transferred from one human to another by linguistic symbols (instructional operations) or by events (behavioral operations). We suspect that there is no pat answer to the problem. In some situations, an event may have more uniform interpretation. In other situations, verbal instructions may be more uniformly interpreted.

These considerations are relevant to the issue of stimulus control versus psychological control (Kiesler *et al.*, 1969) in manipulating the independent variable. The basic question is whether the same objective stimulus situation should be brought to bear on every subject, or whether procedures should vary across subjects in an attempt to bring every subject to a uniform psychological state. The ideal would be a constant stimulus situation which had a uniform effect on every subject. This ideal can seldom be attained in social experiments. People differ widely in their interpretations and reactions to the same object. Therefore, a uniform psychological state might require very different manipulations for different subjects. Opinions diverge widely as to how far an experimenter should vary from strict adherence to set procedures. Most researchers probably compromise to some extent. They have a constant set of procedures, but allow slight variations for a given subject in order to make the manipulations effective for him.

Apparently, Aronson and Carlsmith (1968) feel that the best compromise can be achieved by an event manipulation. This is probably true for some situations, but certainly not all. At any rate, the experimenter should be aware of the behavior-cognition distinction. When planning an experiment both alternative approaches should be considered. If either approach seems feasible, we are inclined to agree with Aronson and Carlsmith (1968) that event manipulations and direct behavioral measures are preferable to the cognitive approach. For several specific techniques for achieving event manipulations, the reader is referred to Aronson and Carlsmith (1968, pp. 39–51).

Chapter 5

GENERALIZING BEYOND THE EXPERIMENT

In this last chapter of Part I, we will discuss several problems with experiments that have been alluded to previously, but were not given systematic consideration. The major topic is the problem of extending the results of an experiment beyond the specific experimental situation—the problem of generalizability.

The distinction between internal and external validity of an experiment will be discussed, and one specific problem, population generality, will be considered in some detail. We will conclude with an analysis of several specific problems such as (a) chronic versus acute manipulations of independent variables, (b) internal analyses of data, and (c) conditions where nonrandom assignment of subjects is appropriate.

Internal and External Validity of an Experiment

The problem of generality has been discussed previously several times. In particular, when we considered demand characteristics, we noted that the subject-experimenter role relationship may limit the extent to which we can generalize our results beyond that particular social relationship.

The basic task of an experiment is to demonstrate the hypothesized relationship between independent and dependent variables. Once that demonstration is made, we may then inquire about the conditions under which the relation will hold. We are really asking how general the relationship is. For example, if a relation can be obtained with just one specific set of operations and one specific dependent measure, that relation is quite limited in value. The general hypothesis we hoped to confirm is thereby restricted to one specific empirical manifestation. Hypotheses are usually stated generally. In actual practice, a test of a hypothesis must always be a specific test, limited to particular procedures with particular subjects at a particular time. Any specific experiment, then, always contains an unknown with regard to generality of the obtained relationships.

The problem of generality can be considered at several levels. At the most immediate level is the question of whether or not an obtained relationship can also be obtained in other experiments using different manipulations and different dependent measures. Such procedural and measurement generality increases our confidence that the original results were not due to chance. More importantly, multiple sets of operations that yield comparable results with multiple dependent measures strongly increase our confidence in the generality of our conceptual hypothesis. The more empirical realizations of it that we can find, the more certain we are that it is a general predictive hypothesis. Generality across procedural operations and measures is, then, very important in hypothesis testing.

Once we are confident in the generality of our hypothesis across experimental situations, we may concern ourselves with whether the relationship can be demonstrated in nonexperimental situations. Essentially, we are trying to discover the class of social situations in which the variable relationship holds true. There are several methods for studying such generality, including survey studies, field experiments, and the technique of the disguised experiment discussed earlier. The special nature of the role relation in the social experiment is only one reason why experimental results may fail to generalize to other social situations. Variable relationships can be exhibited in relatively "pure" form in the laboratory. In other social situations (sometimes referred to as the real world), these variables will often be complexly intertwined and interacting with other variables. Some of these other variables may be so powerful that they obscure the relationship obtained in the experiment. In fact, it may be impossible to detect the experimental relationship in any natural social situation. Such a possibility does not necessarily mean that the experimental relationship is unimportant. If we have some notion about what the third variable might be that is obscuring our relationship, we may be able to incorporate it into our theory and perhaps specify how it is interacting with our experimental independent variable. Of course, if our "theory" consists in just the one hypothesis that we tested in the experiment, we will be in a quandry because we will have no idea why the hypothesis does not hold in natural situations. In that case our experimental hypothesis has rather limited usefulness, even if confirmed 50 times in the laboratory. This eventuality is another argument favoring the development of general social theories. If we have a theory that can predict numerous relationships between several variables, the odds increase that the theory will predict across many social situations, with the experimental situation as just one special case. If we have only one lonely hypothesis that seems to hold only in a tightly controlled experiment, we may well question the value of that experiment.

Once a relationship is established in an experiment, we may wonder if the relationship will hold for other types of people. If the relation holds for college students, does it also hold for children, for old people, for different socioeconomic classes? This is the question of population generality of the obtained relationship. We will give this question special consideration below.

We see, then, that the question of generality has several facets. We are asking not one but several questions. These questions have been discussed in detail by Campbell and Stanley (1963) under the rubrics of *internal validity* and *external validity* of an experiment. "Internal validity is the basic minimum without which any experiment is uninterpretable: Did in fact the experimental treatments make a difference in this specific experimental instance?" (Campbell & Stanley, 1963, p. 175). External validity is concerned with generalizability. "To what populations, settings, treatment variables, and measurement variables can this effect be generalized?" (Campbell & Stanley, 1963, p. 175). Ideally, an experiment would be high in both external and internal validity. In actual fact, the extent of both types of validity will be in doubt in a specific case. As we have indicated, a specific experiment is bound by time, place, procedures, subjects, and measuring instruments, so that it is an empirical question of how far the results may be generalized. Internal validity is threatened by alternative interpretations of the results and by a null hypothesis outcome if a true relationship actually exists between the independent and dependent variables. Essentially, internal validity asks the question of whether obtained effects are attributable to the manipulations of the independent variable, or to some uncontrolled event. Several general classes of such uncontrolled events were discussed by Campbell and Stanley (1963), including history and maturational factors, the sensitizing effect of taking a pretest on test responses a second time, instrumentation effects, certain statistical artifacts, subject selection biases, differential subject loss during the course of the experiment, and complex interactions between any of these variables. The operation of any one of these specific factors is a threat to an obtained relationship because the results may be due to the biasing factor rather than the manipulation of the independent variable.

Internal validity may be increased by careful attention to the formal design of the experiment and by attention to experimenal operations. Assuming an obtained relationship, any procedure that reduces the possibility of an alternative explanation increases internal validity. External validity may be increased in several ways. Replication of the experiment with a variety of operations and measurements provides procedural generality. Replication with samples from different populations provides population generality. Finally, confirming the hypothesis in a variety of situations (including nonexperimental situations) provides setting or situational generality. The problem of setting generality has received rather extensive consideration at various places in this chapter. We will devote our attention to the problems of generalizing to other people—the problem of population generality.

Sampling: The Problem of Population Generality

Psychology has sometimes been accused of building its structure on a weak foundation. There is not a general psychology, but the "psychology of the white rat and college sophomore." To some extent, the criticism has merit. Psychological research is most often done in universities. The majority of social psychological experiments use college students as subjects. The reasons are practical. It is inconvenient and expensive to recruit subjects from other segments of the society. The subject restriction is even more specific in actual practice. Most human experiments use, as subjects, students who are taking an introductory psychology course. In large universities, participating in a certain number of experiments is part of the course requirement. Most of the experiments reprinted in this book used such students as subjects.

Given such selective use of only one group of people, we may wonder whether the body of knowledge we develop has any applicability to the general population. This query is not precisely stated. The notion of a general population is vague. There is not one, but many populations. We may mean all the people living in the United States, but we may also mean all the one-eyed red-heads living in Maine. The point is that we can arbitrarily define a population of interest which we wish to study. In fact, the statisticians tell us that our population is defined by the way we draw our sample. Thus, if we draw our sample from college sophomores, the results of our experiment can be generalized only to college sophomores. Actually, we can generalize only to college sophomores taking an introductory psychology course. Strictly speaking, we cannot generalize to students in other universities, because we did not randomly sample from different universities. It begins to sound very much like we cannot generalize from our college sophomore experiment at all. From the standpoint of formal statistical considerations, we are indeed limited in our ability to generalize. We draw our sample in such a way so that it is in effect unique. How the sample differs or fails to differ from any other group of people cannot be specified. Since we do not know how our particular nonrandom sample may differ from other samples, it follows that logically we cannot generalize beyond our specific sample.

What we are saying essentially is that we do not draw a random sample of people from a well-defined population. We take those people who are available, and they happen to be college sophomores. Of course, given our sample we are very careful to randomly assign them to experimental conditions. Random assignment to conditions was discussed earlier. It is extremely important to have such random assignment in order to control for biasing factors intrinsic to different subjects. If subjects are randomly assigned, we may be relatively certain that they did not differ on some third variable which might provide an alternative explanation for our obtained results. So, in the typical experiment, the researcher is very fussy about random assignment to conditions, but is quite unconcerned about randomly drawing his entire sample in the first place. This may seem anomalous, but in fact the practice can be justified, as we shall see.

Most investigators probably assume intuitively that their results really will generalize to other types of people, even though, on statistical bases, their subject selection procedures preclude such a conclusion. Other experimenters may replicate the study in another university, or an occasional experiment may be reported using people other than students as subjects. So, even if the investigator has not randomly sampled from several types of people (the equivalent of random assignment to conditions within the experiment proper), he may feel intuitively that if he had done such sampling, his results would hold for all those groups.

There is an even stronger reason why some investigators are not bothered by lack of population generality of experiments. Festinger (1959) feels that the main task of an experiment is to discover a relationship between variables. This point is of course completely consistent with our previous discussion. Sampling considerations are not too important as long as one follows random assignment to conditions. Festinger contrasts the experimental study with another type of research, the descriptive study, or, as he calls it, a parametric study. One question we can ask is how much of some attribute exists in a defined population. Or we may be concerned with relative incidence of a characteristic in two different populations. For example, suppose we suspect that blood type differs among racial and ethnic groups. Our research problem becomes that of determining incidence of blood type in defined ethnic groups and making comparisons between groups. For this kind of research, sampling considerations are very important. Suppose we are interested in comparing blood types of blacks and whites. It will not do to test samples of black and white students from an introductory psychology class and expect our results to hold for blacks and whites in general. There are many variables on which our college population differs from the society at large. They are more intelligent, they come from the middle or upper middle socioeconomic class, etc. If the distribution of blood types is differentially related to any of these variables, our conclusions from our college sample would be wrong because we sampled incorrectly. To answer this particular question adequately we would have to draw random samples of blacks and whites from all segments of the society.

As Festinger (1959, p. 361) noted, there are many variables related to the incidence of a characteristic. To control for these variables requires careful sampling. However, the question of hypothesis testing—of showing a relationship between variables—is a fundamentally different question. The difference may be posed as questions about people versus questions about variables. In a certain specific sense, when we are studying the relationship between variables we are not interested in people, per se. We are interested in the relationship between the conceptual variables which we have abstracted from the totality of social behavior. People are required, of course, in order to show our hypothesized relationship, but they are necessary only as "data points" or producers of data. For example, in the hypothesis "frustration leads to aggression" that we discussed earlier, there is no statement about people per se. As social psychologists, we are most interested in frustration and aggression in humans. But the hypothesis is general; presumably it holds for white rats, cockroaches, and elephants, as well as men. The main emphasis is not on species or individual members of a species, but on the concepts and the relation between the concepts. In this specific sense, then, our interest in individual organisms is limited when we are concerned with relations between variables.

Festinger's (1959) point becomes more reasonable now. The overriding concern is to show the relationship. Concerns of sampling (and ultimately generalizing) are secondary to this basic concern. Festinger also believes that relations are relatively robust. Although many variables may affect the incidence of a characteristic, it is much harder to find variables which affect the presence or absence of a relationship.

One implication we wish to draw follows from our fundamental distinction between population questions and relationship questions. Given that the nature of the experiment is to determine relationships, the population question of whether the results will generalize to other groups of people is misdirected. It is misdirected because it asks us to give a population (or incidence of characteristics) answer to a relationship problem. Certainly it is important to know whether the frustration-aggression hypothesis, for example, holds for laborers and farmers as well as college sophomores. But it is important, not because of population differences, but because of variable differences. For example, suppose in our frustration-aggression experiment with college sophomores, we discovered a positive relation between frustration and aggression. However, when we performed the experiment with truck drivers, we discovered a negative relationship. Consistent with our approach of relating variables to each other, we do not conclude that truck drivers are qualitatively different from college students in the incidence of intrinsic personal characteristics. Instead, we conclude there is some third variable, X, which is interacting with our independent variable, frustration, to produce opposite results in our two groups of people.

Thus, the difference between groups is conceptualized not as a population difference, but as a difference in the way variables work. The value of performing the experiment with truck drivers lies not in the discovery of population differences, but in the discovery of the unknown variable X of which we were previously ignorant. Once X is discovered, we can incorporate it into our theory and ultimately have a richer, more predictive theory. At the same time, we have remained consistent with our variable approach—we have extended the network of relationships between variables.

We see, then, that the problem of population generality can be translated into the problem of discovering relationships between variables. This is probably the major reason why most experimenters are not particularly worried about using just college sophomores as subjects. Demonstrating the basic relationship is the main job. Once the relationship is firmly established, we can then concern ourselves with other possible interactive independent variables that might be differentially associated with different social groups. Discovering these interactive relations is important, of course, and we may expect that as social psychology matures, more researchers will begin to sample from a variety of different social groups.

Other Related Problems

There are several remaining problems with regard to generalizing beyond the experiment. These problems involve considerations of both internal and external validity. We will discuss three such problems: (1) chronic versus acute manipulations of variables, (2) internal analyses of data, and (3) conditions under which nonrandom assignment of subjects is appropriate.

Chronic Versus Acute Manipulations

We have stressed the manipulation of independent variables. If we are interested in fear arousal or self-esteem, we attempt to manipulate different amounts of these variables in our subjects. This approach is sometimes called an *acute* manipulation of the variable. Some of our concepts, such as anxiety, self-esteem, hostility, etc., are conceived in such a way so that it makes sense to think of people as possessing a certain *chronic* amount of these variables all of the time. Instead of manipulating these variables, we may measure them in their chronic state, select subjects at appropriate levels on the variables, and then see how they respond on some dependent measure. For example, suppose we are interested in studying the joint effects of anxiety and self-esteem on acceptance of a persuasive communication. We will have two levels (low and high) of each independent variable in a 2×2 factorial design. An acute manipulation would consist of bringing appropriate operations to bear on the subjects who were randomly assigned to one of the four conditions, exposing them to a persuasive communication, and then measuring attitude change.

The chronic approach would involve giving an anxiety test and a self-esteem test to a large group of people. From these tests we obtain measures of their chronic level on each of these two variables. From the total group we select subjects with appropriate combinations of scores to constitute our four experimental conditions. We would need to select subjects who were high in both anxiety and self-esteem, low in both, high in anxiety and low in self-esteem, and low in anxiety and high in self-esteem. After the selection we then expose our four groups to a persuasive communication and measure their attitudes.

In terms of formal design this chronic experiment is identical to the acute experiment. In fact, we would use the same type of statistics in each case to analyze the data. There is a fundamental difference between the two approaches, however. The chronic "experiment" is nothing more than a correlational study which appears at first glance to be a manipulative experiment. As such, it suffers from all the problems of a regular correlational study that were discussed earlier.

Our point is that when a researcher has an option of either a chronic or acute manipulation of his variables, an acute manipulation is usually preferable. This advice is given with some reservation. Although a variable has the same name whether it is measured chronically or manipulated acutely, it may in fact not be the same variable in the two cases. For example, there are several personality tests to assess level of self-esteem. Some people may think poorly of themselves most of the time, while other people have very favorable self-evaluations. This general feeling is what the personality tests hope to measure. In a manipulative experiment, on the other hand, we would attempt to create a brief but intense feeling of self-esteem (either high or low) independent of the subjects' chronic level of self-esteem. There are several techniques to accomplish this variation. One of the more common is to provide the subject with a success or failure experience which is important to him. The performance expectancy experiment by Aronson and Carlsmith in Chapter 6 is a good example of this kind of self-esteem manipulation.

The basic question is whether the two procedures are, in fact, tapping the same concept. Acute self-esteem may have some properties in common with chronic self-esteem, but there are undoubtedly important differences. In fact, the two different approaches may not be commensurate in the sense that they may have no properties in common. Determining the degree of similarity and difference between an acute and a chronic concept requires considerable research. The nature of the chronic measure must be determined. Measures of chronic concepts usually measure other contaminating variables as well. Also, the precise nature of acute manipulations must be specified. Much analytical work is required, as well as research, to determine the similarities and differences. One hopeful approach is to pit both chronic and acute manipulations of the same variable against each other in an experiment and assess their effects on some dependent variable. A good example of this approach was provided in a study by Millman (1968). She was interested in the effects of fearfulness on acceptance of a persuasive communication. On the basis of an anxiety scale, Millman preselected subjects who were high and low in anxiety. Within each level of this chronic condition, she then assigned subjects randomly to a high or low level of an acute manipulation of anxious arousal. Anxiety was manipulated by threatening some subjects with electric shock and omitting the threat for other subjects. Subjects then read a persuasive communication and completed an attitude scale. The results for attitude change showed an interaction between acute anxiety and chronic anxiety. It is evident that chronic anxiety is complexly related to acute anxiety. Such complexity may be found with other concepts as well. This study illustrates well the fact that we cannot assume equivalence between chronic and acute concepts. Determination of such equivalence is a difficult empirical question.

We have emphasized the chronic versus acute distinction because it is very difficult to manipulate some variables in which we may be interested. For example, over a short time period it does not make much sense to talk about manipulating intelligence with a set of experimental operations. We must take a chronic measure (an IQ test) and assign people to high and low intelligence conditions on that basis. Intelligence is certainly a useful concept and we would not want to discard it just because we cannot manipulate it in a one-hour experiment. There are other such important concepts. We wish to make the point that we should do the best job we can in our research. If a variable is manipulable, the acute approach is probably better because we can specify more precisely the concept we are dealing with. If we cannot manipulate the concept, then it is perfectly reasonable to use a chronic measure as a basis for assigning subjects to our independent variable conditions.

When at least two independent variables are to be used, one possibility is to use one chronic variable, and one acute variable. As an example, Hendrick and Page (1970) conducted an experiment concerned with the relation between belief similarity and attraction. Previous research had shown that the more similar a person is to another person in beliefs and attitudes, the more he will be liked (see Byrne, 1969, for a review of this research). Hendrick and Page were interested in how this relation might be affected by variation in self-esteem. People low in self-esteem might actually like dissimilar persons more than similar persons, showing a reversal of the usual relationship. Hendrick and Page were interested in chronic self-esteem because they wanted to tap the subjects' long standing evaluative reactions toward themselves. Therefore, they used a personality test to measure self-esteem. However, they experimentally manipulated belief similarity for each subject. In this way one chronic variable and one acute variable was combined within the same experiment, and some of the difficulties associated with full correlational studies were avoided. At the same time, some insights were gained as to how a personality variable, self-esteem, is related to the experimental relation between similarity and attraction. The combining of acute and chronic manipulations into the same experimental design seems a fruitful approach for many research problems.

Internal Analyses of Data

When an experiment does not work, the researcher may sometimes perform useful additional analyses on the data. Suppose we execute the frustration-aggression experiment and obtain a null hypothesis outcome. Suppose that we had provided a check on our manipulation, for example a rating question, and this check showed no difference between our frustration conditions. However, there was a lot of variability in individual scores. Some individuals were high and some low in frustration regardless of whether they were assigned to high or low manipulations of frustration. What we might do is ignore the manipulation and divide the subjects into high and low frustrated subjects on the basis of their check scores. We would then observe whether the two groups differed in level of aggression. This procedure is sometimes called an internal analysis of the data.

Such supplemental analyses may be useful, particularly when the experiment does not come out as expected. It should be noted, however, that this procedure is not a satisfactory substitute for obtaining an experimental relationship. What we have done is let the subject assign himself to independent variable conditions on the basis of a test score. This procedure violates the principle of random assignment to conditions. In essence, we have changed the study from a manipulative experiment to a correlational study in an attempt to see if any relationship exists at all. The procedure is similar but not identical to the chronic manipulation of variables discussed above. It is not identical because we are using some combination of chronic frustration plus manipulated frustration to assign subjects for the internal analysis. Because of the possibility that the manipulation may interact with the chronic variable, we cannot be sure that we have a "pure" chronic measure of the concept. Internal analyses may be useful, therefore, but they are strictly secondary. If we are going to work with a chronic variable, it would be much better to measure it in advance and assign subjects to conditions before any manipulations are introduced.

Conditions for Nonrandom Assignment

Generally, we have argued strongly for random assignment of subjects to experimental conditions. We have pointed out some of the problems which occur when this principle is violated. There are certain conditions where nonrandom assignment is appropriate. Those conditions are almost always restricted to the case where a subject serves in more than one experimental condition. So far in our discussion, we have assumed that a subject would be in only one condition. For example, in a 2×2 factorial design, subjects would be assigned to one and only one of the four cells. For some experiments it is possible to expose a subject to several conditions and measure his response to each condition. In fact, in the 2×2 design the subject might be in all four conditions. Whether this is possible depends upon the circumstances of the particular experiment. For example, in the performance expectancy experiments in Chapter 6, it probably was not possible to have subjects participate in more than one condition. Once a subject had succeeded or failed, it would have been very confusing to have started over in the opposite condition. In statistical language, there would have been *carryover effects* from one condition to another. The probability of carryover effects seems particularly high in experiments that use an event type of manipulation.

If carryover effects are small, it is advantageous to run subjects in more than one condition. For one thing, individual differences between subjects is measured separately from experimental error. This results in a smaller error term in the statistical analysis (see Chapter 2), and a better chance of showing differences between experimental conditions. Subjects are not randomly assigned to conditions because they participate in all the conditions. However, no bias is involved if there are no carryover effects. In this case, such nonrandom assignment definitely leads to increased power in testing the hypothesis. Experimental designs in which subjects serve in more than one condition are sometimes called *within subject* designs.

The experiment by Hendrick and Costantini in Chapter 8 is an example of such a design. They were interested in whether differences in inconsistency in sets of trait adjectives had an effect on the magnitude of the primacy effect. Subjects responded to all of the adjective sets because problems of carryover effects from one set to another seemed small. Thus, each subject rated both consistent and inconsistent sets, thereby serving in both experimental conditions. As it turned out, there was no difference due to the consistency variable. However, having subjects serve in both conditions provided a much more powerful test than would have been possible if some subjects had evaluated only the consistent sets, and other subjects had evaluated only the inconsistent sets. This particular use of nonrandom assignment can be very useful on occasion, depending upon the nature of the experiment one is conducting.

Concluding Comments

We have discussed in detail a variety of topics. We have looked at the nature of formal theory and the derivation of hypotheses. Much attention was devoted to hypothesis testing. We saw that for a variety of reasons the experiment is the best tool for testing a hypothesis, but it is clear that the experiment is not a foolproof test. Many things can go wrong. Even if an experiment comes out as predicted, the results may be subject to alternative interpretations. We discussed in detail some of the techniques and problems involved in constructing experimental operations and measures. We were concerned with the experiment as a social situation, particularly with such problems as demand characteristics and experimenter bias. The problems of generalizing beyond the experiment was discussed at some length.

We hope that this first part of the book has provided the student with a sound basis for evaluating the chapters which follow. We also hope that it may provide some insights which will be helpful in the design and execution of actual experiments. As you read each of the following chapters there are several things you should keep in mind. First, consider the general theoretical or problem area the chapter is concerned with. We will present a fairly comprehensive overview of the relevant theory at the beginning of the chapter. Pay attention to how well developed each theory is. You will see that none of the theories approach the formal ideal we specified in Chapter 1. There is still considerable difference, however, in the degree of theoretical elaboration.

As you read the research reports, examine carefully the hypothesis that is being tested. Ask yourself whether it seems to follow reasonably from the general theoretical position, or does it seem relatively independent of the general theory? Given the present nature of social psychology, derivations from general theory are loosely made. What seems a reasonable derivation to one person may seem most unreasonable to another. Also ask yourself whether the hypothesis makes sense. You should realize in advance that the researcher is going to claim some support for his hypothesis, otherwise his research would not have been published. But don't take the experimenter's hypothesis for granted—in short don't assume that it is true just because it appears in print. We are not advising an attitude of negativism, but a healthy skepticism of (someone else's) hypothesis is always warranted.

When reading an author's method section, be particularly aware of the actual operations used and the types of measures taken. Ask yourself whether these are reasonable realizations of the particular conceptual variable. You might ponder alternate sets of operations that might have been used. Try to visualize the experiment as an actual social situation. In doing so see if you can think of possible problems. Was the cover story really credible to the subjects? Could particular experimenter biases have been working in the situation? Could the subjects have reasonably guessed the hypothesis?

When studying the first experiment in a chapter, be particularly concerned with alternative explanations for the obtained results. Actually, you know in advance that such alternatives exist because readings were selected which were vulnerable on this point. In fact, we discussed alternative explanations for one of the experiments in considerable detail in an earlier chapter. We feel that you will profit most if you do not wait passively for us to identify the alternatives for you. Actively attempt to come up with an alternative explanation while you are analyzing the first article in the chapter. Then see how your hunches compare with our discussion and that of the following articles.

At the end of a chapter, take a broader look at the research. Did the series of tests of various alternative hypotheses actually lead anywhere? Was the theory clarified in any significant way? Was that particular series of experiments really worth doing?

At the end of the book we add our own evaluative postscript. Between this point and the postscript a considerable amount of hard work is involved. We have provided some of the tools, but the tools can be sharpened and refined only by actual practice. The next five chapters will provide a great deal of such practice. We feel that by the time you reach our postscript, you will have gone a long distance toward the goal of learning to evaluate professional literature. This learning in turn is a major step in the process of becoming a professional social psychologist.

REFERENCES

Abelson, R. P., and Miller, J. C. Negative persuasion via personal insult. *Journal of Experimental Social Psychology,* 1967, **3**, 321–333.

Allport, G. W. The historical background of modern social psychology. In G. Lindzey & E. Aronson (Eds.), *The handbook of social psychology.* (2nd ed.) Vol. 1. *Systematic Positions.* Cambridge, Mass.: Addison-Wesley, 1968. Pp. 1–80.

Aronson, E., and Carlsmith, J. M. Experimentation in social psychology. In G. Lindzey, and E. Aronson (Eds.), *The handbook of social psychology* (2nd ed.) Vol. 2. *Research Methods.* Cambridge, Mass.: Addison-Wesley, 1968. Pp. 1–79.

Barber, T. X., Calverley, D. S., Forgione, A., McReake, J. D., Chaves, J. F., and Bowen, B. Five attempts to replicate the experimenter bias effect. *Journal of Consulting and Clinical Psychology,* 1969, **33**, 1–6.

Barber, T. X., and Silver, M. J. Fact, fiction, and the experimenter bias effect. *Psychological Bulletin Monograph Supplement,* 1968, **70**, (no. 6, part 2).

Beveridge, W. I. B. *The art of scientific investigation.* New York: Vintage, 1950.

Braithwaite, R. B. *Scientific explanation.* New York: Harper, 1953.

Bruyn, S. T. *The human perspective in sociology.* Englewood Cliffs, New Jersey: Prentice-Hall, 1966.

Bryne, D. Attitudes and attraction. In L. Berkowitz (Ed.), *Advances in experimental social psychology.* Vol. 4. New York: Academic Press, 1969. Pp. 35–89.

Campbell, D. T., and Stanley, J. C. Experimental and quasi-experimental designs for research on teaching. In N. L. Gage (Ed.), *Handbook of research on teaching.* Chicago, Ill.: Rand-McNally, 1963. Pp. 171–246.

Campbell, N. *What is science?* New York: Dover, 1952.

Chapanis, N. P., and Chapanis, A. Cognitive dissonance: Five years later. *Psychological Bulletin,* 1964, **61**, 1–22.

Conant, J. B. *On understanding science.* New York: Mentor, 1951.

Dinkines, F. *Introduction to mathematical logic.* New York: Appleton-Century-Crofts, 1964.

Dollard, J., Doob, L., Miller, N., Mowrer, O. H., and Sears, R. *Frustration and aggression.* New Haven, Conn.: Yale University Press, 1939.

Festinger, L. Sampling and related problems in research methodology. *American Journal of Mental Deficiency,* 1959, **64**, 358–366.

Hays, W. L. *Statistics for psychologists.* New York: Holt, Rinehart & Winston, 1963.

Heider, F. *The psychology of interpersonal relations.* New York: Wiley, 1958.

Hempel, C. G. *Philosophy of natural science.* Englewood Cliffs, New Jersey: Prentice-Hall, 1966.

Hendrick, C., and Costantini, A. F. Number-averaging behavior: a primacy effect. *Psychonomic Science,* 1970, **19**, 121–122.

Hendrick, C., and Page, H. A. Self-esteem, attitude similarity, and attraction. *Journal of Personality,* 1970, **38**, 588–601.

Insko, C. A. Verbal reinforcement of attitude. *Journal of Personality and Social Psychology,* 1965, **2**, 621–623.

Insko, C. A. *Theories of attitude change.* New York: Appleton-Century-Crofts, 1967.

Kaplan, A. *The conduct of inquiry.* San Francisco: Chandler, 1964.

Kelman, H. Human use of human subjects: The problem of deception in social psychological experiments. *Psychological Bulletin,* 1967, **67**, 1–11.

Kiesler, C. A., Collins, B. E., and Miller, N. *Attitude change.* New York: Wiley, 1969.

Kuhn, T. S. *The structure of scientific revolutions.* Chicago: University of Chicago Press, 1962.

Marx, M. H. (Ed.) *Theories in contemporary psychology.* New York: Macmillan, 1963.

McCain, G., and Segal, E. M. *The game of science.* Belmont, California: Brooks/Cole, 1969.

Millman, S. Anxiety, comprehension, and susceptibility to social influence. *Journal of Personality and Social Psychology,* 1968, **9**, 251–256.

Mills, J. (Ed.) *Experimental social psychology.* London: Macmillan, 1969.

Nagel, E. *The structure of science.* New York: Harcourt, Brace and World, 1961.

Orne, M. T. On the social psychology of the psychological experiment: with particular reference to demand characteristics and their implications. *American Psychologist,* 1962, **17**, 776–783.

Orne, M. T. Demand characteristics and the concept of quasi-controls. In R. Rosenthal, and R. L. Rosnow (Eds.), *Artifact in behavioral research.* New York: Academic Press, 1969. Pp. 143–179.

Orne, M. T., and Evans, F. J. Social control in the psychological experiment: antisocial behavior and hypnosis. *Journal of Personality and Social Psychology,* 1965, **1**, 189–200.

Ring, K. Experimental social psychology: Some sober questions about some frivolous values. *Journal of Experimental Social Psychology,* 1967, **3**, 113–123.

Rosenberg, M. J. When dissonance fails: on eliminating evaluation apprehension from attitude measurement. *Journal of Personality and Social Psychology,* 1965, **1**, 28–42.

Rosenberg, M. J. The conditions and consequences of evaluation apprehension. In

R. Rosenthal, and R. L. Rosnow (Eds.), *Artifact in behavioral research.* New York: Academic Press, 1969. Pp. 279–349.

Rosenthal, R. *Experimenter effects in behavioral research.* New York: Appleton-Century-Crofts, 1966.

Rosenthal, R. Interpersonal expectations: effects of the experimenter's hypothesis. In R. Rosenthal, and R. L. Rosnow (Eds.), *Artifact in behavioral research.* New York: Academic Press, 1969. Pp. 181–277.

Rosenthal, R., Persinger, G. W., Vikan-Kline, L., and Mulry, R. C. The role of the research assistant in the mediation of experimenter bias. *Journal of Personality,* 1963, **31,** 313–335.

Rosenthal, R., and Rosnow, R. L. The volunteer subject. In R. Rosenthal, and R. L. Rosnow (Eds.), *Artifact in behavioral research.* New York: Academic Press, 1969. Pp. 59–118.

Rudner, R. S. *Philosophy of social science.* Englewood Cliffs, New Jersey: Prentice-Hall, 1966.

Selltiz, C., Jahoda, M., Deutsch, M., and Cook, S. W. *Research methods in social relations.* New York: Holt, Rinehart and Winston, 1959.

Turner, M. B. *Philosophy and the science of behavior.* New York: Appleton-Century-Crofts, 1967.

Underwood, B. J. *Experimental psychology.* New York: Appleton-Century-Crofts, 1966.

Winer, B. J. *Statistical principles in experimental design.* New York: McGraw-Hill, 1962.

Zajonc, R. B. (Ed.), *Animal social psychology.* New York: Wiley, 1969.

Part II

CASE STUDIES IN SOCIAL RESEARCH

Chapter 6

DISSONANCE AND DISCONFIRMED EXPECTANCIES

One of the most pervasive assumptions that people hold concerning their thoughts and actions is that they should be consistent. For example, it would be considered somehow wrong or improper for a person to believe simultaneously that (a) only the most intellectually gifted in a society should receive a college education, and (b) every high school graduate should be required to attend college. These two beliefs are inconsistent with each other. The need to make one's beliefs, values, and actions generally consistent with each other is a motive strongly held by nearly all societies. It is no surprise, then, that social psychologists have investigated this motivation rather thoroughly during the last two decades. This chapter and the next one will examine two specific areas of research that are concerned with the motivation toward consistency.

There are approximately a dozen different theories of cognitive consistency. They differ in details and the predictions they make, and most of these theories have not generated much research. One exception is Festinger's (1957) theory of cognitive dissonance. During the last fifteen years, seven books and perhaps 300 journal articles have been published that are concerned with proving or disproving the theory. In fact, dissonance theory has been the most popular theory in social psychology during the past decade and has provoked more research than any other theory. The basic propositions and applications of the theory will be described in the following section, along with some general criticisms. Given that background, two areas of research will be presented and critically examined, one area in the present chapter and the second in Chapter 7.

Overview of Dissonance Theory

Basic Concepts

The basic conceptual unit of the theory is a *cognition* or *cognitive element,* an undefined term which corresponds to what is usually meant by a belief, an opinion, knowledge, conviction, etc. For example, "It is raining," "I have $20," and "I am against the war," are all cognitive elements. In a given experiment, the experimenter must define the nature and existence of the elements which will occur. Setting up a dissonance experiment so that the proper combinations of cognitive elements do in fact occur is often a demanding and creative challenge.

Two cognitive elements may exist in either a *relevant* or *irrelevant* relation to each other, and two cognitions can interact only if they are relevant. Given relevance, the two elements may support one another, act in concert, produce offshoots, form units, contradict, modify, or conflict with one another. Or, in Festinger's terms, relevant cognitions can either be *consonant* or *dissonant.* Consonance means mutual consistency, and dissonance means mutual inconsistency. The basic definition of dissonance is stated in terms of just two cognitive elements. *Two elements are in a dissonant relation if, considering these two alone, the obverse of one element would follow from the other.* "Obverse" is used in a logical sense. The obverse of the proposition "All A is B" is "No A is not-B." By the obverse of an element, Festinger means its negation (or, for practical purposes, its opposite). Thus two elements A and B are dissonant if not-B follows from A in some psychological sense. For example, the cognition "It is not raining" follows from the cognition "It is a cloudless, sunny day." The two elements "It is raining" and "It is a cloudless, sunny day" would, therefore, be dissonant.

The basic definition of dissonance has received considerable criticism. Some people have noted that the term "obverse" is not quite appropriate.

Also, how can one know when dissonance actually exists? There is a problem as to how one can consider two elements "alone." A major problem involves the meaning of the concept "follow from." It is clear that some kind of implication is intended. It is equally clear that the implication is not a logical implication. Actually, the term "follow from" is to be understood in the sense of a general *psychological implication.* Psychological implication includes logical implication as a special case, but also includes such items as cultural tradition, social definitions of situations, and empirical notions of reality. As an example of empirical implication, assume a person standing outdoors in the rain (without an umbrella). The cognition "I am getting wet" follows from the cognition "It is raining." If one held the cognitions "It is raining," but "I am not getting wet," these two cognitions would be in a dissonant relationship. This relationship derives from the person's assumptions about the nature of empirical reality rather than from any logical inconsistency between the two propositions.

Since the basic definition of dissonance is specified between two single cognitions, one cognition either follows from another cognition or it does not follow. There is no degree of "follow from." This means that in terms of the basic definition dissonance is an all or nothing affair. There is no mechanism for specifying a variable magnitude of dissonance. This situation poses a problem because most experimental tests involve comparisons between conditions where relative magnitudes of dissonance have been created. The problem is solved by assuming that in actual situations, more than two elements are involved. In fact, two "clusters" of cognitions are usually involved. Visualize two separate clusters of marbles separated by some distance. Each marble represents one cognition. Imagine a line connecting a marble in one pile with a marble in the second pile. The line represents a relationship between the two cognitions. This relationship is either consonant (C), or dissonant (D). A great many lines link the two piles; some are D lines, and some C lines. The total magnitude of dissonance in this situation may be represented as a ratio of D to C relations. In this way, a mechanism is provided for varying total magnitude of dissonance from zero continuously up to some maximum level. This matter will be discussed more fully below.

A state of dissonance between two cognitions (or between two sets of cognitions) is considered to be inherently aversive. Dissonance is a negative drive state much like hunger, thirst, or other deficit states. In this sense, dissonance is motivating. When a person is in a state of dissonance, it is assumed that he will attempt to reduce or eliminate it and to avoid situations that will increase it. The greater the amount of dissonance that a person experiences, the greater is his need or motive to reduce it.

It should be noted that there is no answer in terms of the theory as to why dissonance is aversive. In this respect, the parallel between dissonance and other drive states disappears. Presumably, hunger can ultimately be traced to specific physiochemical events in the organism. No such assumption is made for dissonance. However, this difference cannot really be construed as a criticism. A theorist is free to make whatever set of assumptions he feels will be useful. The "aversive assumption" should be considered as a postulate of Festinger's theory, and therefore does not need to be proved.

A second point is that if dissonance is an aversive motivational state, it should manifest itself in overt behavior. That is to say, an experimenter should be able to detect behavioral attempts at dissonance reduction. Most experimental situations have specified such reduction attempts, and observations have been made to see if they occur. The theory has been criticized on this point. Dissonance is never measured directly. Only hypothesized attempts at dissonance reduction are actually measured in experimental situations. Critics (e.g., Chapanis & Chapanis, 1964) maintain that the same behavior is used to claim that (1) dissonance was aroused, and (2) attempts were made to reduce dissonance. Defenders of the theory maintain that one must focus on derivations from a theory. If predictions concerning the final step of dissonance reduction can be made and confirmed, the theory is adequate. It is not necessary to tap into the intervening processes and measure the course of the buildup of dissonance. The argument may be understood better if we consider an analogous case. Suppose that we want to prove that someone is really hungry. Can we rely on our observation of the individual's ravenous eating (i.e., hunger reduction) as evidence that hunger exists? Or must we independently ascertain hunger in some other way (e.g., physiological measures of blood sugar level)? Most people would rely on observation of eating behavior as evidence that hunger had been aroused and was also being reduced. Nevertheless, such independent measures may be useful if they can be feasibly obtained. Very often such measures will be physiological in nature. A few dissonance studies have used physiological measures in an attempt to directly observe the arousal of dissonance (see Zimbardo, 1969, for a review).

Total Magnitude of Dissonance

The total magnitude of dissonance existing between two sets of cognitions depends upon two variables.

1. Importance of the cognitions. Importance is not well defined. Intuitively, it is clear that some cognitions are more important than others.

However, the problem of measuring the importance of cognitions has never been seriously attempted. Conceptually, the importance of a cognition may be considered as a weighting value attached to it: one presumes that the more important the cognitions entering into the dissonant relationship, the more severe will be the dissonance experienced.

2. The second variable determining total magnitude of dissonance is the proportion of dissonant to consonant relations existing between two clusters of cognitions.

Secord and Backman (1964) have provided a useful formalization for representing total magnitude of dissonance between two sets of cognitions. The formula is given below. It should be noted that it is strictly conceptual. No specific predictions can be derived from the formula:

$$\text{Total Magnitude of Dissonance} = \frac{\Sigma w_i D_i}{\Sigma w_i C_i}$$

where D represents a dissonant relation between two elements and C represents a consonant relation. The weights, w_i, represent the importance of the two elements entering into a specific relation. Conceptually all the dissonant relations have been weighted and summed, and represented as a ratio to the summed, weighted consonant relations.

The total magnitude of dissonance may be represented as a fraction that can vary between zero and one. The smaller the numerator term relative to the denominator term, the less the total dissonance. A small numerator term indicates either few dissonant relations or the relative unimportance of the relations, or both.

Total magnitude of dissonance will be greatest when there is an equal proportion of dissonant and consonant relations (with importance held constant). Numerically, dissonance is at a maximum when the ratio approaches 1.0. Presumably, total dissonance cannot exceed 1.0. First of all, cognitions must be somewhat resistant to change. If cognitions did not resist change, any inconsistency in the cognitive apparatus would be immediately resolved. Theoretically, resistance to change is partially determined by the importance of the elements. If the number of dissonant relations exceeded the number of consonant relations, resistance to change of the more resistant relations would be overcome and the dissonance would be resolved. Thus, 1.0 is the hypothetical maximum.

Actually, the conceptual formula is not too useful even as a heuristic, as it is stated. The ratio notion would allow an identical value for two types of situations that differed greatly in their overall importance. Suppose that one is involved in the dilemma of whether to go to a movie or to study. All of the individual cognitions involved are not terribly important. However, the value of the ratio might work out to, say, .75. The same value might be obtained for a much more important situation, such as whether to be drafted, or to defect to Canada to continue one's graduate education. What is needed is some overall weight that represents total importance of all the cognitive elements involved in a given situation. The numerical fraction would then reflect this overall weighting. It is unclear how such a weight would be derived or computationally applied.

Reduction of Dissonance

Dissonance may be reduced in one of two ways.

1. The importance of the elements may be changed. For example, the importance of some of the dissonant relations may be decreased, and/or the importance of the consonant relations may be increased. Suppose that a young man has just graduated from high school and wants to go to college. Many cognitions are consonant with his desire. His parents want him to go. He wants to get a good education. He wants to avoid the draft, etc. However, his girl does not want him to go to college. She wants him to get a job and marry her. The man's cognition that his girl wants to get married now is dissonant with his other cognition that he wants to go to college.

The total magnitude of dissonance that the young man experiences may be reduced by distorting the importance of the consonant relations. He may focus on the reasons he should go to college and magnify them—in short, make them more important. In so doing, the perceived importance of the dissonant cognition is relatively decreased. At the same time he may actively work to decrease the importance of the dissonant thought that his girl wants to get married. He may come to feel that getting married really isn't very important, thereby reducing the impact of the dissonance.

2. The second mode of dissonance reduction involves changing a cognitive element. Two possibilities exist. First, the person may seek out new cognitions that are consonant with present consonant relations. In our example above, the young man may think of several additional reasons why he should go to college. As a potent example, it may occur to the young man that if he goes to college, there will be hundreds of coeds that he might date, many of whom would be more attractive than his present girl.

A second, more effective method of changing cognitions involves changing a dissonant relation so that it is actually consonant. For example, our young man might persuade his girl to believe that he really should go to college. In changing her mind he has in one stroke changed a dissonant relation ("she wants to get married") into a consonant relation ("she wants me to go to college"). Presumably, the young man will go to college and live happily ever after (and probably with a different wife).

Scope of Dissonance Theory

It is obvious that dissonance theory is not rigorously stated, and is, in fact, ambiguous in certain parts. However, from this informal statement a great many conceptual-empirical derivations have been made. The initial statement (Festinger, 1957) had been modified by Brehm and Cohen (1962). Essentially, Brehm and Cohen restrict dissonance theory to those situations in which the individual feels a *commitment* to a given course of behavior, and has a sense of *volition* in selecting that course of behavior. In a later book Festinger (1964) seems to accept Brehm and Cohen's restrictions. In fact, he further restricts the theory himself and argues that dissonance is primarily a *post-decisional* phenomenon. Although the theory has been applied to the effects of decisions ever since it was originated, some people would argue that Festinger was unduly restrictive in his 1964 book. Dissonance theory has been fruitfully applied to behaviors that seem not to involve explicit decision-making. Some of these areas of research are:

1. Decisions—presumably some degree of dissonance is experienced after every decision is made.
2. Insufficient justification—a person who engages in a behavior for which he does not have sufficient justification should experience dissonance.
3. Disconfirmed expectancies—if a person holds a firm expectancy concerning some aspect of his universe, disconfirmation of the expectancy should be a source of dissonance.
4. Sheer informational inconsistency may be a source of dissonance.
5. Inconsistency of social life including conflicting role demands may create a state of dissonance.
6. Sensory inconsistency in one form or another may be handled by the theory.

An Example—Decision Making

As an example of how derivations are made from dissonance theory, the predictions one would make for a choice situation will be illustrated. A choice situation consists of a selection between at least two alternatives, A and B. In the general case, consider that each alternative will have some positive attributes (designated as A+ and B+) and some negative attributes (designated as A— and B—). Choosing between A and B means selecting one alternative and rejecting the other. Suppose the person chooses A. It follows that the positive features of A (A+) and the negative features of B (B—) are consistent or consonant with having chosen A. At the same time the positive features of B (B+) that were given up and the negative features of A (A—) are dissonant with the cognition of choosing A. Thus, in terms of the conceptual ratio, total dissonance in the choice situation (given that A was chosen) may be presented by:

$$\text{Dissonance} = \frac{w_1\,(\mathrm{A}-) + w_2\,(\mathrm{B}+)}{w_3\,(\mathrm{A}+) + w_4\,(\mathrm{B}-)} = \frac{\Sigma w_i D_i}{\Sigma w_i C_i}$$

Assume that the net attractiveness (positive features minus negative features) of each alternative is positive, so that both alternatives are desirable. It is reasonable that dissonance resulting from a choice will be greatest when the net attractiveness of the two alternatives is approximately equal. Given that condition, the ratio approaches a value of 1.00. When the rejected alternative has fewer positive features and more negative features than the chosen alternative, it is clear that the fractional value of the ratio will be much smaller than when the alternatives are equally attractive.

Thus, the explicit prediction is that a person will experience more dissonance when he chooses between two equally attractive alternatives than when he chooses between two alternatives unequal in attractiveness.

A further derivation is that the magnitude of dissonance will be greater the more important the choice is to the person. Choosing between two equally attractive persons for a spouse should be more important (and provoke more dissonance) than choosing between two equally attractive neckties.

Another derivation is that when the net attraction of each alternative is positive, the greater the number of alternatives involved in the choice situation, the more dissonance the person will experience. This derivation follows because, instead of giving up positive features of only one alternative, one must give up the positive features of several alternatives when the choice is made.

Still another informal derivation is that the less the "overlap" between choice alternatives, the greater the dissonance. If two objects were completely identical in attributes, it would not matter which one was chosen —thus no dissonance would exist. More dissonance should exist, for example, if one had to choose between an electric range and freezer than if one had to choose between two identical models of the electric range.

Assume that a person has made a choice. Assume also that there is a commitment to the choice so that it cannot be revoked or reversed. How can the dissonance be reduced? Theoretically there is only one mode of reduction available. The alternatives must be reevaluated. Reevaluation involves a cognitive change in which the person (after the choice) becomes more favorably disposed toward the chosen alternative, and more unfavorable toward the rejected alternative (s). Such spreading apart in attractiveness has the effect of confirming that the person did indeed make the best choice after all.

A dissonance experiment on decision-making typically involves the following situation. In one condition a subject makes a choice between two alternatives previously rated about equal in attractiveness. In a second condition another subject chooses between two alternatives unequal in attractiveness. Some time after the choice, the subjects are asked to rerate the attractiveness of the alternatives. It is expected that in the condition of equal attractiveness, the evaluation of the chosen alternative will be enhanced more (and the rejected alternative lowered more) than in the choice condition where the alternatives were initially unequal in attractiveness. This derivation follows because more dissonance is experienced in the equally attractive choice condition, and more reevaluation is thus necessary to reduce the dissonance.

The example on decisions will suffice to illustrate the manner in which the theory is translated into empirical predictions. It is clear that the derivations are informal, sometimes intuitive, sometimes ingenious. Similar lines of reasoning may be followed to obtain derivations for experiments on insufficient justification for behavior, disconfirmed expectancies, etc. One final point should be noted. In the derivation of predictions for a choice situation, support for the theory depended entirely on the final outcome, e.g., on reevaluation of choice alternatives. Presumably, the reevaluation represents behavioral attempts to reduce dissonance. However, the buildup of dissonance is not measured, only inferred. As was noted earlier, it is this feature of the theory—depending upon the dependent variable as evidence for the process as well as evidence for its attempted reduction—that has aroused most of the conceptual criticism of the theory. However, as a heuristic tool there is no doubt that the theory is exceedingly productive.

Disconfirmed Expectancies and Dissonance

The introductory section above indicated several different ways in which dissonance could be created. One way was a disconfirmed expectancy. We hold expectancies for many events, including our own and other people's behaviors and the inanimate environment around us. The cognitions concerning one's own person, self-expectancies, are probably the most important and affect-laden cognitions held. We expect many things of ourselves. We expect that we will succeed on a job. We expect to behave in an honest, intelligent manner, etc. When we behave in a manner that violates one of our self-expectancies, the inconsistency between our expectancy and the cognition of our behavior creates a state of dissonance.

Actually, Festinger's (1957) theory is not phrased in this way. In the first article in this chapter, Aronson and Carlsmith (1962) theoretically reinterpret dissonance theory as indicated above. As they note (p. 178), the previous research has been based on the assumption "that a person sees himself as good, honest, intelligent, and rational, and consequently expects to behave in a good, honest, intelligent, and rational manner." Aronson and Carlsmith suggest, in effect, that in most of the prior research the dissonance has actually been generated between such a self-expectancy and some behavior that disconfirms the expectancy. Further, the measures of dissonance reduction obtained in the previous experiments may be interpreted as an attempt to maintain or restore the expectation that the person held concerning what his behavior should be.

Aronson and Carlsmith have essentially created a new version of dissonance theory having its own testable implications which probably could not have been derived from the original theory. Their article describes an experimental test of one of these implications. The experimental situation constructed to test the theory is creative and ingenious. They assume that the need to confirm expectancies is a powerful need. Their assumption is put to a stringent test because the need to confirm an expectancy is pitted against another need that is highly prized—the need to achieve. The fact that the need to confirm expectancies wins out over the need to achieve provides strong support for the theoretical reasoning. However, this test contains a difficult problem for empirical research. When two powerful motives are pitted against each other, the outcome will often depend upon the impact of other variables. Often these variables will seem trivial at first glance. What occurs in practice is that the results of such a study may be quite difficult to replicate by other experimentalists. Such is the case with the Aronson and Carlsmith experiment. It is a tribute to their skill as researchers that they were able to obtain their predicted results so clearly. However, other researchers, perhaps equally skilled, sometimes have and sometimes have not been able to replicate their results. Such difficulty often leads to a variety of alternative theoretical interpretations for a given set of data. The articles following Aronson and Carlsmith's article represent attempts to test such alternatives.

In reading the following report, pay particular attention to its method section. The statistical design is simple enough, but the procedures used to construct a test of the hypothesis are rather complex. The manipulation of the independent variables was particularly elaborate. Such complexity may often be necessary to provide an adequate test of the hypothesis, as was indicated in Chapter 4. However, each added empirical step increases the odds that additional unwanted variables will be manipulated, as well as the theoretically significant variables. It is always possible that these extraneous variables may be responsible for the obtained results. While you are reading the report, see if you can think of alternative explanations for the obtained results. Try to visualize the procedures as clearly as possible and imagine their impact on the subject. In other words, try to put yourself in the role of a subject in the experiment, and visualize the possible variables in the situation to which the subject may be responding.

Performance Expectancy as a Determinant of Actual Performance[1]

Elliot Aronson and J. Merrill Carlsmith

In recent years, several theorists have suggested that individuals have a need for cognitive consistency. Typical of these concepts is Festinger's theory of cognitive dissonance (Festinger, 1957; Festinger & Aronson, 1960). According to the theory, when a person holds two ideas which are psychologically inconsistent (dissonant) he experiences discomfort and attempts to reduce the dissonance. The most common method of reducing dissonance is to change or distort one or both of the cognitions, making them more consistent (consonant) with each other.

Virtually all of the experiments which have been conducted to test

[1] From the *Journal of Abnormal and Social Psychology* 1962, **65**, No. 3, 178–182. Received July 13, 1961. Reproduced by permission of the publisher.

This research was partially supported by a grant from the National Institute of Mental Health (M-4387) and by a grant from the National Science Foundation (NSF G-16838), both administered by the senior author. This research was conducted while the junior author was on the tenure of a National Science Foundation fellowship.

At time of writing, the authors were with Harvard University. Current affiliations: Aronson, University of Texas at Austin; Carlsmith, Stanford University.

these theories contain a basic but implicit assumption: that a person sees himself as good, honest, intelligent, and rational and consequently expects to behave in a good, honest, intelligent, and rational manner. In effect, these experiments have contained the tacit assumption that individuals have a high or "good" self-relevant performance expectancy. The existence of this assumption can best be understood by considering a typical experiment.

Ehrlich, Guttman, Schonbach, and Mills (1957) predicted that people who had recently purchased a new car subsequently would read more advertisements about that make of car than about any other make of car. That is, by seeking positive information about the car they had just purchased, they could reduce the dissonance that might be introduced by the few negative qualities of the car. But this hypothesis involves the tacit assumption that these individuals considered themselves to be intelligent, rational people, and, thus, expected to purchase a superior car. Suppose an individual had learned from long hard experience that he is the type of person who never does anything right. Would negative aspects of his newly-purchased car be dissonant with his self-concept? Hardly. In fact, one might predict that such a person would experience dissonance if his car were superior and hence he might expose himself to ads describing cars which he had not purchased. Indeed, a few of the subjects in the experiment did just that. It is highly speculative but perhaps useful to suggest that these subjects may have had a generally negative self-concept, or at least a negative performance expectancy regarding their ability to purchase a superior car.

To generalize from this example, it is suggested that it would be of value to make explicit the role of a person's self-concept in the arousal of dissonance. In most situations, dissonance actually involves a cognition about the self. Thus, instead of stating that dissonance exists between two inconsistent cognitions, it may be more useful to state that dissonance exists between a cognition about the self (i.e., a self-relevant performance expectancy) and a cognition about behavior which is inconsistent with this expectancy. Events which coincide with self-relevant performance expectancies are consonant, pleasant, sought out; events which are discrepant from these expectancies are dissonant, unpleasant, avoided, or minimized.

This formulation leads to the prediction that an individual who has a clear conception of his ability at a given task will experience dissonance if his behavior differs sharply from this expectancy. Thus, if a person expects to do well and does poorly, he will experience dissonance and attempt to minimize this performance. However, this is a rather trivial prediction. Since his performance was objectively poor, we need not appeal to the idea of inconsistency to account for his discomfort. In our culture, people typically are rewarded for doing well and punished for doing poorly. On this basis alone, we would expect this person to minimize poor performance. But what happens to a person who is convinced that he is inept at a given task, and then suddenly discovers that his performance was excellent? Again, with the value placed on good performance in this culture, we would expect him to express feelings of pleasure and satisfaction. Yet, according to our formulation, his excellent performance is inconsistent with his negative performance expectancy, and, thus, should cause discomfort. If a disconfirmed expectancy is a powerful force, then we would predict that this person, conceiving of himself as inept but performing well, will be uncomfortable with this superb performance. A behavioral measure should reflect this discomfort,. even if the person verbalizes satisfaction with the success. Some evidence for this contention is supplied in an experiment by Deutsch and Solomon (1959). In a group task, some subjects were made to feel that they had performed well, others were made to feel that they had performed poorly. Their performance was then evaluated by a teammate. Subjects tended to be more favorably disposed toward a teammate whose evaluations were consistent with her own.

In the present experiment, the theoretical ideas discussed above were tested by (*a*) systematically manipulating an individual's expectancy concerning his ability on a given task and (*b*) systematically manipulating his performance so that it is either consistent or inconsistent with his performance expectancy. The hypothesis is that a performance consistent with a person's expectancy will be consonant (i.e., pleasant, acceptable); a performance inconsistent with his expectancy will arouse dissonance (i.e., will be unpleasant, unaccepted).

Procedure

In general, the procedure involved (*a*) allowing subjects to perform a task; (*b*) presenting some subjects with information which led them to form a high self-concept, or expectancy, regarding their skill on the task, while presenting other subjects with information which led them to form an expectancy of poor performance regarding their skill on the task; (*c*) allowing some subjects to perform in a manner which was consistent with this expectancy while allowing others to perform in a manner inconsistent with their expectancy; (*d*) obtaining a measure of discomfort or displeasure with this performance.

Subjects and Task

The subjects were 40 female undergraduates who were paid volunteers for an experiment "on personality." The experimenter led the subjects to believe that he was interested in correlating interview-type personality tests with short answer, paper-and-pencil tests. The experimenter explained that he was interested in finding a few quick tests which supplied the same information about a person as interviews; he would then be able to save a great deal of time and effort by simply using these tests in lieu of the more cumbersome interviews. The experimenter told each subject that he would like her to take a few of the short tests during this session and that he would interview her (with her permission) at some later date.

As a warm-up, the experimenter administered a short self-rating scale. After the subject completed this test, the experimenter introduced the "next" test which was actually the last test that the subject was to take. This was a bogus instrument which was introduced as an index of social sensitivity and was described as a highly valid and reliable test.

> This test has been widely used with remarkable success by psychologists for several years. Moreover, in my own work, thus far, it has proved to be the most useful of all the short, objective tests I've tried. It is an excellent measure of how sensitive an individual is to other people; i.e., the subjects who score high on this test are the same people who, when interviewed, express a good deal of understanding and insight into other people. Subjects who score low on this test, on the other hand, tend to express a very superficial understanding of other people when interviewed.

The test consisted of 100 cards; on each card were three photographs of young men. The experimenter explained that one of the photos on each card was that of a schizophrenic. The subjects were told that the test measured their ability to judge which of the young men was the schizophrenic. They were told that they could use whatever cues they deemed relevant. The experimenter informed the subjects that some people do extremely well on this test, getting as many as 85% correct; and that some people perform very poorly, getting as few as 20% correct. The experimenter then reiterated that people who score high on this test show a great deal of sensitivity when interviewed, while people who score low show very little sensitivity. Actually, there were no correct answers; the pictures were clipped randomly from an old Harvard yearbook —to the best of our knowledge, none were schizophrenic.

The experimenter explained that it is very difficult for people to judge their performance on the test; that some people who think they do very poorly are among the best performers, and vice versa.

The test was divided into five sections, with 20 cards in each section, and with a 3-minute rest between each section. The experimenter informed the subject that this division was to allow the subject an opportunity to rest at intervals during the test. Actually, it was to afford the experimenter the opportunity to feed the subject specific information about her performance on each section, in order to allow the subject to form a consistent performance expectancy. After the subject had completed each of the first four sections of the test, the experimenter pretended to score the subject's performance by comparing her responses with an answer key. The experimenter then reported a false prearranged score to her. At the end of the fifth section of the test, the experimenter handed the subject an answer key and allowed her to score her own performance, in order to allay any suspicions the subject might have concerning the veracity of the reported scores. Actually this score was also false; the experimenter had recorded the subject's responses in such a manner that, even when the subject scored her own performance, she would receive a prearranged score. After scoring the exam, most subjects whose earlier performance had been disconfirmed asked the experimenter to check the accuracy of their scoring. The experimenter did this and assured them that their scoring was accurate.

The experimenter administered the test by holding each card up until the subject made her choice. He then flipped over the card, recorded her response, and exposed the next card. In order to limit the length of time each subject was exposed to the cards, the experimenter informed the subject that she must make her selection within 10 seconds.

Experimental Conditions

The subjects were randomly assigned to one of four experimental conditions. One half of the subjects were given information about their performance on the first four sections of the test which led them to form a high performance expectancy; the other half were given information which led them to form a low performance expectancy. Specifically, the highs were given scores of 17, 16, 16, and 17, while the lows were given scores of 5, 4, 4, and 5. Then, on the fifth section of the test, one half of each group received a score of 17 while the others received a score of 5. Thus, on the fifth section of the test, (*a*) 10 subjects "performed" in a manner which was consistent with a high expectancy (high-high) ; (*b*) 10 subjects "performed" in a manner which was inconsistent with a high expectancy (high-low) ; (*c*) 10 subjects "performed" in a manner which was consistent with a low expectancy (low-low) ; (*d*) 10 subjects "performed" in a manner which was inconsistent with a low expectancy (low-high) .

Dependent Variable

The subject's reaction to her performance on the fifth section of the test was measured by allowing her to respond to the identical section of the test again. The experimenter could then observe how many of her previous responses she changed; the number of changed responses served as an operational definition of the subject's discomfort with her performance on the fifth section of the test.

This operation was accomplished in the following manner. After the subject completed the fifth section of the test (but before the test had been scored) , the experimenter pretended to be quite chagrined. In response to the subject's inquiry, the experimenter informed the subject that he was supposed to time her speed of performance but had neglected to do so on the fifth section of the test. He then asked the subject to score her own performance while he ruminated in an attempt to decide what to do about his omission. After the subject reported her score, the experimenter recorded it and informed her that he absolutely needed a measure of her time in order to complete his records.

> There's only one thing to do. Would you mind terribly if I asked you to take the fifth section of the test over again? Why don't you just pretend that it's a completely new set of pictures; i.e., respond as if you've never seen the pictures before—that way I can get a fairly accurate measure of the time it takes you to complete the set.

After the subject completed her task, the experimenter explained the true purpose of the experiment and discussed the necessity for the deception. None of the subjects had suspected the purpose of the experiment but none expressed any resentment at having been deceived. On the contrary, most of the subjects expressed a good deal of interest in the design and questioned the experimenter at length regarding several of the methodological details.

Results and Discussion

As mentioned above, the dependent variable used was the number of choices which were changed on the repeat performance of the fifth test. This measure should reflect accurately the amount of comfort or satisfaction with the previous performance. It is obvious that changing no responses will guarantee an identical performance. Changing a large number of responses will guarantee a low score if the previous score was high, and will virtually guarantee a higher performance if the previous score was very low.

Table 1 shows the mean number of responses changed in each of the four conditions. We may consider the high-high condition as a kind of baseline; subjects in this condition should have little pressure to change their responses, since their performance was excellent and conformed with their expectancy. In fact, they changed an average of 3.9 responses, which we may attribute to faulty memory or an attempt to change one or two responses which they had thought were incorrect. In the high-low condition, however, the subjects changed an average of 11.1 responses. We would expect the largest number of changes in this condition, since both variables which might be expected to produce changes were operating here. That is, the performance was both objectively bad and inconsistent with their expectancy. And indeed, the number of responses changed was highest in this condition.

It is the difference between the other two conditions which is most interesting for the hypothesis proposed here, however. In the low-high condition, although the performance was objectively excellent, it was in conflict with the subject's performance expectancy, whereas the low-low condition provided a performance which was objectively poor, but in complete agreement with the expectancy. The results provide clear support for the hypothesis. Subjects in the low-high condition changed an average of 10.2 responses; the mean change in the low-low condition was 6.7. This difference is highly significant ($p < .01$, Mann-Whitney U test). If we interpret the number of responses changed as a measure of dissatis-

TABLE 1
Number of Responses Changed on Repeat Performance

Score expected on fifth test	Score obtained on fifth test	
	Low	High
High	11.1	3.9
Low	6.7	10.2

faction with performance, it seems clear that subjects whose performance was in conflict with their performance expectancy were less satisfied with this performance than subjects whose performance was in harmony with their expectancy. This was true even though the objective performance was far superior for the former group.

Table 2 presents the analysis of variance for these differences. Since the variances were different in the various conditions, an approximation suggested by Smith (1936) and Satterthwaite (1946) was used. This approximation reduces the *df* in the *F* tests from 36 to 26. The analysis of variance shows some effect due to the (reported) performance on the fifth test. The subjects who were told that they had done poorly changed more responses than the subjects who were told they had done well ($F = 8.3$, $p < .01$). This reflects a general desire to do well regardless of expectancy. This desire was apparent in the behavior of the subjects on the first trial. Those subjects who performed well were overtly pleased, those who performed poorly manifested discomfort.

The strongest effect, however, is clearly the interaction. Subjects whose performance was consistent with their expectancies (high-high and low-low) changed fewer responses on the repeat performance than subjects whose performance was inconsistent with their expectancies ($F = 69.8$, $p < .001$). This reflects the drive to confirm a self-relevant performance expectancy regardless of whether the expectancy concerns a positive or negative event.

One possible alternative explanation of these results is that the subjects, having been told that this was a reliable test, were trying to do the experimenter a favor by making their performance seem more reliable. Although we cannot completely reject such an explanation, we can give some informal evidence which seems to us compelling. When the true nature of the experiment was revealed, almost all of the subjects refused to believe the hypothesis. In fact, when the subjects in the low-high condition who had changed a significant number of responses were informed of this, most expressed surprise upon learning that they had changed so many. They attributed changes either to faulty memory or to shifting criteria of judgment.

Although the results were predicted from an extension of dissonance theory, these data also support assumptions contained in several other theories. For example, Lecky's (1945) theory of self-consistency clearly predicts such a result. Similarly, Tolman's (1959) notion that disconfirmed expectancies are unpleasant is consistent with these data. Implicit in Kelly's (1955) theory of personal constructs is the assumption that predictable behavior is desirable. In addition, clinical observations such as Freud's description of the repetition compulsion and Mowrer's (1950)

TABLE 2
Analysis of Variance

Source	*df*	*SS*	*MS*	*F*
Total	39	477		
Treatments	3	329.5	109.8	
Expectancy	1	9.0	9.0	2.2
Fifth trial	1	34.2	34.2	8.3[a]
Interaction	1	286.2	286.2	69.8[b]
Error	36	147.5	4.10	

[a] $p < .01$.
[b] $p < .001$.

concept of the neurotic paradox could be interpreted as being consistent with these data.

Since the result is predicted by all of these theoretical approaches, it is curious that there has been an absence of clear experimental demonstrations of this effect. That is, although several experiments demonstrate the existence of negative affect following the disconfirmation of a positive expectancy, it is more difficult to demonstrate the existence of negative affect following the disconfirmation of a *negative* expectancy. For example, Tinklepaugh (1928) demonstrated that monkeys became quite upset when they expected to find a banana under a cup and found a lettuce leaf instead—even though monkeys normally like lettuce. However, monkeys do prefer bananas to lettuce leaves; when Tinklepaugh attempted to reverse the conditions, the effect did not appear.

It should be noted that the present experiment did not demonstrate the presence of negative affect following a disconfirmed negative expectancy; it showed only that following such a disconfirmation, subjects will take steps designed to reaffirm a negative performance expectancy. In a subsequent experiment (Carlsmith & Aronson, 1961), evidence is presented to show that such a disconfirmation does lead to negative affect.

Summary

Theories of cognitive consistency were extended to account for individual differences in self-relevant expectancies. This extension led to the following prediction: if a person expects to perform poorly in a particular endeavor, a good performance will be inconsistent with his expectancy; he will attempt to reduce dissonance by denying this performance.

In a laboratory experiment, some subjects were led to expect to perform a task excellently—others, poorly. They then performed the task, were given false scores which either confirmed or disconfirmed their expectancies, and were surreptitiously allowed to change their responses on the task. The subjects who were given information which was inconsistent with their performance expectancies changed significantly more of their responses than those who were given consistent information. Thus, subjects who expected to perform poorly but performed well exhibited more discomfort (changed more responses) than subjects who expected to perform poorly and *did* perform poorly.

REFERENCES

Carlsmith, J. M., & Aronson, E. Affectual consequences of the disconfirmation of expectancies. *American Psychologist,* 1961, **16,** 437. (Abstract)

Deutsch, M., & Solomon, L. Reactions to evaluations by others as influenced by self-evaluations. *Sociometry,* 1959, **22,** 93–112.

Ehrlich, D., Guttman, I., Schonbach, P., & Mills, J. Postdecision exposure to relevant information. *Journal of Abnormal and Social Psychology,* 1957, **54,** 98–102.

Festinger, L. *A theory of cognitive dissonance.* Evanston: Row, Peterson, 1957.

Festinger, L., & Aronson, E. The arousal and reduction of dissonance in social contexts. In D. Cartwright & A. Zander (Eds.), *Group dynamics.* Evanston: Row, Peterson, 1960. Pp. 214–231.

Kelly, G. A. *The psychology of personal constructs.* New York: Norton, 1955.

Lecky, P. *Self-consistency, a theory of personality.* New York: Island, 1945.

Mowrer, O. H. *Learning theory and personality dynamics.* New York: Ronald, 1950.

Satterthwaite, F. E. An approximate distribution of estimates of variance components. *Biometrics,* 1946, **2,** 110–114.

Smith, H. F. The problem of comparing the results of two experiments with unequal errors. *Aust. J. council sci. industr. Res.,* 1936, **9,** 211–212.

Tinklepaugh, O. L. An experimental study of representative factors in monkeys. *Journal of Comparative Psychology,* 1928, **8,** 197–236.

Tolman, E. C. Principles of purposive behavior. In S. Koch (Ed.), *Psychology: A study of a science.* Vol. 2. New York: McGraw-Hill, 1959. Pp. 92–157.

Discussion

There are several points of interest concerning Aronson and Carlsmith's experiment. First, the manipulations must have had considerable impact on the subjects. A strong *event* manipulation was used, as discussed in Chapter 4. It is easy to visualize subjects increasing in confidence as they continually "succeeded" on the first four trials. Likewise, it is easy to visualize the discomfort and misery of the subjects who were continually "failed" on the first four trials. Intuitively, it seems reasonable that these event manipulations did create very different performance expectancies for the task.

Similarly, the confirmation-disconfirmation manipulation on the fifth trial seemed equally convincing. One can visualize the surprise and uncertainty of the two groups of subjects who had their expectancies disconfirmed. Such surprise and uncertainty provides phenomenological evidence that dissonance was aroused.

The measurement of the dependent variable was subtle. It involved the technique of the "accident." The experimenter presumably forgot to time the last trial, and that "accident" created a pretext for repeating the trial. Repetition of the trial enabled the experimenter to obtain a *behavioral measure* (see Chapter 4) of change, which presumably reflected an attempt at dissonance reduction.

The results of Aronson and Carlsmith's experiment strongly supported their predictions. A straightforward interpretation would be that people do try to confirm established performance expectancies, and that this need is actually stronger than the need to achieve. However, a number of alternative interpretations for the results may be advanced.

First, consider the experimental situation. A female subject sat facing a male experimenter who showed her a series of 20 cards, each containing three photographs. After each trial of 20 cards, the experimenter orally reported a score to the subject. This situation had the potential for a whole series of artifactual influences that might have determined the results that were obtained.

1. The high reliability and validity of the social sensitivity test was stressed in the instructions to subjects. These instructions may have made subjects feel that they ought to be consistent in their performance because the experimenter expected it of them. Therefore, subjects attempted to behave consistently on the repetition of the fifth trial, not because of dissonance reduction, but because they felt the experimenter's hypothesis demanded such consistency of them. Such reasoning attributes the results to demand characteristics (Chapter 3) of the situation. Aronson and Carlsmith recognized this possibility, but discounted it as a serious alternative because most subjects refused to believe the hypothesis when it was explained to them. However, such postexperimental, introspective data are not definitive. In Chapter 3 we indicated that the postexperimental interview may fail to uncover perceived demand characteristics that subjects have developed because both experimenter and subject have a vested interest in the outcome of the study and may implicitly agree to a pact of silence. Therefore, the demand characteristics alternative is, at this point, a credible alternative explanation for the results.

2. The experimenter certainly had to be on the ball to do his job adequately. In fact, he had to possess a high level of acting skill, and

therein lies a danger. Many opportunities existed for subtle communication of expectancies to subjects. Presumably the experimenter knew the hypothesis. He may inadvertantly have behaved differently toward subjects in different conditions, perhaps signaling his expectancies of hypothesis confirmation to them in subtle ways. There is reason to believe that subjects were very sensitive to such subtle cues in this particular experiment. The instructions that the test was a measure of "social sensitivity" should have aroused considerable *evaluation apprehension* of the type discussed in Chapter 3. It will be recalled that Rosenberg found the strongest effects of experimenter expectancy under conditions of high evaluation apprehension. Certainly the conditions were suitable in Aronson and Carlsmith's experiment for such effects to have occurred.

Some of these possibilities could have been controlled. For example, the experimenter could have been blind to which condition of confirmation-disconfirmation that a subject was in until just before this manipulation was introduced. This procedure would have effectively prevented any differential bias in the experimenter's behavior toward subjects in these two conditions. Also, the entire experiment could have been partially automated by using a slide projector to show the photographs. In this way the experimenter would have had minimal contact with the subject, and therefore less chance of communicating expectancies to her. However, such anonymity would probably have reduced the strength of the manipulation as well. The social interaction involved in the experimenter's successively "succeeding" or "failing" the subject seems an integral part of the strong event manipulation. Nevertheless, such face-to-face interaction may have resulted in the subtle communication of the hypothesis, especially since the experimenter was not ignorant of the hypothesis.

3. The subjects were paid volunteers. Payment plus the fact they were volunteers may have heightened their sense of obligation to the experimenter. It was noted in Chapter 3 that volunteer subjects have a higher need for social approval than nonvolunteers. If Aronson and Carlsmith's female subjects had a high need for approval, we would expect them to be particularly compliant with the demand characteristics of the experiment, and sensitized to the experimenter's expectancy for their behavior. Thus, the fact that volunteers were used adds to the possibility that both demand characteristics and experimenter expectancy effects may have been operating to determine the results.

4. As noted above, subjects in the high and low expectancy conditions probably experienced quite different feelings as the experiment progressed. The high expectancy subjects perhaps felt quite smug about their performance, while the low expectancy subjects may have felt progres-

sively more depressed. The low expectancy subjects may have quit paying serious attention to what they were doing. Therefore, on the fifth block of cards they may not have remembered as well as the high expectancy subjects which faces they initially chose. So there may have been a difference in ability to recall the faces that in some way could have accounted for the obtained results. (See Waterman & Ford, 1965, for a more complete elaboration and attempted test of this hypothesis.)

In the next study, reported by Ward and Sandvold, an attempt was made to test the demand characteristics hypothesis. Pay particular attention to how they proposed to test this alternative. When you read their method section, go back and compare their procedures with Aronson and Carlsmith's procedures. Make a note of all the ways in which the two sets of procedures differed from each other. There is a crucial problem involved in Ward and Sandvold's attempt to test the demand characteristics interpretation. See if you can determine what the problem is before reading the discussion that follows the report of their experiment.

Performance Expectancy as a Determinant of Actual Performance: a Partial Replication[1]

William D. Ward and Kenneth D. Sandvold

A study by Aronson and Carlsmith (1962) indicated that *S*s preferred to fail in order to confirm a failure expectancy than to be successful and disconfirm the expectancy. The present study was a partial replication of the Aronson and Carlsmith study. *E* demands were minimized, and it was expected that the results should have paralleled those of Aronson and Carlsmith if *E* demands in the latter study had not confounded the dependent variable. Forty first-year female nursing students were used. The results indicated that Aronson and Carlsmith's findings might be accounted for by *E* demands. *S*s of the present study behaved as though they preferred to succeed rather than to confirm a failure expectancy.

Aronson and Carlsmith (1962) investigated the effects of the need to confirm performance expectancies. The subjects expecting to fail but who were successful demonstrated behavior suggesting as much discomfort with their performances as those who expected to be successful but who

[1] From the *Journal of Abnormal and Social Psychology* 1963, **67**, No. 3, 293–295. Received March 4, 1963. Reproduced by permission of the publisher.

The subjects of the present study were student nurses in training at the Lakeview Memorial Hospital, Danville, Illinois, and at the Danville Junior College. Appreciation is expressed to the administrators of both of these institutions for their cooperation.

At the time of writing the authors were with the Veterans Administration Hospital, Danville, Illinois. Current affiliations: Ward, State University of New York at Brockport; Sandvold, Oklahoma State University.

failed. The hypothesis, that a performance consistent with a person's expectancy would be pleasant and acceptable and a performance inconsistent with his expectancy would be unpleasant and unacceptable, was considered to have been confirmed. The results suggested that the need for cognitive consistency was greater than the need for achievement.

In order to encourage strong expectancies for failure and success, Aronson and Carlsmith emphasized to their subjects that the task test was highly valid. These authors, in discussing their findings, suggested that this manipulation might have introduced experimenter demands that could have had a confounding effect. Orne (1962) has summarized a great deal of evidence indicating that the demand characteristics of the experimental situation have a profound effect on subjects' experimental behavior.

Considering the fact that the subjects were paid and that the experimenters expressed a great deal of confidence in the task test, the subjects who seemed to prefer failure to the disconfirmation of a failure expectancy might have been motivated by empathy for and a sense of obligation to the experimenters as well as by needs for cognitive consistency. The present investigation was a partial replication of the study by Aronson and Carlsmith. Each of the procedural modifications of the present study was considered to be either irrelevant to comparisons of the two studies or germane to testing possible confounding variables of Aronson and Carlsmith's study. It was predicted that need achievement would be the dominant motivator if experimenter demands were minimized.

Method

Subjects and Task

Forty female, first-year nursing students were selected for the study on the basis of membership in an introductory psychology course taught at a junior college. The course included 42 students; the 2 students not selected as subjects were males. The subjects were randomly assigned to one of four conditions resulting from the independent variables high and low expectancy (HE, LE) for test success and high and low test performance (HP, LP).

The test materials included 100 cards each of which contained three pictures of junior college students. The pictures were old identification card pictures left over from previous years. Five decks of 20 cards were arranged randomly. The task was to select from the three pictures on each card the picture of the person who had the highest intelligence. Each deck of 20 cards was considered to have been one trial.

Procedure

At a pre-experimental class session, the students were told that the class would have an opportunity to take a psychological test. The alleged purpose of taking the test was to provide the students with test experience which could be used to supplement future class discussions. The test was said to have been designed by the experimenters especially for the purpose of classroom illustration. The students were told, in effect, that the test had been used before but that the experimenters did not know about its validity. It was emphasized that it would be necessary for the students to take the test conscientiously in order that the results would provide an adequate example to use in class discussions about psychological tests. An opportunity was given for the students to decline, but none did so.

All subjects were seen individually by the same experimenter, and the order of presentation of the cards was the same for all subjects. Before each subject took the test, she was told that the test was supposed to measure social sensitivity. Social sensitivity was explained in terms of one's ability to judge and understand other people. Individuals were said to differ widely in their scores; some got as many as 85% correct and others got as few as 20% correct. The experimenter marked an answer sheet as the subject responded, and after each trial, he gave the subject a predetermined score. On the first four trials, HE subjects were given scores of 17, 16, 16, and 17, respectively, and LE subjects were told their scores were 5, 4, 4, and 5, respectively. The first four trials were the expectancy trials. On the fifth trial, the performance trial, the HP subjects were told that they had 17 correct, and the LP subjects were given scores of 5.

After the fifth trial, the experimenter indicated that he had forgotten to time the last trial and that this time measure was essential to the test. While the subject scored her own fifth trial, the experimenter ostensibly tried to decide what to do about his omission. After the subject completed her scoring, the experimenter indicated that he would like to give her the last trial over in order to get a time measure. The subject was asked to try to take the fifth trial again as though she had never seen the pictures before. The subjects invariably appeared to cooperate willingly. The subject was then asked not to relate anything about the procedure to any of the other subjects as she might "spoil it for those who have not yet taken the test" and make the experience less effective for class discussion purposes. Follow-up interviews after all subjects had participated indicated that the subjects had not communicated with each other about the details of the procedure. The dependent variable was the number of choices that differed between the first and the second administrations of Trial 5. This was the measure of discomfort associated with confirmation and disconfirmation of expectancies.

Following are the present study procedures which differed from the procedures of the Aronson and Carlsmith study and which were considered to be irrelevant to any differences in results that might have occurred between the two studies. Female nursing students were used instead of female undergraduate university students; there was no time limit on responses; a period of about 30 seconds, instead of 3 minutes, elapsed between trials; pictures of junior college students rather than Harvard students were used; there was no warm-up test administered; and from each card, the subjects were to choose the picture of the most intelligent person instead of the picture of the one who had become schizophrenic. The crucial procedural differences between the two studies had to do with the expressed experimenter confidence in the test and the paying of the subjects. In the present study, the subjects were not paid, and the experimenters communicated disinterest in the validity and reliability of the test.

The suggestion to the subjects in the present study that the task test was of questionable validity might be criticized as having had the effect of creating less intense expectancies than were established in the Aronson and Carlsmith study. However, the authors of the present study considered it important to minimize experimenter demands. Dependence was placed upon providing the same amount of experience with success and failure as was provided by Aronson and Carlsmith in their study.

TABLE 1
Mean Dependent Variable Scores

	LP	HP	
HE	8.1	3.5	5.8
LE	7.1	4.0	5.5
	7.6	3.7	

Results and Discussion

The dependent variable means appear in Table 1, and the summary of the analysis of variance is shown in Table 2. The highly significant performance effect indicated that the subjects did take the test conscientiously. The failure of the interaction to reach significance suggested that the effect demonstrated in the Aronson and Carlsmith study might have occurred as a result of the influence of one or both of the hypothesized confounding procedures.

The results of the present study were not considered to have impugned the theories which regard cognitive consistency as an important motivator. Rather, the present study is interpreted as suggesting that the experimenter demands might account for the findings of Aronson and Carlsmith.

REFERENCES

Aronson, E., & Carlsmith, J. M. Performance expectancy as a determinant of actual performance. *Journal of Abnormal and Social Psychology,* 1962, **65**, 178–182.

Orne, M. T. On the social psychology of the psychological experiment: with particular reference to demand characteristics and their implications. *American Psychologist,* 1962, **17**, 776–783.

TABLE 2
Summary of Analysis of Variance

Source	*SS*	*df*	*MS*	*F*
Expectancy (A)	.62	1	.62	
Performance (B)	148.22	1	148.22	15.50[a]
A × B	5.63	1	5.63	
Within	344.30	36	9.56	
	498.77	39		

[a] $p < .005$.

Discussion

Ward and Sandvold were correct in proposing the demand characteristics alternative because it is quite plausible. The difficulty with their experiment lies in methodology. Actually, the subtitle "A Partial Replication" gives a clue to the problem. They varied many things in their experiment and got results different from Aronson and Carlsmith. They carefully point out differences between the two experiments. Some of the differences are intuitively (but arbitrarily) considered irrelevant. They attempted to reduce demand characteristics by not paying subjects and by downgrading the validity of the test. Other presumably unimportant differences were type of subjects, differences in interstimulus intervals, change in nature of task (i.e., selection of most intelligent face rather than schizophrenic), etc.

Empirically, it is possible that any of these other variables might have caused the differences. Ward and Sandvold should have replicated Aronson and Carlsmith's procedures as closely as possible. If they obtained the same results as Aronson and Carlsmith, they would have a much stronger basis for claiming support for their alternative hypothesis. The conclusion to be drawn is that before you can seriously claim support for an alternative hypothesis, you must be able to reproduce the original findings when you use the original experimental conditions. Obviously, such a procedure is more expensive in time and effort, but is necessary if firm conclusions are to be drawn. Partial replications seldom solve theoretical problems.

If Ward and Sandvold had replicated the original results as well as their actual results under the changed conditions, it still does not follow that their results conclusively refuted Aronson and Carlsmith's expectancy hypothesis. Ward and Sandvold wanted to reduce demand characteristics. By downgrading the validity of the test they may have created less intense expectancies of success or failure, a possibility they recognize in their method section. It would be unclear, then, whether their results were due to a reduction in demand characteristics or to a weakening of the strength of subjects' expectancy. The determination of which alternative is the correct one makes a very important difference. In this case, an independent check on the strength of the expectancy should have been used. If strength of the success-failure expectancy was as strong in the changed replication of the experiment as well as in the replication of the original experiment, then a much stronger case could be made for the demand characteristics interpretation. Ultimately, about all that we can conclude from the second experiment is that under the particular set of experimental conditions that Ward and Sandvold used, subjects attempted to achieve a good score.

There is another difference in procedures between the two experiments that might be important. Ward and Sandvold led subjects to believe that the results of their social sensitivity tests would be discussed in class, a procedural variation not used in Aronson and Carlsmith's experiment. Knowing that their results would be discussed publicly may have greatly enhanced the achievement motivation of Ward and Sandvold's subjects. Cottrell (1965) reasoned that this effect was precisely what had occurred, and in an exceptionally well designed study set about to test his reasoning. Cottrell varied whether or not subjects thought their results would be made public to the class or held private. He ran the subjects in groups of four, one subject in each of the four expectancy-performance conditions. Since all four conditions were run at the same time, the results of the experiment could not be attributed to differences in the experimenter's behavior toward subjects in different conditions. This design feature eliminated the force of one criticism of the original study—differential experimenter behavior in different experimental conditions.

Cottrell's (1965) results did not support his hypothesis concerning public disclosure of scores because there were no differences between public and private conditions. Overall, his results supported Aronson and Carlsmith's findings because there was a significant expectancy by fifth trial interaction. However, the interaction was due mostly to the fact that high expectancy-low performance subjects changed many more of their choices than the high expectancy-high performance subjects. Actually the low expectancy-low performance subjects changed slightly more responses than the low expectancy-high performance subjects. This result was definitely not as strong as the dramatic difference obtained in the original experiment. Overall, then, Cottrell's (1965) results provided only weak support for Aronson and Carlsmith's hypothesis.

Several experiments have shown that subjects in the low expectancy conditions have poorer recall for their choices than subjects in the high expectancy conditions (Waterman & Ford, 1965; Lowin & Epstein, 1965; Brock, Edelman, Edwards, & Schuck, 1965). Waterman and Ford (1965) felt that this differential recall could account for Aronson and Carlsmith's results. However, the recall of subjects in the low expectancy-low performance condition of Waterman and Ford's experiment was virtually the same as the recall of subjects in their low expectancy-high performance condition. This result means that differential memory cannot account for Aronson and Carlsmith's results (Hendrick, 1966) because the low expectancy-high performance subjects changed *significantly* more responses than the low expectancy-low performance subjects. So, even though there may be differences in recall between expectancy conditions, these differences would also have to exist between fifth trial performance conditions before differential recall could account for the original data.

The last paper in this section is a series of studies by Brock and his coworkers. Altogether, seven experiments are reported. These studies are essentially replications of the original experiment which attempted to vary an important conceptual variable—strength of the performance expectancy. As you read the report, notice how "small" procedural differences in the experiments create large differences in the results.

Seven Studies of Performance Expectancy as a Determinant of Actual Performance[1]

Timothy C. Brock, Sheldon K. Edelman, David C. Edwards and John R. Schuck

Aronson and Carlsmith (1962) extended theories of cognitive consistency, particularly dissonance (Festinger, 1957) theory, to predict persons' reactions to inconsistencies between their expected and actual performance. The main finding concerned persons who expected to do poorly but who found themselves performing well. The dissonance aroused between expecting to do poorly and actually doing well was presumably reduced by undoing the good performance, by changing correct responses so as to obtain an event (poor performance) consonant with the person's expectation ("I will perform poorly"). Persons who expected to do poorly, but did well, changed more of their responses than those who expected to do poorly and *did* perform poorly. The present paper reports seven replications of the Aronson and Carlsmith study.

[1] From the *Journal of Experimental Social Psychology,* 1965, **1**, 295–310. Received July 12, 1965.

Supported by grants, GS-343 and GS-606, from the National Science Foundation to the senior author. We are indebted to G. Karas, L. Wolins, R. Peters, L. Becker, B. Clooser, D. McCormick, J. Berns, and K. Harriman for their assistance in various phases of the work. Portions of the data were presented to the Iowa Academy of Science in April, 1963.

T. C. Brock was at the University of Pittsburgh and Iowa State University during the data collections and S. K. Edelman was at Iowa State University.

At the time of writing, Brock was with Ohio State University, Edelman was with the University of Missouri, and Edwards and Schuck were with Iowa State University. Current affiliations: Brock, Ohio State University; Edelman, Kansas State University; Edwards, Iowa State University; Schuck, Bowling Green State University.

Experiment 1

METHOD

Subjects and Task. The *S*s were 55 summer session females at Johnstown College. Forty of the *S*s were assigned randomly to one of the four treatments resulting from High and Low Expectancy and High and Low Performance. After *S*s were run, additional *S*s became available and they were assigned randomly, within the limits of the *E*'s scheduling convenience, to the high expectancy-low performance and low expectancy-high performance conditions.

The stimuli consisted of 100 cards, each of which contained three photographs of female or of male high school students. The pictures were taken from a high school yearbook. Below the pictures appeared the letters *A*, *B*, and *C*. The task was to select from three pictures on each card the picture of the person who "has been committed to a mental hospital because of mental illness."

PROCEDURE

Each *S* was run individually. To begin, the *S* read the following printed instructions.

> Our work concerns the establishment of time standards, that is, how long it takes a person to complete some nationally used psychological tests. Today you will take a nationally used standard test of SOCIAL SENSITIVITY. This test has been widely used with remarkable success by psychologists for many years. Moreover, it has proved to be the most useful of the short objective tests. It is an excellent measure of how sensitive an individual is to other people.
>
> Each card in the pile in front of you contains three pictures, A, B, and C. One of the three pictures on each card is of a person who has been committed to a mental hospital because of mental illness at some time in his or her life. Judge which person has been mentally ill and give your decision by saying out loud A, or B, or C. This test shows some people to be very sensitive, getting as many as 85% correct while others do quite poorly, getting only 5 or 10% correct. Many people, of course, are somewhere in the middle.

Subjects' scores were reported to them at the end of each block of twenty trials. On the first four blocks of twenty trials, high-expectancy *S*s were fed back bogus scores of 17, 16, 16, and 17, respectively, and low-expectancy *S*s were told their scores were 5, 4, 4, and 5, respectively. The first four blocks, eighty trials, were the expectancy blocks. On the fifth block, the performance series, the high-performance *S*s were assigned a score of 17 and the low-performance *S*s were assigned scores of 5. A trial never exceeded ten seconds.

After the fifth block, the *E* said she had forgotten to time the last twenty trials and that a time measure was needed. The *S* was given a faked answer key, allowed to score her own responses on the fifth block, and then the *E* asked the *S* to judge the last twenty cards again "pretending that it's a completely new set of pictures." The *dependent variable* was the number of judgments which were changed in the second presentation of the last twenty cards. Obviously, a person who did very well on the first administration of the fifth block would decrease his score by changing very many of his judgments. A person who did poorly on the first administration of the fifth block would only improve his score by changing very many of his judgments.

DIFFERENCES BETWEEN THE ARONSON-CARLSMITH STUDY (1962) AND EXPERIMENT 1

The *Ss* were inferior intellectually and socioeconomically to the Harvard undergraduates of the Aronson-Carlsmith experiment. There are other variables, too numerous to list here, which undoubtedly distinguish coeds at Johnstown College from those at Harvard. The photographs on the cards were alternately male and female and "mentally ill" was the judgmental dimension instead of "schizophrenic." The elaborate "warmup" and rationale of the Aronson-Carlsmith study were omitted. The *E* was a female undergraduate who was unaware of the hypothesis. (The male graduate student *E* in the Aronson-Carlsmith study presumably knew the hypothesis.) The rest periods provided by Aronson and Carlsmith were omitted.

RESULTS

The results, shown in columns four and five of Table 1, replicated those of Aronson and Carlsmith (column three of Table 1). Table 1 shows the mean number of judgments changed from the first to the second administration of the fifth block of twenty trials. The interaction F, 33.7 ($df = 1, 51$) yielded a p value less than .005. In Experiment 1 the largest number of changes were made by *Ss* who expected to do poorly but found themselves doing well on the last twenty trials. The many differences in procedure, in *Es*, and in *Ss*, between Experiment 1 and Aronson-Carlsmith, increased confidence that Aronson and Carlsmith had reported a reproducible effect.

Experiment 2

The next step was an attempt to vary the strength or clarity of the person's expectancy about his ability to judge mental illness from photos. Aronson and Carlsmith's (1962, p. 178) formulation led "to the predic-

TABLE 1
Mean Dependent Variable Scores for Aronson and Carlsmith and Experiments 1 and 2[a]

Treatment		Aronson and Carlsmith	Experiment 1		Experiment 2	
Expectancy	Performance	Mean	Mean	Variance	Mean	Variance
High	High	3.9	3.5	0.94	4.3	5.12
High	Low	11.1	5.3[b]	7.67	2.7	8.68
Low	Low	6.7	3.7	5.12	2.6	2.04
Low	High	10.2	8.0[c]	5.07	6.0	3.78

[a] Each mean based on $N = 10$, unless otherwise noted.
[b] $N = 19$.
[c] $N = 16$.

tion that an individual who has a *clear* (our italics) conception of his ability at a given task will experience dissonance if his behavior differs sharply from this expectancy." Decreasing the clarity of the expectancy should decrease the resultant dissonance from a disconfirming event. The Aronson-Carlsmith procedure provided an obvious and convenient means of varying the clarity of an expectancy: vary the number of induction trials. Experiment 2 was identical in all respects to Experiment 1 except that the number of induction trials was halved. Instead of four blocks or eighty trials preceding the performance series, only two blocks or forty trials were administered before the final twenty cards. Forty female students from the same population as Experiment 1 were randomly assigned to the four treatments.

An analysis of variance was carried out for the data in the sixth and seventh columns of Table 1. The expectancy $\times$ performance interaction obtained by Aronson and Carlsmith, and in Experiment 1, was reobtained in Experiment 2. The interaction F, 13.1 ($df = 1, 36$), yielded a p value less than .005.

A weaker and/or less clear expectancy about his ability should lead to less dissonance when the person's performance turns out to be inconsistent with that expectancy. Consequently, with forty induction trials instead of eighty, there should be less changing of judgments from the first to the second administration of the performance series. The data tended to support the prediction. The difference of greatest interest is in the low expectancy-high performance condition. The mean for Experiment 1, 8.0, was statistically larger (two-tailed t test $p < .05$) than the mean for Experiment 2, 6.0. Thus, Experiment 2 showed that the strength and clarity of an expectation can be affected by varying the number of induction trials. Presumably, increasing the number of induction trials to 160, or 320, or higher would produce correspondingly larger effects on the dependent variable. It was, however, inconvenient to run so many induction trials and therefore a different means was sought to *increase* the strength of the person's expectancy about the quality of his subsequent performance.

Experiments 3 and 4

In the Aronson-Carlsmith study and Experiments 1 and 2, the *S* received no more than four feedbacks from the experimenter concerning how well he was doing. These were the summary scores at the end of each block of twenty trials. The strength and clarity of the person's belief about his ability should be an increasing function of the amount of feedback from the *E*. Therefore the *E* provided feedback to the *S* after *every* trial instead of only at the end of a block of twenty trials: eighty feedbacks instead of only four.

Method

The *Ss* in Experiment 3, 40 female introductory psychology students at Iowa State University, were randomly assigned to the four treatments by the *E*, a male graduate student who knew the hypothesis. The procedure was the same as in Experiment 1 except that the *E* said "correct" or "wrong" on each trial and the printed instructions included the following:

1. Pick up and look at a card when you hear a click.
2. Say either A or B or C to indicate which person you believe has spent time in a mental hospital because he or she was mentally ill.
3. Continue to look at the card until you hear the click for the next card. (You will be told whether your judgment was correct or incorrect.)

The instructions assured that the *S* continued to look at the card for several seconds after the *E* announced "correct" or "wrong." The "click" was produced on a Hunter timer, a device which was in accord with the rationale given to the *S* about "time standards." A trial never exceeded ten seconds. Summary scores were also given at the end of every block of twenty trials, just as in the Aronson-Carlsmith study and Experiments 1 and 2.

Results

Experiment 3 was designed to increase the strength of *S*'s expectancies about his future performance above the levels produced by Aronson and Carlsmith and by Experiment 1. In Experiment 3, the high-expectancy *S*'s judgment was confirmed 66 times in eighty trials while, in Experiment 1, he received "reinforcement" from the *E* only four times. Similarly, the low-expectancy *S* in Experiment 3 heard "wrong" 62 times; his belief about his poor ability should have been stronger and clearer than that of his low-expectancy counterpart in Experiment 1. Consequently, it was predicted that the dissonance effect, the undoing of correct responses by the low expectancy-high performance *Ss*, would be greater in Experiment 3 than in Experiment 1. The results for Experiment 3, shown in columns three and four of Table 2, clearly contradict the prediction. Table 2 shows no expectancy $\times$ performance interaction ($F = 1.6$). There is a main effect of performance ($F = 34.5$, $df = 1, 36$) significant at beyond the .005 level: those who found themselves doing poorly on the fifth block changed their responses when they were given an opportunity to do so. There was, however, still a tendency for the low expectancy-high performance *Ss* to change more than the high expectancy-high performance *Ss*: the difference between the means of 7.0 and 4.7 yielded a two-tailed *t* significant at the .05 level. Nevertheless, the results were opposed to the derivation that increasing the clarity of an expectancy should in-

TABLE 2
Mean Dependent Variable Scores for Experiments 3 and 4[a]

Treatment		Experiment 3		Experiment 4	
Expectancy	Performance	Mean	Variance	Mean	Variance
High	High	4.7	2.44	4.8	5.51
High	Low	11.0	4.00	10.8	5.07
Low	Low	11.0	16.44	11.4	4.04
Low	High	7.0	8.00	5.9	4.32

[a] Each mean based on $N = 10$.

crease the amount of dissonance, and consequent alteration of the dissonance-producing event. The derivation required that Experiment 3 produce *more* change than Aronson and Carlsmith and Experiments 1 and 2 in the low expectancy-high performance condition. This was clearly not the case. At this point it was decided to replicate Experiment 3, by sampling 40 *S*s from a slightly different population, female summer session students at Iowa State University, and by using a different male graduate student *E* who did not know the hypothesis. The results for Experiment 4, shown in the fifth and sixth columns of Table 2, repeated those for Experiment 3: a very significant main effect of performance ($F = 69.8$) and no expectancy × performance interaction ($F < 1$).

Discussion of Experiments 1, 2, 3, and 4

Why were we unable to reproduce the results of the Aronson-Carlsmith (1962) experiment when the *E* told the *S* on *every* trial whether his judgment was correct or wrong? Frequent feedback from the *E* should have augmented the strength and clarity of the *S*'s expectancy about his subsequent performance (Rotter, 1954, p. 113, 165–168; Good, 1952). The clearer and stronger the expectancy, the greater should be the dissonance-arousing effect of a disconfirming event. Since the results did not bear out this derivation, several alternative interpretations were considered.

In one interpretation of the failure to replicate under feedback conditions, attention is called to the ease with which *S*s can reverse concepts to correspond with a changed pattern of reinforcement. During Trials 1 to 80 of Experiment 3, the low expectancy-high performance *S* has been experiencing many "wrongs" together with a small proportion of "corrects." Before Trial 80 he has never received "correct" twice in a row. When, on Trials 81, 82, 83, etc., he begins to hear "correct" more frequently and, indeed, consecutively, he quickly revises his pessimism about his ability to judge mental illness from faces. Some dissonance may have occurred on Trial 82 or 83 but that dissonance may have been supplanted on subsequent trials (84, 85, 86, etc.) by a high expectancy. After twenty trials (81 to 100) consisting mainly of "correct" the low expectancy has been extinguished and the *S* believes he has become proficient at judging mental illness from pictures. Hence, there would be little pressure to change "right" answers to confirm a previous low expectancy because that low expectancy has been relinquished. Tests of the foregoing interpretation required a design in which two groups can be compared: (*a*) persons given feedback on the Performance Series only and (*b*) persons given feedback on the Expectancy Series only. Group *a* should show the effect we have been describing: for Trials 81 to 100 they receive trial-by-trial feedback and quickly alter whatever prior expectancies they developed from the previous four end-of-block summary scores. Thus group *a* will show only a main effect of Performance, just as in Experiment 3. Group *b*, however, should show the dissonance effect when the single summary announcement of performance scores conflicts with the expectancies developed under trial-by-trial feedback. The plans for Experiments 5 and 6 are shown in relation to previous experiments in Table 3. The interpretation predicts only a performance main effect in Experiment 5. In Experiment 6 the performance $\times$ expectancy interaction should be obtained.

A second interpretation, suggested by Aronson (personal communication), emphasized the psychological effect of hearing "wrong" repeatedly versus only at the end of a block of twenty trials. Under the former condition more "frustration" was perhaps engendered as well as a "higher achievement drive." In Aronson's words, "it may be that the subjects in the low-low condition may simply be sick of hearing the word 'wrong' over and over and over again and, therefore, may be willing to do almost anything to hear the word 'right'—even if it means performing in a manner which is inconsistent with their expectancies!" Aronson's suggestion was tested in two ways. First, the low-low groups in Experiments 3 and 4 were compared with the low-low group in Experiment 5. The low-low

TABLE 3
Presence or not of Feedback ("Correct" or "Wrong") on Every Trial in the Aronson-Carlsmith (1962) Study and Experiments 1 to 6

Expectancy series[a]	Performance series	Experiments
No F	No F	Aronson-Carlsmith, 1, 2
F	F	3,4
No F	F	5
F	No F	6

[a] F = Feedback on every trial.

groups in Experiments 3 and 4 should have changed more of their Performance Series responses than the low-low group in Experiment 5 because the former groups heard "wrong" for the first 80 trials while the latter did not. A second test compared the low-low group in Experiment 5 with the low-low groups in Experiment 6. The latter group should change more Performance Series responses if the frustration-engendering or achievement-arousal interpretation has validity.

The third interpretation concerns the nature of the conceptual work performed by the *S*s in the high and low expectancy conditions. Post-experimental interviews suggested that many *S*s were forming hypotheses about cues which might betoken mental illness. Some *S*s said they looked at the eyes, others noticed the mouth, and so forth. The high-expectancy *S* was reinforced more than 75% of the time for whichever particular hypothesis he was entertaining. He was therefore unlikely to try out very many hypotheses; he was likely to stick with one or two discriminative cues simply because they seemed to be effective. The low-expectancy *S*, on the other hand, was forced to generate new hypotheses because most of his hypotheses and choices about discriminative cues were quickly overruled by the *E*. The low-expectancy *S*, more frequently than the high-expectancy *S*, was "looking for alternatives" (Schroder and Rotter, 1952). The rational coping possibly instigated in the low-expectancy *S* in Experiment 3 may have contributed to his reluctance to undo correct responses and his eagerness to change wrong ones when given the opportunity to do so. An indirect evaluation of this interpretation was made by asking each *S* to write down her thoughts while she was judging faces. The protocols were scored for number of attributes allegedly used to detect mental illness.

Experiments 5 and 6

Method

Experiments 5 and 6 were identical with Experiment 3, except that in Experiment 5, feedbacks on Trials 1 to 80 were omitted, and in Experiment 6, feedbacks on Trials 81 to 100 were omitted.

At the end of the experiment, the *S* was given about five minutes to reply to the following printed instructions. "Please list the thoughts and ideas occurring to you while you were judging the faces. List *everything* that came to your mind. Your detailed remarks here will greatly aid our psychological research." These protocols were scored without knowledge of the *S*'s treatment assignment. The scorer counted the number of cues, traits, attributes, etc., which the *S* said she used to judge mental illness.

Data from one *S* was discarded because of negativism and from another, because she had "worked for a psychologist" and expressed extreme suspicion. Three cell *N*s are larger than 10 due to the *E*'s oversight.

RESULTS AND DISCUSSION

The results for Experiments 5 and 6 are shown in Table 4. In both experiments the only statistically reliable effect was the main effect of performance. Low performers changed more of their answers than high performers, just as in Experiments 3 and 4. The absence of a dissonance effect in Experiment 6 was surprising and leaves assessment of the first interpretation lacking in definitiveness.

According to the second interpretation, hearing "wrong" over and over again may have engendered frustration and heightened willingness to violate expectancies in order to elicit "correct." Thus the low-low groups in Experiments 3, 4, and 6 should show more response change than the low-low group in Experiment 5 which had no feedback for the first 80 trials. Since the means for the former groups were 11.0, 11.4, and 9.7, while the mean in Experiment 5 was 12.1, the interpretation was discredited.

The third interpretation, which implied more hypothesis exploration by low-expectancy *S*s, was tested by counting the number of attributes of the stimuli which the *S* said she noticed in order to judge whether the person had been mentally ill. The mean number of attributes mentioned by high expectancy-high performance *S*s in Experiments 5 and 6 were 3.7 and 3.4, respectively; the corresponding scores for low expectancy-low performance *S*s were 3.6 and 3.0. The slight nonsignificant tendency for high-high *S*s to report using more attributes than the low-low *S*s was opposed to the interpretation. The mean scores in the high-low and low-high conditions did not differ reliably from the overall mean of about 3.4. Hence, there was no evidence in support of the possibility that high-expectancy *S*s differed from low-expectancy *S*s in the kind of conceptual work they were performing.

TABLE 4
Mean Dependent Variable Scores for Experiments 5 and 6[a]

Treatment		Experiment 5		Experiment 6	
Expectancy	Performance	Mean	Variance	Mean	Variance
High	High	4.2	1.11	3.3	2.44
High	Low	9.1[b]	13.88	6.7[c]	3.20
Low	Low	12.1	11.89	9.7[d]	6.64
Low	High	3.4[c]	4.50	4.2[b]	2.75

[a] Each mean based on $N = 10$, unless otherwise noted.
[b] $N = 9$.
[c] $N = 11$.
[d] $N = 12$.

Experiment 7

Persistence of a main effect of performance and failure, after Experiments 1 and 2, to reobtain higher change scores under low expectancy-high performance than under low expectancy-low performance, made us suspect that doing poorly on the judgment task may affect *S*s' recall of prior stimulus-judgment associations and *S*s' subsequent "learning" of new connections. One purpose of Experiment 7 was to investigate directly the possibility that low-expectancy *S*s differed from high-expectancy *S*s in their ability to recall their previous judgments. Evidence of poorer recall under low expectancy was reported by Lowin and Epstein (1965) and Waterman and Ford (1965) after the present data collection began.

Another objective of Experiment 7 was to repeat the experiment of Aronson and Carlsmith (1962) in a different experimental context. Experiments 1 and 2 reproduced the critical expectancy × performance interaction. This seems clear. However, failure to obtain the interaction in subsequent experiments employing somewhat different procedures, and the failure of other investigators,[2] raised the question of the appropriate domain to which the phenomenon can be generalized.

Additional aims concerned the implications of the stimuli for alternative interpretations. Although no evidence for differential hypothesis invention was obtained in Experiment 5 and 6, there was great between-subject variability. Photos of faces, some of which allegedly represent mentally ill persons, evoked a wide range and variety of responses. In the present experiment the photos were replaced with Munsell color strips and the task was changed to judgment of relative "brightness" in order to impoverish our *S*s with respect to cues for hypothesis invention. In addition, by employing a less "social" and more "psycho-physical" task we might minimize whatever contribution "social sensitivity test" may have made to arousal of sensitivity to "demand" (Ward and Sandvold, 1963) characteristics. Finally, the stimuli were selected so that they

[2] Others have failed to replicate Aronson and Carlsmith (1962): A. H. Buss (1964, personal communication), Silverman and Marcantonio (1965), Lowin and Epstein (1965), and Ward and Sandvold (1963). Cottrell (1965) reported a significant expectancy × performance interaction, but the mean score under low expectancy-high performance was not reliably greater than the mean score under low expectancy-low performance. It was the undoing of good performance by low-expectancy persons which was so striking in the original Aronson-Carlsmith data (1962, p. 181). To be considered "successful" a replication must reproduce a statistically significant difference in which the change score for low expectancy-high performance exceeds that for low expectancy-low performance. By this criterion the only successful reproductions known to the writers were those of Experiments 1 and 2 in the present series.

were actually identical in subjective "brightness." Thus variations in recall would be assignable almost entirely to the treatments and not to the complex effects of subject stimuli interaction.

Experiment 7 included the four cells of the original Aronson-Carlsmith (1962) design and two additional conditions comparable to those of Lowin and Epstein (1965) in which recall of previous judgments was requested.

Method

The procedure was the same as that of Experiment 3 with the following exceptions: scores were announced only at the end of a series of twenty trials, as in Aronson and Carlsmith (1962), and Experiments 1 and 2; the stimuli and task concerned "brightness" rather than "social sensitivity," as described below; seven instead of ten *Ss* from the same population (Iowa State University coeds) were randomly assigned to the four experimental conditions and fourteen *Ss* to each Memory condition.

Stimuli. Instead of photos, each of the 100 cards in the five twenty-card series contained three Munsell Glossy Papers from the Munsell (1963) Cabinet Edition. The

TABLE 5
Identification Labels for Munsell Glossy Papers[a] Used as Stimuli in the Fifth Series of Experiment 7

Trial	Value	Chroma	Stimulus hue		
			A	B	C
1	7	2	10RP	10YR	10B
2	6	6	10R	5G	10PB
3	5	4	10R	5P	10G
4	7	4	5PB	5R	5Y
5	4	6	10B	10PB	10BG
6	5	6	10B	10RB	5G
7	6	6	10G	5GY	10BG
8	6	4	10GY	10P	5YR
9	4	6	5GY	10P	10RP
10	5	6	10G	10Y	10R
11	4	6	5R	5RP	10G
12	4	4	10P	10B	5YR
13	4	4	5B	5PB	5BG
14	7	1	5PB	5Y	5R
15	4	2	10Y	10GB	5YR
16	7	4	10P	10RP	10GY
17	5	4	10RP	5YR	5BG
18	6	4	5B	5BG	5R
19	5	6	5GY	5G	10BG
20	7	2	10GY	5R	5BG

[a] Munsell, 1963.

papers were labeled A, B, and C. To illustrate, the papers used in the fifth series are tabulated with their Munsell notation in Table 5. Note that on every trial only hue varied; value and chroma, the factors which contributed to subjective "brightness," were the same. For example, on the first trial of the fifth series the hues red-purple, yellow-red, and blue, had identical degrees of lightness (value = 7) and saturation (chroma = 2).

Instructions to Subjects

The subjects read the following printed instructions:

Iowa State University Time Study: Brightness Sensitivity Inventory

Explanation: Our work concerns the establishment of time standards, that is, how long it takes a person to complete some nationally used psychological tests. Today you will take a nationally used standard test of BRIGHTNESS SENSITIVITY. This test has been widely used with remarkable success by psychologists for many years. It has proved to be the most useful of the short objective tests. It is an excellent measure of how well an individual can judge brightness in colors of differing hue and saturation. BRIGHTNESS SENSITIVITY is an important ability. It is involved in art, photography, home decoration, as well as simple enjoyment of the visual world.

Each card in the pile in front of you contains three colors, A, B, C. One of the three colors on each card is actually brighter than the other two. Which color seems brighter than the other two to you? Judge which color is brighter and then give your decision by saying out loud "A" or "B" or "C." This test shows some people to be very sensitive, getting as many as 85% correct while others do quite poorly, getting only 5 or 10% correct. Many people, of course, are somewhere in the middle.

Instructions: 1. Pick up and look at a card when you hear a click; 2. Say either A or B or C to indicate which color seems brighter to you; 3. Continue to look at the card until you hear the click for the next card; 4. At the end of a set of twenty cards you will be given your score.

Memory Conditions. There were two memory conditions, high and low expectancy. At the end of the fifth series, instead of scoring their response sheets while the *E* fixed his timer, the memory *S*s were told: "This is a memory test, I want you to go through the fifth series again giving as many as possible of the same answers as you just gave me."

At the end of the experiment, the *S*s wrote their thoughts about their experience by following the same printed instructions used in Experiments 5 and 6, except that "colors" was substituted for "faces."

Results and Discussion

The change scores are shown in Table 6. Analysis of variance of the four replication means yielded only one reliable ($p < .05$) effect: low

TABLE 6
Dependent Variable Scores for Experiment 7

Treatment			
Expectancy	Performance	Mean[a]	Variance
High	High	4.86	4.15
High	Low	9.43	14.95
Low	Low	9.57	18.62
Low	High	8.57	8.28
High	Memory[b]	6.29	14.23
Low	Memory[b]	8.93	8.35

[a] Each mean based on $N = 7$, unless otherwise noted.
[b] $N = 14$.

performance *S*s changed more responses than high performance *S*s. The *F* was 4.72 with 1 and 24 degrees of freedom. The *F*s for the expectancy main effect and the expectancy $\times$ performance interaction were 2.26 and 1.94, respectively. With 1 and 24 *df* an *F* of 2.93 is needed for significance at the .10 level. (A variance-stabilizing square-root transformation, $(x)^{1/2} + (x + 1)^{1/2}$, did not affect these *F*s, either in absolute or relative magnitudes.)

For the memory conditions, the mean number of changes under low expectancy exceeded the mean number under high expectancy and the difference was reliable by *t* test ($t = 2.78$, $p < .02$). The same result, it is recalled, was obtained by Lowin and Epstein (1965) and Waterman and Ford (1965) even though their memory instructions differed somewhat. Hence, low-expectancy *S*s have poorer recall than high-expectancy *S*s of their prior judgments. "Correcting" the four replication means for memory did not affect the incompatibility of the results with the expectancy theory prediction.

The present memory data suggested that when the *S* is given a low score at the end of a series of trials, memory for his responses suffers. Although the present memory *S*s did not score their fifth series it is reasonable to infer from earlier studies[3] that they developed accurate expectancies about their performance over the previous eighty trials. The finding that low-expectancy *S*s "forget" their responses more than high-expectancy *S*s suggested that differential memory loss also occurred at the end of the performance series, when the *S* has just scored his own

[3] In the Lowin-Epstein (1965) study *S*s were asked to estimate their scores before the announcement of the score by the *E*. In Cottrell (1965) *S*s were asked to guess what score they would get on a new set of cards. In both studies, the data clearly showed that subjects had learned to expect poor or good performance depending upon their assignment to low or high expectancy.

responses. If so, within each expectancy condition, high-performance *S*s should exhibit better recall than low-performance *S*s. Recall by high-performance *S*s excelled recall by low-performance *S*s in both the Lowin-Epstein (1965) and Waterman-Ford (1965) experiments. However, in both studies the differences were not statistically reliable. Hence, the conclusion that the recurring performance main effect can be attributed to differences in recall must remain tentative. Undoubtedly the desire to do well rather than poorly contributed importantly to the performance main effect.

A memory impairment explanation may account for the persistent tendency of low expectancy-high performance *S*s to change more than high expectancy-high performance *S*s. (In the present study the low-high mean, 8.57, was statistically larger, two-tailed t test $p < .02$, than the high-high mean, 4.86.) Low-expectancy *S*s have learned to discount the correctness of their judgments so that by the time they get to the last twenty trials they may be guessing wantonly. Hence, there is no appreciable "saving" when the low-expectancy *S* is given an opportunity to score his responses for the fifth series.[4]

If a *S* has been doing poorly for the first four series his learning (incidental or otherwise) of the stimulus-response associations on the fifth series will be inferior to that of a *S* who has been doing well on the first four series. In sum, receiving a low score adversely affects (a) recall of previous judgments and (b) learning of subsequent stimulus-judgment associations.

Achievement Motivation and Hypothesis Invention

The postexperimental protocols were scored for indications of achievement motivation and attempts at hypothesis invention.[5] The mean number of achievement motivation statements under low expectancy-low

[4] Cottrell (1965) presented data showing that treatment during the first four series overweighs any possible effects on expectancy of performance on the fifth series. When asked to guess what score they would get on a new set of cards, Cottrell's low expectancy-high performance *S*s gave a mean estimate of 3.12, while the corresponding mean for the low expectancy-low performance *S*s was 3.00. These values were virtually the same.

[5] Achievement was indicated by statements such as "like the feedback from the experimenter," "worried about whether I was giving correct answer," "tried harder," "wondered how I could improve my score," "didn't feel I was doing well enough," "envied people who could get a score of 85% correct." Hypothesis invention was scored by counting the number of attributes of the stimuli which the subject said she employed to judge "brightness." Typical statements were "I chose all green," "the one I saw first," "rejected purples and browns," "my first impression," "I chose the larger square," "used the reflection from the light," "chose the lighter color."

performance was .60, a value not reliably greater than the high expectancy-high performance mean, .30. For the high-expectancy memory condition the mean was .50 and for the low-expectancy memory condition the mean was .66. These values were also not reliably different. Overall evidence of achievement motivation arousal was meager.[6]

The overall mean hypothesis invention score for the four replication conditions was .33. In Experiments 5 and 6 the over-all mean hypothesis invention score was 3.60. Hence, the present use of Munsell colors, instead of human faces, significantly impoverished the *S*s with respect to cues for hypothesis invention. The mean hypothesis invention score for the high expectancy-high performance and low expectancy-low performance conditions was the same, .40. The low-high mean, .44, and the high-low mean, .14, did not differ reliably from each other or the overall mean. Similarly no reliable difference was obtained between the high-expectancy memory condition mean, .50, and that of the low expectancy memory condition, .33. Here, as in the Experiments 5 and 6, slightly greater evidence of hypothesis invention was exhibited by the high-expectancy *S*s. An interpretation which relies on greater hypothesis invention by low-expectancy *S*s is clearly discredited.

General Discussion

The conditions under which low expectancy-high performance *S*s will change more of their responses than low expectancy-low performance *S*s are still unknown. Although Experiments 1 and 2 confirmed Aronson and Carlsmith (1962), subsequent data collections by ourselves and others (see footnote 2) have consistently failed to supply replication. The possibility that the trial-by-trial feedback of Experiments 3 and 4 engendered differential frustration and/or rational coping was discredited by Experiments 5 and 6.

[6] Examination of the Lowin-Epstein (1965) procedures seemed to weaken further the achievement motivation view. Lowin and Epstein found no difference in change scores between conditions which might have been expected to induce different amounts of achievement motivation. In the first condition, *S*s had to phone Dr. Lowin "through the departmental offices" to make an appointment and "the experiment was conducted in his private office." "Dr. Lowin of the Social Psychology Department maintained a professor-student role relationship (with his *S*s) at all times." Subjects were paid and test items were mounted on IBM cards. In the second condition, a graduate student ran unpaid volunteers using 3-inch $\times$ 5-inch file cards.

Lowin and Epstein intended to vary status of the *E*. While they undoubtedly succeeded, motivation to perform well was probably varied as well. Absence of differences on the dependent variable between the Lowin-Epstein "status" conditions suggested that arousal of achievement motivation does not affect change scores over and beyond whatever effect is produced by low versus high performance.

Experiments 5 and 6 also discouraged the possibility that the dissonance aroused by an inconsistent score on the performance series is so evanescent that it does not affect change behavior. Analysis of hypothesis invention in Experiments 5, 6, and 7 offered no support for the possible interpretation that low expectancy *S*s are performing a different kind of conceptual work than high-expectancy *S*s. Doubt has been cast by Silverman and Marcantonio (1965) on Ward and Sandvold's (1963) contention that "demand qualities" (Orne, 1962) may determine consistency-seeking behavior by low expectancy-high performance *S*s.

One is left with the repeatedly obtained main effect of performance and evidence from Experiment 7 suggesting that this effect can be explained in terms of differences in recall of previous judgments as well as in terms of motivation to do well. Whether or not Aronson and Carlsmith's (1962) expectancy theory can be fruitfully extended to increase understanding of performance deficit is dependent upon easy replication of their major result. The paradigm should be uncontaminated by "learning" artifacts and by the arousal of motives competitive with consistency-seeking behavior.

Summary

Seven experiments were performed to explore the effects of expectancy-performance inconsistency on the undoing of correct responses (Aronson and Carlsmith, 1962). Experiments 1 and 2 reproduced the expectancy $\times$ performance interaction; the dissonant effect of high performance on low expectancy was significantly reduced from 1 to 2 by reducing the number of trials used to induce expectancy in 2. Experiments 3 to 7 failed to yield an expectancy $\times$ performance interaction. Experiments 3 to 6 examined the effects of trial-by-trial feedback on expectancy strength and hypothesis invention. Experiment 7, which included conditions requiring recall of previous judgments, suggested that the repeated finding of greater response change by low-performance *S*s may be explained by differences in memory as well as by differences in motivation to do well.

REFERENCES

Aronson, E., & Carlsmith, J. M. Performance expectancy as a determinant of actual performance. *Journal of Abnormal and Social Psychology*, 1962, **65**, 178–182.

Cottrell, N. B. Performance expectancy as a determinant of actual performance: a replication with a new design. *Journal of Personal and Social Psychology*, 1965, **2**, 685–691.

Festinger, L. *A theory of cognitive dissonance*. Evanston: Row, Peterson, 1957.

Good, R. A. The potentiality for changes of an expectancy as a function of the amount of experience. Unpublished doctoral thesis, 1952, Ohio State University.

Lowin, A., & Epstein, G. F. Performance expectancy as a determinant of actual performance: some additional variables. *Journal of Experimental Social Psychology*, 1965, **1**, 248–255.

Munsell Color Company. *Munsell system of color notation*. Baltimore: Munsell Color Company, 1963.

Orne, M. T. On the social psychology of the psychological experiment: With particular reference to demand characteristics and their implications. *American Psychologist*, 1962, **17**, 776–783.

Rotter, J. B. *Social learning and clinical psychology*. Englewood Cliffs: Prentice-Hall, 1954.

Schroder, H. M., & Rotter, J. B. Rigidity as learned behavior. *Journal of Experimental Psychology*, 1952, **44**, 141–150.

Silverman, I., & Marcantonio, C. Demand characteristics vs. dissonance-reduction as determinants of failure-seeking behavior. *Journal of Personality and Social Psychology*, 1965, **2**, 882–884.

Ward, W. D., & Sandvold, K. D. Performance expectancy as a determinant of actual performance: a partial replication. *Journal of Abnormal and Social Psychology*, 1963, **67**, 293–295.

Waterman, A. S., & Ford, L. H. Performance expectancy as a determinant of actual performance: dissonance reduction or differential recall? *Journal of Personality and Social Psychology*, 1965, **2**, 464–467.

Discussion

It would be satisfying to be able to conclude, after the previous seven experiments, that the mysteries of performance expectancy have been solved. Such is obviously not the case. In fact, one study mentioned in the Brock *et al.* article by Silverman and Marcantonio (1965) adds further to the confusion. The latter tested the demand characteristics hypothesis by nicely varying the reliability-validity instructions. However, they included only the two low expectancy conditions within each level of instructions. Their results were puzzling because they supported neither the demand interpretation nor the expectancy disconfirmation interpretation. The same note of puzzlement is evident in the Brock *et al.* discussion section. The conditions under which performance effects or expectancy effects may be obtained still seem elusive.

Although the results of Brock *et al.* Experiments 3–7 do not allow clear conclusions to be drawn, the results for Experiments 1 and 2 do permit some conclusions with respect to the first two articles reprinted in this chapter. Brock *et al.* enumerated a number of differences between their Experiment 1 and the Aronson-Carlsmith study. There were differences in subject populations, stimulus materials, and initial warmup and rationale. They did maintain the stress on the excellence of the social sensitivity test. And, very importantly, the experimenter was a female who was unaware of the hypothesis, in contrast to the Aronson-Carlsmith experiment. Despite these changes, the results of the original experiment were replicated.

What do these changes allow us to conclude? First, some procedural differences may not be important, as Ward and Sandvold suggested. Second, the fact that the experimenter was ignorant of the hypothesis allows the tentative conclusion that communication of differential expectancies is not a viable alternative interpretation. This alternative seemed very plausible for the original experiment, as was noted in the discussion following the Aronson-Carlsmith study.

By exclusion, the stress on the validity of the social sensitivity test seems to be an important variable. Brock *et al.* replicated the original results when they used the high validity instructions; Ward and Sandvold did not replicate the results when they did not emphasize high validity of the test. But if high validity instructions are important, it is still not clear whether the effect works via a demand characteristics interpretation or by creating an intense expectancy of failure or success.

The results for Brock *et al.*, Experiment 2, do not yield much insight. They attempted to vary strength of the expectancy by reducing the number of expectancy trials. They had no independent check on the expectancy manipulation. The pattern of the results was very similar to that obtained in Experiment 1. The comparison of the low expectancy-high performance means for the two experiments is not very convincing evidence that strength of the expectancy was successfully varied across the two experiments. In addition, there is a puzzling problem of why the means for the high expectancy-low performance condition were so low in both Experiments 1 and 2 (see Table 1 in Brock *et al.*). Subjects in that condition should have shown greater changes. Brock *et al.* do not discuss the matter. In a sense, this particular result can be interpreted as a partial failure to replicate. Subjects in this condition neither tried to succeed nor to reconfirm a disconfirmed high performance expectancy. Such results suggest caution in the interpretation of the (more interesting) low expectancy-high performance results of the two experiments.

Thus, even Experiments 1 and 2 in the Brock *et al.* series do not provide much information concerning the demand characteristics interpretation. Also, the peculiar results for the high expectancy-low performance conditions leave a sense of puzzlement and uncertainty about these data.

The reader is within his rights to wonder how the performance expectancy studies have helped to advance social psychology. Were they a contribution to the science or is this research area a dead-end? It is too early to say with any certainty. Brock's criticism that extension of a new hypothesis depends upon ability to replicate is certainly valid. However, the original results were quite clear and all the proposed alternatives have fared badly. Also, Brock provided two replications (for low expectancy conditions) and Cottrell (1965) provided a weak third. The original results and the replications cannot simply be ignored. They must be explained, and if no viable alternative can account for the results, presumably the original explanation stands. However, it stands in a sense by default. Researchers now realize that performance expectancy is a "sticky" area. The conditions under which the expectancy effect can be replicated are not well understood. This lack of consistent replicability suggests caution in generalizing the hypothesis.

It seems clear that the expectancy research in this tradition has arrived at a temporary cul-de-sac. A spate of reports appeared in 1965 but no studies have appeared since then. The original experiment generated considerable interest, even excitement. Besides the published articles, there were perhaps an even larger number of unpublished Masters' theses and Ph.D. dissertations dealing with the problem. By a criterion of generating more research, Aronson and Carlsmith's hypothesis and experimental paradigm must certainly be counted as a success. Several scholars increased the length of their publication vita in the process, a not unimportant motivation in the life of the professional researcher. However, the answer to the substantive question, "How does expectancy determine performance?" must remain undecided. The final verdict is not yet in. It is possible that this research area may become merely a footnote in the history of social science. It is also just as possible that the research will stimulate some future experimenter to create a better experiment, perhaps with a new design that overcomes some of the difficulties inherent in the original design. If such an event occurs, who can say that the performance expectancy excursion was not worthwhile?

REFERENCES

Brehm, J., & Cohen, A. C. *Explorations in cognitive dissonance.* New York: Wiley, 1962.

Chapanis, N. P., & Chapanis, A. Cognitive dissonance: five years later. *Psychological Bulletin,* 1964, **61,** 1–22.

Cottrell, N. B. Performance expectancy as a determinant of actual performance: A replication with a new design. *Journal of Personality and Social Psychology,* 1965, **2,** 685–691.

Festinger, L. *A theory of cognitive dissonance.* Stanford: Stanford University Press, 1957.

Festinger, L. (Ed.). *Conflict, decision and dissonance.* Stanford: Stanford University Press, 1964.

Hendrick, C. Comment on Waterman and Ford's dissonance reduction or differential recall. *Journal of Personality and Social Psychology,* 1966, **3,** 706–707.

Lowin, A., & Epstein, G. F. Does expectancy determine performance? *Journal of Experimental Social Psychology,* 1965, **1,** 248–255.
Secord, P. F., & Backman, C. W. *Social psychology.* New York: McGraw-Hill, 1964.
Silverman, I., & Marcantonio, C. Demand characteristics versus dissonance reduction as determinants of failure-seeking behavior. *Journal of Personality and Social Psychology,* 1965, **2,** 882–884.
Waterman, A. S., & Ford, L. H. Performance expectancy as a determinant of actual performance: Dissonance reduction or differential recall? *Journal of Personality and Social Psychology,* 1965, **2,** 464–467.
Zimbardo, P. G. (Ed.) . *The cognitive control of motviation.* Glenview, Ill.: Scott, Foresman, 1969.

Chapter 7

DISSONANCE AND SEVERITY OF INITIATION

The last chapter illustrated one approach to the study of dissonance theory. There are many such areas of research on the theory. Typically, an experimental paradigm is developed to test a particular derivation from the theory, and several different experiments are conducted within that paradigm. The articles in the present chapter are no exception. A basic paradigm was created by Aronson and Mills in the first article to test the dissonance prediction that unpleasant effort involved in initiation into a new group increases the attraction felt toward that group. This basic paradigm was then used in the two studies following the Aronson and Mills' article to test various alternative interpretations for Aronson and Mills' results.

It will be apparent that the paradigm created by Aronson and Mills differs radically from the experimental paradigm used by Aronson and Carlsmith in the performance expectancy studies. Indeed, these two different sets of experimental arrangements may even be testing different versions of the basic theory: in effect, testing the goodness of two different theories. We will pursue this point further in our discussion following the Aronson and Mills' article. The point we wish to emphasize here is that a very influential theory, such as dissonance theory, will often generate several different empirical traditions. The differing traditions are built around the differing sets of techniques, procedures, and measuring instruments that are used in the construction of an experimental paradigm. One consequence is a certain amount of ambiguity, even confusion, concerning how two different empirical traditions relate to each other. It is often difficult to see the connection even when the two areas of research are presumably supporting the same theory. Two problem areas exist, one at the level of the general theory, and the other at the level of research methodology. As suggested above, the two empirical traditions may actually be testing two different versions of the general theory, rather than just one general theory. Such may be the case with "performance expectancy" and "severity of initiation." This problem arises because the general theory was not stated well enough so that precise unequivocal predictions could be derived.

The second problem area concerns alternative interpretations for the results of a given experiment. As you read the series of articles in this chapter, you will notice that the issues concerning alternative interpretations are quite different from those in the performance expectancy chapter. One generalization that can be drawn is that alternative interpretations usually stem from the ways in which specific procedures and methods were used in an actual concrete experiment. We noted in Chapter 2 that an alternative interpretation means that essentially some other *conceptual* independent variable determined the results, rather than the intended independent variable. However, the only reasonable entry into the visualization of other independent variables is the actual set of empirical procedures used in an initial experiment. Thus, alternative interpretations usually revolve around experimental methodology. It follows that the intense concerns with testing and countertesting alternative hypotheses will be quite different when different experimental paradigms are used. Therefore, the issues in this chapter will be different from those in the previous chapter, even though both chapters are concerned with dissonance theory.

The content issue in the present series of experiments is an interesting one. Human groups seem to have the peculiar property of requiring some set of standards for entry into their membership. Such standards may vary from the trivial to the esoteric, but quite often some form of *initiation* into the group is required. As preparation for the readings in this chapter it will be helpful to review some material on initiation rituals.

Initiation Ceremonies

Human beings in all cultures have certain universal experiences during the course of their life (Endleman, 1967, p. 262). Among these universals are the developmental progression of birth, infancy, childhood, adolescence, adulthood, old age, and death. These "stages" stem from the biological nature of man, and all cultures in one form or another deal with these various stages in the life cycle of mankind. Very often various rituals, educational practices, and specified forms of behavior are required for the transition from one stage to another. In general, such practices are called *rites of passage.* During such transitional periods of one's life, very specific behavioral sequences may be enacted by some significant segment of the individual's community. These behavior sequences are often highly stylized and formalized, typifying what we usually mean by a ceremony. When the ceremony focuses on the individual and his change from one stage or type of life to another, we speak of an initiation ceremony or initiation rite.

Such initiation rites have many functions in different cultures. One factor seems to predominate, however. Initiation rites seem to serve as a signal that the individual is changing the status of his group membership in some significant way. Anthropologists have studied initiation rites rather intensively in primitive cultures. One rather common initiation rite for males occurs at the onset of puberty. Many primitive societies have elaborate sets of rituals which symbolize the end of that part of the life cycle known as childhood and the beginning of what is defined as adulthood. Such ceremonies are much more common for males than for females, and often are highly charged emotionally. With respect to group membership, such ceremonies serve to notify members of the society that the boy is leaving the category "child," or more fully "child of a woman," and is entering the category "man" or "man of the men."

Our society does not have well defined puberty rituals. Perhaps for females, buying the first bra is mildly symbolic of the transition to womanhood. For males, getting one's drivers license at age sixteen may have some connotations of achievement of virile masculinity. But beyond these minor incidents we have no dramatic puberty rites. However, western society has many other types of initiations into groups. Several examples come readily to mind. Joining fraternities and sororities on college campuses is one example. Graduation from college is perhaps the most salient symbol of induction into middle-class adult society. It is an interesting point that graduation ceremonies are extremely important to relatives and friends but tend to be denigrated by the graduate himself. Why this is so is not clear. Often such ceremonies do seem perfunctory, even worthless, but as long as our society continues to value education so highly, the graduation ceremony is likely to persist.

Other examples of initiation into groups abound. Fraternal organizations in American society often have elaborate initiation rituals. Taking an occupational role within a corporate organization, particularly a "white-collar" role, has elements of an initiation ceremony. A grace period is given the novice during which he is entitled to an extra measure of courtesy and consideration from the old members. His social mistakes are readily forgiven because he is not yet accustomed to the set of rules by which people love and hate each other within that particular organization. Inevitably, but subtly, there comes a time when he is no longer defined as a new member, and then he receives his measure of privilege and punishment the same as other members of the group.

Severity of Initiation and Group Attraction

One phenomenon that soon becomes apparent is that groups differ greatly in the severity of the initiation of new members into the group. For example, puberty initiation rites vary widely around the world, ranging from no ceremony at all to very brutal behaviors including genital operations, physical deprivation and punishment, and social isolation. Whiting, Kluckhohn, and Anthony (1958) studied anthropological data on 56 societies with respect to the presence or absence of severe puberty initiations. They were primarily interested in the functions that such ceremonies serve for a society. They reasoned from a psychoanalytic basis that such initiations may serve to reduce intense father-son conflict as the son approaches adulthood, and, more generally, reduce male-male conflict within the society.

Whiting *et al.* (1958) reasoned that such conflict would be more or less probable depending upon the particular child rearing experiences in the society. Specifically, they reasoned that in societies which have extremely nurturant mother-child relations for a long period during infancy, the child will experience intense loneliness and envy of the father when the time inevitably comes that the father is once again the central figure in the mother's life. Presumably, the child's seething rage at the father is suppressed during the formative years, but is in danger of breaking into open conflict at the onset of puberty. The function of the male initiation ceremony at puberty is to force an identification with the males of the group, a taking in of the male value structure, in short, to develop a set of intense positive attitudes toward the male sex role. In this way conflict is avoided and group solidarity is maintained.

Whiting *et al.* (1958) tested this hypothesis as follows. They classified the 56 societies according to whether or not there were exclusive mother-son sleeping arrangements at birth, and whether there was a long post-partum sex taboo. This classification served as their independent variable. The dependent variable was presence or absence of severe puberty initiation ceremonies. The hypothesis was that societies which have mother-son sleeping arrangements and long taboos on resumption of intercourse should have severe initiation ceremonies, while societies lacking in these characteristics should not have severe initiations. The results strongly supported the hypothesis.

The research described above is a classic and important example of a correlational study. It provided impressive support for the theoretical rationale. It is literally impossible to test such a hypothesis with a manipulative experiment in the laboratory. But, as indicated in Chapter 5, we do the best job we can with whatever tools are available; in this case the tool was a correlational study. However, as noted previously, correlational findings are particularly susceptible to alternative interpretations. In the example above, Young (1962) proposed the alternative hypothesis that the presence or absence of initiation ceremonies reflects the degree of male solidarity within a society which is manifested in the existence of exclusive male organizations. Young (1962) was able to show that when the presence-absence of exclusive male organizations was held constant, the relation between mother-son arrangements and initiation ceremonies was greatly reduced. However, Young's counter-hypothesis was also supported only by correlational evidence and was itself susceptible to alternative interpretations. The important point to be drawn is that hypotheses are very difficult to substantiate with correlational evidence.

The classic example of a severe initiation in our own society is the ritual to which a new inductee into the military is subjected. Typically, such a ritual includes uniform dress and equipment, rather harsh interpersonal relations with military superiors, total separation from all aspects of civilian life, and severe mental and physical hazing. Endleman (1967) believes that these rituals serve the function of stripping away the previous civilian self-identity and creating a new military identity. The intensive indoctrination presumably fosters a strong positive identification with military norms and values, ultimately enabling the recruit to face military combat as a "real soldier." An underlying assumption seems to be that a very mild initiation would not result in the required identification; consequently failure as a combat soldier would be the result.

These examples suggest that many groups operate under the assumption that a severe initiation into the membership ranks will result in greater identity with and attraction to the group. Aronson and Mills provide a rigorous experimental test of that hypothesis in the following article. From this point on, we will be less concerned with the group identification aspect of the hypothesis. Instead we will focus on how the hypothesis provided more or less support for dissonance theory, and the discussion following each experiment will focus on various alternatives to the dissonance explanation. However, it should not be forgotten that the content of the hypothesis has considerable social significance beyond any consideration of dissonance theory. The research reported below indicates, in a rather rigorous way, that people seem to be more attracted to groups that require a severe initiation than to groups requiring only a mild initiation. This finding is of potential social usefulness; we will return briefly to this point at the end of this chapter.

The Effect of Severity of Initiation on Liking for a Group[1]

Elliot Aronson and Judson Mills

It is a frequent observation that persons who go through a great deal of trouble or pain to attain something tend to value it more highly than persons who attain the same thing with a minimum of effort. For example, one would expect persons who travel a great distance to see a motion picture to be more impressed with it than those who see the same picture at a neighborhood theater. By the same token, individuals who go through a severe initiation to gain admission to a club or organization should tend to think more highly of that organization than those who do not go through the severe initiation to gain admission.

Two questions are relevant here: (1) Is this "common observation" valid, that is, does it hold true when tested under controlled conditions? (2) If the observation is valid, how can it be accounted for? The relationship might be simply a result of differences in initial motivation. To

[1] From the *Journal of Abnormal and Social Psychology,* 1959, **59,** 177–181. Received June 9, 1958. Reproduced by permission of the publisher.

This research was partially supported by a grant from the National Science Foundation, administered by Leon Festinger. The authors are grateful to Leon Festinger for his help and encouragement during the planning and execution of the study.

At the time of writing, Aronson was with Stanford University and Mills was with the U. S. Army Leadership Human Research Unit, HumRRO. Current affiliations: Aronson, University of Texas at Austin; Mills, University of Maryland.

take the case of initiations, persons who initially have a strong desire to join a particular club should be more willing to undergo unpleasantness to gain admission to it than persons who are low in initial interest. Therefore, a club that requires a severe initiation for admission should be joined only by those people with a strong desire to become members. On the other hand, a club that does not require a severe initiation should be joined by some individuals who like it very much, and by others who are relatively uninterested. Because of this self-selection, one would expect persons who are members of clubs with severe initiations to think more highly of their club, on the average, than members of clubs without severe initiations.

But is there something in the initiation itself that might account for this relationship? Is severity of initiation positively related to group preference when motivation for admission is held constant? Such a relationship is strongly implied by Festinger's (1957) theory of cognitive dissonance. The theory of cognitive dissonance predicts this relationship in the following manner. No matter how attractive a group is to a person it is rarely completely positive, that is, usually there are some aspects of the group that the individual does not like. If he has undergone an unpleasant initiation to gain admission to the group, his cognition that he has gone through an unpleasant experience for the sake of membership is dissonant with his cognition that there are things about the group that he does not like. He can reduce this dissonance in two ways. He can convince himself that the initiation was not very unpleasant, or he can exaggerate the positive characteristics of the group and minimize its negative aspects. With increasing severity of initiation it becomes more and more difficult to believe that the initiation was not very bad. Thus, a person who has gone through a painful initiation to become a member of a group should tend to reduce his dissonance by over estimating the attractiveness of the group. The specific hypothesis tested in the present study is that individuals who undergo an unpleasant initiation to become members of a group increase their liking for the group; that is, they find the group more attractive than do persons who become members without going through a severe initiation.

Method

In designing the experiment it was necessary to have people join groups that were similar in every respect except for the severity of the initiation required for admission —and then to measure each individual's evaluation of the group. It was also necessary to randomize the initial motivation of subjects (*S*s) to gain admission to the various groups in order to eliminate systematic effects of differences in motivation. These requirements were met in the following manner: volunteers were obtained to participate in group discussions. They were assigned randomly to one of three experimental conditions: a *severe* initiation condition, a *mild* initiation condition, and a *control* condition. In the severe condition, *Ss* were required to read some embarrassing material before joining the group; in the mild condition the material they read in order to join the group was not very embarrassing; in the control condition, *Ss* were not required to read any material before becoming group members. Each *S* listened to the same tape recording which was ostensibly an ongoing discussion by the members of the group that he had just joined. *Ss* then evaluated the discussion.

The *Ss* were 63 college women. Thirty-three of them volunteered to participate in a series of group discussions on the psychology of sex. The remaining 30, tested at a somewhat later date, were "captive volunteers" from a psychology course who elected to participate in the group discussions on the psychology of sex in preference to several other experiments. Since the results obtained from these two samples were very similar, they were combined in the analysis presented here.

Each *S* was individually scheduled to "meet with a group." When she arrived at the experimental room, she was told by the experimenter (*E*) that he was conducting several group discussions on the psychology of sex. *E* informed her that she was joining a group that had been meeting for several weeks and that she was taking the place of a girl who had to leave the group because of scheduling difficulties. *E* stated that the discussion had just begun and that she would join the other members of the group after he had explained the nature of the experiment to her. The purpose of the foregoing instructions was to confront *S* with an ongoing group and thus make plausible the recorded discussion to which she was to be exposed.

E then "explained" the purpose of the experiment. He said that he was interested in investigating the "dynamics of the group discussion process." Sex was chosen as the topic for the groups to discuss in order to provide interesting subject matter so that volunteers for the discussion groups could be obtained without much difficulty. *E* continued as follows:

> But the fact that the discussions are concerned with sex has one major drawback. Although most people are interested in sex, they tend to be a little shy when it comes to discussing it. This is very bad from the point of view of the experiment; if one or two people in a group do not participate as much as they usually do in group discussions because they are embarrassed about sex, the picture we get of the group discussion process is distorted. Therefore, it is extremely important to arrange things so that the members of the discussion group can talk as freely and frankly as possible. We found that the major inhibiting factor in the discussions was the presence of the other people in the room. Somehow, its easier to talk about embarrassing things if other people aren't staring at you. To get around this, we hit upon an idea which has proved very successful. Each member of the group is placed in a separate room, and the participants communicate through an intercom system using headphones and a microphone. In this way, we've helped people relax, and have succeeded in bringing about an increase in individual participation.

The foregoing explanation set the stage for the tape recording, which could now be presented to the *S* as a live discussion conducted by three people in separate rooms.

E then mentioned that, in spite of this precaution, occasionally some persons were still too embarrassed to engage in the discussions and had to be asked to withdraw from the discussion group. *S* was asked if she thought she could discuss sex freely. She invariably answered affirmatively. In the control condition *S* was told, at this point, that she would be a member of the group.

In the other two conditions, *E* went on to say that it was difficult for him to ask people to leave the group once they had become members. Therefore, he had recently decided to screen new people before admitting them to the discussion groups. The screening device was described as an "embarrassment test" which consists of reading aloud some sexually oriented material in the presence of *E*. *S* was told that *E* would make a clinical judgment of her degree of embarrassment, based upon hesitation, blushing, etc. and would determine whether or not she would be capable of participating in the discussion group. He stressed that she was not obligated to take this test, but that she could not become a member unless she did. Only one *S* declined to take the test. She was excluded from the experiment. It was also emphasized, at this point, that the "embarrassment test" was a recent innovation and that the other members had joined the group before it was required for admission. These instructions were included in order to counteract any tendency to identify more strongly with the group as a result of feelings of having shared a common unpleasant experience. Such a process could conceivably bring about a greater preference for the discussion group on the part of *S*s in the severe condition, introducing ambiguity in the interpretation of the results.

In the severe condition, the "embarassment test" consisted of having *S*s read aloud, from 3×5 cards, 12 obscene words, e.g., fuck, cock, and screw. *S*s also read aloud two vivid descriptions of sexual activity from contemporary novels. In the mild condition, *S*s read aloud five words that were related to sex but not obscene, e.g., prostitute, virgin, and petting. In both the severe and the mild conditions, after each *S* finished reading the material, she was told that she had performed satisfactorily and was, therefore, a member of the group and could join the meeting that was now in progress.

It was of the utmost importance to prevent the *S* from attempting to participate in the discussion, for if she did, she would soon find that no one was responding to her statements and she would probably infer that the discussion was recorded. To insure their silence, all *S*s were told that, in preparation for each meeting, the group reads an assignment which serves as the focal point of the discussion; for this meeting, the group read parts of the book, *Sexual Behavior in Animals*. After the *S* had indicated that she had never read this book, *E* told her that she would be at a disadvantage and would, consequently, not be able to participate as fully in this discussion as she would had she done the reading. He continued, "Because the presence of a participant who isn't contributing optimally would result in an inaccurate picture of the dynamics of the group discussion process, it would be best if you wouldn't participate at all today, so that we may get an undistorted picture of the dynamics of the other three members of this group. Meanwhile, you can simply listen to the discussion, and get an idea of how the group operates. For the next meeting, you can do the reading and join in the discussion." *S*s were invariably more than willing to comply with this suggestion. The above instructions not only prevented *S* from attempting to participate in the discussion but also served to orient her toward the actual content of discussion.

Under the guise of connecting the *S*'s headphones and microphone, *E* went into the next room and turned on the tape recorder. He then returned to the experimental room, put on the headphones, picked up the microphone, and pretended to break into the discussion which supposedly was in progress. After holding a brief conversation with the "members of the group," he introduced the *S* to them. Then he handed the headphones to her. The tape was timed so that at the precise moment that *S* donned her headphones, the "group members" introduced themselves and then continued their discussion.

The use of a tape recording presented all *S*s with an identical group experience. The recording was a discussion by three female undergraduates. It was deliberately designed to be as dull and banal as possible in order to maximize the dissonance of the *S*s in the severe condition. The participants spoke dryly and haltingly on secondary sex behavior in the lower animals, "inadvertently" contradicted themselves and one another, mumbled several *non sequiturs,* started sentences that they never finished, hemmed, hawed, and in general conducted one of the most worthless and uninteresting discussions imaginable.

At the conclusion of the recording, *E* returned and explained that after each meeting every member of the group fills out a questionnaire expressing her reactions to the discussion. The questionnaire asked the *S* to rate the discussion and the group members on 14 different evaluative scales, e.g., dull-interesting, intelligent-unintelligent, by circling a number from 0 to 15. After completing the questionnaire, *S* made three additional ratings, orally, in response to questions from *E*. Nine of the scales concerned the *S*'s reactions to the discussion, while the other eight concerned her reactions to the participants.

At the close of the experiment, *E* engaged each *S* in conversation to determine whether or not she was suspicious of the procedure. Only one *S* entertained definite suspicions; her results were discarded.

Finally, the true nature of the experiment was explained in detail. None of the *S*s expressed any resentment or annoyance at having been misled. In fact, the majority were intrigued by the experiment and several returned at the end of the academic quarter to ascertain the results.

Results and Discussion

The sum of the ratings for the 17 different scales provides an index of each *S*'s liking for the discussion group. The means and *SD*s for the three experimental conditions for this measure are presented in Table 1. Means and *SD*s are also presented in Table 1 separately for the eight scales which tapped the *S*s' attitudes toward the discussion and the seven scales which tapped their attitudes toward the participants. The significance of the differences between the means for the different conditions were determined by *t* tests. The *t* values and significance levels are presented in Table 2.

Examination of Table 1 shows that *S*s in the severe condition rated both the discussion and the participants higher than did those in the control and mild conditions. The overall difference between the ratings by *S*s in the severe condition and *S*s in the control condition reaches the .01% level of significance. The over-all difference between the ratings by *S*s in the severe initiation condition and *S*s in the mild initiation condition reaches the .05 level.

These differences cannot be explained by differences in initial motivation to become members of the group, since *S*s (with varying degrees of motivation) were randomly assigned to the three experimental conditions. The differences in liking for the group must be considered a consequence of the unpleasant experience. The results clearly substantiate the

TABLE 1
Means of the Sum of Ratings for the Different Experimental Conditions

Rating scales	Control (N = 21)	Mild (N = 21)	Severe (N = 21)
	Experimental conditions		
Discussion (9)			
M	80.2	81.8	97.6
SD	13.2	21.0	16.6
Participants (8)			
M	89.9	89.3	97.7
SD	10.9	14.1	13.2
Total (17)			
M	166.7	171.1	195.3
SD	21.6	34.0	31.9

hypothesis: persons who undergo a severe initiation to attain membership in a group increase their liking for the group. This hypothesis follows directly from Festinger's theory of cognitive dissonance. According to the theory, *S*s in the severe initiation condition held the cognition that they had undergone a painful experience to become members of the discussion group. Then they listened to a dull, banal discussion. Negative cognitions about the discussion which they formed from listening to it were dissonant with the cognition that they had undergone a painful experience to gain membership in this group. The presence of dissonance leads to pressures to reduce it. *S*s in this condition could reduce their dissonance either by denying the severity of the initiation or by distorting their cognitions concerning the group discussion in a positive direction. The initiation of the *S*s in the severe condition was apparently too painful for them to deny—hence, they reduced their dissonance by overestimating the attractiveness of the group.

TABLE 2
Significance Levels of the Differences between Experimental Conditions

Rating scales	Control-severe	Mild-severe	Control-mild
	Differences between conditions		
Discussion (9)	$t = 3.66$	$t = 2.62$	$t = .29$
	$P < .001$[a]	$P < .02$	N.S.
Participants (8)	$t = 2.03$	$t = 1.97$	$t = .15$
	$P < .05$	$P < .10$	N.S.
Total (17)	$t = 3.32$	$t = 2.33$	$t = .49$
	$P < .01$	$P < .05$	N.S.

[a] The P values given are based on both tails of the t distribution.

There was no appreciable difference between the ratings made by *S*s in the control condition and those made by *S*s in the mild condition. It would seem that the mild condition was so devoid of unpleasantness as to constitute little investment in the group. Hence, little dissonance was created. If any dissonance did occur in this situation it would be more realistic for the *S* to reduce it by minimizing the pain of the initiation, than by distorting her cognitions concerning the discussion. Thus, it is not an initiation per se that leads to increase in liking for a group. The initiation must be severe enough to constitute a genuine investment and to render it difficult to reduce dissonance by playing down the extent of the pain involved.

An examination of Table 1 shows that the rating scales concerning the discussion show greater differences between the conditions than the scales dealing with the evaluations of the participants in the discussion. There are at least two possible explanations for this result: (*a*) It may be easier for people to express negative criticism about an impersonal discussion than about the people involved. Thus, *S*s in the control and mild conditions may have inflated their ratings of the participants to avoid making negative statements about fellow college students. (*b*) It is possible that *S*s in the severe condition had less need to distort their perception of the participants than of the discussion itself. The dissonance of the *S*s in the severe condition resulted from the actual discussion: they experienced dissonance between going through an unpleasant experience and taking part in worthless uninteresting discussions. The most direct way for them to reduce this dissonance would be to change their perceptions of the discussion in a positive direction. The participants in the discussion were peripheral to the cause of dissonance. If *S*s in the severe condition had less need to distort their perceptions of the participants than their perception of the discussion, their evaluations of the participants could be expected to be closer to the evaluations of the participants made by *S*s in the control and mild conditions.

Summary and Conclusions

An experiment was conducted to test the hypothesis that persons who undergo an unpleasant initiation to become members of a group increase their liking for the group; that is, they find the group more attractive than do persons who become members without going through a severe initiation. This hypothesis was derived from Festinger's theory of cognitive dissonance.

College women who volunteered to participate in discussion groups were randomly assigned to one of three experimental conditions: A *severe* initiation condition, a *mild* initiation condition, and a *control* condition. In the severe condition, subjects were required to read some embarrassing material before joining the group; in the mild condition the material they read in order to join the group was not very embarrassing; in the control condition, subjects were not required to read any material before becoming group members. Each subject listened to a recording that appeared to be an ongoing discussion being conducted by the group which she had just joined. Afterwards, subjects filled out a questionnaire evaluating the discussion and the participants. The results clearly verified the hypothesis. Subjects who underwent a severe initiation perceived the group as being significantly more attractive than did those who underwent a mild initiation or no initiation. There was no appreciable difference between ratings by subjects who underwent a mild initiation and those by subjects who underwent no initiation.

REFERENCE

Festinger, L. *A theory of cognitive dissonance.* Evanston: Row, Peterson, 1957.

Discussion

Aronson and Mills' experiment is deservedly a classic in social psychology. The experiment is relevant to a very common occurrence in everyday life, i.e., initiation into groups. More importantly, the experiment seems to provide a rather clear test of one derivation of dissonance theory. Since the test was successful, the results provided strong support for the theory. Finally, the procedures used to stage the experiment were carefully designed, though quite elaborate. The manipulation of the independent variable was an integral part of the cover story. The final measurement of the dependent variable probably seemed quite natural from the subject's point of view.

Technically, the experiment was smooth, polished, and sophisticated, and the results supported the hypothesis. Superficially, one might suppose there were no problems with the experiment. Such is not the case. First of all, the theoretical interpretation of the results is not very rigorous. The dissonance interpretation was that dissonance was aroused between the cognitions of unpleasant initiation effort and the cognitions that the discussions were actually worthless. Such dissonance was subsequently reduced by enhancing the attractiveness of the group. Another equally plausible dissonance interpretation derives from the expectancy confirmation effect discussed in the previous chapter. The severe versus mild initiations may have created different expectancies for the group's performance. Subjects in the severe initiation condition may have had a much stronger expectancy of an interesting discussion, which was more strongly disconfirmed by the banal discussion. Because of the greater dissonance in this case, the need to reconfirm the initial expectancy would be greater, and greater reevaluation of the group might be expected in an attempt at dissonance reduction.

Thus, one may justifiably question whether the dissonance effect was due to "justification for unpleasant effort expenditure," or to "reconfirmation of a disconfirmed expectancy." Both explanations are based on dissonance theory considerations, but it makes an important difference which (if either) is correct. One might argue that the expectancy interpretation is preferable because it seems a more general explanation.

Actually, it would be quite easy to test the expectancy interpretation. What is required is the manipulation of the independent variable, but prior to listening to the discussion a measure of what subjects expected of the group discussion is taken. In fact, Aronson and Mills' same dependent variables in a slightly modified form would do nicely for this task. If subjects in the severe initiation condition showed greater anticipated favorableness than subjects in the mild initiation condition, good evidence would exist that the manipulations created differing expectancies.

However, such an outcome would pose problems for any dissonance interpretation. Consider for a moment this hypothetical outcome in relation to the actual results obtained by Aronson and Mills. The two sets of data would be quite similar. But the results for the two new conditions we have proposed above would have been obtained without any intervening dissonant cognitions. Recall that the dull, boring task was necessary to provide a source of cognitions dissonant with the knowledge of having engaged in the embarrassment test. If no such set of dissonant cognitions existed, then obviously a dissonance interpretation would be inappropriate. For a dissonance interpretation to still be valid, the following relations would have to hold. Assume the difference between severe and mild conditions was significant when measures were taken in advance of listening to the tape. In the conditions of actually listening to the tape, the difference between severe and mild conditions would have to be significantly greater than the difference noted above. Such an increase in the difference between severe and mild conditions would provide evidence that something above and beyond a mere expectancy difference was occurring. And that "something" could reasonably be interpreted as attempted dissonance reduction. Such results would appear as a statistical interaction between the severity conditions and the proposed prelistening, postlistening measurement conditions. The nature of interactions was discussed in Chapter 2, and at this point the reader might want to plot graphically the pattern of the interaction that would be required to support the dissonance hypothesis.

The above discussion is quite speculative because the proposed research with the anticipation conditions has not been done. Beyond the difficulty in discriminating between two dissonance interpretations of the Aronson and Mills' experiment, there are several nondissonance alternatives to their results. Most of these alternatives were discussed in some detail in Chapter 2 (see Fig. 5). As indicated in that chapter, most of the bases for alternative interpretations involve the impact that the severe initiation condition might have had on subjects. Reading obscene material may have effectively served as a manipulation of several possible independent variables.

One of these alternative interpretations (the dependency explanation) was tested in the following article by Schopler and Bateson. Notice that in their experimental design they included a crucial replication of the original Aronson and Mills' experiment. Without such a replication, the results obtained in their new conditions would have been largely uninterpretable, and the value of their study would have been greatly diminished.

A Dependence Interpretation of the Effects of a Severe Initiation[1]

John Schopler and Nicholas Bateson

The term "dependence" is customarily used as a personality construct. In this usage it denotes the degree to which one person requires others to satisfy his needs; its obverse is independence—a state in which the person is able to generate his own gratifications. Dependence has also been defined as a characteristic of an interpersonal relationship. Thibaut and Kelley (1959) represent this point of view in that they define one

[1] From the *Journal of Personality,* 1962, **30,** 633–649. Received May 16, 1962.

This study was conducted in the program of the Organization Research Group of the Institute for Research in Social Science, which is supported by the Office of Naval Research [Nonr-855 (04)]. We are grateful to Dr. Jack Brehm for his suggestions in the initial stages of the experiment and to Dr. John Thibaut for his advice and encouragement throughout.

At the time of writing, Schopler and Bateson were with the University of North Carolina. Schopler is currently with the University of North Carolina at Chapel Hill; Bateson is in London, England.

member's dependence in a dyad as a direct function of the range of outcomes (i.e., the discrepancy between the most and least pleasant experiences) that he has enjoyed or may enjoy. A person's degree of dependence varies from relationship to relationship; in one he may be highly dependent, in another less so. A person's degree of dependence can vary *within* a relationship also: at one moment he may be highly dependent upon it; at another, he may perceive that the range of available outcomes has decreased and that his dependence has been correspondingly reduced. Interpersonal dependence, then, is flexible in a way in which dependence as a personality attribute is not. The research reported in this paper is based on the Thibaut and Kelley system, which specifies certain consequences of high interpersonal dependence.

Before applying the dependence formulation to the *E–S* interaction in laboratory experiments, it will be necessary to summarize the position of Thibaut and Kelley. They view a person as having a repertoire of behavior sequences which comprises all the responses he is capable of enacting. When two people interact they select behavior sequences from their repertoires. The pairing of behavior sequences, during the course of interaction, yields a series of outcomes, each of which has a particular subjective utility to the individual on a goodness–poorness dimension. The pairing of only two behavior sequences would be sufficient to establish a range of outcomes, but even in brief interactions many more outcomes are sampled. The lower limit of the range is the worst outcome a person will endure without leaving the relationship, while the upper limit is set by the best available outcome. It should be noted that in some relationships a person's degree of dependence may be greater than the range of actual outcomes experienced because a wider range is *potentially* available. The *E* who threatens to use electric shock on a *S* or promises him two dollars for participating in the experiment has made an outcome salient to the *S* even though it may never actually be administered to him.

Thibaut and Kelley define interpersonal power with the same concepts used to define dependence. A person's degree of power in a relationship is measured by the range of outcomes through which he actually does or potentially could move his partner. An individual's degree of power over a partner is therefore coextensive with that partner's degree of dependence. For example, if the *E* increases his power over the *S* by promising him he can earn some amount between 0 and $50, instead of some amount between 0 and $2, the *S*'s dependence also increases.

All interpersonal relationships involve some degree of dependence and power. This paper describes a situation in which high dependence is created by causing an individual to endure some very poor outcomes in the relationship while he knows that some very good ones are also attainable. From a simple outcome-maximization hypothesis it follows that he will take steps to avoid getting any more of the very poor outcomes and that he will try to obtain the very good outcomes. If his efforts are successful, he will restrict the range of outcomes he actually receives to the good ones only.

One way in which an individual can thus alter his range of experienced outcomes is by influencing his partner to produce certain behavior sequences of high outcome value. In order to employ this technique, the individual must have some counter-power over his partner, as without power he can have no influence. In the situation that this paper deals with the individual is at first in a position of low counter-power. He therefore has to increase it. Power can be increased by extending the range through which the partner can be moved. For example, the positive end of the range can be extended through such behaviors as flattery or praise, while the negative end can be extended by developing the ability to injure, harm, or molest. Such techniques reduce the range of outcomes the individual is liable to experience because his partner is now more vulnerable to experiencing a reduction of good outcomes and must take this into account when selecting the behavior sequences he is going to enact. When the more dependent member of the dyad is successful in increasing his counter-power, the partner's actual power is not changed, but his usable power is limited. In other words, the extent to which he can profit by using that power (i.e., by giving the individual poor outcomes as well as good) is curtailed.

One way of dealing with high dependence is to conform to the powerful partner's wishes, attitudes, and opinions. In these terms, conformity means selecting the behavior sequences which are seen as desired by the partner. Such conformity can serve the function of increasing the counter-power of the conformist and thereby of reducing the range of experienced outcomes.

This point can best be illustrated when the more powerful member, A, states an opinion that he wishes his partner, B, to adopt, although it will be assumed to hold true any time A states or implies a preference among B's behaviors. By giving an opinion he wishes his partner to adopt, A is in effect both making B fully cognizant of what little power he does have at present and is indicating that B can increase his power. He teaches B about his (B's) present power resources in the following way. A demonstrates to B that he prefers some of B's behaviors (namely, those which indicate B's adoption of the opinion) over others (namely, those which indicate that B has not adopted the opinion). In this way A makes salient to B the fact that B can move him through a range of outcomes. The relationship between the two men is now one of mutual dependence: each has the ability to reward or punish the other. If A now gives low outcomes to B, B can retaliate by indicating to A that he has rejected A's opinion. If A wishes to maximize the outcomes he receives from B, and assuming that he has no strong dislike for B, he will have to eliminate from his repertoire those behaviors that give poor outcomes to B. Therefore B's conformity should have the effect of restricting the range of outcomes he experiences in interaction with A to the good ones only. Moreover, the request that B adopt his opinion also presents B with the prospect of, in future, increasing his power over A. If B complies with A's request, the mere act of obedience is likely to be gratifying to A, as is the fact that B has provided consensual validation for A's opinion.

The Thibaut and Kelley system could be used to analyze a number of different social relationships. The present paper will focus only on certain laboratory situations where it seems evident that the conditions for creating dependence have been met, i.e., a more powerful person (the *E*) has moved another person (the *S*) through a wide range of outcomes, and where the dependent person is likely to be motivated to lessen his dependence because he has endured some very poor outcomes. *E*s often capitalize on the transitory nature of most experimental interactions along with the seeming docility or excessive cooperation of the average sophomore "volunteer" to induce a wide range of outcomes. This general format is found in many experiments dealing with a wide variety of topics. Because the constructs contained in most psychological theories do not point to specific operations by which hypotheses can be tested, there is wide latitude in the selection of a laboratory situation by which a given hypothesis will be tested. Insofar as a particular situation is capable of producing dependence which the *S* wishes to lower (and frequently the tasks *S* must perform are fairly unpleasant) it is possible that the *E–S* interaction will lead to results that reveal as much about a theory of dependence as they do about the specific theory under investigation.

A particularly striking example of dependence-producing conditions is evident in an experiment conducted by Aronson and Mills (1959). These authors deduced from Festinger's dissonance theory that *S*s who had to endure pain in order to join a group would like that group more than *S*s who were given easy access. Their experiment contained three different treatments. In one of these, the severe condition, the *S*s were allowed to join a group ostensibly discussing sex only after proving their qualifications by passing a thoroughly unpleasant embarrassment test. *S*s in the control condition joined the group without being tested, while *S*s in the mild condition received an innocuous test. All *S*s then heard their group having a very dull discussion, which, unknown to the *S*s, had been previously recorded. The significantly higher ratings of the discussion and the participants given by the severe *S*s, compared to those of the mild or control *S*s, were taken as evidence for dissonance reduction.

It is also possible to interpret the high ratings as a response to dependence. The *S*s in the severe condition were moved through a wide range of outcomes by the *E*. They had to endure the unpleasant outcomes associated with the embarrassment test, on the one hand, and in all likelihood experienced a mixture of relief and pride upon learning that they had "passed" the test, on the other. The *S*s in the control and mild conditions were obviously not subjected to such an extensive range of outcomes. The procedure of the severe condition produced higher dependence and greater necessity for increasing power than the procedures of the other two conditions. One of the likeliest ways of increasing power which was available to *S*s in this situation was to conform to the opinion of the *E*, who strongly implied that the *S*s would like the discussion. The high ratings given by the *S*s in the severe condition can therefore be interpreted as a power-gaining strategy of conforming to the opinion of the *E*.

In order to assess some of the effects of experimentally creating dependence, as well as to set the dissonance interpretation against the dependence interpretation, the Aronson and Mills procedure was replicated in all important details with the addition of two conditions. The specification for these two new conditions presented a number of difficulties. It was, of course, essential to preserve the dissonance-producing elements contained in the initial experiment, while also introducing a new variable which might differentiate dependence from dissonance effects. It is possible to cite several sources of cognitions in the original experiment which might have contributed to the experience of dissonance. For instance, the severity of the initiation procedure might have produced high expectations about the superb quality of the discussion to be heard, expectations which would be dissonant with the objective characteristics of the discussion. Or possibly the recruitment procedure of having the *S*s volunteer was critical in that the *S*s were personally responsible for getting involved in the unpleasant proceedings. Although dissonance might have been created by cognitions arising from several sources, the dissonance formulation which was to be tested by the new conditions was the one stressed by Aronson and Mills, who had stated:

> According to the theory, *S*s in the severe initiation condition held the cognition that they had undergone a painful experience to become members of the discussion group. Then they listened to a dull, banal discussion. Negative cognitions about the discussion which they formed from listening to it were dissonant with the cognition that they had undergone a painful experience to gain membership in this group (p. 180).

It was this formulation then that served as a guide in the decisions about the changes to be made in the two new conditions. In one of these the *E*'s opinion was made explicit (but was negative rather than positive), while in the other condition the *S*s were led to believe that they had power over the *E*. The condition in which the *E* made his opinion explicit was identical to the original severe condition except that after the *S* had been told that he had "passed" the test the *E* made a short, pejorative comment about the discussion the *S* was about to hear. If creation of dependence leads to increased agreement with the *E*'s opinion, the ratings of these *S*s should be low. The prediction from the dissonance formulation was thought to be in the opposite direction. The *E*'s disparaging remarks obviously could not affect the cognitions about the initiation procedure, but presumably they would contribute, to some extent, to the weight of negative cognitions about the discussion. Dissonance should therefore be increased. Partial support for this effect is provided by Brehm (1960). He found that *S*s who were committed to performing an unpleasant task increased their liking for it after reading a supposedly expert report that disparaged it.

In the other new condition the *S*s were given power over the *E*. The operational definition of this condition produced a number of problems. Effective power, that is, power that leads to lessened dependence, can exist only if the *S* feels that his outcomes are improving through his own impact on the *E*. However, if this improvement were permitted, these *S*s would not endure the same degree of pain and therefore could not be expected to experience the same amount of dependence as the *S*s in the severe condition. One experimental solution for this dilemma would be to institute, in place of the embarrassment test, a ritual that gradually decreased in severity. The *S*s with increased power could then be led to believe that the diminishing pain resulted from the power they possessed while the severe group would perceive the decrease merely as a standard sequence imposed by the *E*. Because different parts of the embarrassment test could not be scaled for degree of pain, it was impossible to incorporate this manipulation into the framework of the Aronson and Mills experiment.

It was decided instead to translate increased power over the *E* into the operation of telling the *S*s before the start of the experiment that after the session was over they were to evaluate the *E* on his general competence. This was presented as a standard procedure that obviously had significance for his employment future, but one that was not based on their particular *E*'s incompetence. It should be emphasized again that this power was nonfunctional: the *S*s could not directly reward or punish the *E* while he was delivering the low outcomes to them.

It was thought that dissonance theory would predict ratings comparable to those of the severe group because the increased power did nothing to alter the dissonance-producing cognitions. We would predict lower ratings because the *S*'s increased power should lessen the necessity for using conformity as a power-gaining strategy.

Our third innovation to the procedure used by Aronson and Mills was the inclusion of a number of rating scales on which the *S*s rated, among other things, their degree of embarrassment. Aronson and Mills had said that *S*s in the severe condition

> . . . could reduce their dissonance either by denying the severity of the initiation or by distorting their cognitions concerning the group discussion in a positive direction. The initiation of the *S*s in the severe condition was apparently too painful for them to deny—hence, they reduced their dissonance by overestimating the attractiveness of the group (p. 180).

While this assumption may be true, it is conceivable that dissonance might be reduced by the denial of having been embarrassed. The extension of this reasoning would be, then, that degree of recorded embarrassment would be positively associated with degree of overvaluation of the discussion. Our own theoretical position will be stated when we present the results.

To summarize briefly, four groups were constituted: a control, where *S*s had easy access to the group; a severe, where *S*s had painful access; a disparage, where *S*s had painful access and the *E* made a negative comment; and an increased power condition, where *S*s had painful access and were able to rate the *E*. The four major hypotheses to be tested were:

1. *S*s in the severe group would rate the discussion more favorably than the control *S*s, thus repeating the Aronson and Mills findings.

2. *S*s in the disparage condition would rate the discussion less favorably than *S*s in the severe condition.

3. *S*s in the increased power condition would rate the discussion less favorably than *S*s in the severe condition. Dissonance theory had already generated hypothesis 1, but it was thought that it would make an opposite prediction for hypotheses 2 and 3. Furthermore, from dissonance theory hypothesis 4 was also predicted.

4. The degree of embarrassment reported by *S*s would be positively associated with ratings of liking of the discussion.

Method

The *S*s were 60 girls aged between 18 and 23 drawn from introductory psychology and sociology courses in which participation in experiments was required. In contrast to the Aronson and Mills procedure or recruiting subjects, none of them had any expectations about the nature of the experiment in which they would be participating.

The experimental procedure employed adhered closely to that described by Aronson and Mills. In order to test the hypotheses the two new conditions and the control group had to differ in certain procedural details from the severe group. These differences will therefore be described after the routine for the severe group has been presented.

Each *S* in the severe condition was met by the senior investigator who led her directly to a small room where she was introduced to the *E*. *E* began an elaborate subterfuge by giving her the impression that she was about to join a group discussing sex. Other members of the group were not in the same room because it had been found that the discussion went best when participants were not in face to face contact. The discussion therefore took place over an intercom system. Nevertheless, in the past some *Ss* still had been too embarrassed "to join in properly" and *S* was asked if she thought she could discuss sex freely. (To this question all but two *Ss* replied affirmatively, though some with evident reluctance.) *E* then informed her that it was difficult to ask people to leave the group once they had started and therefore he had instituted an "embarrassment test" which he was going to administer to her, although this had not been required of the present members of the group. He would make a clinical judgment of her reactions, and if she passed she would be allowed to join the group. For the test the *S* had to read out in a loud, clear voice five obscene words, which were presented one at a time on three-by-five cards. Next the *S* was required to free associate to four words and finally she had to read aloud a short passage taken from Henry Miller's *Tropic of Cancer*. After completing the test each *S* was told she had passed. However, because *S* had not read the book under discussion for that day she could only listen to, but not participate in, the discussion.

E then went out of the room ostensibly to connect *S*'s loudspeaker to the ongoing discussion, actually to switch on a tape-recorder. This began to play a very dull and uninformative discussion of sexual characteristics in animals. When *E* came back into the room he plugged a microphone into the wall and pretended to break into the discussion in order to introduce the *S*. The group members then introduced themselves, whereupon *E* "broke into" the discussion a second time in order to explain that *S* would not be taking part this time. Again the discussion was resumed. *E* ostentatiously unplugged the microphone and left the room.

At the end of the discussion, which lasted about twenty minutes, *E* returned and gave *S* a questionnaire containing 10 16-point rating scales. Like the Aronson and Mills scales these were numbered from 0 to 15. On them she made five ratings of the content of the discussion and five of the participants in the discussion. The content was rated as dull–interesting, unpleasant–pleasant, not informative–informative, roundabout–to the point and superficial–deep; the participants as cold–warm, unfriendly–friendly, unintelligent–intelligent, insincere–sincere and rude–considerate.

After *S* had completed this form *E* handed her another headed "Confidential Rating Sheet." This sheet contained a number of 11-point rating scales, numbered from 0 to 10, including one item each on degree of embarrassment, degree of felt influence over *E*, degree of liking for *E*, and *E*'s degree of competence. It also provided a space for any further comments *S* wished to make about the experiment. In order to minimize the possible usage of power strategies in marking these items, *E* asked *S* not to hand the scales back to him personally but to place them in a special envelope.

The experiment now being over, *E* explained its true nature to *S* and interrogated her in order to find out whether she had been suspicious about the deception. Several *Ss* showed a mild degree of suspicion; none showed enough to warrant the discarding of her data.

The *Ss* in the disparage condition received identical treatment except that after they were informed that they could not participate in the discussion *E* added:

> Actually I don't think you'll lose anything by not taking part today. Other groups who've discussed this chapter have produced rather feeble discussions. It really is pretty dull, and the discussion today probably won't be at all exciting.

The induction of the increased-power manipulation was accomplished at the start of the experiment. The senior investigator showed *S* four rating scales she was to fill out at the end of the experiment which were ". . . aimed at getting at how good a job the experimenter is doing." She could make several ratings of *E*'s effectiveness and could recommend whether he should be dismissed, evaluated further, retained, or promoted. In order to avoid the implication that the *E* was particularly incompetent, this was presented as a standard procedure for all psychology experiments. *S* was then introduced to *E* and had an identical series of experiences to that of the *Ss* in the severe condition.

The control condition was distinguished by a pale version of the embarrassment test. *Ss* merely had to read out in a loud, clear voice the words, "boyfriend," "breast," and "sex." It should be noted that this corresponded to the mild condition of Aronson and Mills. We omitted their control group who received no embarrassment test nor any of the subterfuge justifying its administration. Because the subterfuge might itself contribute to raising expectations about the discussion we reasoned that their mild condition would serve as a more adequate control.

Results and Discussion

The mean ratings of embarrassment and of influence are presented in Table 1. For the embarrassment ratings the control group mean was compared to the means of the other three conditions by *t* test. The control group had a significantly smaller variance than the other conditions, beyond the .01 level by *F* test,[2] probably indicating a "ceiling effect" on the one-item scale, and therefore comparisons were made following the procedure recommended by Edwards (1954, pp. 273–274). The severe and the disparage conditions differed significantly from the control, whereas for the increased power condition the difference only approached statistical significance. The ratings of influence over the *E* were obtained to evaluate the success of inducing increased power. Table 1 shows that the increased power group had a significantly smaller mean than the other three conditions, a difference that was opposite to the one intended; in addition, it had a significantly smaller variance than the severe or control groups, probably again indicating a ceiling effect on the scale. The induction of embarrassment apparently was successful, while the induction of increased power appears to have failed. These results will have a bearing on the main findings and will be discussed further below. The results

[2] All probability values reported are based on two-tailed test.

TABLE 1
Mean Ratings of Degree of Embarrassment and Influence for Each Condition[a]

Rating scales	Severe	Control	Disparage	Increased power
Embarrassment				
M	4.27	2.20	5.87	3.67
SD	2.55	1.06	2.83	2.56
t ratio for control condition vs.—	2.92	—	4.71	2.06
p	<.02	—	<.01	<.10
Influence				
M	2.67	3.00	2.07	1.07
SD	2.66	2.83	1.53	1.39
t ratio for increased power condition vs.—	2.06	2.37	1.87	—
p	<.10	<.05	<.10	—

[a] In each condition $N = 15$.

for ratings of liking for *E* and *E*'s competence are presented in Table 2. Both of these items were included to check on the similarity of perceptions of *E* by *S*s in each condition. As can be seen from the table, no significant differences existed among the four experimental groups.

Tests of the Hypotheses

It was predicted that the means of the disparage, increased power, and control groups for ratings of the content and participants would be lower than the means of the severe group. No predictions were made about

TABLE 2
Mean Ratings of Degree of Liking for *E* and Competence of *E* for Each Condition[a,b]

Rating scales	Severe	Control	Disparage	Increased power
Liking				
M	8.80	8.40	8.20	8.07
SD	1.72	1.56	1.78	2.02
Competence				
M	9.40	9.00	9.40	9.27
SD	0.91	1.31	1.03	0.83

[a] In each condition $N = 15$.
[b] None of the mean differences between conditions for either liking or competence approaches significance by *t* test.

relationships between the disparage, increased power, and control conditions. Significance tests were made on the differences between the ratings of the severe group and the ratings of the other three groups. The means, standard deviations, and relevant t ratios are presented in Table 3. Mean differences for ratings of content between the severe and both the control and disparage groups reach acceptable levels of significance, but the mean difference between severe and increased power does not. The mean differences for the ratings of the participants only approach acceptable levels of significance, but show similar trends to the ratings of content. The differences between the severe and control groups are not quite as striking as those obtained by Aronson and Mills for their equivalent conditions, the severe and mild, respectively. In order to be able to compare means directly, all total scores were divided by the number of items contributing to the total, thus obtaining mean scores for each group on a 16-point scale. These are presented in Table 4 where it can be seen that, on the whole, the means for the two experiments are similar. The lower means found in the present study may indicate that our taped discussion was even duller than the original one, or that the differences in subject recruitment had a consistent effect. It therefore seems that the various minor differences in our experimental procedure had no appreciable effect on the results.

The ratings of *content,* then, give confirmation to two of our predictions while failing to confirm the third. We found, as Aronson and Mills had before, that the differences between conditions on rating of par-

TABLE 3
Mean and Standard Deviation of Discussion Ratings for Each Condition with t Tests between Severe and Other Conditions[a]

Rating scales	Severe	Control	Disparage	Increased power
Content (5)				
M	47.8	39.2	37.1	41.1
SD	9.8	11.2	13.2	17.4
t ratio for severe condition vs.—	—	2.24	2.53	1.29
p	—	$<.05$	$<.02$	n.s.
Participants (5)				
M	62.9	59.7	59.5	64.9
SD	8.5	10.9	9.3	10.3
t ratio for severe condition vs.—	—	.89	1.06	.57
p	—	n.s.	n.s.	n.s.

[a] In each condition $N = 15$.

TABLE 4
Mean Ratings of the Discussion Obtained by Aronson and Mills and in the Present Study

Rating scales	A & M "severe"	Present "severe"	A & M "mild"	Present "control"
Content	10.8	9.6	9.1	7.8
Participants	12.2	12.6	11.2	11.9

ticipants were less striking than the differences on rating of content. They explained this in part by saying: "It may be easier for people to express negative criticism about an impersonal discussion than about the people involved." We would propose in addition that to praise the participants would be a rather weak power strategy, since *E* could hardly be held responsible for the personality characteristics of people drawn at random, as the *S*s believed, out of the regular subject pool.

The confirmation of the prediction that the severe group would value the discussion more highly than the control (hypothesis 1) shows that this Aronson and Mills finding can be obtained even under slightly altered conditions of subject procurement and experimental technique. Of course the successful replication gives no direct evidence on whether the dissonance or dependence interpretation is more appropriate. Considering only these two conditions there is a suggestive piece of indirect evidence, however. Our initial assumption was that *S*s in the severe condition would show a high level of general emotional tension as a result of the wide range of outcomes they had experienced. This tension would be manifested in high involvement with *E*, who had been responsible for providing the most extreme of these outcomes; it was this assumption that originally led us to a dependence interpretation. An indication that this assumption was correct is provided in the replies *S*s gave to the open-ended question on the confidential rating sheet, which asked them if they had any further comments about the experiment. Their replies were coded into two categories: long comments (i.e., at least one full-length sentence); short or no comments (less than one full-length sentence). As this was the first opportunity that *S*s in the severe or control groups had to express themselves freely, it was felt that a long comment would imply the release of greater emotional tension than a short comment or no comment. It was found that 12 *S*s in the severe condition and 3 in the control made long comments, while 3 in the severe and 12 in the control made short or no comments. The chi-square test of these frequencies resulted in a chi-square of 10.7, which is significant beyond the .005 level of confidence. To provide an index of personal involvement with *E*, replies were further coded according to whether or not they mentioned *E*. Five replies out of 15 in the severe condition were found to mention *E*, but none of the 15 Control *S*s mentioned him.

The confirmation of the prediction that when an *E* makes a negative comment about a discussion, the *S*s will give it a lower rating than when *E* implies approval (hypothesis 2), lends some support to the dependence effects involved in the initiation procedure. A more critical test of this effect would involve the addition of another control group in which *S*s hear the disparaging remark, but do not have to take the initiation test. (This would also provide comparability to the design used by Brehm in the experiment cited previously.) It therefore is possible to view these results as indicating the direct effect of negative information on the evaluation of a complex stimulus situation. However, if this were the case the disparaging remark would merely block one avenue of reducing the dissonance aroused by the discrepant cognitions of having endured pain for something worthless, which, presumably, would still have to be reduced. The disparage group did not deny embarrassment (their mean rating of embarrassment was the highest mean obtained), nor did they display deviant ratings on the other measures which might have indicated dissonance reduction. In line with the reasoning presented in the introduction, however, it is still possible that the lowered ratings of the disparage group were a consequence of the experimentally created dependence and served the same function as the inflated ratings did for the severe group.

The prediction made from dissonance theory that embarrassment would be positively associated with rating of content (hypothesis 4) was tested by dividing each condition at the median for rating of embarrassment. The ratings of the discussion for the group above the median were then compared to those of the group below by a Mann-Whitney test (Siegel, 1956, pp. 116–118). It was found that the *S*s in the severe and increased power conditions whose ratings fell above the median for extent of embarrassment made lower ratings of the content and the participants than the *S*s whose embarrassment ratings were below the median. The differences were significant beyond the .05 level of confidence. No significant differences were found for *S*s in the control or disparage conditions.

These relationships are the opposite to those we deduced from the Aronson and Mills statement of dissonance theory but are susceptible to a dependence interpretation. If we assume that all *S*s who took the severe embarrassment test experienced, as a result, approximately the same low level of outcomes, we would infer that those who rated themselves as unembarrassed must in addition have experienced some good outcomes during the first part of the experiment. The range of outcomes, therefore, that these people received would have been rather extensive. And their high ratings of discussion content are interpreted as a response to high dependence.

The effect of attempting to increase an *S*'s amount of power in this experiment remains unclear. The prediction that the increased power group would value the discussion less than the severe group (hypothesis 3) was not confirmed. The manipulation of increased power did not produce the effects intended, although it appeared to have had considerable impact on the *S*s. It will be recalled that their ratings of felt influence were significantly *lower* than those of the other conditions. Furthermore, the variability of their ratings of the discussion was the largest of the four conditions, different from the severe group at beyond the .05 level of confidence by *F* test. Inspection of the frequency distributions of ratings of content for all conditions revealed that the increased power condition had the largest range and was bimodal, whereas the distributions of the other three conditions were approximately normal. In light of these features it now seems that the power given by requiring a postexperimental rating of the *E* accentuated the lack of actual power during the experiment, since *S*s in the increased power condition could not prevent themselves from experiencing very poor outcomes. The conflict caused by possessing apparent power in what was actually a powerless situation was perhaps resolved according to the various preferences of the individuals. Differences in the preferred mode of resolution may account for the extreme variability and apparent bimodality of ratings given by these *S*s.

In conclusion, the present experiment provides substantial evidence for the replication of the main finding reported by Aronson and Mills, despite slightly altered conditions of subject procurement and experimental technique. The evidence presented for the dependence interpretation and against the dissonance interpretation of the effects of the severe initiation is not entirely conclusive. However, the lowered ratings of content made by *S*s in the disparage condition, the greater number of written comments made by the *S*s in the severe group, and the internal analysis of the embarrassment ratings, when taken together, are suggestive in pointing to the critical role of the *S–E* interaction in determining the *S*'s responses.

Summary

Aronson and Mills have reported an experiment in which they found that *S*s who had difficult entrance to a boring discussion group made more favorable ratings of the discussion than *S*s who had easy access, thereby confirming a prediction based on dissonance theory. Their procedure for inducing difficult access adequately represented the conditions for creating high dependence as defined by Thibaut and Kelley, because the *E* had to inflict a highly unpleasant experience upon the *S*, thus demonstrating his power over her and her dependence upon him. From the Thibaut and Kelley model of behavior the Aronson and Mills results were interpreted as indicating that the *S*s attempted to lessen their dependence by conforming to *E*'s implied attitude that they would like the discussion.

In order to evaluate the adequacy of the Aronson and Mills interpretation against a dependence interpretation, two of their conditions were repeated and two new conditions were added. The new treatments, termed disparage and increased power, attempted to maintain the dissonance-producing features of the Aronson and Mills procedure. In the disparage condition *E* stated openly that he thought that the *S* would not like the discussion, while in the increased power condition the *S* was given some power over *E*. The results from the former condition were in accord with a dependence interpretation, while results from the latter condition were ambiguous. The major finding of Aronson and Mills was also obtained, with slightly altered conditions of subject procurement and experimental technique.

REFERENCES

Aronson, E., & Mills, J. The effect of severity of initiation on liking for a group. *Journal of Abnormal and Social Psychology,* 1959, **59,** 177–181.

Brehm, J. W. Attitudinal consequences of commitment to unpleasant behavior. *Journal of Abnormal and Social Psychology,* 1960, **60,** 379–383.

Edwards, A. L. *Statistical methods for the behavioral sciences.* New York: Rinehart, 1954.

Siegel, S. *Nonparametric statistics for the behavioral sciences.* New York: McGraw-Hill, 1956.

Thibaut, J. W., & Kelley, H. H. *The social psychology of groups.* New York: Wiley, 1959.

Discussion

In their introduction Schopler and Bateson very carefully delineated their own alternative interpretation for Aronson and Mills' results. Essentially, they stated that their dependency hypothesis would also predict the same results that Aronson and Mills obtained. Their next step was most important. They discriminated two further sets of empirical conditions similar to the original conditions, but differing in certain significant ways. These two experimental conditions were structured so that dissonance theory reasonably made one kind of predicted outcome for the new conditions, but dependency theory made exactly opposite predictions. The logic was such that if the results for the two new conditions supported the dependence interpretation, then, by inference, Aronson and Mills' results were also due to dependency rather than dissonance. This approach is a fairly standard way of testing alternative hypotheses.

In terms of strict logical inference this approach may not be valid. It is perfectly possible, empirically, that in the Aronson and Mills' conditions dissonance was indeed the critical process at work, while in Schopler and Bateson's two new conditions a dependency process was at work. But although possible, this "different process" view would be considered unlikely. The reasons are pragmatic rather than logical. First, there is the principle of parsimony in explanation. Never use two explanations if one will suffice. Second, the power of the theory to handle many situations is an important empirical consideration. If Aronson and Mills' theory could account for only two sets of empirical conditions, while Schopler and Bateson's theory could account for four, then the latter is more powerful and therefore more desirable. Of course we have simplified here. The ability of dissonance theory to account for many other diverse empirical areas would have to be considered before we summarily dismissed Aronson and Mills' interpretation on the basis of our comparison of two-versus-four empirical conditions.

The actual results of Schopler and Bateson's experiment were somewhat disappointing. The increased power manipulation apparently failed; indeed the checks (see their Table 1) on the manipulation indicated that an effect opposite to that intended occurred. That is, subjects in this condition perceived themselves as having significantly less power than subjects in any of the other conditions. If this result is reliable, these data pose problems for the dependence interpretation. The reason is that there were no differences in ratings of the discussion between the increased power and severe initiation conditions. Given the significant difference in perceived influence, such a difference in ratings of content would be expected. However, too much importance probably should not be attributed to this point. The difference in perceived influence was only marginally significant, and it is unclear why the manipulation "backfired." Schopler and Bateson offered one suggestion in their discussion, but all such possibilities are necessarily post hoc. The best conclusion probably is that the results for the increased power condition have no relevance one way or another in interpreting the data for the other conditions.

Thus we are left with the results of the disparage condition only to compare the merits of the dependence interpretation with the dissonance interpretation. As noted, the results were as predicted. Subjects in the disparage condition rated the content of the discussion significantly less favorably than subjects in the severe condition. This difference supports the dependence interpretation. A critical question must be raised at this point concerning Schopler and Bateson's assumption of what dissonance theory would predict for the disparage condition. They assumed that dissonance theory would predict the same result as for the severe condition. But would it? We think not, particularly not an expectancy confirmation version of dissonance theory. The reasoning is that the embarrassment test may have created the beginning of an expectancy for an interesting discussion. However, the experimenter promptly demolished that expectancy with the information that the discussion would be boring. Therefore, there was no dissonance to be reduced following the presentation of the dull discussion. It follows that the discussion would not be evaluated very favorably, and indeed it was not.

The results for embarrassment provide some support for this notion (Table 1). Subjects in the disparage condition showed the highest embarrassment scores. If we assume this mean score as a baseline, subjects in the severe condition showed less embarrassment. This reduction in embarrassment could certainly be an avenue for dissonance reduction, a possibility that Aronson and Mills noted in their introduction.

Thus the results for the disparage condition are not fatal for the dissonance interpretation. Additionally, the differences for ratings of the participants were nonsignificant, certainly a bothersome aspect of the data. Problems such as these led Schopler and Bateson to conclude that the evidence in favor of their interpretation was "not entirely conclusive." Indeed it was not. In fact, a good dissonance theorist would interpret their data as quite consistent with dissonance theory. We must conclude that the test of the dependence alternative was ambiguous, and that the results overall provided almost no support for the proposed alternative explanation.

The last article in this chapter was discussed in Chapter 2. In reading Gerard and Mathewson's experiment, pay particular attention to how they designed the study. Note especially the various conditions included to rule out different alternative explanations. As noted in Chapter 2, this is a "high risk" experiment because the procedures departed radically from Aronson and Mills' procedures. Had the results not come out rather precisely as predicted, the study would have been of little value, because divergent results are usually uninterpretable when procedures are radically different.

The Effects of Severity of Initiation on Liking for a Group: A Replication[1]

Harold B. Gerard and Grover C. Mathewson

This experiment represents an attempt to rule out a number of alternative explanations of an effect found in a previous experiment by Aronson and Mills. This effect, that the more a person suffers in order to obtain something, the greater will be the tendency for him to evaluate it positively, was predicted from dissonance theory. By modifying the original experiment in a number of ways, and applying additional treatment variations, these other hypotheses were effectively ruled out, thus lending considerable additional support to the original "suffering-leading-to-liking" hypothesis.

The experiment by Aronson and Mills (1959), in which a positive relationship was found between the severity of initiation into a group and subsequent liking for that group, is open to a variety of interpretations other than the one the authors give. The purpose of the experiment to be reported here was an attempt to rule out some of the more cogent of these alternative interpretations.

The observation that people often tend to value highly things for which they have suffered or expended a great deal of effort can be interpreted as having been due to dissonance reduction. The hypothesized process involved assumes that knowledge held by the person that he had suffered or expended a great deal of effort for a desired goal is inconsistent with knowledge that the goal or certain aspects of it are worthless. Such inconsistencies produce psychological dissonance which is unpleasant and the individual will attempt to reduce this unpleasantness by cognitive work. In this case he can either distort his beliefs about the amount of suffering or effort he expended by coming to believe that it was less than he had previously thought or he can distort his belief about

[1] From the *Journal of Experimental Social Psychology,* 1966, **2**, 278–287. Received October 18, 1965.

This experiment was conducted by the junior author as part of an undergraduate senior tutorial. We gratefully acknowledge the financial support provided by grant No. MH 1181701 from the National Institute of Mental Health and grant No. GS 392 from the National Science Foundation.

At the time of writing the authors were at the University of California at Riverside. Gerard is currently at the University of California at Los Angeles; Mathewson is in Loma Linda, California.

the worthlessness of aspects of the goal by coming to believe that these aspects were really not worthless. In their study, Aronson and Mills attempted to create a laboratory situation in which the latter hypothesized process could be examined. Let us review that experiment in some detail so that we may then point up the basis for the other interpretations of the data.

The subjects were college coeds who were willing to volunteer for a series of group discussions on the psychology of sex. The ostensible purpose of the study was presented to the subject as having to do with the investigation of group dynamics. Before any prospective member could join one of the discussion groups she was given a "screening test" to determine her suitability for the group. The severity of this screening test (or initiation) was varied; in the "severe" treatment the subject read obscene literature and a list of dirty words out loud to the experimenter (who was a male), whereas in the "mild" condition the subject read sexual material of an innocuous sort. The subject was told that the screening test had been necessary in order to weed out people who were too shy to discuss topics related to sex. After the initiation, each experimental subject was informed that she had passed the test and was therefore eligible for membership in the group. She was led to believe that the group she was to join had been formed several weeks ago and that she was to take the place of a girl who had to drop out. Her "participation" in her first meeting with the group was limited to "overhearing" via headphones what was presented to her as an ongoing discussion by the group on aspects of sexual behavior in animals. The reason she was given for not being able to participate actively in the discussion was that the other three girls had prepared for the discussion by reading a book on the sexual behavior of animals. It was also suggested to her that overhearing the discussion without participating in it would give her an opportunity to get acquainted with how the group operates. What she heard was not an ongoing discussion but was instead a standardized recorded discussion on the sexual behavior of animals that was extremely boring and banal. The discussion was contrived to be worthless in order to maximize the dissonance of the subject in the "severe" initiation group, since the knowledge that she had suffered to get into the group would be dissonant with finding out that the discussion was worthless.

After hearing the taped recording, the subject was asked to evaluate the discussion and the participants on a number of semantic differential-type scales. A control group was also run in which the subjects evaluated the discussion without having received any initiation whatsoever. The findings of the experiment supported the derivation from dissonance theory, namely that the subjects in the severe treatment evaluated the discussion more favorably than did the mild or control subjects. A dissonance theory interpretation conceives of the severe initiation as confronting the subject with the "problem" of having suffered for something that was later found to be worthless and the prediction is based upon how that problem is "solved." One of the reasons why the results are important and provocative is that they are exactly opposite to what a strict application of secondary reinforcement theory would predict in which it would be expected that the unpleasantness of the initiation would "rub off" and generalize to the discussion.

While the results are consistent with dissonance theory, they lend themselves to a variety of other, quite plausible interpretations. For example, there is an entire *family* of interpretations that derives from the fact that the content of the initiation and the content of the discussion are so closely related, both having to do with sex. One could argue that the initiation aroused the girls sexually to a greater extent in the severe as compared with the mild treatment and they were therefore more anxious to get into the group in order to pursue the discussion of sex. Along similar lines, one could also argue that the girls in the severe treatment did not know the meaning of some of the dirty four-letter words and believed that they could find out their meaning by joining the discussion group. This is a variation of the uncertainty-affiliation hypothesis. Still another possibility is that the subjects in the severe treatment were intrigued by the obscene material and the dirty words and may have believed that, if not now, sometime in the future these things would be discussed by the group. One could continue to list related interpretations based upon the assumed arousal of one or another motive in the severe treatment that might be satisfied by joining the discussion group (thus making the group more attractive).

Another possible interpretation, a "relief" hypothesis, is that the reading of the obscene material built up anxiety which was subsequently reduced by the banal, innocuous material of the group discussion. Since the discussion was responsible for reducing the anxiety, it took on positive value for the subject in the severe treatment.

Schopler and Bateson (1962) find partial support for a "dependency" interpretation of the Aronson and Mills findings. Following Thibaut and Kelley (1959), Schopler and Bateson suggest that, as contrasted with the mild initiation, the severe initiation induced in the subject dependence upon the experimenter. This, according to them, occurred because the experimenter had "moved" the subject in the severe treatment through a "wide range of outcomes," consisting of the unpleasant shock and the pleasantness associated with the pride experienced by the severe subject upon learning that she had passed the test. Subjects in the mild condition had not experienced this range of pleasantness of outcome and hence were less dependent. Also, their argument continues, somehow the subject assumed that the experimenter expected her to like the discussion. Due to the assumed differential dependency induced by the initiation treatments, the subject in the severe treatment was more concerned with pleasing the experimenter than was the subject in the mild treatment, and hence attempted to a greater extent to meet his expectations by indicating to him that she liked the discussion.

Chapanis and Chapanis (1964) suggest an "afterglow" hypothesis to explain the data. All subjects in the experiment were told that they had passed the embarrassment test. Presumably, subjects in the severe treatment perceived the test as being more difficult than did subjects in the mild treatment and, according to Chapanis and Chapanis, they therefore may have had a greater sense of accomplishment. This self-satisfaction somehow rubbed off onto other aspects of the task situation, including, presumably, the group discussion. This might then account for the severe subjects' more positive disposition toward the discussion.

Still another even more plausible interpretation of quite a different sort is that any experience following the severe initiation, which we assume was unpleasant, would by contrast seem more pleasant than it would following the mild initiation. It is important that this rather simple "contrast" hypothesis, which is a compelling explanation of the Aronson and Mills data, be ruled out, if possible.

A problem in the experiment related to the first set of interpretations concerns the nature of the initiation itself. Was the severe initiation really more unpleasant than the mild one? The authors do not report any check of the success of the experimental manipulation in producing differences in unpleasantness. Without the assurance that this all-important requirement was met, certain other interpretations of the data are quite plausible. It is not unlikely that many of the subjects in the severe treatment found the experience pleasant and exciting.

The experiment we shall report here is an attempt to replicate, not so much in fact but in spirit, the Aronson and Mills study, in order to counterpose the dissonance interpretation of the results against the other interpretations discussed above.

Method

An Overview of the Design

Two basic treatments were compared, one in which the subject received electrical shocks as part of an initiation procedure and one in which she received shocks as part of a psychological experiment, the "noninitiate" treatment. Within each of these treatments, half of the subjects received strong shocks and half received weak shocks. Half of the severe and half of the mild initiates were told that they had passed the screening test, whereas the other half of each were not told whether they had passed. After the shocks, all subjects heard and then evaluated a boring and worthless group discussion about cheating in college. The "initiates" believed that this was a recording of a previous meeting of the group that they were slated to join, whereas the "noninitates" evaluated the discussion as just one of a series of stimuli to which they were being exposed.

Procedure

The subjects were 48 female undergraduate volunteers contacted at random from the student body of the University of California at Riverside. All subjects were first contacted by telephone. During the telephone contact a subject selected to be an initiate was asked whether or not she would like to volunteer for a discussion club that was to discuss the problem of morals on university campuses. The noninitiates were asked, during the telephone contact, whether they would like to volunteer to be a subject in a psychological experiment. Thus, half of the subjects reported to the laboratory believing that they were going to be members of a discussion club whereas the other half believed that they were participating in a psychological experiment. The procedure followed during the experimental session was essentially the same for both initiates and noninitiates. The noninitiate condition was introduced in an attempt to rule out the contrast and relief hypotheses. If the unpleasant experience represented by the initiation was not seen as instrumental to joining the discussion club and the same effect was found as in the Aronson and Mills experiment, both alternative explanations would receive support. If, however, the initiates showed the effect and the noninitiates did not, both the contrast and relief hypotheses would have been effectively ruled out. We might expect a secondary reinforcement effect in the noninitiate condition which would manifest as a negative relationship between the unpleasantness of the shocks and the evaluation of the discussion, the assumption being that the effect produced by the shocks would generalize to the discussion.

When the initiate arrived in the laboratory she was seated in an isolation booth and was told:

> In the past we have had considerable difficulty with some of the girls who have joined these discussion clubs. The problem is that some people cannot maintain an attitude of objectivity during the discussion. When this happens, naturally the discussion tends to deteriorate and emotions run very high. In order to avoid this difficulty in the future we have just instituted a screening test to weed out those girls who would tend to let their emotions run away with them during a discussion. You are the first person to whom we will be administering the test, which is a very good one, that has been used by psychologists for many years. It consists of determining your physiological reaction to a series of stimuli. We do this by hooking you up to these electrodes (the experimenter shows the subject a pair of dummy GSR electrodes) that detect changes in your skin resistance during the test which is done with the aid of this recorder (the experimenter shows the subject a small strip-chart recorder). By your response on this chart we can tell how objective you are likely to be under conditions represented by the morals discussion.

The subject was told that she was the first one to take the test in order to eliminate the possibility that she would want to be in the group in order to compare her reactions to the test with those of the girls already in the discussion group.

The noninitiate was told when she arrived at the laboratory, "You are going to be a subject in a psychological experiment which involves your being exposed to a variety of different kinds of stimuli. We are going to determine your reaction to these stimuli with the aid of these electrodes (the experimenter shows the subject the GSR electrodes) which are hooked up to this instrument (the experimenter shows the subject the strip chart recorder)."

All subjects were hooked up to the electrodes and received exactly the same sequence of stimuli which was designed to be a credible screening test for the initiate. The sequence consisted of a spray of perfume from an atomizer placed in the ceiling of the subject's booth, a series of slides of paintings projected on the wall in front of the subject's booth (the paintings were: Roualt, *The Apprentice;* Picasso, *Madame Picasso, Portrait of A. Vollard, Figure by the Sea;* La Tour, *Self Portrait;* Matisse, *Landscape;* and Klee, *Girl Possessed*). Each painting was presented for 15 seconds with a 15-second pause between presentations. After all of the paintings were shown, the subject was fitted with headphones and heard the shooting sequence in Copland's ballet, *Billy the Kid.* Finally, the subject received the critical stimuli which were a series of three shocks delivered 15 seonds apart by a Lafayette inductorium. In the severe treatment the shocks were quite strong whereas in the mild treatment they were barely supraliminal. This method of varying suffering would be more likely, on the face of it at least, to produce greater uniformity of psychological state within each of the two suffering levels than the method used by Aronson and Mills. Using electric shock to produce suffering effectively separates the content of the initiation from the content of the discussion. If the Aronson and Mills effect were to be found by using shock, this would rule out the family of interpretations that are all based upon the similarity of content of the two phases of the experiment.

Aronson and Mills informed all of their subjects that they had passed the screening test. The subject, thus, had acquired that for which she had suffered. It was inappropriate in the present experiment to inform the noninitiates as to how they had done in responding to the sequence of stimuli since they had not been told that they were taking a test. In order to control for this difficulty, half of the initiates were told, after receiving the shocks, that they had passed the screening test, whereas the other half were treated like the noninitiates by not receiving any feed-back concerning their performance on the screening test. This "told" versus "not-told" factor was counterbalanced across the severe and mild initiates. More importantly, this treatment also enables us to test the Chapanis and Chapanis "afterglow" hypothesis, the plausibility of which is based on the assumption that the pleasure experienced in passing the severe initiation generalized to the group discussion. If those subjects who were told that they had passed showed the Aronson and Mills effect and those who were not given this information did not show the effect, the afterglow explanation would be supported. The Schopler and Bateson dependence hypothesis would also be supported if the Aronson and Mills effect replicated in the told but not in the not-told treatment, since the assumed broader range of outcomes experienced by the severe subject depends on the pleasure experienced by the subject upon learning that she had passed the test.

All subjects then listened to a five-minute tape recording of three girls having a discussion of cheating in college. This discussion was absolutely worthless, consisting mostly of hemming, hawing, clearing of throats, and pauses. The initiate was told that this was a recording of a previous discussion of the group that she was slated to join.

The noninitiate was merely asked to listen to the discussion as one of the sequence of stimuli. Aronson and Mills presented the recording as an ongoing discussion. This difference in procedure in our initiate treatment did not seem to us to be critical.

In the final phase of the experiment, all subjects evaluated the discussion using semantic differential-type scales similar to those used by Aronson and Mills. Eight scales dealt with the qualities of the participants and eight with qualities of the discussion itself. Each scale was numbered from 0 to 15, the polarity of the scales being alternated in order to counteract any response bias. After this evaluation sheet was filled out, the subject was administered a postexperimental questionnaire which asked her to rate the pleasantness or unpleasantness of the various stimuli. The subject's evaluation of the shocks on this questionnaire was, of course, the check on the manipulation of suffering.

Results

The two shock levels clearly induced different degrées of pleasantness. The postquestionnaire contained a 7-point scale on which the subject rated the pleasantness of the shocks. The difference between the two shock conditions was extremely large ($p < .001$ by chi-square[2]) with the majority of subjects in the severe condition indicating that the shocks were "extremely unpleasant." No subjects in the mild treatment found the shocks more than only "mildly unpleasant."

The discussion evaluation data are shown in Table 1. The figures in the table represent the means of the pleasantness ratings for both the participant and the discussion evaluation, summed over the eight scales used for each. Tables 2 and 3 present the analysis of variance for each of the two evaluations. We see a clear main effect of the initiation factor. When the subject anticipated joining the group whose discussion she

TABLE 1

The Effects of Severity of Shock, Initiation, and Feedback on Evaluation of the Group Discussion[a]

	Initiate				Noninitiate	
	Mild shock		Severe shock			
	Told	Not told	Told	Not told	Mild shock	Severe shock
Participant rating	11.5	26.1	31.1	41.0	19.8	13.2
Discussion rating	11.0	15.6	27.0	28.2	9.1	5.8

[a] The larger the number, the more favorable the evaluation.

[2] Chi-square was used as a test of significance because the distribution in the severe treatment was skewed.

TABLE 2
Analysis of Variance of the Participant Evaluation

Source	*SS*	*df*	*MS*	F^b
Initiation (I)	1276	1	1276	8.28
Severity (S)	1045	1	1045	6.78
I × S	1504	1	1504	9.77
Told (T)	1201	1	1201	7.80
S (I) × T[a]	45	1	45	
Error	6471	42	159	

[a] Interaction of feedback (told versus not-told within the initiate condition).
[b] F .05 = 4.07; F .01 = 7.27.

had heard, she tended to evaluate both the discussion and the participants more highly than she did when there was no such expectation. This shows a general "effort effect" in line with dissonance theory. There was also a main effect of severity that is accounted for by the initiates. The crucial degree of freedom that concerns us here is the interaction between initiation and severity which also yields a significant F-ratio. A t test applied within the initiates and within the noninitiates shows that both trends, which are opposite, are significant, the trend in the initiate treatment being stronger ($p < .01$) than the trend in the noninitiate treatment ($p < .05$). Whether or not the initiate received feedback about her performance on the screening test (the told versus not-told variations) appears not to have interacted with severity of the shock. We do see, however, that for the participant evaluation there does seem to be a main effect of feedback. Informing the subject that she had passed the test appears to have reduced the evaluation of the participants.

Since there was some variation in both the severe and mild shock conditions in the perception of unpleasantness by the subject, we were in a position to do an internal analysis of the data by examining the correlation between *perceived* severity of the shock and liking for the group discussion. On the basis of dissonance theory we would expect a positive

TABLE 3
Analysis of Variance of the Discussion Evaluation

Source	*SS*	*df*	*MS*	*F*
Initiation (I)	1811	1	1811	13.22
Severity (S)	850	1	850	6.20
I × S	835	1	835	6.09
Told (T)	69	1	69	
S (I) × T	23	1	23	
Error	5774	42	137	

relationship only within the initiate condition. The overall correlation with the initiate treatment is .52 for the participant rating and .45 for the discussion rating ($p < .01$ for both correlation coefficients). The corresponding correlations in the noninitiate treatment are .03 and .07.

Discussion

The data from the experiment strongly support the "suffering-leading-to-liking" hypothesis and effectively rule out a number of other interpretations of the original experiment by Aronson and Mills. Our data for the initiate treatment are much stronger than those in the first experiment. This is probably attributable to the shock manipulation which undoubtedly produced more uniform within-treatment levels of suffering. The fact that the content of our suffering manipulation was divorced from the content of the group discussion eliminates the family of interpretations of the Aronson and Mills data that invoke some motive for wanting to affiliate that would be assumed to be greater in the severe than in the mild initiation treatment. The fact that there was an interaction between the initiate and severity factors eliminates the contrast and relief hypotheses. Both hypotheses predict the same difference under the initiate and the noninitiate treatments. We see instead an effect within the noninitiate treatment that supports a secondary reinforcement interpretation; the more severe the shock the *less* the subject liked the discussion. The internal correlation analysis adds further support for the suffering-leading-to-liking hypothesis and further weakens the contrast and relief hypotheses, since within the initiate treatment the greater the perceived suffering was the greater the subject liked the group discussion, whereas no such relationship was found within the noninitiate treatment.

Both the Chapanis and Chapanis afterglow and the Schopler and Bateson dependence hypotheses depend upon the subject having had a success experience after learning that she had passed the screening test. This success experience is presumed to have been greater in the severe than in the mild initiation treatment. Greater liking for the discussion under the severe initiation should, therefore, according to both hypotheses, occur under the told but not under the not-told treatment. The lack of such an interaction effectively rules out both hypotheses.

Feedback did have a main effect on the evaluation of the participants. The high evaluation of the participants in the not-told as compared with the told condition may reflect a desire to be in the group. When informed that she had passed the screening test and would be in the group, the subject reduced her evaluation. Objects that a person is not sure he can have may appear more attractive to him under certain circumstances than similar objects that he already possesses. Having suffered or expended effort in order to acquire the object may be just such a circumstance. This effect was not predicted and our interpretation, therefore, must be considered as highly speculative.

REFERENCES

Aronson, E., & Mills, J. The effect of severity of initiation on liking for a group. *Journal of Abnormal and Social Psychology*, 1959, **59**, 177–181.

Chapanis, N. P., & Chapanis, A. Cognitive dissonance: five years later. *Psychological Bulletin*, 1964, **61**, 1–22.

Schopler, J., & Bateson, N. A dependence interpretation of the effects of a severe initiation. *Journal of Personality*, 1962, **30**, 633–649.

Thibaut, J., & Kelley, H. H. *The social psychology of groups*. New York: Wiley, 1959.

Discussion

The experiment by Gerard and Mathewson illustrates a phenomenon that seldom occurs in social psychology, namely, generality of a relationship across tremendous variation in procedural methodology. The experiment may be considered a conceptual replication. An attempt was made to create the necessary conditions to obtain the relevant functional relation between variables. This attempt involved a complete change in the nature of the task (shock versus obscene words), and numerous other procedural changes as well. Such generality across methods increases our confidence greatly in the relationship between our conceptual independent and dependent variables.

At the same time that methods generality was demonstrated, an entire series of alternative interpretations were ruled out. Indeed, the main reason for changing the nature of the task was to rule out all sex-relevant interpretations. In this sense the experiment was very efficient—generality was demonstrated with the same tools by which alternative interpretations were ruled out. These two aspects of the research, plus the fact that the results were so clear, allow us to state that the Gerard and Mathewson experiment is one of the very best pieces of social research. All of the possible alternative interpretations were ruled out. Insko (1967, p. 251) feels that Gerard and Mathewson did not rule out the dependence interpretation because they did not account for the results of the disparage condition in Schopler and Bateson's experiment. However, we have already indicated that those results do not pose a severe problem for the dissonance formulation, and indeed may even support an expectancy version of the theory. Therefore the dissonance interpretation is left as the only strong contender.

For several reasons, the two noninitiate conditions in Gerard and Mathewson's experiment provided an important set of results. Traditional reinforcement theory would predict that through the process of stimulus generalization, the pain of a severe initiation would transfer to the subsequent group discussion. Therefore, a reinforcement theory would predict that the discussion should be more favorably evaluated in the mild initiation condition. Exactly those results were obtained in the noninitiate conditions (see Table 1). Therefore, the results in the initiate conditions indicate that something very different was going on there. Presumably that "something" was dissonance aroused by the discrepancy between a severe initiation and the consequent dull discussion.

As we have indicated, all the proposed alternative explanations were effectively ruled out. Does this fact therefore prove dissonance theory? No, of course not. The theory was supported but it is certainly possible to conceive of still another alternative interpretation which might be supported by new research. In fact, we may propose one that was mentioned briefly earlier. In everyday life people learn that there is usually a positive correlation between how valuable something is and the amount of energy and effort that one must expend to earn it. One consequence of this particular social learning is that if we engage in some task requiring much effort, we may strongly anticipate that the consequences will be highly rewarded. In other words we will have a "set" for a rewarding experience. This set may be so strong that we will actually feel the follow-up experience was rewarding even when an objective observer would feel otherwise. Particularly, in "social reality" there is often no good way to evaluate just how rewarding an experience actually is. It is very likely that the subjects in the initiation experiments had no good basis for evaluating the worth of the sex discussions. Therefore, they may have used their knowledge of the severity of the initiation to infer that the discussion must have been worthwhile. This interpretation is in part a variant of Bem's (1965; 1967) self-perception theory which attempts to account for dissonance phenomena in terms of the subject's inferences about his own behavior, rather than in terms of dissonance as a motivating drive.

The interpretation is also related to Asch's directed impression theory of person perception that will be discussed in Chapter 8. The notion is that the strong initial set created by the severe initiation causes later experience to be assimilated to the initial impression. The initial impression is that the initiation was difficult, and that the following discussion should lead to many rewards. If the later experience is ambiguous at all (as such a discussion might be to some extent), then the assimilation will occur.

Although this alternative theory is not well developed, it has some plausibility. A relevant test within the framework of Gerard and Mathewson's paradigm would be as follows. Severity of initiation would be varied as in their experiment. In addition, the worth of the group discussion would be varied at several levels, including mild and severe anticipation conditions in which subjects rate the impending discussion before they hear it. A difference between these two conditions would imply that subjects were set to be rewarded for a severe initiation, assuming that the severe condition was rated more favorably. Support for dissonance theory would require an even greater difference between the two conditions when subjects actually listened to the dull discussion. Further, if different groups received different discussions scaled in terms of increasing "goodness," subjects in the mild initiation conditions should increase their positive evaluations much more rapidly than subjects in the severe initiation condition. This derivation follows because the mild conditions experience no dissonance, and should be responding only to the actual quality of the discussion. However, subjects in the severe initiation should be responding to strong dissonance reduction pressures in the very dull discussion condition, presumably resulting in favorable evaluations. But as the quality of the discussions increase, dissonance should be decreasing. It follows that favorability should increase very slowly (and perhaps even decrease) as the quality of the discussion increases.

This proposed experiment would allow both the set effect and a dissonance effect to occur. The test of dissonance theory would be a rather stringent one because support for the theory would require an interaction having a rather precise form. In the past, the conduct of crucial experiments was rather popular. The idea seems to have been to design an experiment so that if one theory was proved "true," the other had to be proved "false," and vice versa. We now know that such crucial experiments are almost never definitive. In fact, they are näive. Reality is complex, and there may be nuggets of truth in many different theories. On occasion, a more sophisticated approach to research will allow support of more than one theory within the same experimental design. The experiment suggested above offers such a possibility, because the pattern of results could potentially support both the set theory and dissonance theory. Of course, the pattern of the results could also support only one theory and discredit the other. Otherwise, the experiment would not be very interesting to conduct.

So far we have discussed this area of research almost entirely in terms of support for different theories of social behavior. However, the content of the research does seem to have some practical implications that should not be overlooked. The research seems to indicate that people are more attracted to groups under severe than under mild conditions of initiation. The generality of this result across methods indicates that the effect is robust. There is no reason why actual groups could not use this nugget of information to enhance the cohesive forces within their group membership. Of course it is easy to overgeneralize. The nature of the initiation is probably very important. For example, if the severe initiation consisted of brutal personal attacks of old members against new members, increased attraction might very well not occur. At any rate, we believe that the empirical result is sufficiently well established in the laboratory so that a careful field experiment using actual groups is warranted.

REFERENCES

Bem, D. J. An experimental analysis of self persuasion. *Journal of Experimental Social Psychology*, 1965, **1**, 199–218.

Bem, D. J. Self-perception: An alternative interpretation of cognitive dissonance phenomena. *Psychological Review*, 1967, **74**, 183–200.

Endleman, R. *Personality and social life*. New York: Random House, 1967.

Insko, C. A. *Theories of attitude change*. New York: Appleton-Century-Crofts, 1967.

Whiting, J. W. M., Kluckhohn, R., & Anthony, A. The function of male initiation ceremonies at puberty. In E. Maccoby, T. Newcomb, and E. Hartley (Eds.), *Readings in social psychology*. New York: Holt, Rinehart & Winston, 1958.

Young, F. W. The function of male initiation ceremonies: a cross-cultural test of an alternative hypothesis. *American Journal of Sociology*, 1962, **67**, 379–396.

Chapter 8

PRIMACY–RECENCY IN PERSONALITY IMPRESSION FORMATION

One of the more intriguing areas of research in social psychology is the investigation of the manner in which we form impressions of other people. The importance of being able to form an accurate "picture" of the people with whom we interact can hardly be overestimated. If we are to function properly, we must be able to predict how our actions will affect others and how they will react. If we have formed an accurate impression of others, then we are more likely to be able to predict their reactions to subsequent events. The problem, of course, is contained in the word "accurate," and in the fact that we rarely have complete knowledge of another person, i.e., we usually base our impressions on very limited amounts of information.

There have been relatively few theoretical statements about the process of impression formation. Much of the work in the area has been of a straight empirical sort in which subjects are given information about another and each is asked to form an impression of the other. Independent variables such as the amount of information given, the internal consistency of the information, and the spacing in time of the information have been manipulated. All the studies that we will discuss in this chapter have been concerned with one such variable—the order in which the information about another person is received. Suppose someone were described to you as being "intelligent, artistic, optimistic, humorless, unruly, and crafty." Chances are that you would have a more favorable impression of him than if he had been described as "crafty, unruly, humorless, optimistic, artistic, and intelligent." If, in fact, your final impression was more favorable after the first order, we would call this a primacy effect. If your impression was more favorable after the second, we would call this a recency effect. A primacy effect is simply the giving of more "weight" to the early items of information received about another, while a recency effect means that you attach more significance to the last items of information.

Much of the current work on primacy-recency in impression formation has developed out of earlier work on primacy-recency in persuasion, and there remains a great deal of common interest between the two lines of research. One could easily make the case that primacy-recency in impression formation is a subcategory under the more general topic of primacy-recency in persuasion. After all, when we are trying to form an impression of another person, we are really dealing with him as a concept about which we are seeking information.

Primacy-Recency in Persuasion

Almost fifty years ago Lund (1925) performed a very simple experiment which has since given rise to a great deal of controversy and research. Lund presented subjects with a brief communication advocating, for example, that a protective tariff was a wise policy for the United States. He then had the subjects indicate on an attitude scale the extent of their agreement with the communication, after which they were presented with a second communication which took the point of view exactly opposite to that of the first communication, i.e., that a protective tariff was not a wise policy for the U. S. The subjects then filled out the attitude scale a second time.

Counterbalancing was employed so that primacy-recency effects could be evaluated. That is, half of the subjects were presented the affirmative version first, while half were given the negative version first. Thus, if subjects given the affirmative version first ended up more in favor of the protective tariff and subjects given the negative version first ended up less in favor of the protective tariff, Lund assumed he would have evidence for a primacy effect. That, in fact, is what happened, and the subtitle of his research report was "The law of primacy in persuasion."

Such results, if upheld, would be extremely important. In a trial setting, it would imply that a defendant would have less chance of being acquitted if the prosecution's case were presented first. Such immediate extrapolations to real-life settings are dangerous. The real-life setting usually differs in many ways from the experimental setting. The most obvious difference between Lund's design and the presentation of evidence to a jury is that the jury does not reach a verdict after the prosecution's presentation and a second verdict after the defense's presentation. It may be that the primacy effect would not have been obtained by Lund if subjects had not indicated their agreement with the first communication before being exposed to the second. As Hovland and Mandell (1957) point out, the simple act of administering an opinion questionnaire after the first communication . . . "may have had the effect of requiring the subjects to review the arguments, formulate their own conclusions, and put their position 'on record'. . . . Thus . . . 'freezing' opinion and . . . causing individuals to be less likely to change their opinions once they had committed themselves on a questionnaire [p. 14]."

Some evidence in support of this possibility comes from an experiment by Cromwell (1950). The subjects in Cromwell's experiment were not required to indicate their own opinion on an issue until after they had been exposed to both affirmative and negative communications on the issue. Lund's design and results might be summarized as: First Communication, Questionnaire, Second Communication, Questionnaire → Primacy. Cromwell's design and results were: First Communication, Second Communication, Questionnaire → Recency.

Many people would be tempted to conclude at this point that the failure to obtain primacy effects in Cromwell's study must mean that the primacy effects in Lund's experiment were due to the "commitment" resulting from subjects expressing their opinions on the questionnaire after the first communication. Strictly speaking, however, comparison of the results of these two studies is not warranted. The results could be meaningfully compared only if we were sure that the presence or absence of the questionnaire after the first communication was the only difference between the two experiments. We are certainly not sure of that. Lund's study was performed many years before Cromwell's, with a different subject population, in a different setting, with a different procedure, with a gap in time between the first and second communications, etc. Any or all of these differences might be a factor in the different results. What was called for was a study which controlled all these aspects while, at the same time, it manipulated the presence or absence of a questionnaire after the first communication.

Hovland and Mandell (1957) set up an experimental design which incorporated both the Lund and Cromwell designs. Some subjects were requested to answer a questionnaire after the first communication, others were not, while all subjects filled out a belief questionnaire after both communications had been read. Three groups of subjects were put through the Lund replication procedure, and three groups through the procedure in which there was no intervening questionnaire between the first and second communications. The results were not very informative. Of the three groups put through the Lund procedure, two showed a nonsignificant recency effect, and one a significant primacy effect. Of the three groups put through the procedure without the intervening questionnaire, two showed nonsignificant primacy effects, and one a nonsignificant recency effect.

In attempting to come to grips with their failure to replicate clearly the Lund results, Hovland and Mandell decided to try a second experiment in which they would again follow Lund's procedure as closely as possible, but would use more "up-to-date" topics. The topics chosen for the second experiment concerned the sale of antihistamines without a prescription and the feasibility of atomic submarines (the study was carried out in 1949). Again, the results were not supportive of Lund's results. In fact, the only significant effect was a recency effect ($p < .01$) with the atomic submarine issue.

Hovland and Mandell sought to explain the differences between their results and Lund's in terms of the differences between the conditions of learning and of acceptance which were present in the experiments. For example, in Lund's research (but not Hovland and Mandell's) the experimenter was the regular classroom instructor. Thus, the motivation to learn and accept the first communication was probably higher in Lund's experiment. The second communication would not have met with the same reception, i.e., the students might have thought they were being tricked.

There are a number of other procedural factors which might explain the discrepant results, but Hovland and his colleagues were still interested in the "commitment" hypothesis. Hovland, Campbell, and Brock (1957) introduced a stronger form of commitment by requiring some subjects to write out their opinions for publication in a pamphlet after being exposed to the first communication. The prediction was, simply, that these subjects would be less influenced by a subsequent opposing communication than would subjects who had not publicly stated their opinion after the first communication. The data indicated some support for the hypothesis, but the effect was very weak.

A second experiment was carried out in which an attempt was made to strengthen the commitment manipulation even more. Subjects in the commitment condition of the experiment were told that the opinion statement they made after the first communication would be printed in their high school newspaper the following week. The result was similar to the first experiment. The commitment to an opinion following the first communication reduced the effect of the second communication. Hovland *et al.* (1957) maintain that the results ". . . appear to highlight the importance of socially mediated rewards. . . . An individual's close daily associates expect him to behave in a consistent and reliable manner. Under such circumstances an individual who contemplates revocation of a position he has publicly maintained may well anticipate some disparagement and negative social reinforcement from his associates if his attitude change becomes known to them. When the change in attitude remains anonymous, these effects are much less clear-cut [pp. 31–32]."

In the studies by Hovland and Mandell (1957) and Hovland *et al.* (1957) the interpretations involve a reinforcement analysis of the function of commitment in producing a primacy effect. The interpretations are loose, however, and are not particularly compelling. McGuire (1957) attempted to apply a more precise learning theory analysis to order effects within a communication. He hypothesized that if one received a series of messages from the same source, the receipt of each message could be viewed as a conditioning trial. The response to be conditioned was agreement with the source. Agreement with the source would be reinforcing for the subject if the source were arguing for something that the subject himself desired. For example, if the subject were a college student with a 7:00 A.M. class and the source were arguing that 7:00 A.M. classes should be abolished, agreement with the source would be reinforcing. A conditioning trial would have occurred. On the other hand, if the source were arguing that 6:00 A.M. classes should be begun—an undesirable state of affairs from the subject's point of view—agreement with the source is not reinforcing and an extinction trial would have occurred.

Applying this analysis to order effects, McGuire hypothesized that "when those messages supporting the likelihood of pleasant contingencies were presented first and those supporting the likelihood of unpleasant contingencies offered later, a greater total amount of agreement with the message contents would be evoked than when the messages were presented in reverse order, i.e., with the undesirable messages followed by the desirable ones [pp. 99–100]." To check on this hypothesis, McGuire exposed subjects to four communications from the same source. For each subject, two of the communications (H) took the position that an event which the subject had previously rated as desirable would, in fact, occur. The other two communications (L) argued that an event which the subject had previously rated as undesirable would occur. For half the subjects the communications were presented in the H-L order, and for the remaining subjects in the L-H order. Though somewhat weak, the results appeared to support the hypothesis. Subsequent to receipt of the communications, subjects in the H-L condition indicated greater overall agreement with the communicator's positions than did subjects in the L-H condition. Further, it appears that the order-effect was not due to a difference in the perception of the credibility of the communicator.

While the problems concerning order effects in persuasion were far from being solved at this point, at least two characteristics of the studies summarized thus far should be noted. First, the value of replications of research has been made apparent. Lund, on the basis of one experiment, postulated a "Law of Primacy in Persuasion." Hovland and Mandell, who were really interested in the "why" of the discrepancy between Lund's primacy effect and Cromwell's recency effect, found that they were unable to replicate Lund's results. Lund's results[1] appear to have been produced by any one of a number of extraneous variables and not by the variable of order of presentation which he was manipulating. The value of replications in different settings is, partly, that the extraneous variables are usually different. Hence, if the extraneous variables produced the first set of results, those results will not be replicated.

The second point we would like to make about the above studies is that a trend toward greater precision, not only of problem statement but of methodology, is apparent. Precision is not always the ideal in psychology. There are times when vague hunches and loose methodology are called for, but one of the things that has most impressed us in preparing this book is that in each of the content areas we cover, understanding of the processes involved appears directly related to the precision with which an investigator manipulated and controlled the variables he was interested in.

The trend toward refined methodology of primacy-recency studies was continued by Miller and Campbell (1959). So far we have looked at commitment and conditioning as possible factors in producing primacy-recency effects. Miller and Campbell were interested in the time intervals

[1] The "results" may not actually have been reliable at all. No significance tests are reported.

between the measures and communications as a possible factor in producing primacy or recency effects. One of the well-established findings in psychology is that memory for learned material decays in a negatively accelerated fashion. Applying this simple principle to the primacy-recency question, several predictions emerge which relate passage of time to memory for competing messages. To generate their predictions, however, Miller and Campbell made one additional assumption. They noted that there does appear to be some advantage, as far as acceptance is concerned, for the first information or message received—a primacy or prior entry effect. Applying these two assumptions, they set up four conditions which are represented in Figure 11.

Inspection of Figure 11 reveals the bases for Miller and Campbell's predictions. In condition 1, there is not enough difference between the strength of association for communications A and B for either primacy or recency to be predicted. A similar situation occurs in condition number 4. In condition number 2, however, the strength of association to communication A is sufficiently higher than that for communication B, so a primacy effect was predicted. In condition number 3, the strength of association for communication B^1 is sufficiently higher than that for communication A, so that a recency effect was predicted. These predictions were, in fact, borne out by the data that Miller and Campbell collected.

Thus, we have another determinant of primacy-recency. Hovland and

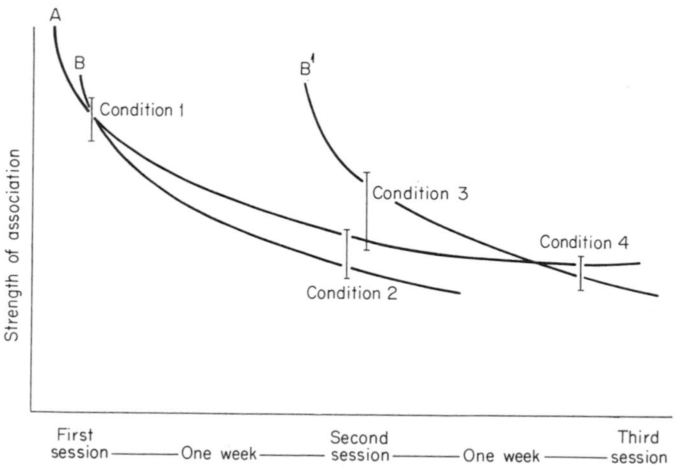

Fig. 11. Hypothetical forgetting curves for two competing communications with an added primacy effect; the primacy effect is represented by the higher initial starting point and final asymptote of line A in comparison with lines B or B^1. (From Miller and Campbell, 1959.)

his associates were interested in commitment to an opinion after only one communication as a producer of primacy effects. McGuire demonstrated that "conditioning" of the agreement response can also produce primacy effects. Miller and Campbell have demonstrated that the time intervals between the communications themselves and between the communications and the measures of effectiveness can be important determinants of whether or not one obtains primacy or recency.

It is important to realize that had Miller-Campbell based their predictions solely on forgetting curves, they would have predicted only recency effects. In order for them to predict primacy effects they had to make the additional assumption of a prior entry effect, i.e., of an advantage for the first message. This means ". . . an initially higher level for the first message at its onset than for the second message at its highest and, correspondingly, a higher eventual asymptotic level of strength for the first message than for the second. Under this assumption, a manifest or net primacy can occur . . . [but] . . . note that such a primacy effect does *not* occur *instead of* a recency effect but, rather, *in addition* to a recency effect [Miller and Campbell, 1959, pp. 2–3]."

A model devised by Anderson and Hovland (1957) and tested by Anderson (1959) also predicts a recency effect, but for quite different reasons. The basic assumption made in the model is that the amount of change produced by an influence attempt is directly related to the amount of change advocated. For example, suppose someone believes that the proper amount of sleep each night is eight hours. The above assumption is that that person would change his opinion more in response to a communication advocating only six hours of sleep per night than in response to one advocating seven hours of sleep per night. This is a very simple assumption. Anderson and Hovland present the following equation for X_1, the opinion after exposure to a communication advocating position C:

$$X_1 = X_0 + S\,(C - X_0)$$

In the equation, X_0 represents the initial opinion and S is a proportionality factor. Anderson and Hovland (1957) give the following example to illustrate the operation of the model in a pro-con presentation:

> . . . it will be assumed that the initial attitude of the recipient is 5; that the position of the con communication is 2, and that of the pro communication 8, on the attitude continuum; and that each communication moves the recipient halfway from his current position toward the position of the communication presented (i.e., with no change in susceptibility to influence). Then after presenting the pro communication, the new attitude will be $X_1 = 5 + \frac{1}{2}\,(8 - 5) = 6.50$; change $= +1.50$. Presenting now the con communication, the new attitude will

be $X_2 = 6.5 + \frac{1}{2}\ (2 - 6.5) = 4.25$; change $= -2.25$. . . . An important implication for the problem of order effects is readily seen. With no change in susceptibility of the recipient (e.g., no commitment effect, no increased attentiveness, etc.) we should *not* anticipate that the two communication effects will cancel. . . . Rather, it is to be expected that a recency effect . . . will be produced [pp. 160–161].

An additional prediction from the model is that if a subject is presented a series of communications all arguing for position *C* (and assuming the proportionality factor *S* is constant), one would obtain an exponential growth curve for the subject's opinion as a function of the number of communications he had received. The growth curve would, of course, approach *C* as an asymptote. Suppose, for example, the scale distance between the subject's initial position, X_0, and the position advocated by the communication is 4 units, and that $S = \frac{1}{2}$. Then, in response to the first communication, the subject will move 2 units toward *C* (i.e., $\frac{1}{2} \times 4 = 2$). The distance between the subject's position and the position advocated by the communications is now 2 units. In response to the second communication, the subject will move 1 unit (i.e., $\frac{1}{2} \times 2 = 1$). In response to the third communication, he will move .5 units (i.e., $\frac{1}{2} \times 1 = .5$), etc. Anderson (1959) presented subjects with prosecution and defense arguments from a court trial under a number of different conditions and, in general, found strong support for the above two predictions, a recency effect and the exponential growth of opinion in response to a series of communications advocating the same position.

Anderson had made one other prediction which was not supported by his data. Suppose that some subjects are given a communication advocating position A, followed by a communication advocating position B, and other subjects are given the two communications in B-A order. "If each group is then administered the same sequence of further communications, the mean opinions of the two groups will converge toward equality [p. 372]." This prediction was not fully supported by the data, a consequence which led Anderson to the following formulation. He assumed that an opinion has "two components: a basal component which is relatively little affected by the communication once it is formed, and a superficial component which is quite labile, and which obeys the original model [p. 379]." Anderson admits that this is largely speculation, but it has a familiar ring. It often seems that our impressions of others follow a similar model. That is, once our "basal impression" of another has been formed, it seems to be little affected by new, and often contradictory, information that we receive about the other. Such a statement is at best tremendously oversimplified, of course, and at worst totally incorrect.

Let us focus in, then, on what is known about primacy-recency effects in impression formation.

The studies that we have discussed thus far are obviously of importance to impression formation, and the separation of studies of primacy-recency in persuasion from studies of primacy-recency in impression formation has been maintained simply for clarity of exposition. As we will see, the trends and findings of studies in the two areas are very similar.

Primacy-Recency in Impression Formation

The classic paper in the area of impression formation was published by Asch in 1946. In it he reports the results of ten experiments in which subjects were read short lists of adjectives describing a person and were asked to form an impression of that person. The most widely known of those ten experiments are the ones which deal with the centrality of particular traits. Of interest here, however, are his experiments VI, VII, and VIII which deal with the effects of the order in which the traits are presented.

In the first of these experiments, Asch selected six traits which seemed to him to range from highly favorable (intelligent) to highly unfavorable (envious). The traits were read to two groups of subjects and the subjects were then asked to write out a brief sketch of the person described by the traits, as well as to indicate which adjectives from a check list applied to the person. The first group was read the list in descending order: A. intelligent-industrious-impulsive-critical-stubborn-envious. For the second group, the traits were read in the reverse order, i.e., the most unfavorable quality first and the most favorable last: B. envious-stubborn-critical-impulsive-industrious-intelligent. The two groups of subjects ended up with quite different pictures of the "person" described by the set of traits.

Asch quotes (p. 270) from the descriptions written by subjects to illustrate the nature of the difference between the impressions produced by the two orders:

> A—The person is intelligent and fortunately he puts his intelligence to work. That he is stubborn and impulsive may be due to the fact that he knows what he is saying and what he means and will not therefore give in easily to someone else's idea which he disagrees with.
>
> B—This person's good qualities such as industry and intelligence are bound to be restricted by jealousy and stubbornness. The person is emotional. He is

unsuccessful because he is weak and allows his bad points to cover up his good ones.

The adjective check list data reveal similar sorts of differences in impression. More of the subjects who were read list A saw the stimulus person described by the list as generous, happy, restrained, strong, etc. Thus, these subjects had, in general, a much more favorable impression than did subjects exposed to the list in reverse order. The effect is clearly a primacy effect, but what interpretation are we to give?

Asch argues that the first few traits give a direction to the impression, and that the following traits are interpreted with respect to that direction. This is nicely illustrated in the two quotations above. The trait "stubborn" has a very favorable connotation in the first quote, i.e., it is the stubbornness of an intelligent person who knows he's right. In the second quote it is tied with jealousy and connotes a certain childish pettiness about minor points. There was obviously an active interpretive process going on. Subjects were not just accepting the individual traits as elements to be summed for the total impression. Instead, they seemed to interpret each new trait in light of the ones they had already received.

In his next experiment (number VII), Asch (1946) decided to try a set of traits in which there was no gradual change in the favorableness of the set as there had been in the preceding study. Instead he used one "highly dubious trait" (evasive) and this trait was introduced at either the beginning or end of a set of otherwise favorable traits. Again, two groups of subjects were used; subjects in the first group heard the traits read in this order: intelligent-skillful-industrious-determined-practical-cautious-evasive. Subjects in the second group were read the traits in this order: evasive-cautious-practical-determined-industrious-skillful-intelligent. As expected, the results were quite similar to those of the preceding experiment. Subjects exposed to the first order formed more favorable impressions than those exposed to the second order.

In the next study (number VIII), Asch (1946) took the sequence of traits: intelligent-industrious-impulsive-critical-stubborn-envious, and divided it into two parts: A. intelligent-industrious-impulsive, and B. critical-stubborn-envious. Subjects in one group were read the two sets separately and were told that each set of three traits described a different person. They were asked to form an impression of each of these two people, to write out a sketch for the two, and then to respond to the adjective check list for the two. Following all this, they were told that the six traits actually described one person, and that they should form an impression of that person. A second group of subjects was told at the outset that the two lists of traits described only one person. The latter subjects were asked to form an impression of one person who had all six traits.

The subjects who had initially formed impressions of two distinct people, and who had committed themselves to these impressions in writing the sketches they were asked to write, experienced a great deal of difficulty in merging these two impressions into one. On the other hand, subjects who had initially been told that only one person was being described by the six traits seemed to experience little difficulty in forming an impression of that person.

These studies seem to point to three important factors. First is that we see what appears to be strong evidence for a primacy effect in impression formation, and that old saw about "first impressions" may really have something to it. Second, the last experiment noted above returns to the factor of commitment which we discussed in connection with the work of Hovland and his associates. Third, Asch's notion that the earliest information about another person sets the tone or direction for the interpretation of later information is an intriguing possibility, and we shall return to it later.

Luchins (1957) felt that fuller descriptions of the stimulus person were needed if one wanted to investigate primacy-recency in impression formation. Specifically, Luchins felt that Asch had erred in giving subjects lists of *discrete traits* and having them attempt to form an impression of the person described by those traits. Luchins argued that in a typical real-life setting we are not given such lists; rather, we base our impressions on the behavior of others.

Thus, Luchins constructed two paragraphs, both describing someone named Jim. In the first of these, E, Jim was described as outgoing and friendly. In the second, I, Jim was described as withdrawn and introverted. In neither of the paragraphs was a list of Jim's characteristics or traits given, however. Each paragraph described only a sample of Jim's behavior. The two paragraphs follow (Luchins, 1957, pp. 34–35).

> E—Jim left the house to get some stationery. He walked out into the sun-filled street with two of his friends, basking in the sun as he walked. Jim entered the stationery store which was full of people. Jim talked with an acquaintance while he waited for the clerk to catch his eye. On his way out, he stopped to chat with a school friend who was just coming into the store. Leaving the store, he walked toward school. On his way out he met the girl to whom he had been introduced the night before. They talked for a short while, and then Jim left for school.
>
> I—After school Jim left the classroom alone. Leaving the school, he started on his long walk home. The street was brilliantly filled with sunshine. Jim walked down the street on the shady side. Coming down the street toward him, he saw the pretty girl whom he had met on the previous evening. Jim crossed the street and entered a candy store. The store was crowded with students and he noticed

a few familiar faces. Jim waited quietly until the counterman caught his eye and then gave his order. Taking his drink, he sat down at a side table. When he had finished his drink he went home.

Using these two paragraphs as his basic stimulus material, Luchins carried out a number of experiments on primacy-recency in impression formation.

The first experiment utilized four conditions. In one condition subjects read the E paragraph and then indicated whether they thought Jim to be friendly or unfriendly. In the second condition subjects read only the I paragraph before indicating whether they thought Jim to be friendly or unfriendly (shy). In the remaining two conditions, subjects read both the E and I paragraphs which were run together as one paragraph, but some read the two in IE order, and others in EI order. The responses of those exposed to the IE order were very much like those who read only the I description. Conversely, the responses of those exposed to the EI order were very much like those who read only the E description. In short, there were strong primacy effects for those subjects who read both the E and I descriptions of Jim.

In his second experiment, Luchins utilized essentially the same procedure—i.e., four conditions E, I, IE, and EI—but included a large number of dependent measures in an attempt to gather more information about the impressions formed by subjects in each of the four conditions. The new dependent measures asked a number of questions about Jim, and each subject was asked to write a brief sketch describing his impressions of Jim. Again, strong primacy effects were apparent. Only about one-fifth of the subjects who read both paragraphs (in IE or EI order) wrote descriptions of Jim which appeared equally influenced by both E and I blocks of information. Questioning of a sample of subjects from the EI and IE conditions revealed that the majority of them were unaware that the two paragraphs were contradictory.

A third experiment yielded similar results. Strong primacy effects were even evident in items that subjects inferred about Jim, items which were not mentioned in the paragraphs. Also, about two-thirds of the subjects exposed to the EI and IE paragraphs said they noticed either no or only slight discrepancies in the descriptions.

There are a number of possible explanations for the primacy effect obtained, and Luchins discusses six. First, it is quite possible that someone who notices discrepancies in the description of Jim could explicitly decide that one of the paragraphs is the "true" Jim, and respond on the basis of that paragraph. This did, in fact, happen with a few subjects, but Luchins assures us that this was a very infrequent occurrence. Two other possible, but unlikely, explanations concern serial learning effects and interference. Serial learning effects refer to the finding from experimental psychology that humans, when asked to learn a list of items, learn the first and last items most quickly. Interference refers to the possibility that learning of the second paragraph may have been hindered by the previous learning and memory of the first paragraph. Neither of these explanations seems appropriate here. The amount of "learning" required appears too small for these phenomena to play a role.

A more likely explanation is Luchins' suggestion that subjects may have paid more attention to the first than the second paragraph. Most people assume that others are consistent in their behavior. Thus, they may have attended closely to the first paragraph to get a picture of Jim, and then skimmed over the second paragraph assuming that it was "just more of the same." Related to this is the fifth possibility mentioned by Luchins, i.e., that subjects accepted the first paragraph as being the "true Jim" and were then more critical of the second paragraph, perhaps discounting it as due to a bad day that Jim had had.

The interpretation that Luchins finally puts his faith in is a version of the old idea of set. In experimental psychology, set refers to a readiness to perceive or respond in a certain way. This is clearly related to Asch's idea that the first few traits give a direction to the impression formed. The later traits are interpreted in light of the embryonic impression formed on the basis of the first few traits. If the primacy effect is due to a set being established by the first trait or first few traits, then the primacy effect should be reduced if we introduce variables which "break" the set. To check on this possibility, Luchins conducted the following experiment.

One group of subjects was given the standard EI or IE materials to read. A second group of subjects was warned, prior to reading about Jim, against letting their first impression dominate. A third group of subjects read the E (or I) paragraph, were warned about making snap judgments, and then read the I (or E) paragraph. A fourth group of subjects read the E (or I) description, performed some simple arithmetic tasks, and then read the I (or E) description. The results were as predicted. The standard primacy effect appeared in the group exposed only to the EI or IE material. The primacy effect was reduced among subjects who had been warned in advance against making snap judgments. A slight recency effect appeared when subjects were warned against snap judgments between reading the E and I material. Finally, performance of an unrelated task between reading the E and I description resulted in a pronounced recency effect—i.e., the description read last was most influential in determining the final impression.

The results appear to offer some support to the set notion, but the data are somewhat ambiguous. Are the recency effects in the interpolated warning and interpolated task conditions really due to a break in set? A simpler explanation is simply that these two conditions had a longer time interval between the first description and the measurement of effects. Subjects in the other two conditions were given no time out between reading the first and second descriptions. The work by Miller and Campbell (1959) which we referred to earlier would lead us to expect that time is an important variable in such experiments, and the time factor was uncontrolled in Luchins' experiment.

Another problem with Luchins' work is that he used only the two paragraphs about Jim and did not sample a variety of such stimulus materials to see if other such descriptions would produce the same effects. There might be something peculiar to these two paragraphs which produces primacy effects. In the following article, Anderson and Barrios (1961) point out several other shortcomings and address themselves specifically to the question of what happens to order effects when one is exposed to a number of communications on separate issues. The article by Anderson and Barrios also exemplifies a turning toward greater precision and control in the study of impression formation. Anderson and Barrios return, in their discussion section, to a consideration of alternative hypotheses of impression formation, and their methodology provides a way of checking out the contribution of these alternative possibilities.

Primacy Effects in Personality Impression Formation[1]

Norman H. Anderson and Alfred A. Barrios

Studies in communication research have reached no consensus as to the effect of order of presentation. The pro-con versus con-pro paradigm leads sometimes to primacy effects (greater effect of the first communication) and sometimes to recency effects. Although some progress has been made in the study of the relevant variables (Anderson, 1959; Hovland *et al.*,

[1] From the *Journal of Abnormal and Social Psychology*, 1961, **63**, No. 2, 346–350. Received October 6, 1960. Reproduced by permission of the publisher.

This research was supported by Grant M-3502 (A) from the National Institute of Mental Health.

At the time of writing the authors were with the University of California at Los Angeles. Current affiliations: Anderson, University of California at San Diego; Barrios, East Los Angeles Community College.

1957a; Luchins, 1958; Miller & Campbell, 1959), the situation is far from clear.

One limitation of most work is the small number, typically two, of communications involved. Two experiments (Anderson, 1959; Weld & Roff, 1938) have used reasonably long sequences of communications on a single topic. However, no work has been done to assess practice effects over a sequence of communications on separate topics. Both lines of attack are desirable, not only because they simulate everyday situations more closely, but also for theoretical reasons. Thus, Hovland (1957b) has emphasized some of the ways in which prior familiarity with the topic might influence reception and acceptance of the communications. Analogous considerations would apply when a sequence of different topics is used, and various practice effects might also be important. The two cited paradigms would thus be expected to be useful in bringing the relevant psychological processes under closer experimental scrutiny.

The present experiment was designed to study order effects over a sequence of communications on separate issues. The classic paper of Asch (1946) suggested the use of personality adjectives in order to get a large body of relatively homogeneous material. Asch's results, as well as those of Luchins (1957, 1958), indicated that under the specific experimental conditions employed here, primacy effects would be obtained for the initial trials. However, it was thought that with continued practice the primacy effect would decrease and perhaps become a recency effect.

Method

Subjects

Volunteers who were fulfilling a class requirement in introductory psychology were assigned randomly to the various conditions within each experiment. Sex was balanced in Experiment 1 but not in Experiment 2. The *N*s for the two experiments were 64 and 24, respectively. Subjects were examined individually.

Stimuli

A set of 328 adjectives descriptive of personality characteristics were picked on the basis of familiarity by the experimenter and were then given a rough scaling based on the responses of 10 judges. The judges rated each adjective on a six-point Favorable-Unfavorable scale which had an additional "X" rating for unfamiliar words. The 25 adjectives that received an X were not used. The mean ratings of the remaining adjectives ranged from 0.1 to 4.8, with a rating of 5 corresponding to Very Favorable. The 48 adjectives in the range 4.0–4.3 will be called H; the 48 adjectives in the range 1.2–2.5 will be called L. Table 2 shows some of the adjectives that were used.

Procedure

Subjects were told that they would be read a number of sets of adjectives, each set describing a different person, and that they should try to form an impression of the kind of person the adjectives described. The instructions indicated that they were to think of the six adjectives as having been given by six different people who knew that person well. After the experimenter read each set, the subject indicated his response numerically in terms of a rating scale typed on a card in front of him. This eight-step scale ranged from +4 to —4, the neutral response being disallowed. An identifying label was placed by each number using the various combinations of Favorable and Unfavorable, with Highly, Considerably, Moderately, and Slightly as modifiers.

Experiment 1

Each subject judged 61 or 62 sets of six adjectives each. One of these sets was the same as that used by Asch (1946, Experiment VI). It was used as the first set for half the subjects, and as the last set for the other half. Within each of these halves, the set was given in forward order to half the subjects and in reverse order to the other half. Those subjects who received this set as their first set also received it as their last set.

The remaining sets were of five types. Type HL consisted of three adjectives in the H range followed by three adjectives in the L range of scale values. Type LH had three L adjectives followed by three H adjectives. Type GD was a sequence of six adjectives gradually descending from H to L in scale value. Type GA gradually ascended from L to H. Type R consisted of six adjectives chosen similarly to the other sets but arranged in random order within a set. Twelve sets of each type were constructed randomly subject to the restriction that no adjective appear twice in any set and that each adjective be used about equally often.

Six ordered blocks of 10 sets each were constructed randomly subject to the restriction that two sets of each type appear in each block. Four sequences of 60 sets were obtained using four different permutations of the six blocks. From these four sequences, four additional sequences were formed by reversing the order of the adjectives in the 60 sets. The GD, GA, and R sets were completely reversed in order. However, the H and L subsets in the HL and LH sets were simply interchanged without disturbing the order of the three adjectives within either subset.

The adjectives of each set were read by the experimenter at an approximate rate of one adjective each 3 seconds. Three trials were given each minute until all the sets had been judged.

Experiment 2

Each subject judged 90 sets of two adjectives each, 30 HL, 30 LH, 15 LL, and 15 HH. These sets were constructed as in Experiment 1 and balanced for type in ordered blocks of 30 sets each. Half the subjects received the sets in one sequence; the other half received the same sequence but with the order of the two adjectives in the LH and in the HL sets reversed.

The main independent variable was the time between the reading of the first and second adjectives of a set. Each subject judged one block of 30 sets at each of three time intervals: 0, 2, and 4 seconds. All six possible sequences of time intervals were used in a latin square design. Successive blocks were separated by 1 minute during which the subject was told that a new tempo would be used for the following block.

Results

EXPERIMENT 1

If an HL set produces a higher response than the corresponding LH set, then the first subset of three adjectives had a stronger effect than the second subset, within at least one of the two sets. Positive HL-LH differences, and positive GD-GA differences thus represent primacy effects. These two difference scores were computed for each subject using the several adjectives of each type in a given block of trials.

The results are shown in Fig. 1 which plots mean difference scores for the four main experimental conditions as a function of trial blocks. It is seen that there is a strong primacy effect which equals 0.69 averaged over all conditions. Although the effect decreases somewhat over trials, it does not appear to be approaching zero. Females show more primacy than males but this sex difference resides largely in the HL-LH sets. Indeed, the sexes are not too far apart on the GD-GA curves and, compared to these, the males are lower and the females are higher on the HL-LH curves.

The analysis of these data was performed on the difference scores summed over all 60 trials and is given in Table 1. Since a difference score was used, the F for Mean shows a significant primacy effect. Although the

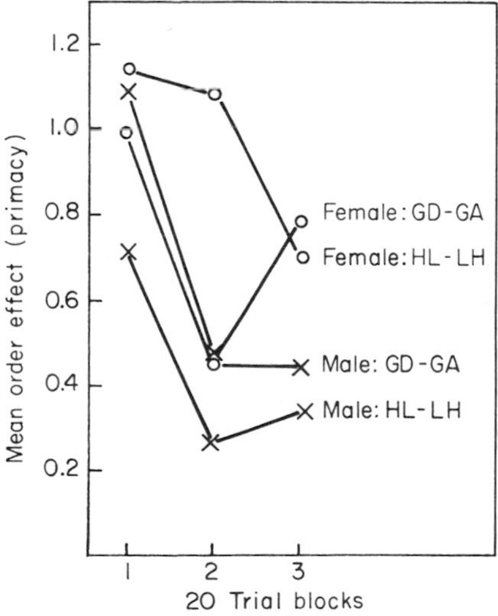

Fig. 1. Mean primacy scores as a function of sex, type of set, and trial blocks. (Experiment 1.)

TABLE 1
Analysis of Variance of Order Effect Scores Summed over All Trials

Source	*df*	*F*
Mean	1	48.38[a]
Sex	1	2.23
Error (b)	62	(183.81)[b]
Type	1	.02
Sex × Type	1	8.03[a]
Error (w)	62	(83.77)[b]

[a] $p < .05$.
[b] Error mean squares in parentheses.

main effect of Sex is not significant, the significant Sex × Type interaction verifies the comments on sex differences made in the preceding paragraph. A trend test showed that the decline of the primacy effect with trials was significant ($F = 12.27$, $df = 1/60$).

The absolute responses, as distinguished from the difference scores, are also of interest. The mean response over all descending sets (HL and GD) was 0.94, and the mean response over all ascending sets (LH and GA) was 0.25. This latter value is quite close to the mean response of 0.32 for the R sets. Since the adjectives for the R sets were from the same pool as for the other sets, the asymmetry of these results suggests that the primacy effect has its source in the initial adjectives of the descending sets. However, this suggestion must be viewed with caution since, although the HL-LH and GD-GA order effects were almost identical, the mean response to GA and LH sets was 0.48 and 0.02, respectively.

Results from the set used by Asch (1946) were consistent with the above. When this set was given first, the means were 0.87 and —0.94 for the GD and GA orders, respectively. The primacy effect of 1.81 was significant ($F = 6.87$, $df = 1/30$). The primacy effect was just half as large when the set was given last and this was nonsignificant, even when all 64 subjects were used.

Of the 48 critical sets used, all but 5 gave a primacy effect. The descending versions of the 6 sets which showed the greatest overall mean primacy effect are listed in Table 2.

Experiment 2

The overall mean scores for the HH, HL, LH, and LL sets were 2.68, 0.80, 0.76, and —1.27, respectively. The analysis of variance was performed on the HL-LH scores computed for the three successive blocks of 30 trials. Neither time interval nor trial blocks approached signifi-

TABLE 2
Mean Response to Six Sets Showing Strongest Primacy Effects

Type	Words	Descending order	Ascending order	Mean primacy
GD	smart, artistic, sentimental, cool, awkward, faultfinding	1.38	−0.72	2.10
HL	determined, tolerant, gentle, stubborn, forgetful, tricky	1.62	−0.16	1.78
GD	orderly, entertaining, humble, cool, calculating, moody	1.84	0.44	1.40
HL	efficient, scholarly, smart, crafty, faultfinding, unruly	0.66	−0.66	1.32
GD	warm, independent, optimistic, reserved, tough, faultfinding	1.69	0.41	1.28
HL	patriotic, perfective, generous, softhearted, uninhibited, humorless	1.84	0.59	1.25

cance. The 95% confidence interval for the overall mean order effect was 0.04 ± 0.12. It thus seems reasonable to conclude that the true order effect is rather small when only two adjectives are used. Supporting evidence is found by comparing Error (b) to Error (w) which tests for individual differences. The resulting F ($df = 17/36$) was 1.19. Because of the great power of the F test with this many df, it seems reasonable to conclude that true individual differences in the order effect are also quite small when only two adjectives are used.

Discussion

The primacy effect that was found is striking. Over the first block of 10 trials, the mean difference in response obtained from simply reversing the order of the six adjectives was 1.12. This is a respectable part of the eightpoint scale, especially since few subjects used the full scale range. Moreover, the result is not due to some peculiarity of the particular sets used since they were constructed randomly and since a primacy effect was observed in 43 of the 48 sets. However, it is not clear how far the results may be generalized beyond the experimental situation used here. The need for some caution in this respect is indicated by the work of Luchins (1957, 1958) who finds that the order effect changes with variations in the procedure.

The decline in primacy over the later trials has a number of possible causes. It may be that, despite the use of the random sets, the pattern of good and bad words in the remaining sets brings about an increased tendency to take account of all the words in each set. This possibility could perhaps be tested by reducing the relative frequency of the critical sets. A progressive loss of interest in the task might also influence the primacy effect, a hypothesis which would be testable by inserting a rest and motivating instructions partway through the session. A third possibility is that adaptation to the experimental situation and practice in integrating the material are the governing factors. If so, the decrement in primacy found here indicates that caution should be used in generalizing results of studies employing only one or two communications.

The results of an earlier experiment (Anderson, 1959) were interpreted as suggesting the existence of two opinion components. The basal component, once formed, was quite resistant to change whereas the surface component was readily influenced by the successive communications. The present data would be consistent with the two-component hypothesis if it were assumed that a strong basal component was formed over the first three but not the last three adjectives within a given set. Thus for an HL set, the surface component induced by the three H adjectives would be approximately canceled by the surface component induced by the three L adjectives. However, the basal component induced by the three H adjectives would persist to produce a response toward the Favorable end of the scale. For the corresponding LH set, the basal component would tend to produce a response toward the Unfavorable end of the scale, and the difference between the two would constitute the primacy effect.

The two-component hypothesis is thus not inconsistent with the present data but other explanations cannot be ruled out. In particular, the primacy effect may result from a progressive decrease in attention over the adjectives of a given set. Attention decrement could presumably be reduced by more stringent control or at least tested by asking subjects to recall the adjectives (McGuire, 1957).

It should also be noted that in the present situation the basal component would be equivalent in effect to and perhaps explainable in terms of Luchins' (1957) Einstellung, or Asch's (1946) concept of direction. However, a two-component interpretation suggests a test which the other two formulations do not. For consider the order effect paradigm defined by the two sets, HLH′L′ versus HLL′H′, in which the first six adjectives are the same in both sets and the last six differ only in order of presentation. According to hypothesis, only the surface component is affected over the last six adjectives and hence (Anderson, 1959) the paradigm should yield a recency effect. Although this prediction must be considered rather speculative, the use of this and similar paradigms should prove valuable in the study of opinion and impression formation.

Experiment 2 was designed on the assumption that a considerable crystallization of impression had occurred in the first half of the sets in Experiment 1. It was thought that the primacy effect would increase as increased time was allowed for the first adjective to sink in. Even though the reduction from six to two adjectives was expected to decrease the overall effect, the finding of negligible order effects in Experiment 2 came as a surprise in view of the strong primacy obtained in Experiment 1. The results of Experiment 2 thus give no evident support to Asch's (1946) hypothesis that the first adjective sets up a directed impression in terms of which the later adjectives are interpreted. However, the combined results of the two experiments give some basis for speculating that the critical events leading to primacy in Experiment 1 occurred at the second and third adjectives.

Summary

Sets of Favorable and Unfavorable adjectives descriptive of general personality characteristics were constructed so as to test for effect of order of presentation of the adjectives. The sets were read to subjects who were asked how favorable an impression they had of the person described by the set of adjectives.

In Experiment 1, 64 subjects each judged some 60 sets of six adjectives each. Strong primacy effects were found although there was some decrement over trials. Females showed greater primacy than males for sets in which the change from Favorable to Unfavorable (and vice versa) was abrupt. However, there was little sex difference when the change was gradual.

In Experiment 2, 24 subjects each judged 90 sets of two adjectives each, with intervals of 0, 2, and 4 seconds between the adjectives. Time interval had no observable effect and order of presentation was also nonsignificant.

REFERENCES

Anderson, N. H. Test of a model for opinion change. *Journal of Abnormal and Social Psychology,* 1959, **59,** 371–381.

Asch, S. E. Forming impressions of personality. *Journal of Abnormal and Social Psychology,* 1946, **41,** 258–290.

Hovland, C. I., Mandell, W., Campbell, Enid H., Brock, T., Luchins, A. S., Cohen, A. R., McGuire, W. J., Janis, I. L., Feierabend, Rosalind L., & Anderson, N. H. *The order of presentation in persuasion.* New Haven: Yale University Press, 1957. (a)

Hovland, C. I. Summary and implications. In C. I. Hovland *et al., The order of presentation in persuasion.* New Haven: Yale Univer. Press, 1957. Pp. 129–157. (b)

Luchins, A. S. Experimental attempts to minimize the impact of first impressions. In

C. I. Hovland *et al., The order of presentation in persuasion.* New Haven: Yale Univer. Press, 1957. Pp. 62–75.

Luchins, A. S. Definitiveness of impression and primacy-recency in communications. *Journal of Social Psychology,* 1958, **48,** 275–290.

McGuire, W. J. Order of presentation as a factor in "conditioning" persuasiveness. In C. I. Hovland *et al., The order of presentation in persuasion.* New Haven: Yale Univer. Press, 1957. Pp. 98–114.

Miller, N., & Campbell, D. T. Recency and primacy in persuasion as a function of the timing of speeches and measurements. *Journal of Abnormal and Social Psychology,* 1959, **59,** 1–9.

Weld, H. P., & Roff, M. A study in the formation of opinion based upon legal evidence. *American Journal of Psychology,* 1938, **51,** 609–628.

Discussion

As we mentioned earlier, the article by Anderson and Barrios (1961) appears to represent a turning point in the study of impression formation. Greater control over the stimulus material is one of the salient improvements when these two experiments are compared with earlier research. For example, in the first of the experiments by Asch (1946) that we discussed in the introduction to this chapter, the traits which were presented to subjects were selected because they "seemed to range from highly favorable (intelligent) to highly dubious (envious)." There was no independent check on whether or not subjects did perceive the ordering as ranging along the continuum which Asch assumed. Anderson and Barrios (1961) did institute a check on the perceptions of the adjectives that they used as stimuli. They had a group of judges rate each of a list of potential stimulus adjectives on a six point "favorableness" scale. The adjectives actually used were selected on the basis of the mean ratings assigned by these judges. Thus, they did not have to trust their intuitions as to whether subjects would see "artistic" as being more or less favorable than "smart."

One of the nice features of the first experiment Anderson and Barrios reported is that a large number of sets of adjectives were used. Asch had used one set of six adjectives and there was the distinct possibility that his results might have been peculiar to that set of adjectives. When primacy effects are obtained with a large number of different sets of adjectives, we feel more confident that the finding is a true effect and not an idiosyncracy of one particular selection of adjectives.

The relationship between experiments I and II in the Anderson and Barrios (1961) paper is puzzling, however. In experiment I, subjects were read sets of six adjectives, each set supposedly describing a different person. The adjectives within each set were read at a rate of about one every three seconds. This procedure produced strong primacy effects which, even though the magnitude decreased over trials, were still present after sixty such sets. One of several possible explanations for such primacy effects was advanced originally by Asch (1946) ; he said that the initial adjectives in a set form the seeds of an impression which then influences the interpretation of the later adjectives in a set. Anderson and Barrios reasoned that if one manipulated the time allowed for this initial impression to "sink in," one should be able to enhance or reduce the primacy effect. If the Asch interpretation were correct, the primacy effect would be enhanced when the subject had a longer time to think about the first information received, and reduced when there was no time for the initial impression to crystallize. What was called for, then, was to repeat the first experiment with a number of added conditions in which the time interval between adjectives in a set was manipulated.

Unfortunately, this was not done. Anderson and Barrios used only sets of two adjectives each in their second experiment. Hence, they did not replicate the conditions of the first experiment and the second experiment does not give us any information on the "crystallization of impression" hypothesis. There is another curious thing about the second experiment that involves the time intervals selected (0, 2, and 4 seconds) . The time interval between adjectives in the first experiment was "approximately three seconds." In view of the hypothesis they were investigating, it would have made sense to include in the second experiment a time interval significantly shorter than three seconds (0, which was included) , and a time interval significantly longer than three seconds (which was not included) .

Thus, the hypothesis proposed by Asch, and the related two-component hypothesis proposed by Anderson (1959) , remain in contention as explanations for the primacy effect in impression formation. Another possibility is mentioned by Anderson and Barrios (1961) , i.e., the attention decrement hypothesis, suggesting that subjects may simply pay less attention to the later adjectives in a set. Luchins (1957) referred to a similar idea earlier when he argued that we expect others to be consistent and after attending to the first information we receive about another we pay less attention to later information expecting it to be "more of the same." We do not seem to have eliminated any of the explanations for primacy. We do have a paradigm in the first experiment by Anderson and Barrios that seems to be a reasonably precise methodology for pursuing the various explanations.

In a brief review Lana (1964) found the set hypothesis to be the most adequate explanation for primacy when the stimulus materials were unfamiliar to the subject. However, there are several explanations he did not consider, and since 1964 there has been a great deal of research on primacy-recency in impression formation.

Anderson and Norman (1964) wanted to see if the primacy effect found by Asch (1946), Anderson and Barrios (1961), and others would obtain when the descriptive items were not descriptive of a person. "Thus, the subject was read a set of items describing a person, or a meal, or a newspaper, or a week in his life, and asked how much he would like the event or object so described (Anderson and Norman, 1964, p. 467)." For example, when the subject was presented items in a "meal set" he was asked to judge how much he would like a meal which consisted of six dishes (like steak, turnips, sherbet, etc.). One of the nice features of the Anderson and Norman study was that the stimuli were individually tailored for each subject. That is, in a preliminary session subjects had rated how much they liked each of a number of foods. From these ratings, foods were selected which the subject had rated as very likeable (H) and as unlikeable (L). Sets of six foods were then composed on the basis of these ratings so that order effects could be studied (HHHLLL) or (LLLHHH).

The findings revealed primacy effects with foods, adjectives, and headlines, but not when the stimuli were "life events." Anderson and Norman argue that the primacy effect obtained with food items is evidence against the set or directed impression explanation of primacy. "For foods, an interpretation of the primacy in terms of contextual shifts in meaning is not even plausible. Certainly, the objective meaning of 'turnips,' say, should be the same whether it precedes or follows 'sherbet' (p. 470)." They propose the attention decrement hypothesis as a more likely interpretation of the primacy, i.e., the latter items are presumed to carry less weight in the total impression than the early items. The failure to obtain primacy effects with the life event items is interpreted as probably due to the subjects' familiarity or affective involvement with the stimulus materials. This does not sound too plausible since subjects were undoubtedly familiar and affectively involved with the various foods. It does appear, however, that the Anderson and Norman study casts some doubt on the set interpretation of primacy effects.

Stewart (1965) reasoned that if the subject were asked to respond after each new adjective in a series, he would be forced to pay attention even to the last items in a series. While a primacy effect obtained with such a procedure would call the attention decrement hypothesis into question, it would not rule out the set interpretation. Stewart's results were not clear cut, but he seems to have found a primacy effect when the response was obtained only after all the items were presented, and a recency effect when the subject responded after each item in the series.

The major ambiguity in his data is that he failed to obtain recency with the continuous mode in one of two replications. In general, however, Stewart favors the Anderson and Hovland (1957) model which we described earlier as the most appropriate explanation for the recency effect that he did obtain. It will be recalled that the Anderson-Hovland model predicts a recency effect and that the main assumption involved is that the amount of change obtained is directly related to the amount of change advocated.

Anderson and Jacobson (1965) proposed yet another interpretation for primacy effects, an interpretation which is reminiscent of one proposed earlier by Luchins (1957). Luchins had found that some subjects who were exposed to the IE or EI paragraphs about "Jim" noticed the inconsistencies and made a decision to respond in terms of only one of the paragraphs. In effect, subjects discounted the other paragraph. Anderson and Jacobson (1965) used triads of adjectives in which one adjective was inconsistent with the other two. Their results appear to favor the inconsistency discounting hypothesis except when subjects were explicitly told to give each adjective equal weight.

One of the questions that occurs, then, is whether primacy effects would occur when the adjectives used to describe the hypothetical stimulus person were not so blatantly inconsistent as in the Anderson and Jacobson (1965), Anderson and Barrios (1961), and other studies. Some evidence on this question is presented in the following article. Primacy, a phenomenon which Lund (1925) believed to have the status of a "law," seems to be a will-o'-the-wisp, at the mercy of all sorts of minor changes in experimental procedure. Even a paradigm such as Anderson's which appears very well controlled, indeed, is full of possibilities for unintended artifacts to creep in.

Application of a Linear-Serial Model to a Personality-Impression Task Using Serial Presentation[1]

Norman H. Anderson

Ss saw 3 or 6 personality-trait adjectives 1 at a time in serial order; they were told that each set described a person whom they were to rate on likeableness. The sets of

[1] From the *Journal of Personality and Social Psychology* 1968, **10**, No. 4, 354–362. Received February 6, 1968. Reproduced by permission of the publisher.

This work was supported by National Science Foundation Grants GB-3913 and GB-6666. I wish to thank Gwendolyn Alexander for her assistance in running this experiment.

At the time of writing the author was with the University of California at San Diego.

adjectives were chosen to test 3 theoretical questions: (*a*) the addition of mildly polarized to highly polarized words decreased the polarity of the responses; this rules out an additive model but favors an averaging model; (*b*) in 2 exact tests applicable to both models, supportive results were obtained with favorable adjectives but a discrepancy was obtained with unfavorable adjectives; this discrepancy was the same as in previous work and would be consistent with an averaging formulation if mild negative adjectives had lower weight than more extreme negative adjectives; (*c*) a recency effect was observed for sequences in which all adjectives had the same polarity but different value; this result supports a discounting interpretation of the primacy effects that have been obtained in previous work in which the sequences contained both positive and negative stimuli.

In social situations, one's opinions and judgments are usually based on various different pieces of information. The processes that govern the integration of this information are of considerable interest. This experiment studies this integration problem in an experimental task based on serial presentation of trait information about personalities.

A substantial amount of related work has already been done in connection with testing a linear model for information integration (cf., Anderson, 1962, 1968b). In this formulation, the judgment is assumed to be, in effect, a weighted sum of the subjective values of relevant stimuli. With appropriate experimental design, analysis of variance may then be used to give a rigorous, quantitative test of the model. For the case of stimuli presented simultaneously, several experiments have given considerable support to this formulation. For serial presentation, however, previous experiments using social stimuli (e.g., Anderson, 1959, 1965b) have not employed a corresponding test of goodness of fit.

Serial presentation is more realistic because one's daily judgments are usually based on information accumulated over time. But it is also more complicated because the effect of a given stimulus may depend on its temporal position. Indeed, order of presentation is known to be important in a variety of tasks (e.g., Hovland, 1957; Lana, 1964; McGuire, 1966; Rosnow, Holz, & Levin, 1966).

Fortunately, the linear integration model can still be directly applied to serial presentation by allowing the weight, or importance, of each stimulus to depend on serial position. With appropriate experimental procedure, analysis of variance may still be used to get an exact test of the goodness of fit of the data to the model (Anderson, 1964a). Such a test of the model is also important in the estimation and interpretation of the serial position curve, including primacy and recency effects.

A special feature of the present design is that each stimulus sequence contains only positive or only negative information. This is important, and considerable pains were taken to implement it by preselection of the stimuli on an individual basis. Stimulus sequences constructed in this way do not have the potential inconsistencies of the usual order effect sequences, which include both positive and negative information. As a consequence, the data bear on the interpretation of the primacy effect usually obtained with the present task in terms of a discounting (Anderson & Jacobson, 1965) of the later adjectives from being inconsistent with the earlier adjectives. In addition, the use of unipolar sequences allows a critical test between the averaging and adding forms of the general model, parallel to that given previously for simultaneous presentation (Anderson, 1965a).

Method

Subjects were shown sequences of three or six personality-trait adjectives one at a time. They were told that the adjectives described a person whom they were to rate on a likeableness scale. The main independent variables were the value and the serial pattern of the adjectives in the various sequences, and these were chosen to test specified hypotheses. In addition, three different response modes were employed. In the continuous, final, and intermittent conditions, respectively, subjects rated after each successive adjective, after the last adjective only, or after the third and sixth adjectives only.

Stimulus Construction

To get high precision in the critical tests, it was necessary to construct sequences with adjectives of specified value for each individual subject. Accordingly, a preliminary session was given in which each subject selected groups of six adjectives that were about equal for him.

The basic adjectives were four sublists of 32 adjectives chosen from a master list on which normative data were available (Anderson, 1968b). These four sublists, the same as used in previous work, are denoted by H, M^+, M^-, and L, standing for high, moderately high, moderately low, and low, respectively. All adjectives were typed on 3×5-inch cards, and each sublist was split into two packets of 16 cards. From each packet, the subject was given 12 cards and selected a group of 6 that seemed about equally likable or dislikable as personality traits. After all eight groups had been thus chosen, the subjects checked each one and were allowed to improve it by exchanging with the four remaining cards of each packet.

In this way, each subject selected two groups of six equated adjectives from each of the four scale ranges, H, M^+, M^-, and L. From these selections, 32 sequences of adjectives were constructed for each subject. The 16 sequences of favorable adjectives are shown in Table 1. There were 16 complementary sequences constructed of L and M^- adjectives in the same manner.

Twelve of the 16 sets of Table 1 were constructed from one group of six H adjectives and one group of six M^+ adjectives. The subscripts 1–6, which were paired with particular adjectives by random choice, indicate the stimulus balancing that was employed. For example, Sets 3a and 3b are equivalent, while Set 10a is merely Set 3a in reversed order. The subscripts 11–16 in Sets 2ab and 4ab denote a different group of adjectives.

Sets 2ab and 4ab of Table 1 were used to give additional data on a central question

TABLE 1
Experimental Sequences of Favorable Adjectives

Set no.[a]	Adjective sequence
1a	$H_3H_1H_2$
1b	$H_4H_6H_5$
2a	$H_{11}H_{12}H_{13}$
2b	$H_{14}H_{15}H_{16}$
3a	$H_1H_2H_3M_1{}^+M_2{}^+M_3{}^+$
3b	$H_4H_5H_6M_4{}^+M_5{}^+M_6{}^+$
4a	$H_{13}H_{12}H_{11}M_{11}{}^+M_{12}{}^+M_{13}{}^+$
4b	$H_{16}H_{15}H_{14}M_{14}{}^+M_{15}{}^+M_{16}{}^+$
9a	$M_3{}^+M_1{}^+M_2{}^+$
9b	$M_4{}^+M_6{}^+M_5{}^+$
10a	$M_3{}^+M_2{}^+M_1{}^+H_3H_2H_1$
10b	$M_6{}^+M_5{}^+M_4{}^+H_6H_5H_4$
13a	$H_2H_3H_1H_6H_4H_5$
13b	$H_5H_4H_6H_1H_3H_2$
14a	$M_2{}^+M_3{}^+M_1{}^+M_6{}^+M_4{}^+M_5{}^+$
14b	$M_5{}^+M_4{}^+M_6{}^+M_1{}^+M_3{}^+M_2{}^+$

[a] Set numbers correspond to Table 2; a and b denote the two instances of each set type. Subscripts 1–6 denote six particular adjectives at each polarity; Subscripts 11–16 (Sets 2ab and 4ab) denote a second group of six particular adjectives. Sequences of negative adjectives were constructed similarly.

of this experiment. That is, an additive formulation would predict a higher response to Sets 4ab than to Sets 2ab. The second groups of six H and M^+ adjectives were used for these last four sets, and the subscripts 11–16 were assigned to particular adjectives by random choice.

PROCEDURE

The adjectives of each set were typed on 8½ × 11-inch sheets and positioned in a flat exposure apparatus on a table. The experimenter exposed the adjectives by stepping a 7 × 15-inch mask down the sheet of paper. In the mask were two slits, 3 × ¾ inches in size. One slit exposed the adjectives; the other exposed a 2-inch line when a response was required, and otherwise a blank space. The two slits were offset so that no adjective was visible when the response was made.

The 2-inch line exposed by the second slit represented a like-dislike scale. Subjects gave their judgments by making a slash mark on the line. This graphic scale was used in preference to a numerical scale in order to avoid memory effects in the continuous condition in which subjects revised their ratings after each added adjective. The graphic scale has the added potentialities of being sensitive to small changes in response and of avoiding number preferences.

The subject read each adjective aloud as it was shown. Each adjective was exposed for approximately 1 second. The mask was then advanced one step to expose a blank space under each slit for approximately 1 second, and then advanced again to expose the next adjective or a response line. Between the last adjective and the final response there was a 4-second interval during which the subject was to "think about your overall impression of the person."

Three response modes were used. In the final condition, subjects rated the person only once, after all the adjectives had been presented. In the continuous condition, the person was rated after each successive adjective. In the intermittent condition, ratings were given after the third and sixth adjectives of the sequence.

For the continuous condition, the total times required for sequences of three and six words were approximately 16 and 27 seconds, respectively.

The 32 experimental sets were presented in shuffled order for each subject. Four common filler sets were also included, after the third, eighth, fifteenth, and twenty-fourth experimental sets. Each filler contained both positive and negative adjectives, less extreme than the H or L adjectives, and without obvious inconsistency. Their main purpose was to break up the patterning in the experimental sets which were all homogeneous in polarity.

Instructions

The subject was told to imagine that the adjectives on each sheet described a single person, and that each adjective was accurate and equally important; that he should decide how much he himself would like the person, that there was no right or wrong answer; that he should simply give his own opinion; and that he should try to spread his responses over the whole response line.

The serial presentation procedure was explained by analogy to real life in which one ordinarily gets to know a person step by step.

Further, subjects in the continuous and intermittent conditions were told that each response should be made on the basis of all the accumulated information, and that changes in opinion were only natural as more information was obtained.

Four practice sets were given, common to all subjects. Two of these were mixed M^+ and M^- adjectives, and two were end anchors consisting of very high and very low adjectives. Questions were then answered, and the main points of the instructions repeated before proceeding to the experimental sets.

Subjects

Subjects were 88 undergraduates who were paid $2.50 for the two ½-hour sessions. There were 40 subjects in the final condition, and 24 each in the other two conditions. Half the subjects were of either sex, and within each sex they were randomly assigned to conditions.

Results

Terminal Response

The terminal responses, given after all the adjectives had been presented, are the most important. Table 2 gives the response means, averaged over subjects and over the two instances of each set type. These data answer several specific questions that will be considered in turn.

Order of Presentation. The experimental design assesses the effect of

TABLE 2
Mean Likableness Response at End of Adjective Sequence as a Function of Sequence of Adjectives and Response Condition

Set no.	Set words[a]	Response condition			
		Final	Continuous	Intermittent	*M*
1	HHH	16.44	16.98	16.00	16.47
2	HHH	16.46	16.46	16.06	16.35
3	$HHHM^+M^+M^+$	14.46	14.23	14.23	14.33
4	$HHHM^+M^+M^+$	15.20	15.25	15.19	15.21
5	LLL	1.49	1.48	1.58	1.51
6	LLL	1.02	1.58	1.69	1.36
7	$LLLM^-M^-M^-$	3.12	2.92	3.23	3.10
8	$LLLM^-M^-M^-$	2.62	3.71	3.10	3.05
9	$M^+M^+M^+$	11.96	11.04	10.08	11.20
10	$M^+M^+M^+HHH$	14.92	14.88	14.02	14.66
11	$M^-M^-M^-LLL$	2.51	2.23	2.52	2.44
12	$M^-M^-M^-$	5.28	6.06	6.65	5.86
13	HHHHHH	17.41	17.79	17.48	17.53
14	$M^+M^+M^+M^+M^+M^+$	12.29	11.23	11.67	11.83
15	$M^-M^-M^-M^-M^-M^-$	4.42	5.79	5.75	5.16
16	LLLLLL	.91	1.00	1.35	1.06

[a] Adjectives listed in the order presented. H, M^+, M^-, and L denote adjectives of high, mildly favorable, mildly unfavorable, and low value. Because of the balancing in the experimental design, Sets 2, 4, 6, and 8 figure in comparisons only in the upper half of the table, not in the lower half.

presenting the same adjectives in different orders. For positive stimuli, the comparison is between Sets 3 and 10, that is, between $3H3M^+$ and $3M^+3H$. The response to the first set is somewhat lower, a recency effect. However, the difference of .33 fell short of significance.

The corresponding comparison for negative stimuli is based on Sets 7 and 11. The response of 3.10 to $3L3M^-$ is larger than the response of 2.44 to $3M^-3L$, again a recency effect. The difference of .66 is significantly greater than 0 ($F = 10.37$, $df = 1/82$).

The theoretical interpretation of these order effects is quite uncertain. Within the present formulation, they are considered to reflect differential weighting of the initial and later stimuli. This problem will be discussed in more detail below when the complete response curves for the continuous condition are examined.

Serial Integration Model. The design provides two tests of quantitative predictions of the general model, one for positive and one for negative stimuli. These two predictions are:

$$R(6H) + R(6M^+) = R(3H3M^+) + R(3M^+3H)$$
$$\text{and } R(6L) + R(6M^-) = R(3L3M^-) + R(3M^-3L)$$

where R denotes the response to the stimulus sequence in parentheses. The model derivation allows weight or importance to vary with serial position, but assumes that all stimuli at a given serial position have the same effective weight.

To test the first prediction, the combined response to Sets 13 and 14 is to be compared to the combined response to Sets 3 and 10 in Table 2. The corresponding means are 14.68 and 14.50, respectively, and the difference of .18 points does not approach significance. It may be noted, incidentally, that the four sets form a 2×2 design in which the cited difference score is just the interaction.

The second prediction, for negative stimuli, compares Sets 15 and 16 to Sets 7 and 11. The means are 3.11 and 2.77, respectively, and the difference of .34 points is just significant ($F = 4.30$, $df = 1/82$).

This pair of results parallels that for simultaneous presentation (Anderson, 1965a). There also the prediction was verified for positive stimuli but not for negative stimuli. In the earlier report, it was noted that the discrepancy could be interpreted as evidence for a special case of the general formulation in which the stimulus values are averaged. This interpretation rested on the assumption that the L adjectives had greater natural weight than the M⁻ adjectives. The response to a set with equally many Ls and M⁻s would then be shifted from the stimulus midpoint toward the stimulus with greater weight. The direction of the discrepancy is the same in the present data which supports the earlier interpretation, and suggests that the test of fit reflects no more than an inaccuracy in the simplifying assumption of equal weighting.

There is one further aspect of the discrepancy with the negative stimuli that needs comment. In the statistical analysis, response condition was also significant. Inspection of Table 2 shows that the continuous and intermittent, but not the final, response conditions are discrepant from the model prediction. This naturally casts doubt on the interpretation of the discrepancy in terms of differential weighting since that would, presumably, imply that the final condition should show the same discrepancy as the other two conditions. More detailed inspection of the data suggests that the between-conditions difference is located in the lower response to $6M^-$ in the final condition. This between-conditions difference is consistent since it appears also for $3M^-$, but it does not shed any obvious light on the above interpretation.

Averaging Versus-Adding. Further evidence on the averaging interpretation is also embodied in the design. The empirical test is straightforward. Sets 1 and 2 contain three H adjectives; Sets 3 and 4 contain added favorable information, namely, three M^+ adjectives. This added favorable information must raise the response according to any summative formulation. In contradiction, the response to the 3H3M$^+$ sets is 1.64 points lower than the response to the 3H sets.

A similar critical test, for negative information, is given by Sets 5 to 8. An additive model would predict a more negative response from 3L3M$^-$ than from 3L, but the observed difference is again in the other direction. In both cases, of course, the result is consistent with an averaging formulation.

Both results are quite reliable. For the comparison between 3H and 3H3M$^+$, the analysis yielded $F = 36.86$, $df = 1/82$. For the difference between 3L and 3L3M$^-$, $F = 75.06$, $df = 1/82$.

These results are not peculiarities of the order of presentation. In Set 10 (3M$^+$3H) the order of presentation is reversed compared to Sets 3 and 4. Because of the stimulus balancing, Set 10 is properly compared only with Set 1. However, the difference of 1.81 points favors the averaging formulation and is statistically significant ($F = 31.09$, $df = 1/82$). The similar comparison for negative stimuli is based on Sets 5 and 11. Here the difference between the response of 2.44 to 3M$^-$3L and 1.51 to 3L again favors an averaging formulation ($F = 23.19$, $df = 1/82$).

Set-Size Effect. The data show the usual effect of set size. For each stimulus value the response to sets of six adjectives is more extreme than the response to sets of three adjectives. This effect has some immediate relevance since it validates the choice of M$^+$ and M$^-$ stimuli.

The present set-size effect is consistent with previous experiments that have also employed serial presentation (Anderson, 1959; Fishbein & Hunter, 1964; Stewart, 1965). It has theoretical interest since it rules out the most simple averaging model. That is, if the response were the average of the scale values of the stimuli actually presented, a set of three Hs and a set of six Hs would yield the same response. This situation can be handled theoretically by assuming that the subject averages an initial or neutral impression in with the values of the overt stimuli (Anderson, 1959, 1967b). In this form, the averaging model then predicts the response to be a growth curve function of set size, and this has been verified in all the above cited work. The effect can be seen more directly when continuous responding is used as illustrated in Fig. 1 below.

Response Mode and Sex. Each of the above analyses included Response Condition and Sex as between-subjects variables. All tests were made by analysis of variance, and all results significant at the .05 level are reported. Somewhat surprisingly, there was relatively little effect of Response Condition on the size of the terminal response. It was significant only in the one test already mentioned. The data show some scattered

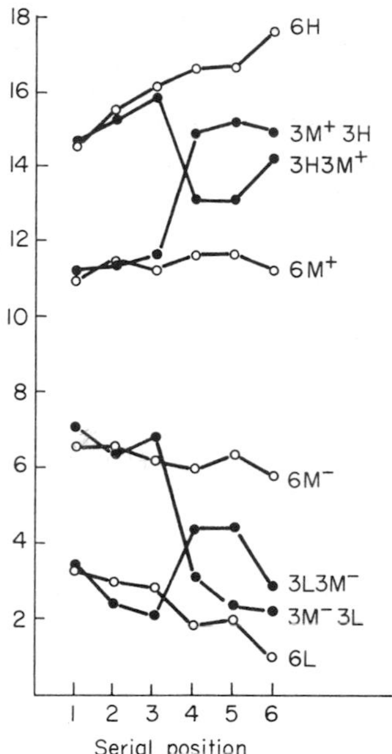

Fig. 1. Mean impression as function of serial position in continuous responding condition.

between-conditions differences with some tendency for the final condition to give lower responses to negative stimuli. However, two further tests, based on the five homogeneous sets of each polarity, failed to yield significant differences.

Sex was significant in most of the separate analyses, with the female response being more extreme. In the two tests just cited, the female mean was 1.43 higher for positive stimuli and .72 lower for negative stimuli, both differences being significant. As is usually the case, comparison of different populations presents methodological difficulties, and these data naturally give no warrant for concluding that the underlying impression is different in males and females. The given result may simply reflect different semantic habits in using the response scale.

Intermediate Responses

Subjects in the continuous condition responded after each adjective so that a complete response curve may be obtained for each sequence. These response curves for sets of six adjectives are shown in Fig. 1. The curves reflect the development of the person-impression as additional information is received.

The curves for the sets of three adjectives are not included since they duplicated information in Fig. 1. The data for the intermittent condition at Serial Position 3 are also omitted. They were, on the whole, about the same as the corresponding data for the continuous condition; the between-conditions differences were somewhat less than the differences at Serial Position 6 in Table 2 and showed no systematic pattern.

The most interesting comparison in Fig. 1 concerns order of presentation. Sets 4 and 8 of Table 2 were excluded to allow comparison of order of presentation unconfounded with stimulus differences. Thus, $3M^{+}3H$ and $3H3M^{+}$ represent equivalent information presented in opposite orders, and similarly for $3M^{-}3L$ and $3L3M^{-}$. Each pair of curves shows two effects: recency and finality.

The recency effect is represented graphically by the crossing of the paired curves at Serial Position 4. Thus, $3M^{+}3H$ yields a higher response than $3H3M^{+}$ at each of the last three serial positions. Similarly, $3M^{-}3L$ yields a lower response than $3L3M^{-}$ over the last three serial positions, also a recency effect.

To test this recency effect, the two orders of presentation and the three last serial positions were combined as a 2×3 design. The overall recency was significant both for the positive and the negative stimuli ($F = 7.32$ and 7.58, respectively, $df = 1/22$).

The finality effect is seen in the reversal of trend at the last point for Sets $3H3M^{+}$ and $3L3M^{-}$. The marked upward jump at the last point would seem to reflect a latent effect of the initial H adjectives. Similarly, the downward jump at the last point of Set $3L3M^{-}$ suggests a latent effect of the initial L adjectives.

This finality effect was unexpected, and a completely suitable test of its reliability is not available. On a post hoc basis, however, it seemed reasonable to test the null hypothesis that the difference in response at Positions 5 and 6 was 0. The mean upjump for the $3H3M^{+}$ curve in Fig. 1 was 1.10; the other $3H3M^{+}$ data showed an even larger upjump of 1.82 points. The test was made on the combined data and yielded $F = 18.65$, $df = 1/22$. For the negative stimuli, the mean downjump from Position 5 to 6 is 1.50 in the plotted curve. The other $3L3M^{-}$ data showed a downjump of 1.02. The test on the combined data yielded $F = 14.22$, $df = 1/22$.

These tests were suggested by inspection of the data and must therefore be interpreted cautiously. However, the effect occurs consistently in the data and the F ratios are large enough to give some warrant for considering the finality effect to be real.

The order effect curves of Fig. 1 require a brief discussion in relation to two previous reports. They differ in two respects from curves obtained by Stewart (1965) with a fairly similar task. The second limb of Stewart's curves shows a gradual change toward recency, whereas here the recency appears abruptly at Serial Position 4. Also, Stewart found differences between his final and continuous conditions, with primacy in the former and no primacy or recency in the latter. The present final condition exhibits recency and this difference, as well as the abrupt recency in the continuous condition, may reflect the present use of adjectives of the same polarity in each set as discussed below. The general agreement between the present continuous and final data provides a safeguard on the main theoretical results of this report.

Finally, it may be noted that the finality effect, if real, may be interpretable in terms of a two-component hypothesis of opinion structure (Anderson, 1959). In this view, the immediate shift to recency at Serial Position 4 would reflect the action of the superficial component, whereas the basal component would produce the finality effect during the terminal pause in the stimulus presentation. Here, of course, as above, it must be realized that the shape of the continuous curves may depend heavily on the time intervals used in the sequence.

The remaining curves of Fig. 1 are for sets in which all six adjectives have equivalent value. These curves have theoretical interest since they represent the set-size effect for serial presentation. Although the sequences are too short to be conclusive, the curves for Sets $6M^+$ and $6M^-$ seem to have reached an asymptote as would be predicted by an averaging model. The shape of the curves for Sets 6H and 6L is not entirely clear since the last point on each shows a larger change than might be expected in view of the first five points. Since this may only reflect a tendency to use the endpoints of the response scale (Anderson, 1967b), detailed analysis of these curves does not seem justified here. Further work in this direction will probably require closer attention to scale end effects and more extensive use of end anchors.

Several people (e.g., M. Brewer, G. S. Leventhal, R. S. Wyer, Jr.)[2] have suggested that this set-size effect results simply from an increase in confidence as information accumulates. No doubt confidence does increase with each successive adjective in Set 6H, for instance, but this may merely reflect the processes involved in the information integration without playing any causative role in the impression response. The present data suggest that confidence alone is not a sufficient explanation. In Sets $6M^+$ and $6M^-$ confidence should increase steadily over successive stimuli. On the confidence interpretation, then, there is no reason to expect the impression curves to level off at intermediate values as they do in Fig. 1. The mixed sets, such as Sets $3H3M^+$ and $3M^+3H$, also pose difficulties for a confidence interpretation. It might not be unreasonable to argue, for instance, that the M^+ adjectives in Set $3H3M^+$ decrease confidence since, even though they add positive information, they in-

[2] Personal communications.

crease the variance of that information. That argument, however, would not be able to account for the increase in the curve for Set 3M+3H as the H adjectives are added. Nevertheless, the confidence question is quite interesting. However, further speculation is unwarranted here since the problem is open to direct experimental attack.

Discussion

Two main theoretical questions will be considered here. The first concerns the general model for serial information integration; the second concerns the interpretation of the serial order effects.

On the first question, the results are fairly straightforward. The quantitative predictions were satisfied under all three response conditions for positive stimuli, but there was a discrepancy in two conditions for negative stimuli. The pattern of these results is similar to that obtained previously with simultaneous presentation (Anderson, 1965a). As noted above, it is possible to account for this discrepancy if the general formulation is specialized to an averaging model, with greater weighting of the more polarized stimuli.

Added support for an averaging interpretation is found in two qualitative tests. For both positive and negative stimuli, adding mildly polarized to highly polarized information decreased the polarity of the response. This contradicts an additive model, but is consistent with an averaging interpretation, just as in the cited report on simultaneous presentation.

On the whole, therefore, the present and previous reports allow some optimism over this approach to information integration. Although the empirical tests have been mainly limited to the personality-impression task, similar results may be expected with other stimuli (Anderson, 1965a, 1967b).

In this connection, one methodological comment deserves special note. In the present data, the critical test between averaging and adding was considerably more reliable than in the previous report. Although comparison of serial with simultaneous presentation is risky, it seems likely that the increase in reliability flows in large part from the stimulus preselection employed here. This allows a very close matching of stimulus values for each individual with a consequent reduction in error variability (cf., Anderson, 1965b; Table 2). Constructing sets of stimuli for each separate subject is costly, of course, but may well be worth the gain in precision as well as in validity.

The data also bear on a second theoretical problem; the cause of the primacy effect that is usually obtained in this task under a standard set of conditions. This primacy was first obtained by Asch (1946), who interpreted it in terms of an assimilation of the meaning of the later adjectives toward the meaning of the earlier adjectives. Recent work has uniformly favored an alternative hypothesis that the primacy results from a decrease in the weight rather than a shift in the meaning of the later adjectives (Anderson, 1965b; Anderson & Barrios, 1961; Anderson & Hubert, 1963; Anderson & Norman, 1964; Stewart, 1965). These experiments also supported the idea that the serial decrease in weight stemmed from a decrement in attention over successive serial positions, and this seemed especially clear in the straight-line primacy curves obtained from a generalized order effect paradigm (Anderson, 1965b).

However, a second possible cause of a serial decrease in weight was suggested by the finding that subjects discount, that is, give lower weight to, affectively inconsistent stimuli (Anderson & Jacobson, 1965). That experiment used simultaneous presentation, but it was noted that primacy with serial presentation could result from discounting. It is easy to see that any such discounting would be directional, producing lower weights for the later stimuli. In LLLHHH, for instance, the first H is to be integrated by itself into the weightier impression based on the three Ls. Discounting would then tend to work against the first H. Somewhat the same situation would then also apply to the second and third Hs.

The present design allows a test between these two explanations of a serial decrease in weight. Previous work has used sequences with both positive and negative stimuli, whereas the present sequences contain stimuli of only one polarity.

Simple attention decrement would produce primacy for either kind of sequence. On the discounting hypothesis, in contrast, primacy would not obtain with the present sequences since they do not embody affective or semantic inconsistency. That primacy was not obtained here argues, therefore, that the primacy in previous experiments was caused by a discounting process.

At the same time, the present recency effect is consistent with recency effects that have been obtained under comparable conditions with averaging of psychophysical stimuli (Anderson, 1967a; Parducci, Thaler, & Anderson, 1968) and numbers (Anderson, 1964b). The cause of this recency is not known, but it probably stems jointly from forgetting of the earlier stimuli (e.g., Miller & Campbell, 1959), and from a natural tendency to overweight the immediately present stimulus in a sequence as assumed in the linear operator model of previous work (Anderson, 1964a; Anderson & Hovland, 1957).

In accordance with the above view, recency would be generally expected, and a necessary though not sufficient condition for primacy would be inconsistency among the stimulus items. Whether this view has any generality is difficult to say since the primacy-recency area is especially marked by conflicting results (e.g., Hovland, 1957; Lana, 1964; McGuire, 1966; Rosnow *et al.,* 1966). However, since most work in the area has in fact used stimuli of mixed polarity, conflicting results might be expected on the present view. With such stimuli, tendencies toward primacy and toward recency would be operating together, and the net resultant could depend heavily on experimental details. For the personality-adjective task, at least, this seems to be true empirically. Ordinarily strong primacy is obtained, but this is eliminated or changed to recency by relatively simple experimental manipulations (Anderson & Hubert, 1963; Stewart, 1965). The above view, it should be noted, allows for but does not explain this shift from primacy to recency. Some additional mechanism, such as attention, would still be needed for this purpose.

The checkered history of the primacy-recency problem indicates the need for courage if not caution in any theoretical analysis. The present view at least has the merit of being easily tested. For instance, it requires primacy to vary directly with amount of discounting, and discounting can be manipulated fairly easily.

REFERENCES

Anderson, N. H. Test of a model for opinion change. *Journal of Abnormal and Social Psychology,* 1959, **59,** 371–381.

Anderson, N. H. Application of an additive model to impression formation. *Science,* 1962, **138,** 817–818.

Anderson, N. H. Note on weighted sum and linear operator models. *Psychonomic Science,* 1964, **1,** 189–190. (a)

Anderson, N. H. Test of a model for number-averaging behavior. *Psychonomic Science,* 1964, **1,** 191–192. (b)

Anderson, N. H. Averaging versus adding as a stimulus-combination rule in impression formation. *Journal of Experimental Psychology,* 1965, **70,** 394–400. (a)

Anderson, N. H. Primacy effects in personality impression formation using a generalized order effect paradigm. *Journal of Personality and Social Psychology,* 1965, **2,** 1–9. (b)

Anderson, N. H. Component ratings in impression formation. *Psychonomic Science,* 1966, **6,** 279–280.

Anderson, N. H. Application of a weighted average model to a psychophysical averaging task. *Psychonomic Science,* 1967, **8,** 227–228. (a)

Anderson, N. H. Averaging model analysis of set size effect in impression formation. *Journal of Experimental Psychology,* 1967, **75,** 158–165. (b)

Anderson, N. H. A simple model for information integration. In R. P. Abelson, E. Aronson, W. J. McGuire, T. M. Newcomb, M. J. Rosenberg, & P. H. Tannenbaum

(Eds.), *Theories of cognitive consistency: A sourcebook.* Chicago: Rand McNally, 1968. (a)

Anderson, N. H. Likableness ratings of 555 personality-trait words. *Journal of Personality and Social Psychology,* 1968, **9,** 272–279. (b)

Anderson, N. H., & Barrios, A. A. Primacy effects in personality impression formation. *Journal of Abnormal and Social Psychology,* 1961, **63,** 346–350.

Anderson, N. H., & Hovland, C. I. The representation of order effects in communication research. In C. I. Hovland (Ed.), *The order of presentation in persuasion,* New Haven: Yale University Press, 1957.

Anderson, N. H., & Hubert, S. Effects of concomitant verbal recall on order effects in personality impression formation. *Journal of Verbal Learning and Verbal Behavior,* 1963, **2,** 379–391.

Anderson, N. H., & Jacobson, A. Effects of stimulus inconsistency and discounting instructions in personality impression formation. *Journal of Personality and Social Psychology,* 1965, **2,** 531–539.

Anderson, N. H., & Norman, A. Order effects in impression formation in four classes of stimuli. *Journal of Abnormal and Social Psychology,* 1964, **69,** 467–471.

Asch, S. E. Forming impressions of personality. *Journal of Abnormal and Social Psychology,* 1946, **41,** 258–290.

Fishbein, M., & Hunter, R. Summation versus balance in attitude organization and change. *Journal of Abnormal and Social Psychology,* 1964, **69,** 505–510.

Hovland, C. I. Summary and implications. In C. I. Hovland (Ed.), *The order of presentation in persuasion.* New Haven: Yale University Press, 1957.

Lana, R. E. Three interpretations of order effects in persuasive communications. *Psychological Bulletin,* 1964, **61,** 314–320.

McGuire, W. J. Attitudes and opinions. In P. Farnsworth (Ed.), *Annual review of psychology.* Vol. 17. Palo Alto: Annual Review Press, 1966.

Miller, N., & Campbell, D. T. Recency and primacy in persuasion as a function of the timing of speeches and measurement. *Journal of Abnormal and Social Psychology,* 1959, **59,** 1–9.

Parducci, A., Thaler, H., & Anderson, N. H. Stimulus averaging and the context for judgment. *Perception and Psychophysics,* 1968, **3,** 145–150.

Rosnow, R. L., Holz, R. F., & Levin, J. Differential effects of complementary and competing variables in primacy-recency. *Journal of Social Psychology,* 1966, **69,** 135–147.

Stewart, R. H. Effect of continuous responding on the order effect in personality impression formation. *Journal of Personality and Social Psychology,* 1965, **1,** 161–165.

Discussion

Anderson's results are somewhat surprising with respect to order effects. Specifically, both the $3H3M^+$ versus $3M^+3H$ and $3L3M^-$ versus $3M^-3L$ comparisons yielded recency effects. It would have been expected, on the basis of previous research (Stewart, 1965), that these comparisons would produce primacy effects under the final mode of responding, and recency effects under the continuous mode. Inspection of Table 2 in Anderson's article (Sets 3 versus 10 and 7 versus 11) reveals that recency carried the day under both response modes. In the following article, Hendrick and Costantini (1970) propose that the recency obtained was an artifact of Anderson's procedure. Before going on to that article, however, let us briefly note two design refinements that Anderson introduced and two design flaws in addition to the one that Hendrick and Costantini discuss.

The first refinement in procedure was the use of stimulus sequences which contained only positive or only negative information. This allows one to rule out the "discounting hypothesis" as a major source of variance in the results. It still remains possible, of course, that discounting inconsistencies was a major factor in producing primacy effects in the studies by Luchins (1957) and Anderson and Barrios (1961). Had Anderson (1968) really wanted to investigate the discounting hypothesis, he should have included two more sets in his experiment (HHHLLL and LLLHHH). If these sets had produced primacy with the various response modes and the LLLM⁻M⁻M⁻ and M⁻M⁻M⁻LLL sets had not, he would have been in an excellent position to argue that the primacy effects were due to discounting.

A second procedural improvement in the Anderson article was the use of a continuous response scale. That is, when a subject was ready to give a judgment, he made a slash mark on a line running from like to dislike. Earlier experiments (e.g., Stewart, 1965) had required subjects to give a numerical rating (say, between 1 and 8) in making their judgments. As Anderson (1968) notes "... (the) graphic scale was used in preference to a numerical scale in order to avoid memory effects in the continuous condition in which subjects revised their ratings after each added adjective. The graphic scale has the added potentialities of being sensitive to small changes in response and of avoiding number preferences [p. 355]."

One of the flaws in Anderson's (1968) procedure has to do with the instructions given the subjects. On page 356 he states that "... subjects in the continuous and intermittent conditions were told that each response should be made on the basis of all the accumulated information and that changes in opinion were only natural as more information was obtained." This sounds very reminiscent of one of Luchins' (1957) experiments in which subjects were forewarned against forming snap judgments. *Procedurally,* however, the important point is that subjects in the continuous and intermittent conditions were given these instructions while subjects in the final conditions were not. Had recency been obtained in the continuous conditions but not in the final conditions, these instructions would have been sufficient explanation for the different results. The requirements of good control dictate that everything except the independent variable be constant across conditions.

A second source of possible contamination is evident in a close inspection of the continuous and final conditions. Consider the interaction between the subject and the experimenter in the continuous condition. The experimenter exposes an adjective, the subject pronounces it, the experimenter moves the mask over the adjective and exposes a response line, the subject marks down his response, and the experimenter goes on to the next adjective. By the manner in which he acknowledged the subject's response in moving on to the next item, the experimenter could very well have influenced what that next response would be. It is true, of course, that the experimenter acknowledges the subjects' pronouncing the adjective by moving on even in the final conditions—but this is constant across the final and continuous conditions. The point is, simply, that there was much greater opportunity for the experimenter to influence unintentionally the subjects in the continuous condition than in the final condition. While we have no data to show that this did occur, the burden is always on the researcher to show that such contaminating influences could not reasonably have been operating.

In the following article, Hendrick and Costantini (1970) point up another unintended influence in Anderson's procedure. In reading their Experiment II, however, pay close attention to their descriptions of the experimental conditions and the differences between those conditions.

Effects of Varying Trait Inconsistency and Response Requirements on the Primacy Effect in Impression Formation[1]

Clyde Hendrick and Arthur F. Costantini

Attention decrement and inconsistency discounting are competing explanations of primacy effects in impression formation. Two relevant experiments are reported in which subjects rated persons described by serially presented trait adjectives. In the first experiment affective inconsistency between traits was varied. The discounting hypothesis was not supported because a primacy effect was obtained that was independent of variation in intertrait consistency. This result conflicted with results reported by Anderson, who found recency with traits low in inconsistency. However, Anderson had

[1] From the *Journal of Personality and Social Psychology,* 1970, **15,** No. 2, 158–164. Received August 11, 1969. Reproduced by permission of the publisher.

The authors are indebted to Norman H. Anderson for his comments on an earlier version of the manuscript.

Request for reprints should be sent to Clyde Hendrick, Department of Psychology, Kent State University, Kent, Ohio 44240.

At the time of writing both authors were with Kent State University; Costantini is currently with the University of Connecticut.

subjects pronounce each trait, a novel response requirement. The second experiment tested the interpretation that the recency effect was due to the novel requirement. Subjects rated persons described by sets of consistent or inconsistent adjectives, and subjects either pronounced or did not pronounce each adjective. Primacy was obtained without pronunciation, and recency was obtained with pronunciation. Variation in inconsistency had no effect. The results did not support discounting, but were consistent with the attention decrement hypothesis.

Beginning with Asch's (1946) classic studies of impression formation, several experiments have found a primacy effect when subjects are asked to evaluate a person described by serially presented trait adjectives (e.g., Anderson, 1965b). Asch suggested a change-in-meaning interpretation in which the initial traits in the series set up a directed impression that shifts the meaning of the later traits toward the initial direction. This interpretation has not been supported empirically, but it has been difficult to rule out conclusively. Another interpretation views the primacy effect as due to a progressive decrease in attention over the adjectives in a set (Anderson, 1965b). A third interpretation is that the primacy effect reflects a motivated discounting process in which subjects attempt to resolve the affective inconsistency existing between adjectives in a set (Anderson & Jacobson, 1965). The present research attempted to assess the relative merits of the attention decrement and inconsistency discounting explanations of the primacy effect.

The attention decrement notion has an appealing simplicity, since all that is assumed is a change in weight assigned to stimuli, rather than a change in meaning or evaluative strength of the stimuli themselves. Support for the concept was provided by Anderson and Hubert (1963), who had subjects recall the adjectives after giving their evaluative responses to sets of serially presented traits. This procedure presumably tended to equalize attention to all adjectives in the set. In this situation the primacy effect disappeared and in some conditions a recency effect was obtained. Additional support for attention decrement was obtained by Stewart (1965), who attempted to equalize attention to the traits by having subjects respond evaluatively after each individual trait was presented. A recency effect was obtained with this "continuous mode" of responding, and the traditional primacy effect when the typical "final mode" of responding was used.

A possible problem with the aforementioned studies is that the additional response requirements imposed on the subjects may have created a variety of interfering tendencies that resulted in a situation very different from the standard primacy task. For example, having subjects give evaluations after each trait in the series (Stewart, 1965) may have psychologically released them from the obligation to remember the preceding traits once the evaluation was made. Such a tendency would leave the last adjective in the series more salient, and a recency effect would be expected.

Anderson and Jacobson (1965) have noted that the primacy effect might be due to a discounting process. They presented sets of three adjectives to subjects in which one adjective was either affectively or antonymically inconsistent with the other two adjectives. Both types of inconsistency resulted in discounting of the odd adjective, and there was no difference between the two types in amount of discounting. This experiment was not directly relevant to the primacy issue since simultaneous presentation of the stimuli was used, the sets contained only three traits, and discounting instructions were varied explicitly. The results are indirectly relevant, however, because in the typical primacy study a tremendous amount of inconsistency is usually built into the adjective sets. Stimulus persons are usually described by six or eight traits. Half the traits are desirable, and the other half are undesirable. The two types of information are likely to be perceived as strongly inconsistent by the subject, and pressures may be created to resolve the inconsistency.

One mode of inconsistency resolution would be to discount part of the stimulus information. Since the information comes in blocks of desirable-undesirable (or vice versa), one strategy would be to discount an entire block. Inconsistency reduction would be served by discounting either the first block of adjectives (yielding a recency effect) or discounting the second block (yielding a primacy effect). On strictly logical grounds, inconsistency resolution would occur equally well regardless of which block was discounted. However, a theoretical argument may be made for discounting later rather than earlier information in a stimulus sequence. The argument would assume that to some extent an impression has organizational qualities. Subjects do seem to average scale values of individual traits to arrive at an overall evaluation (Anderson, 1965a). However, they also work with the information, organizing it into a coherent impression of a person (Asch, 1946). The first several traits in a series should be most important for developing and organizing the impression simply because the subject starts with a base line of zero information. Just at the point where the impression begins to stabilize, the subject receives the inconsistent information. If one assumes a principle such as "organization inhibits reorganization" (Scott, 1968), a least effort rationale is provided why the later information should be discounted to resolve the inconsistency. Discounting earlier information would require reorganizing the entire impression. The developing initial impression or organization would inhibit such a tendency. Therefore, the most likely version of the discounting hypothesis would predict a primacy effect in the impression task.

It is interesting that the motivated discounting interpretation of the primacy effect is mathematically similar to the attention decrement interpretation. Both notions assume a decrease in weight across the serial positions of a stimulus sequence. The decrease should occur differently in the two cases, however. The attention decrement model would predict a smooth linear decrease in weights across serial positions. The discounting hypothesis would predict an abrupt change in weight at the serial position where inconsistency is introduced.

Basically, the inconsistency discounting hypothesis maintains that serial position weights are sensitive to amount of inconsistency, while the attention decrement hypothesis does not make such an assumption. This difference in assumptions leads to different experimental predictions. If the primacy effect is due to inconsistency discounting, then as the degree of inconsistency in sets of descriptive adjectives increases, the magnitude of the primacy effect should increase also. The attention decrement hypothesis would not predict any differences in the amount of primacy as a function of variation in inconsistency.

Two experiments relevant to these predictions are reported. In the first experiment the amount of inconsistency in sets of descriptive traits was varied and the magnitude of the primacy effect was observed as a function of the variation in inconsistency. The traditional final mode of evaluative responding was used with serial presentation of stimuli. In the second experiment stimulus inconsistency and response requirements were both varied. The final mode of evaluative responding was used, but subjects either did or did not pronounce each stimulus word as it was presented.

Experiment I

Method

Subjects gave evaluative ratings of stimulus persons described by serially presented trait adjectives. Each person was described by a set of six adjectives, three high and three low in desirability. The sets were constructed so that for half of the sets the desirable traits were very inconsistent with the undesirable traits. For the other half of the sets the inconsistency between desirable and undesirable traits was minimal.

Stimulus Construction. On the basis of Anderson's (1968b) list of traits, a dictonary of antonyms and synonyms, and intuition, a number of sets of six adjectives were constructed. Each set was composed of three desirable traits that were relatively homogeneous in meaning (e.g., energetic, vigorous, resourceful), and three undesirable traits likewise relatively homogeneous (e.g., withdrawn, silent, helpless). Much initial trial and error work was devoted to finding blocks of three highly desirable (H) traits that did not seem to conflict or be inconsistent with a block of three low desirable (L) traits. Let such a set be designated generally by HL(+). Two such specific sets, using different traits and designated $H_1L_1(+)$ and $H_2L_2(+)$, were constructed with the stipulation that when the three low traits in one set were joined with the three high traits in the other set, the new set thus formed would contain strong inconsistency between the high and low traits. Two additional sets, designated $H_1L_2(-)$ and $H_2L_1(-)$, were formed in this manner. This procedure was essentially a control for specific words used in forming sets and ensured that each specific adjective would be used in both consistent and inconsistent sets.

The four sets of six traits formed in this manner were considered as one stimulus replication. Several such replications were constructed and tested in a preliminary rating study. In that study subjects were asked to rate on an 11-point scale the probability that a person could possess the three low traits, given that he possessed the three high traits. On the basis of the probability ratings of the initial study, four stimulus replications were selected for use in the primacy study. In each replication the mean probability ratings for the two HL(+) sets were significantly larger than the mean ratings for the two HL(—) sets. Since the construction of the 16 stimulus sets entailed considerable work and may be more useful generally, they are included verbatim in Table 1. The mean probability rating for each set is shown in the third column of the table.

Procedure. When a subject arrived for the experimental session, the nature of the impression task was briefly explained. Subjects were told that several sets of traits, each describing a different person, would be read to them. Their task was to form an impression of the person and rate him in terms of the favorability of their impression. A cardboard scale with numbers 1–8 was placed in front of the subject. An identifying label was printed under each number (e.g., highly favorable under 8 and highly unfavorable under 1). Subjects were told that each adjective in a set was contributed by a different individual who knew the person, and since different individuals may view a person in different ways, perfect consistency of description should not be expected. Subjects were also told that the same word might appear several times in the description of different persons.

The experimenter read the adjectives at a steady rate of one word every three seconds. Subjects ordinarily called out their numerical response within five seconds after the sixth word in the set was read to them.

The subjects rated 32 experimental sets and four additional sets. The 32 experimental sets were the HL and LH orders of presentation of the 16 sets shown in Table 1. In addition, there were two initial warm-up sets consisting of one set of six traits of neutral scale value, and a second set containing both desirable and undesirable traits. Two additional anchor sets were used. One set contained only highly desirable traits, and the second set only undesirable traits. One of the two sets was always read to the subject after the eleventh and twenty-second experimental sets.

Each set of traits was printed on a 5 × 8-inch card. The deck of cards was randomly shuffled for each subject with the stipulation that a given set and its reverse order not follow each other consecutively.

Subjects. Twenty-five females from an introductory psychology course participated as subjects. Each subject was run individually. The experimenter was a female who had no particular expectations concerning the outcome of the experiment.

Results

The mean ratings for the HL and LH orders of presentation for each experimental set are shown in columns 4 and 5 of Table 1. The mean

TABLE 1
Experimental Sets, Mean Probability, and Mean Primacy per Set

Set	Traits	Probability[a]	Order of presentation HL	Order of presentation LH	HL-LH[b]
$H_1L_1(+)$	Energetic, vigorous, resourceful, stubborn, dominating, egotistical	.770	5.36	4.44	.92
$H_2L_2(+)$	Trusting, patient, respectful, withdrawn, silent, helpless	.786	6.16	5.12	1.04
$H_3L_3(+)$	Bold, daring, adventurous, reckless, immature, foolhardy	.886	4.00	3.44	.56
$H_4L_4(+)$	Trustworthy, dependable, loyal, shy, passive, timid	.859	6.88	6.52	.36
$H_5L_5(+)$	Self-disciplined, logical, intelligent, gloomy, cynical, moody	.636	5.20	4.08	1.12
$H_6L_6(+)$	Cheerful, humorous, good-natured, noisy, boisterous, childish	.747	5.44	4.72	.72
$H_7L_7(+)$	Polite, agreeable, cooperative, mediocre, dull, uninteresting	.718	5.04	4.16	.88
$H_8L_8(+)$	Self-confident, sharp-witted, active, irritable, careless, grouchy	.581	4.40	3.68	.72
M		.748	5.31	4.52	.79
$H_1L_2(-)$	Energetic, vigorous, resourceful, withdrawn, silent, helpless	.200	5.40	4.84	.56
$H_2L_1(-)$	Trusting, patient, respectful, stubborn, dominating, egotistical	.400	5.52	4.68	.84
$H_3L_4(-)$	Bold, daring, adventurous, shy, passive, timid	.216	5.92	5.80	.12
$H_4L_3(-)$	Trustworthy, dependable, loyal, reckless, immature, foolhardly	.261	4.92	4.36	.56
$H_5L_6(-)$	Self-disciplined, logical, intelligent, noisy, boisterous, childish	.322	5.36	4.40	.96
$H_6L_5(-)$	Cheerful, humorous, good-natured, gloomy, cynical, moody	.254	5.16	4.48	.68
$H_7L_8(-)$	Polite, agreeable, cooperative, irritable, careless, grouchy	.261	4.88	4.04	.84
$H_8L_7(-)$	Self-confident, sharp-witted, active, mediocre, dull, uninteresting	.252	5.00	4.20	.80
M		.271	5.27	4.60	.67

[a] The probabilities shown are the mean ratings of likelihood in the preliminary study that the person possessing the first three H traits could also possess the three L traits.

[b] A positive HL-LH score indicates a primacy effect.

HL-LH primacy-recency score is shown in the last column of Table 1. All of the sets showed a primacy effect ranging from a low of .12 for Set H_3L_4 (—) to 1.12 for Set H_5L_5 (+).

The main point of interest was whether the magnitude of the primacy effect for the HL (+) sets differed from the effect for the HL (—) sets. The mean primacy effect for the eight HL (+) sets was .79, while the mean effect for the eight HL (—) sets was .67. The difference of .12 was in the direction opposite to that predicted by the discounting hypothesis. The sixteen HL-LH difference scores for each subject were reduced to two scores by averaging over the eight HL (+) sets, and over the eight HL (—) sets. A repeated measures analysis of variance was used to test the significance of the difference between the two set types. The results indicated that the mean difference of .12 was far from significance ($F < 1$, $df = 1/24$).

A second question concerned whether the overall primacy effect was significant. An average primacy score was calculated across the 16 sets for each subject. The mean of these scores was .73. This mean was tested against a theoretical mean of zero. The mean of .73 was significantly greater than zero ($F = 27.09$, $df = 1/24$, $p < .005$) indicating that a reliable overall primacy effect occurred.

Another test of the discounting hypothesis may be made by direct examination of the HL and the LH mean ratings. If discounting of the second block of information occurs under inconsistency, the HL (—) mean should be more positive than the HL (+) mean. Also the LH (—) mean should be more negative than the LH (+) mean. Inspection of Table 1 shows that the HL (+) mean was 5.31 and the HL (—) mean was 5.27. The difference between the means was a trivial .04. The LH (+) mean was 4.52 and the LH (—) mean was 4.60. The difference was only .08 and was in the direction opposite to that predicted by the discounting hypothesis.

Discussion

The results of the first experiment clearly indicate that with serial presentation, variation in the amount of intertrait consistency did not produce differential primacy. Therefore, the data offered no support for the inconsistency discounting hypothesis. The results do provide de facto support for the attention decrement hypothesis, since the latter would not predict any difference in amount of primacy between the HL (+) and HL (—) sets.

It should be noted that the results cannot be attributed to some peculiarity of the stimulus sets or to lack of variation in amount of stimulus inconsistency. The mean probability rating was .748 for the eight HL (+) sets and .271 for the HL (—) sets, and the mean probability differences were highly significant within each stimulus replication. Also, since the same traits were used in both HL (+) and HL (—) set types, a control was provided for specific adjectives used in constructing sets.

While the first experiment was in progress, Anderson (1968a) reported a study showing a recency effect when unipolar sets were used (e.g., highly desirable and moderately desirable traits). This result was obtained with both a continuous mode (Stewart, 1965) and a final mode of evaluative responding. Presumably, strong inconsistency did not exist in these unipolar sets, so that the recency effect indirectly supports the inconsistency discounting hypothesis. However, in Anderson's (1968a) study, subjects were required to pronounce each stimulus word as it was presented, a procedure not used in any of the other primacy studies. This procedure may have forced the subjects to pay more attention to all the adjectives than would have occurred without pronunciation. Also, pronunciation of the later traits in the series may have interfered with retention of the earlier traits. If such events occurred, a recency effect would be expected regardless of which mode of evaluative responding was used. One implication of the interpretation given above is that if the pronunciation procedure were used with the sets shown in Table 1, a recency effect should be obtained for both HL (+) and HL (—) set types. That implication was tested in the second experiment.

Experiment II[2]

METHOD

The design of the second experiment used the same basic procedures that were used in the first experiment. The main variation was that half the subjects were randomly assigned to a pronunciation condition in which they pronounced each adjective after it was presented, and gave an evaluation of the stimulus person at the end of the series of adjectives. The other half of the subjects were assigned to a regular condition which involved only an evaluation of the stimulus person at the end of the series of adjectives. The regular condition served as a partial replication of the first experiment, and it was predicted that a primacy effect would be obtained for both consistent and inconsistent set types. In contrast a recency effect was predicted for the pronunciation condition for both set types.

Stimulus Sets. Three of the four stimulus replications used in the first experiment were used in the second experiment. Since each replication consisted of four sets, there

[2] The authors are indebted to Rhoda Lindner for suggesting the feasibility of the second experiment.

were twelve different adjective sets used altogether. Six of the sets contained strong affective inconsistency and the other six sets were consistent. Since both HL and LH orders of presentation were used, each subject rated twenty-four experimental sets. In addition there were three warm-up sets, and ten anchor sets mixed with the experimental sets. Anchor sets consisted of either all H traits, all L traits, or H and L traits in random order.

Subjects and Procedure. Forty-four students from an introductory psychology class participated individually as subjects. Eighteen of the subjects were males and twenty-six were females. Half the subjects were randomly assigned to the regular response condition and the other half were assigned the pronunciation condition. When a subject arrived for the experimental session, the nature of the impression task was briefly explained. Subjects were told that several sets of traits, each describing a different person, would be read to them. Subjects in the pronunciation condition were asked to pronounce each trait word out loud after the experimenter pronounced it. The subject's task was to form an impression of the person and rate him in terms of the favorability of the impression. A cardboard scale with numbers from 1 to 8 with identifying labels (e.g., highly favorable under 8 and highly unfavorable under 1) was placed in front of the subject. Subjects were told that each adjective in a set was contributed by a different individual who knew the person, and that perfect consistency in the description should not be expected.

The experimenter read the adjectives in the regular condition at a steady rate of one word every three seconds. In the pronunciation condition the experimenter read the next word in the series immediately after the subject had repeated the previous word. Most subjects called out their numerical response within five seconds after the sixth word in the set was presented. Each set of adjectives was printed on a 5 × 8-inch card and the deck of cards was randomly shuffled for each subject, except that a given random order was presented to one subject each in both the regular condition and the pronunciation condition. An additional requirement was that a given set and its reverse order not follow each other consecutively.

Results

An HL-LH difference score was calculated for each of the 12 experimental sets for each subject. The six difference scores for the consistent sets were averaged, as were the six difference scores for the inconsistent sets, to provide two primacy-recency scores for each subject. The means of these primacy-recency scores are shown in Table 2 for the response conditions and for the set types. The mean shown in each cell is based on 22 subjects. The means shown in Table 2 strongly supported the predictions. A mean primacy effect of .636 was obtained when subjects gave only a final evaluation of the stimulus person. When subjects were required to pronounce each adjective, a mean recency effect of —.379 was obtained.

The data were analyzed by analysis of variance. The subject sums for the six sets within each set type were used rather than averages for calculational convenience. A summary of the analysis is shown in Table 3.

TABLE 2
Mean Primacy-Recency Effects: HL-LH[a]

Set type	Response mode: Regular	Pronunciation	M
Consistent	.621	−.409	.212
Inconsistent	.652	−.348	.304
M	.636	−.379	

[a] Positive means indicate a primacy effect and negative means indicate a recency effect.

The analysis for response mode indicated that the mean of .636 for the regular condition was significantly larger than the mean of —.379 for the pronunciation condition ($F = 25.80$, $df = 1/42$, $p < .001$). Variation in trait consistency had no effect in either of the response conditions. The mean primacy of .621 for the consistent sets in the regular condition was virtually the same as the mean of .652 for the inconsistent sets. This result replicates the results of the first experiment. Similarly, the mean recency of —.409 for the consistent sets in the pronunciation condition was almost the same as the mean of —.348 for the inconsistent sets. These small differences are reflected in the nonsignificant main effect ($F < 1$) for set type shown in Table 3. Whether primacy or recency was obtained depended entirely on the response requirements imposed on the subjects, and not at all on the variation in inconsistency.

The marginal column means shown in Table 2 were also tested against zero. The mean primacy of .636 for the regular condition was significantly greater than zero ($F = 24.47$, $df = 1/21$, $p < .001$). The mean recency effect of —.379 for the pronunciation condition was significantly less than zero ($F = 6.14$, $df = 1/21$, $p < .05$). Thus each effect considered separately was reliable.

TABLE 3
Summary Analysis of Variance

Source	df	MS	F
Response mode (A)	1	816.18	25.80[a]
Error	42	31.63	
Set type (B)	1	1.63	—
A × B	1	.19	—
Error	42	11.60	

[a] $p < .001$.

Discussion

The results of the second experiment support the interpretation given for the conflicting results between Anderson's (1968a) experiment and the results of the first experiment. When subjects were required to give only a final evaluative response, primacy was obtained. But when subjects were additionally required to pronounce each word as it was presented, recency effects were obtained. Variation in inconsistency was not a significant variable in either of the two experiments. By implication, the results of Anderson's (1968a) study may be attributed to response requirements instead of lack of inconsistency among the stimuli.

The results of the present experiments provide no support for the inconsistency discounting hypothesis. The results of both studies are consistent with the attention decrement hypothesis. One generalization that seems to be slowly emerging from the primacy studies is that when verbal stimuli are used, a primacy effect may be generally expected when one final evaluative response is given to the stimulus set. When evaluative responding is required after each item (Stewart, 1965), when recall of the stimuli is required (Anderson & Hubert, 1963), or when pronunciation of the stimuli is required as in Anderson (1968a) and the second experiment, recency effects are obtained. All of these procedures presumably redistribute attention across the stimuli in the series and the results accordingly suggest the attention decrement interpretation.

References

Anderson, N. H. Averaging versus adding as a stimulus combination rule in impression formation. *Journal of Experimental Psychology,* 1965, **70**, 394–400. (a)

Anderson, N. H. Primacy effects in personality impression formation using a generalized order effect paradigm. *Journal of Personality and Social Psychology,* 1965, **2**, 1–9. (b)

Anderson, N. H. Application of a linear-serial model to a personality-impression task using serial presentation. *Journal of Personality and Social Psychology,* 1968, **10**, 354–362. (a)

Anderson, N. H. Likableness ratings of 555 personality-trait words. *Journal of Personality and Social Psychology,* 1968, **9**, 272–279. (b)

Anderson, N. H., & Hubert, S. Effects of concomitant verbal recall on order effects in personality impression formation. *Journal of Verbal Learning and Verbal Behavior,* 1963, **2**, 379–391.

Anderson, N. H., & Jacobson, A. Effects of stimulus inconsistency and discounting instructions in personality impression formation. *Journal of Personality and Social Psychology,* 1965, **2**, 531–539.

Asch, S. E. Forming impressions of personality. *Journal of Abnormal and Social Psychology,* 1946, **41**, 258–290.

Scott, J. P. *Early experience and the organization of behavior.* Belmont, Calif.: Brooks/Cole, 1968.

Stewart, R. H. Effect of continuous responding on the order effect in personality impression formation. *Journal of Personality and Social Psychology,* 1965, **1**, 161–165.

Discussion

The problem of how to compare and evaluate competing alternative explanations for a phenomenon is an extremely complex one. It is made more difficult by the fact that there is very little of a general nature that can be said about alternative explanations. One can exhort others to be as careful as possible, to make sure they include all the appropriate control conditions, etc., but in the end one is faced with explanations that are idiosyncratic to the particular procedures that were employed in a given study. Consider, for example, Hendrick and Costantini's (1970) summary statement of their findings ". . . The results of both studies are consistent with the attention decrement hypothesis [p. 163]." It does, indeed, appear that primacy occurs when the subject is not forced to pay attention to each adjective (their regular response mode) and recency occurs when the subject is forced to pay attention to each adjective (their pronunciation response mode). This is "consistent" with the attention decrement hypothesis. But think about it for a moment. Is their data really evidence for the attention decrement hypothesis.

On page 162 they state that ". . . The experimenter read the adjectives in the regular condition at a steady rate of one word every three seconds. In the pronunciation condition the experimenter read the next word in the series immediately after the subject had repeated the previous word." The problem is really a logical one. Suppose we know, for example, that every time A is absent and B is present, X occurs. Further, when A is present and B is absent, Y occurs. Can we then say that X occurs because A is absent? No, of course not. As far as we know, the necessary conditions for X to occur are for A to be absent and B to be present.

In short, Hendrick and Costantini's (1970) pronunciation condition not only forced the subject to pay attention to every adjective, but it also took away the intervals between adjectives during which subjects in the regular condition could let the adjectives "sink in." Thus, their results say no more about the attention decrement hypothesis than they do about the crystallization of initial impression hypothesis (Asch, 1946; Anderson and Barrios, 1961). It would have been nice, for purposes of distinguishing these two explanations, if Hendrick and Costantini (1970) had included a condition in which subjects were required to pronounce each adjective and were allowed a few seconds after each pronunciation for the adjective to sink in before the experimenter read the next word.

The question of appropriate controls and appropriate control conditions is a recurring question in all experimental research. As Boring (1969) points out "... in the specification of a variable one always remains uncertain as to how exhaustive the description is. Artifacts adhere implicitly to specification and, when they are discovered, ingenuity may still be unable to circumvent them. When they are not discovered, they may persist for a year or a century and eventually turn out to be the reason why a well-established fact is at long last disconfirmed. For this reason scientific truth remains forever tentative, subject always to this possible eventual disconfirmation [p. 9]."

In this chapter we have been primarily concerned with alternative explanations and have devoted relatively little space to other methodological problems. In part, our concentration on alternative explanations in the area of impression formation has been due to the comparative precision with which questions can be investigated in the paradigm used by Anderson. We will return to other methodological difficulties in the following two chapters. Before doing that, however, we need to say a few words about impression formation research.

It has probably already occurred to the reader that the studies referred to in this chapter have gotten increasingly further away from "impression formation" as we know it in everyday life. One could, in fact, raise serious questions about the relevance of any of these experiments to the actual way in which we form impressions of others. This is a serious problem. The Anderson paradigm is a highly artificial one and while the studies we have cited do seem to be "zeroing in" on certain variables important in information processing, they tell us little about person perception.

There are signs, however, that impression formation research is entering an exciting new era. Recent advances in clustering (Johnson, 1967) and multidimensional scaling (Kruskal, 1964) offer the possibility of rigorously analyzing free descriptions of other persons and allowing inspection of the basic dimensions and categories that people use in forming impressions of others. The interested reader is referred to Rosenberg and Sedlak (1969) and Rosenberg and Jones (1971) for a description of these procedures.

REFERENCES

Anderson, N. H. Test of a model for opinion change. *Journal of Abnormal and Social Psychology,* 1959, **59**, 371–381.

Anderson, N. H., & Hovland, C. I. The representation of order effects in communication research. In C. I. Hovland *et al.* (Eds.), *The order of presentation in persuasion.* New Haven: Yale University Press, 1957, 158–169.

Anderson, N. H., & Jacobson, A. Effect of stimulus inconsistency and discounting instructions in personality impression formation. *Journal of Personality and Social Psychology,* 1965, **2**, 531–539.

Anderson, N. H., & Norman, A. Order effects in impression formation in four classes of stimuli. *Journal of Abnormal and Social Psychology,* 1964, **69**, 467–471.

Asch, S. E. Forming impressions of personality. *Journal of Abnormal and Social Psychology,* 1946, **41**, 258–290.

Boring, E. C. Perspective: Artifact and control. In R. Rosenthal and R. L. Rosnow (Eds.), *Artifact in behavioral research.* New York: Academic Press, 1969, 1–11.

Cromwell, H. The relative effect on audience attitude of the first versus the second argumentative speech of a series. *Speech Mongraphs,* 1950, **17**, 105–122.

Hovland, C. I., Campbell, E. H., and Brock, T. The effects of "commitment" on opinion change following communication. In C. I. Hovland *et al.* (Eds.), *The order of presentation in persuasion.* New Haven: Yale University Press, 1957, 23–32.

Hovland, C. I., & Mandell, W. Is there a "law of primacy in persuasion?" In C. I. Hovland *et al.* (Eds.), *The order of presentation in persuasion.* New Haven: Yale University Press, 1957, 13–22.

Johnson, S. C. Hierarchical clustering schemes. *Psychometrika,* 1967, **32**, 241–254.

Kruskal, J. B. Multidimensional scaling by optimizing goodness of fit to a nonmetric hypothesis. *Psychometrika,* 1964, **29**, 1–27.

Lana, R. E. Three theoretical interpretations of order effects in persuasive communications. *Psychological Bulletin,* 1964, **61**, 315–320.

Luchins, A. S., Chapter 4, Primacy-recency in impression formation, and Chapter 5, Experimental attempts to minimize the impact of first impressions. In C. I. Hovland *et al.* (Eds.), *The order of presentation in persuasion.* New Haven: Yale University Press, 1957, 33–75.

Lund, F. H. The psychology of belief. IV. The law of primacy in persuasion. *Journal of Abnormal and Social Psychology,* 1925, **20**, 183–191.

McGuire, W. J. Order of presentation as a factor in "conditioning" persuasiveness. In C. I. Hovland *et al.* (Eds.), *The order of presentation in persuasion.* New Haven: Yale University Press, 1957, 98–114.

Miller, N., & Campbell, D. T. Primacy and recency in persuasion as a function of the timing of the speeches and measurements. *Journal of Abnormal and Social Psychology,* 1959, **59**, 1–9.

Rosenberg, S., & Jones, R. A. A method for investigating and representing a person's implicit theory of personality: Theodore Dreiser's view of people. Unpublished manuscript, Rutgers University, 1971.

Rosenberg, S., & Sedlak, A. Structural representations of perceived personality trait relationships. Paper presented at the Seminar on Scaling and Measurement, University of California, Irvine, June, 1969.

Stewart, R. H. Effect of continuous responding on the order effect in personality impression formation. *Journal of Personality and Social Psychology,* 1965, **1**, 161–165.

Chapter 9

FOREWARNING AND ANTICIPATORY ATTITUDE CHANGE

There are many different ways in which research proceeds. One way, exemplified in the chapter on expectancy, is for a prediction derived from a general theory to be applied to a particular problem area. A primary advantage of a good theory is that it can be used to make predictions in a number of different empirical areas. For example, dissonance theory has something to say about the processes that occur when one's expectancies are disconfirmed, but it also has something to say about the very different area of effort justification.

Suppose someone has worked extremely hard and deprived himself for years so that he could get through graduate school, obtain a Ph.D., and become a college professor. Suppose, further, that he "makes it," but that he is extremely unhappy in his new position. Clearly, our young professor has two dissonant cognitions: (1) "I worked for years to become a college professor," and (2) "I am very unhappy as a college professor." Presumably, rational people would not work for years to become unhappy. Several things might occur, according to dissonance theory. Our young academician might begin to differentiate the goal. That is, he might convince himself that he is unhappy as a faculty member at institution A, but, if he were at institution B, life would be wonderful. He might also begin to accentuate aspects of his job which he did like—to make them more important and convince himself that he really is quite happy. Dissonance theory would predict either or both of these reactions: differentiation of the goal and/or a reshuffling of priorities on our professor's happiness ladder. The alternative is too difficult. To admit that one has spent years working for a goal which is not very pleasant once attained is too damaging to one's self and hence unlikely to occur.

A primary advantage of a theory is that it helps in organizing our knowledge of the world. Problems and processes which appear quite diverse superficially can be organized and understood in terms of a single conceptual structure. The processes that ensue when one exceeds one's expectancies and when one's effort leads to a negative outcome may be quite similar. The advantage of beginning with a theory is a great one.

But suppose that something interesting occurs and there is no theory to explain it. One of the most exciting ways in which research can proceed begins with the observation of an unexpected and unexplained phenomenon. Such observations are often discarded or forgotten as the researcher pursues the topic that he was investigating when the unexpected phenomenon presented itself. Sometimes the new finding is intriguing enough so that it becomes the focus of research. If the new finding does become the focus of attention, how is research to proceed? One way is to propose one or more tentative explanations and then set up the necessary conditions for a test or demonstration of the tentative explanations.

Here, then, we are working from phenomena to explanation and back to phenomena. One could argue, of course, that all theories originate with observation of phenomena so that this method is not really different from research that is within the tradition of testing an existing general theory. There is a difference, however, in terms of freedom of inquiry and room for creativity available to the researcher. Can he come up with plausible and, hopefully, accurate explanations of what he has observed? Can he set up a well designed experiment to try out the adequacy of these explanations? Or must the new and exciting phenomena be crammed into some already existing theoretical mold?

The three articles of the present chapter focus on a topic for which the existing theoretical molds were inadequate. Research interest was focused on the topic as the result of what was originally a serendipitous and statistically nonsignificant finding.

Forewarning and Attitude Change

Over a decade ago, Carl Hovland (1959) called attention to some intriguing discrepancies between laboratory and field studies of attitude change. He pointed out that in experiments the audience is usually initially opposed to the position advocated in the communication to which they are exposed. Thus, there is a great deal of room for attitude change as a result of hearing the communication. In field studies, however, a process of self selection might be occurring. That is, members of the audience who are opposed to the position that is to be advocated in the communication might not expose themselves to it. One would hardly expect to find many Democrats at a speech given by the local Republican Party leader. The audience would be composed mostly of people of similar political persuasion. Hence, one would expect the speech to change few attitudes. Everyone already agrees with the speaker.

While such self selection on the part of the audience might account for the smaller change in the field settings, it is relatively uninteresting. If you agree with a speaker, one would expect that your attitude would not change as a result of listening to the speaker (other things being equal). But perhaps the process is a little more subtle. Perhaps the important question is whether or not the audience knows in advance what position the speaker is going to take. If that is the case, then we might expect Democrats at the Republican's speech—but Democrats with a difference. They would arrive with their defenses all worked up and ready to do battle. Another possibility is that the Democrats would come but would simply not listen to the speech. The important variable might then be whether or not the audience knew in advance what position the speaker was going to take. This is a somewhat more interesting possibility because it is not immediately clear how knowledge of the speaker's position would inhibit or promote attitude change. Do the opposed members of the audience simply not listen? Do they sit there and silently refute each point made by the speaker? How important is it that they have specific defenses prepared in advance? McGuire and Papageorgis (1962) set out to investigate the extent to which forewarning of an impending attack on one's beliefs helps develop resistance to the attack.

McGuire and Papageorgis (1962) worked with health issues on which there was a generally believed "correct position" which most people had seldom or never heard attacked. For example, one of the beliefs they used was "Everyone should get a chest X-ray each year in order to detect any tuberculosis symptoms at an early stage." Since these beliefs had never been attacked, they were considered analogous to an organism raised in a germ free environment. The authors argued that "just as we develop the disease resistance of a person raised in a germ free environment by pre-exposing him to a weakened form of the virus so as to stimulate, without overcoming, his defenses, so also we would develop the resistance to persuasion of a person raised in an ideologically asceptic environment by pre-exposing him to weakened forms of the counterarguments, or to some other belief threatening material strong enough to stimulate, but not so strong as to overcome, his belief defenses (McGuire and Papageorgis, 1962, p. 25)."

In earlier studies (McGuire and Papageorgis, 1961; Papageorgis and McGuire, 1961) the relative effectiveness of different types of pre-attack defenses had been investigated. In general, supportive defenses which simply gave positive reasons for maintaining the already held belief were found to be less effective in conferring resistance to subsequent attack than were refutational defenses which involved "mentioning counterarguments (the threatening material) against the belief but weakening these counterarguments by explicitly refuting them (McGuire and Papageorgis, 1962, p. 25)."

Following up these earlier studies, McGuire and Papageorgis (1962) hypothesized that telling someone in advance (forewarning) that his beliefs are about to be attacked would motivate more resistance to the subsequent attack than if there is no forewarning. Presumably the forewarning contains an element of threat which stimulates one's defenses. This being the case, the supportive defenses should gain more when coupled with the forewarning of impending attack than the refutational defenses should gain, since the latter already contain defense stimulating threats. Both of these predictions were borne out by the data. When subjects were forewarned that their beliefs were going to be attacked, the defenses were more effective in bestowing resistance to the subsequent attacks. Furthermore, this was primarily due to the heightened effectiveness of the supportive defenses when accompanied by forewarning of an impending attack.

Happily, for our purposes, McGuire and Papageorgis included two control conditions in which subjects were exposed to neither an attack or defense message. They were simply forewarned or not of an impending attack on their beliefs. Data from these conditions indicated that forewarning per se caused some opinion change toward greater agreement with the impending attack. The finding was not statistically significant, but it was intriguing.

Two questions might have occurred at this point. First, is the finding "for real?" That is, could an appropriately designed study demonstrate the finding at an acceptable level of significance? Second, if it is a true phenomenon and not a statistical quirk, what is the explanation? Holding the first question in abeyance, what are some possible explanations for such postwarning preattack opinion change?

The Postwarning Preattack Interval

There have been a number of studies on the effects of forewarning on the reception of a subsequent message, but does forewarning of an attack have any effect before the message arrives? That is, are there any systematic influences operating in the postwarning preattack interval? There are several reasons for thinking that there might be.

Consider for a moment the information that warning of an impending attack conveys. The warning alerts one to the fact that someone else holds a different position on the issue. According to dissonance theory (Festinger, 1957), this information alone is sufficient to create some pressure toward changing the opinion. The magnitude of the pressure would, of course, be somewhat dependent on the identity of the person holding the discrepant opinion. One would hardly expect much pressure to change one's belief that teeth should be brushed after every meal if forewarned of an impending attack on that belief by the President of the Artificial Denture Manufacturer's Association. But if the source of the impending attack were not so easily dismissed as having an ulterior motive, there is at least the possibility here of precommunication opinion change. That is, learning that a different opinion from one's own does exist on a given issue may create some pressure to change one's own opinion—particularly if that different opinion is held by a highly respected other person. But then this analysis is not particularly compelling because we know that there are people who disagree with us on just about everything. Let us briefly look at other processes that might be operating in the postwarning preattack interval.

Reactance theory (Brehm, 1966) postulates that people may be viewed as having a set of free behaviors, any one of which they could engage in at will. If one of a person's free behaviors is threatened or eliminated, that person is said to experience "psychological reactance"—a motivational state directed toward safeguarding or restoring the free behavior in question. It is possible that when one is forewarned of an impending attack on one of his beliefs, that he will view this as a threat to his freedom to hold the opinion that he does. According to Brehm (1966, p. 94),

"When a person experiences reactance from having his freedom to hold his own opinion threatened, he will attempt to re-establish his freedom by not taking the position advocated by the communicator." Thus, reactance theory would predict that under some conditions (where the freedom to adopt any position on the issue is of high importance, for example) forewarning of any impending attack might actually cause one to change his opinion *away from* the position to be advocated in the impending attack. Since we are searching for possible explanations of why forewarning causes one to change his opinion *toward* the position to be advocated in the impending attack (as in the McGuire and Papageorgis, 1962 study), we will let this brief mention of reactance theory serve as our sole reminder that processes may be operating in the other direction.

Two related notions that might predict movement toward greater agreement with the position to be advocated in an impending attack on one's beliefs are demand characteristics (Orne, 1962) and ingratiation (Jones, 1964). The eagerness to please and to be thought a good subject are well documented motives (see Chapter 3) operating in the typical undergraduate who serves in psychological research. Furthermore, most of the issues used in research on forewarning and attitude change are relatively innocuous and unimportant to subjects. If the subject takes the forewarning of an impending attack on his belief as evidence that the experimenter would like to change that belief, it is quite conceivable that the subject changes his belief at that point, "without further ado," simply because it appears to be the result that the experimenter desires.

Another possible mechanism that may account for postwarning precommunication opinion change is fear arousal (Janis, 1962; 1967). It is not too farfetched to think of a forewarning of an impending attack on one's beliefs as making one afraid. In Janis' (1967) analysis of fear arousal, he points out that a "key assumption is that a person's level of reflective fear is roughly proportional both to the perceived probability of the dangerous event materializing and to the anticipated magnitude of the damage, if it does materialize [p. 170]." But even if a threatening forewarning of an impending attack on one's beliefs did arouse fear, what does that fear produce? Janis postulates three behavioral consequences of reflective fear: (1) heightened vigilance, (2) a tendency to seek reassurances, and (3) an increased probability that the person will develop "new attitudes involving a compromise between vigilance and reassurance tendencies [1967, p. 172]."

The last of the three is the most interesting. Unfortunately, it is not really clear what Janis meant by "will develop new attitudes." If we assume that a forewarning really does arouse fear, then perhaps the "new attitude" is one of greater agreement with the impending attack. But do all forewarnings arouse fear? If we are to use fear arousal as an explanatory mechanism for attitude change in the postwarning preattack phase, there are many assumptions that must be made. Is it really reasonable to think of precommunication opinion change as reducing fear? While the fear arousal-reduction sequence seems a possible explanation for postwarning precommunication opinion change, the details and assumptions of the process need to be spelled out in greater detail before predictions could be tried out in the laboratory.

So far we have specified several processes which at least might account for postwarning precommunication opinion change. First, the forewarning may serve to inform that someone else holds an opinion discrepant from one's own and this may create pressure to change the opinion. Second, the forewarning may serve simply as a cue to cooperative subjects that the experimenter would like for them to change their attitudes—that is, the forewarning is a demand characteristic of the experimental setting. Third, the subject may be actively trying to ingratiate himself with the experimenter by changing his attitudes as a result of the forewarning. Finally, forewarning may be fear-arousing. The subject may be afraid of exposing himself or being exposed to arguments which oppose his opinions on certain issues. The main problem with each of these explanations is that they have not been spelled out in sufficient detail to allow empirically meaningful tests and comparisons.

In the following article, McGuire and Millman make yet another explanation for postwarning precommunication opinion change and put it to an experimental test. They postulate the operation of a face-saving ploy as the main result of a threatening forewarning of an impending attack on one's beliefs. In reading the McGuire and Millman article, note how the authors first spell out the boundary conditions of their version of self-esteem theory. By boundary conditions we mean simply the conditions under which the theory would be expected to hold. Note also how self-esteem theory might be considered a refined and well articulated subtheory within the fear arousal framework proposed by Janis.

One should always remember that the most important parts of an article are usually the Method and Results sections. If the authors clearly indicate the conditions under which their data were obtained and clearly present those data, then the data are always available even though the currently popular theoretical interpretations may change. Each manipulation should be carefully thought through—"does this procedure really manipulate the variable of interest?" In the McGuire and Millman article, is the emotional-technical manipulation adequate?

It is also worth keeping in mind that the impetus for this experiment arose from the statistically trivial finding reported by McGuire and Papageorgis (1962). "Self-esteem theory," at least this particular version of it, is a creative attempt to explain a novel and unexpected finding.

Anticipatory Belief Lowering Following Forewarning of a Persuasive Attack[1]

William J. McGuire and Susan Millman

It was predicted (and found) that forewarning a person that he is about to receive strong persuasive attacks on specified beliefs which he holds will result, under our experimental conditions, in an anticipatory lowering of these beliefs. Further predictions were made and confirmed that this anticipatory lowering due to warning will be greater on emotional than on technical issues, but that the actual attacks, when they do come, will lower beliefs on the technical issues more than those on the emotional issues. Finally it was predicted that both the forewarnings and the actual attacks will be more effective in lowering belief if the predesignated sources were respectable rather than disreputable ones. This prediction was confirmed as regards the attacks but not the forewarnings. These predictions were derived from self-esteem theory, but it was pointed out that dissonance theory could predict similar outcomes and that, in fact, both theories had heuristic value despite being rather equivocal on most of the points at issue.

It has been suggested earlier (McGuire & Papageorgis, 1962) that forewarning a person of an impending persuasive attack may have a paradoxical effect: the warning, whatever its effect on resistance to the attack when it comes, may itself weaken the belief that is designated as the intended target. The prediction that forewarning of attack results in an anticipatory lowering of the belief prior to the attack can be derived from several alternative sets of assumptions, but in designing the present study we were guided by what we call "self-esteem" theory.

This theory posits that people tend to be anxious about their ability to resist social pressure; the person suspects that he will prove more susceptible to influence than he would like to appear to himself and to others. Hence, when told in advance that certain beliefs (which he happens to accept) are about to be exposed to skillful persuasive attacks, the person worries that he will succumb to the arguments and appear gull-

[1] From the *Journal of Personality and Social Psychology* 1965, **2**, No. 4, 471–479. Received May 4, 1964. Reproduced by permission of the publisher.

The research reported here was supported by a grant from the National Science Foundation, Division of Social Sciences.

At the time of writing both authors were with Columbia University. Current affiliations: McGuire, Yale University; Millman, Polytechnic Institute of Brooklyn.

ible. An elegant self-esteem preserving (and face-saving) maneuver in this situation is for the person to decide, before the attack comes, that he did not really hold the target belief in the first place. To this end he will moderate his belief away from his initial position (which is to be attacked) when he gets the warning. Then when the attack comes, it will reduce his belief to the given point, but the change from just before to after attack will be less for this forewarned person, who has subtly traversed part of the distance between the warning and the attack, than it will be for the unforewarned person. In Janis' (1962) terminology, the individual responds to warning of persuasive attack in a way that will provide reassurance, rather than by hypervigilance.

Clearly, the psychological availability and suitability of this anticipatory-lowering strategy depends on a number of factors. Hence, we introduced several additional variables into the design to test some of these further implications about conditions likely to interact with the forewarning-of-attack variable in inducing anticipatory lowering of belief. First, we added a type-of-issue variable, since the believer's need to make use of this strategy will be more pronounced to the extent that a change of belief following the attack is clearly indicative of gullibility rather than of something more commendable. If the issue is a technical matter-of-fact one, rather than an emotional unverifiable one, the person could ascribe any opinion change after the attack to a commendable openness to evidence and ability to take in new information, rather than to a socially undesirable inability to stand up for one's own opinion. Second, we introduced a positive versus negative source-valence variable. The believer is likely to use the anticipatory lowering strategy to the extent he expects the impending attack to produce a great deal of change. If he expects that it will come from a highly persuasive source he should show more anticipatory change than if he expects an attack from a less effective, negative source.[2]

The above predictions all deal with main or interaction effects of the forewarning of attacks, prior to any actual attacks. As described above, self-esteem theory does not predict that the forewarning will mitigate the effect of the attack when it comes. We did, however, introduce the additional variable of attack versus no attack into the design to check this assumption of no effect and also because self-esteem theory did predict

[2] A third relevant factor is the ambiguity of the believer's initial opinion on the issue. If he is already clear in his own mind (and especially if he is publicly committed) to an initial stand on the issue prior to the forewarning of attack, it would hardly be feasible to employ this face-saving anticipating lowering strategy. Initial ambiguity was not manipulated in the present study because there are two earlier studies bearing on it (McGuire & Anderson, 1959; Sears, Freedman, & O'Connor, 1964).

that the actual-attack manipulation would interact with our other two variables, type of issue and source credibility, in determining the final belief levels.

The actual attacks should be more effective against the technical than the emotional issues, since, as discussed above, changing one's opinion on a technical issue can be interpreted as an openness to information, intellectual flexibility, and ability to assimilate new information (all desirable traits), rather than to the undesirable gullibility that is more clearly indicated by a yielding on the controversial, emotional issues. It will be noted that the very principles that required our predicting that the forewarning would have a *greater* impact on emotional than on the technical issues, requires our predicting that the actual attacks will have a *lesser* impact on these emotional than on the technical issues. It also follows from self-esteem theory that the attacks will have more persuasive impact if attributed to highly respectable sources rather than to disreputable ones, on the assumption that it is less damaging to self-esteem to have yielded to a reputable person.

Method

General Procedures

Participation in the experiment required one 75-minute session. The 96 subjects were run in small groups ranging from 12 to 20 during the regular class meetings of the various sections of an educational-methods course. All of the materials and measures were administered silently to the subjects by means of preprogramed mimeographed booklets that were designed to allow each of the participants at a given administration to be serving in a different condition.

The experiment was explained to the subjects as designed to develop a test of analytic thinking ability that could be used by the Federal government in selecting technical personnel for the Foreign Service, the CIA, and other sensitive agencies. To justify the mechanical, preprogramed administration procedure, the subjects were told that the study was being conducted cooperatively by several large universities and hence it was necessary for us to exercise care in keeping the conditions highly standardized from college to college. To those ends, all of the instructions were printed in their test booklets. These instructions were to be read silently by the students and no further questions could be asked of the experimenter. Also, the time allowance had been carefully predetermined and the subjects were requested to work on a given page only during the time provided for it, and not to turn ahead or back at any time, except when instructed by the experimenter to turn to the next page.

The first pages of all booklets told the students that the test section of the booklet contained reading passages that had been written by skillful specialists on the topics being discussed, who were endeavoring to convey their points of view. The students would be required to read these passages analytically, and then their own opinions on these issues would be measured. The instructions continued by stating that a wide variety of passages were being pretested and that different passages would go to different people, but four of the possible topics were listed to give them an idea of the type of issues to be discussed. This listing constituted the forewarning of attack: for any one subject four additional items went unmentioned and constituted the "no-forewarning" condition. The four mentioned issues included two technical ones and two emotional ones; the four unmentioned issues were similarly subdivided.

Next followed the prior description of the source. Subjects in the high source-credibility condition were told the passages would come from editors of learned journals in the areas discussed, the passage being taken from reports (urging the actions indicated) that they had made as chairmen of Presidential Advisory Committees to which they had been appointed by either President Eisenhower or President Kennedy. The other half of the subjects (in the low source-credibility condition) were told the passages come from highly skilled criminals who had been convicted of rather distasteful crimes which carried heavy penalties, the passages being taken from part of their skillful defense testimony, arguing for the point indicated.

The subject then read persuasive messages, on four different issues, each of a length that filled a single-spaced letter-sized sheet. Before each message was a short description of its source (depicting him in detail as a presidential advisor and editor, or as a skilled criminal, depending on the source condition for that subject) for which the subject received one minute to read. Four minutes were allowed for reading the persuasive message itself, and to pick out and underline the principle clause in each of its three paragraphs (these underlining tasks having been introduced to assure attention to the passages). The four messages received by any one subject include two on forewarned issues (one technical and one emotional) and two on issues that had not been mentioned in advance (again a technical and an emotional issue). The subjects were then asked to fill out an opinionnaire designed to measure their personal opinions on all issues, their responses to this opinionnaire providing the dependent-variable scores.

MATERIALS

The eight issues used included four emotional and four technical ones. The four emotional ones were as follows: the high likelihood of further Communist takeovers in Latin America; the difficulties of developing a cure for cancer; the probability of a serious economic depression in the United States; and the growing likelihood of a third world war. The four noncontroversial technical issues included: the growing shortage of laboratory animals for experimental research; the failure of the earth sciences to aid in finding oil deposits; the continuing need for propeller planes in commercial aviation; and the likely abolition of the sales tax. Prestudy revealed that initial opinions of college students were preponderantly on the opposite sides of the issues from those stated above. Since in the forewarnings of attack the messages were represented as taking an extreme stand on the unpopular sides of the issues, practically all of the subjects could anticipate receiving messages arguing for a position far removed from their own initial positions on each of the forewarned issues.

The message on each issue was about 600 words long, broken into three paragraphs. The first paragraph described the thesis of the message and stated that informed people were largely in agreement with the point expressed. Two of the "many" reasons why the experts were in agreement with the thesis were then stated, and the following two paragraphs developed these reasons in detail. The tone of presentations was

TABLE 1
Final Belief Level in All Conditions[a]

Persuasive condition \ Type of belief	Emotional		Technical	
	Positive source	Negative source	Positive source	Negative source
No warning, no attack	9.29	9.53	9.79	9.55
Warning, no attack	8.60	8.76	9.66	9.39
No warning, attack	7.87	8.73	6.83	7.67
Warning, attack	7.71	8.48	7.00	7.94

[a] Scores are the means based on a 15-point scale, with the attacks aimed at lowering the mean. Each cell mean based on 48 subjects.

scholarly and the arguments used were rational ones making use of statistics and technical analyses of the situation.

The final opinionnaire that furnished the dependent variable scores contained 50 items, 6 dealing with each of the eight issues and 2 repeated items to allow a reliability check. Each item was in the form of a statement paraphrasing the thesis of the message on that issue. The subject was asked to indicate his agreement with each statement by circling a number between 1 and 15 on a scale immediately beneath the statement. The 6 statements dealing with any issue were counterbalanced for acquiescence when presented to the subjects, but in analyzing the data these raw scores were converted so that, in the present paper, the closer to 15.00 the reported condition mean, the less successful was the attack or warning in reducing the belief.

Design and Subjects

The study included four two-level experimental variables in a $2 \times 2 \times 2 \times 2$ design, including: warning versus no warning, attack versus no attack, emotional versus technical issues, and high- versus low-credibility sources. The first three were within-subject variables. Hence, each subject served in eight conditions, each on a separate issue, so that eight issues were required (four technical and four emotional). The specific issues were systematically rotated around the experimental conditions from subject to subject. The fourth (source-credibility) variable was the only between-subject manipulation of theoretical interest, and 48 subjects served in the high-credibility condition and another 48 in the low.

The subjects were 99 students taking an educational-methods course required for a teacher's certificate. Most of them were recent college graduates in liberal arts who had gone into elementary or secondary school teaching and needed this and other educational-methods courses to qualify for a permanent teacher's certificate. The experiment had not been announced in advance and all students who came to the regular class meeting (about 90% of total enrollment) were used in the study, except that the data of the last three students who would have constituted a part of a thirteenth replication and resulted in unequal n's among conditions, were excluded to make statistical analyses more convenient, thus reducing the total N from 99 to 96. Some characteristics of the 96 subjects used were as follows; 88% were females; the age range was from 20 to 55 years.

Results

Main Effects of Warning

Our main hypothesis was that the warning per se would produce an anticipatory lowering of the beliefs, prior to the actual attacks. The appropriate data for testing this prediction are the mean belief levels in the "warning, no-attack" row of Table 1 as compared with the mean of the "no-warning, no-attack" row. The difference between the respective means, 9.10 and 9.54, is significant at the .05 level. (We used the residual within-subjects variance as the error term.) The effect of warning on the impact of the actual attack is negligible: the belief level in the "warning and attack" row is 7.78, which is almost identical with that in the "no-warning, attack" row, 7.77. Each of these "attack" means is significantly ($p < .001$) lower than the corresponding "no-attack" mean.

Hence, as predicted, the warning itself reduces the belief and so does the actual attack, but the two effects are not additive. The belief ends up after attack about 1.77 points below the prewarning level, whether or not it was preceded by a warning. What the warning seems to do is to move the believer in advance part of this distance, about .44 point, so that when the attack comes he has only to move the remaining 1.33 points. The forewarned person, by subtly adjusting his belief prior to the attack, has to face the fact that he was swayed from before to after the attack only three-fourths the distance he would have to admit changing had he not been forewarned.

Interaction with Type of Issue

Self-esteem theory yielded the predictions that the forewarning of attack would produce more anticipatory lowering on the emotional than on the technical issues, but that the attacks themselves would produce more of an effect on the technical than on the emotional issues. The results in the no-attack conditions confirm the prediction about the effect of the warning. After the warning (as can be seen in the "warning, no-attack" row of Table 1) the belief levels on the emotional issues go down to 8.68; while on the technical issues they go down only to 9.52, the difference between these two levels being significant at the .01 level. This difference in postwarning levels cannot be attributed to initial difference in belief levels for the two types of issues. The actual change from before to after the warnings is .73 point for the emotional issues ($p < .05$), while the corresponding change for the technical issues is a statistically trivial .15 point.

As predicted, the direction of this effect is reversed as regards the impact of the actual attacks. The most appropriate data for testing this effect is found in the "no-warning, attack" row of Table 1 (though the slightly less relevant "warning, attack" rows also give clear results, as can be seen in the table). The attacks reduce the belief levels on the technical issues to 7.25 while reducing the belief levels in the emotional issues only to 8.30, a difference significant at the .01 level. Because of this predicted reversal between effect of warning and effect of attack, the warning reduces the emotional beliefs 66% of the distance that the attacks will eventually reduce them; while with the technical beliefs, the warnings reduced the distance they are changed by the attacks by only 6%, the difference in absolute magnitudes being significant at the .001 level. Obviously, as the self-esteem formulation would indicate, much more use was made of the warnings to reduce the apparent amount of yielding on the emotional than on the technical issues.

Interactions with Type of Source

According to self-esteem theory, both the warning and the actual attacks should be more effective in reducing the beliefs when the attacks are attributed in advance to respectable rather than to disreputable sources. The predicted source differential was not confirmed with respect to warning, as can be computed from the "warning, no-attack" row of Table 1. The belief level after forewarning of attacks by reputable sources was 9.13, which is only trivially different from the 9.07 level in the disreputable source condition. This was the only prediction from self-esteem theory to fail to receive confirmation. This exception will be discussed further below.

The prediction about the effect of this source variable on the persuasive impact of actual attacks can be tested most appropriately in terms of the data in the "no-warning, attack" row of Table 1 (though it can be seen that the results in the slightly-less-relevant "warning, attack" row are almost identical). When the attacks were attributed to high-credibility sources they reduced the beliefs to 7.35 and where attributed to low-credibility sources, only to 8.20, a difference in the predicted direction, significant at the .05 level. (While residual within-subject variance was used to test the significance of effects involving the previously discussed within-subject variables, we here, to test the source-credibility effects, employed the larger between-subjects residual variance as the error term.) As can be seen in the "no-attack" rows of Table 1, these postattack levels represent changes from almost identical preattack levels in the two credibility conditions, tending to rule out their being attributable to chance differences in the initial levels.

Discussion

Several points about the present study call for further discussion. We shall comment, in turn, upon a revision in our initial theoretical formulations that is suggested by the failure to confirm one of the source-credibility predictions; upon some peculiarities in the present experimental design that may have had an effect on the outcome; and, finally, upon some related earlier findings and alternative theoretical formulations relevant to the present results.

Source Credibility and the Effect of Warning

In retrospect, it seems possible that the reason our source-credibility manipulation had no impact on the effectiveness of the warning was that we failed to consider sufficiently analytically the various components of source credibility. Specifically, we made our theoretical derivation in terms of the believer's expectation of the persuasiveness of the source, but our actual manipulation affected also, and perhaps especially, the believer's perception of the respectability of the source. What we would predict on the basis of self-esteem theory is quite different for these two components, perceived effectiveness and perceived respectability.

In practice, the two components are probably highly correlated, in that a person probably expects typically that he will be more influenced by respectable than by disreputable sources; hence, there is some justification for our attempt to manipulate perceived effectiveness by varying the predesignated respectability of the source. Nevertheless, the source inductions we used here were unfortunate for two reasons. First, our descriptions stressed the persuasive effectiveness of all our sources, even the disreputable ones. The latter were represented as unsavory criminals, it is true, but were also called "skillful," and "highly intelligent and specialists in the areas they were discussing," and "highly motivated to get their views across." The source descriptions were phrased in this manner in order that the warnings might arouse, as required for our main prediction, an appreciable threat to the belief. We may, in accomplishing this aim, have negated the differential in anticipated effectiveness of the two types of sources. A second theoretical problem arising from our "respectability" manipulation is that it introduces another consideration suggested by self-esteem theory, namely, the question of how embarrassing it would be to yield to a given source. Obviously, it should be more painful to self-esteem to admit one had been persuaded a given amount by an unsavory criminal than by a scholarly presidential advisor.

Hence, our specific manipulation of source credibility may inadvertently have set two considerations raised by self-esteem theory in opposition to one another. On the basis of their perceived effectiveness, we would predict more impact of warning with the positive than negative sources. On the other hand, equating for expected persuasiveness, we would predict less anticipatory change with the positive source, since any anticipated change due to the attack would be less ego dystonic if produced by the positive rather than by the disreputable sources. In the present study, our failure to find any difference due to the source manipulation may have resulted from the mutual cancellation of these two factors. A study could be designed to test this revision by orthogonally varying these two components of source valence: high- versus low-respectability and high- versus low-anticipated persuasive effectiveness. Our revised self-esteem formulation would predict that the effect of the warning would be inversely related to the former and directly related to the latter.[3]

Possible Effects of the Present Experimental Design

We have already indicated in Footnote 2 why we used the less sensitive after-only experimental design, comparing the end-of-experiment belief levels on forewarned versus nonforewarned issues. The before-after design might have eliminated some individual difference and issues variance from the error term, but it would have had the undesirable effect of taking away some of the believer's saving ambiguity about his initial belief levels, and ambiguity is required to make psychologically feasible the use of the anticipatory-lowering strategy as a self-esteem saving device.

A second aspect of the present design that calls for some comment is our introduction of the warning manipulation as a within-subject variable. All subjects served in a forewarning condition on some issues, and in a no-forewarning condition on others. It is possible that our warning all subjects of forthcoming attacks on at least some issues would tend to produce a generalized wariness in the subjects that would to some extent wipe out the effect of the specific warning variable on one issue versus another. We considered the alternative design of introducing forewarning as a between-subject manipulation with some subjects in a

[3] The study by Sears *et al.* (1964) mentioned in Footnote 2 reports one finding relevant to this issue. Their uncommitted subjects responded with less anticipatory change when forewarned of exposure to a two-sided discussion rather than to a debate. According to Sears *et al.* this difference occurred because the believers perceived the debates as more likely to be effective than the two-sided discussions.

forewarning condition and others in a no-forewarning condition. However, we felt that too much ambiguity is introduced by the need to interpret the induction used for the no-forewarning subjects (to balance the forewarning induction used for the other subjects) as in the Allyn and Festinger (1961) study. The difference between two such inductions tends to be open to alternative interpretations, as Festinger has himself recently admitted (Festinger & Maccoby, 1964). Hence, we decided to risk the loss of sensitivity entailed by the within-subject manipulation, in return for more clear-cut comparability of the warning and no-warning conditions. It may be that the lack of effect of warning on the persuasive impact of the attacks is due to this design decision. As far as self-esteem theory is concerned, no such effect is predicted, but it is predicted by other theorists. Allyn and Festinger (1961) and Freedman and Sears (1965) have been able to derive such a prediction from dissonance theory, though Festinger and Maccoby have presented an alternative distraction explanation. The "overheard" versus intent-to-persuade study of Walster and Festinger (1962) makes a similar analysis, but again an alternative explanation is possible since their sources always argued in a "desirable" direction. The above studies found some support for the prediction, but it was usually confined to highly involved believers. A theory that forewarning lowers the credibility of the attacking source (Hovland & Mandell, 1952) likewise could predict an attack-mitigating effect of forewarning.

Relations to Other Theories and Results

When we originally commented on the possibly belief-weakening effect of forewarning of attack (McGuire & Papageorgis, 1962), we accounted for it in terms of dissonance theory. We still feel dissonance theory could account for the present results. The two formulations, dissonance theory and self-esteem theory, have rather similar logical status, each being a guiding principle of heuristic value rather than a formalized system. The basic notion of dissonance theory is that people tend to behave in such ways as will minimize discrepancies among their cognitions; the basic notion of self-esteem theory is that people behave so as to maximize their self-esteem. Each could, without violence, be made a special case of the other: thus, within dissonance theory, behaving to maximize self-esteem could be looked upon as a minimizing of discrepancy between the real and ideal-self; alternatively, within self-esteem theory, behaving so as to reduce cognitive discrepancies could be regarded as maximizing one's concept of oneself as internally consistent. Worchel and McCormick (1963) find the two theories useful in conjunction.

Dissonance theory is, of course, worked out in much more detail than is self-esteem theory: there is certainly nothing in the latter so thoroughly developed as the trivium of "importance, commitment, and volition," as elaborated by Brehm and Cohen (1962) to supplement the basic notion of discrepancy. Still, the notion of self-esteem has not been neglected either, and the raw materials for its development lie conveniently at hand in Wylie's (1961) review. Beginnings of an opposition of a self-esteem theory to dissonance theory are found in the work of Deutsch (Deutsch, 1961; Deutsch, Krauss, & Rosenau, 1962; Deutsch & Solomon, 1959). We do not, by any means, wish to suggest that self-esteem theory should be further developed to the level of dissonance theory. One such theory is quite enough.

We avoided using dissonance theory in deriving the present prediction because some of its proponents (Brehm & Cohen, 1962; Festinger, 1964) have chosen to oppose dissonance with conflict theory by saying that the former requires that the cognitive change occur after the decision, while conflict theory (Janis, 1959a, 1959b) requires that the cognitive change be predecisional. We regard this distinction as a rather uninteresting one and quite difficult to apply to the present situation. Brehm and Cohen themselves point out that this difficulty of application will often arise. However, if the distinction be a valid, testable one (as is indicated by some interesting studies in Festinger, 1964) it seemed somewhat inappropriate to use dissonance theory to predict an "anticipatory" change. One could, of course, attribute the postwarning change to the discrepancy between the believer's initial opinion and the information contained in the warning that an expert source holds a very different opinion, rather than an anticipatory change to avoid the coming dissonance that would otherwise result from the discrepant information to be contained in the attack. According to this reinterpretation, there should be as much belief lowering if we merely mention to the believer that the expert source holds the discrepant opinion, as if we forewarn him that this source is moreover about to present an attack on the belief. Dissonance theory predicts an equal change in the two conditions and self-esteem theory predicts more change with the additional forewarning of attack. The point remains to be tested.

A further reason why we avoided using dissonance theory in this study was that it seemed more equivocal than self-esteem theory as regards its predictions in the present situation (though, as we have seen in our discussion of the lack of source effect, self-esteem theory is not free of equivocality either). We were unable to decide, for example, if dissonance theory would predict that the effect of warning would be greater with emotional beliefs or with technical ones. On the one hand, beliefs on emotional issues would tend to be tied in with more cognitions and hence any change would introduce more discrepancies and higher dissonance (Festinger, 1957) than a change on the cognitively more isolated technical issues. Hence, perhaps we should predict that with the more cognitively articulated emotional issues, there would be less postwarning lowering of beliefs and perhaps even a postwarning strengthening of the belief to bolster it against the coming attack (Abelson, 1959; Cohen, 1962). On the other hand, perhaps dissonance theory implies the reverse, because the emotional issues would tend to be more important and involving to the believers than would the technical issues. It would, therefore, be more dissonant to hold opinions discrepant from those of significant other people on such issues (Zimbardo, 1960) and, hence, the forewarning would have more belief-lowering impact with these emotional issues. We were unable to decide which of these two opposing processes suggested by dissonance theory would have the greater influence under the present experimental conditions.

Nor was it clear what predictions would follow from dissonance theory about the effect of forewarning on the persuasive impact of the attacks themselves under our experimental conditions. Both theory and findings tend to be ambiguous on this point, as described earlier in this section. Dissonance theory would also readily yield predictions of interactions between source respectability and the emotional versus technical issue variable in determining the impact of the warnings and of the attack. However, as can be seen in the various rows of Table 1, there is no sign of any such interaction in the obtained data.

We have already pointed out that self-esteem theory is itself equivocal about what effect our source manipulation should have on the impact of the warning. It must be admitted further that it is also somewhat equivocal regarding the other variable, emotional versus technical issues. We predicted (and found) more anticipatory lowering after forewarning on the emotional issues, because yielding to the attack on these would be more damaging to the self-esteem. But, on the other hand, one's initial, prewarning belief might tend to be clearer on these more thought-about controversial, emotional issues. If so, there would be less of the saving ambiguity shrouding initial beliefs on the emotional issues and less psychological availability of responding to warning with the esteem-saving tactic of anticipatory lowering.

Thus, in the present study, as in so many others, we can use formulations like self-esteem or dissonance theory to deduce predictions, at least some of which are interesting and nonobvious, and a large number of which are confirmed by the experiment designed to test them. And yet, for all their heuristic value, these theories remain so vague and unformulated that, in the very experimental situations used, they can often be made with a little ingenuity (or even without it) to yield opposite predictions. It appears that during the prehistory of a science, even equivocal theories offer heuristic utility.

REFERENCES

Abelson, R. P. Modes of resolution of belief dilemmas. *Journal of Conflict Resolution,* 1959, **3**, 343–352.

Allyn, J., & Festinger, L. The effectiveness of unanticipated persuasive communications. *Journal of Abnormal and Social Psychology,* 1961, **62**, 35–40.

Brehm, J., & Cohen, A. R. *Explorations in cognitive dissonance.* New York: Wiley, 1962.

Cohen, A. R. A dissonance analysis of the boomerang effect. *Journal of Personality,* 1962, **30**, 75–88.

Deutsch, M. The interpretation of praise and criticism as a function of their social context. *Journal of Abnormal and Social Psychology,* 1961, **62**, 391–400.

Deutsch, M., Krauss, R. M., & Rosenau, N. Dissonance or defensiveness? *Journal of Personality,* 1962, **30**, 16–28.

Deutsch, M., & Solomon, L. Reactions to evaluations by others as influenced by self-evaluations. *Sociometry,* 1959, **22**, 93–112.

Festinger, L. *Theory of cognitive dissonance.* Evanston, Ill.: Row, Peterson, 1957.

Festinger, L. (Ed.) *Conflict, decision and dissonance.* Stanford Univer. Press, 1964.

Festinger, L., & Maccoby, N. On resistance to persuasive communications. *Journal of Abnormal and Social Psychology,* 1964, **68**, 359–366.

Freedman, J. L., & Sears, D. O. Warning, distraction, and resistance to influence. *Journal of Personality and Social Psychology,* 1965, **1**, 262–266.

Hovland, C. I., & Mandell, W. An experimental comparison of conclusion-drawing by the communicator and by the audience. *Journal of Abnormal and Social Psychology,* 1952, **47**, 581–588.

Janis, I. L. Decisional conflicts: A theoretical analysis. *Journal of Conflict Resolution,* 1959, **3**, 6–27. (a)

Janis, I. L. Motivational factors in the resolution of decisional conflicts. In M. R. Jones (Ed.), *Nebraska symposium on motivation: 1959.* Lincoln: Univer. Nebraska Press, 1959. Pp. 198–231. (b)

Janis, I. L. The psychological effects of warnings. In G. W. Baker & D. W. Chapman (Eds.), *Man and society in disaster.* New York: Basic Books, 1962. Pp. 55–92.

McGuire, W. J., & Anderson, L. Effect of prior commitment and forewarning of attack on resistance to persuasion. Unpublished manuscript, University of Illinois, 1959.

McGuire, W. J., & Papageorgis, D. Effectiveness of forewarning in developing resistance to persuasion. *Public Opinion Quarterly,* 1962, **26**, 24–34.

Sears, D. O., Freedman, J. L., & O'Connor, E. F. The effects of anticipated debate and commitment on the polarization of audience opinion. *Public Opinion Quarterly,* 1964, **28**, 617–627.

Walster, E., & Festinger, L. The effectiveness of "overheard" persuasive communication. *Journal of Abnormal and Social Psychology,* 1962, **65**, 395–402.

Worchel, P., & McCormick, B. L. Self-concept and dissonance reduction. *Journal of Personality,* 1963, **31**, 588–599.

Wylie, R. *The self concept.* Lincoln: Univer. Nebraska Press, 1961.

Zimbardo, P. Involvement and communication discrepancy as determinants of opinion change. *Journal of Abnormal and Social Psychology,* 1960, **60,** 84–94.

Discussion

Seldom are authors as explicit in spelling out the shortcomings of their research as McGuire and Millman. Probably the most interesting of their posthoc analyses is the new and more detailed look at the "components" of source credibility. If, as self-esteem theory posits, people really are concerned about their ability to resist social influence, it should be very damaging to self-esteem to yield to someone of low-reputability. That prediction, and its converse, that it should not be damaging to self-esteem to yield to someone of high reputability, make sense.

Their other new source prediction is less clear. McGuire and Millman state that one of the reasons they avoided using dissonance theory "was that it seemed more equivocal than self-esteem theory as regards its predictions in the present situation [p. 477]." Unfortunately, their posthoc analyses have added whatever equivocality was missing in the earlier version. They point out that "a study could be designed to test this revision by orthogonally varying these two components of source valence: high- versus low-respectability and high- versus low-anticipated persuasive effectiveness. Our revised self-esteem formulation would predict that the effect of the warning would be inversely related to the former and directly related to the latter [p. 476]." The second new prediction then is that a source reputed to be highly effective should produce more anticipatory belief lowering than one reputed to be not very effective. Whether or not this prediction follows from self-esteem considerations is certainly arguable. It is quite possible to maintain that it would be much more damaging to self-esteem to yield to someone who was known to be an ineffective speaker. In any event, the next article, by Papageorgis (1967), presents some data on these new source predictions arrived at by McGuire and Millman. Before going on, however, there are some other questions to consider.

Recall for a moment the emotional-technical issues that McGuire and Millman used. It is less than clear (see Table 1), for example, that the probability of a serious economic depression is any less of a technical issue than the likely abolition of the sales tax. The only definition offered of this variable is that a technical issue is a "matter-of-fact" one and an emotional issue is an unverifiable one. It is certainly a "matter-of-fact" that it has been difficult to find promising leads for a cancer cure. Yet

TABLE 1
Issues Used By McGuire & Millman (1965)

Emotional	Technical
1. Likelihood of Communist takeovers in Latin America	1. Shortage of lab animals
2. Difficulties of finding a cure for cancer	2. Failure of earth sciences to find oil deposits
3. Probability of a serious depression	3. Continuing need for propellar planes
4. Likelihood of World War III	4. Likely abolition of sales tax

this was used as an emotional issue. Likewise, the probability of a serious economic depression is no less verifiable than the likely abolition of the sales tax. Yet one of these was classed as a technical issue and the other as an emotional issue. To put it simply, it appears that whatever the issue variable was, it was not emotionality-technicality. It could have been involvement, interest, importance for the subjects—we just do not know. Only careful research will tell.

McGuire and Millman (1965) point out several factors that might limit the generality of their results even if the results had been flawless. Probably the most serious of those is that the same subjects participated in both warning and no-warning conditions. As the authors note, "it is possible that our warning all subjects of forthcoming attacks on at least some issues would tend to produce a generalized wariness in the subjects that would to some extent wipe out the effect of the specific warning variable on one issue versus another [p. 476]." As we shall see, subsequent research has still not dealt with this problem. It may be a nonproblem, but coupled with the ambiguity of the issue dimension it may be a serious problem.

In the experiment reported in the following article, Papageorgis set out to gather data on two questions raised by McGuire and Millman in their discussion section. First, Papageorgis manipulated the two components of source credibility that McGuire and Millman supposed to have been working against each other (reputability and effectiveness). Second, he set up a condition which he hoped would contribute to an understanding of whether or not dissonance theory would adequately account for the data gathered by McGuire and Millman.

Unfortunately, there appears to be a fatal flaw in Papageorgis' procedure. Try to imagine yourself as a subject serving in the experiment and see if you think there would be any problem from the subject's point of view. There was a great deal of information for the subjects to take in and process in a very short period of time.

Anticipation of Exposure to Persuasive Messages and Belief Change[1]

Demetrios Papageorgis

One hundred and fifty undergraduates were told that they would listen to speeches advocating positions opposite to their initial beliefs and that the effect of these speeches on their opinions would be measured. Warnings about forthcoming speeches were given on four issues, and the effectiveness and reputability of their sources were varied orthogonally in order to test predictions from self-esteem theory. The topic and direction of argument of a fifth speech was announced, but *S*s were told that they would not hear it. The inclusion of this condition allowed comparison between predictions derived from self-esteem and cognitive balance theories. Postwarning beliefs of *S*s favor the balance interpretation of forewarning and suggest that belief change following warning may not be anticipatory. A compromise interpretation in terms of variable orientations toward belief expression is presented.

Most of the experimental research in opinion change is carried out with the purpose of the experiment disguised from the subjects. Implicit in this method is the assumption that the persuasive message will lose some or all its impact if the subject is told or discovers (i.e., is intentionally or unintentionally forewarned) that an attempt to influence his opinions is about to be made. Experiments that have used forewarning in an enforced-exposure context have given only partial support to this assumption, and have also contributed other findings of considerable interest (Allyn & Festinger, 1961; Freedman & Sears, 1965; Kiesler & Kiesler, 1964; McGuire & Millman, 1965; McGuire & Papageorgis, 1962; Mills & Aronson, 1965).

Among these other findings are belief changes, in a direction opposite to the subject's initial position, that are found following the forewarning, but prior to any attack with the persuasive messages (McGuire, 1966; McGuire & Millman, 1965; McGuire & Papageorgis, 1962; Sears, Freedman, & O'Connor, 1964). The label "anticipatory" lowering or change of belief is applied often to this phenomenon (McGuire, 1966): the change is assumed to be a defensive response by the subject who, expecting to be gullible to the persuasive messages and thus lose self-esteem, shifts his position closer to the position that he anticipates in the forthcoming attacking message. Depending on the extent of the shift and the

[1] From the *Journal of Personality and Social Psychology* 1967, **5**, No. 4, 490–496. Received May 5, 1966. Reproduced by permission of the publisher.

William J. McGuire made several helpful suggestions on an earlier version of this report.

The author is with the University of British Columbia.

position that the subject will eventually assign to the message, he may attain the postmessage luxury of perceiving himself as less gullible than he would have otherwise (Deutsch, Krauss, & Rosenau, 1962; McGuire & Millman, 1965).

In their recent study, McGuire and Millman obtained evidence that supports the anticipatory, self-esteem explanation of postwarning belief change. They found that forewarning about emotional unverifiable issues significantly changed preattack beliefs when these beliefs were compared to those expressed by subjects who had not been forewarned or who had been forewarned about technical, matter-of-fact issues; in addition, forewarning about technical issues did not change preattack beliefs. These findings support the self-esteem interpretation because opinion change in response to a factual communication is less threatening to one's self-esteem. The same investigators also hypothesized that forewarning of attack by a disreputable source would produce greater change in preattack beliefs than would forewarning of attack attributed to a reputable source; subsequent persuasion by the reputable source would be less injurious to self-esteem. This prediction was not supported. McGuire and Millman, however, pointed out that the source manipulation they used created differential reputability only within a context of high source effectiveness, and thus may have failed to maximize the difference in overall source persuasiveness needed for an adequate test of self-esteem predictions. The present study includes an attempt to overcome this difficulty. As suggested by McGuire and Millman, it introduces an orthogonal variation of source effectiveness and reputability whereby conditions of high and low source effectiveness are paired with conditions of high and low source reputability. If these source manipulations are successfully induced, self-esteem theory would predict that preattack beliefs will show greater change following forewarning about a forthcoming message attributed to a source of (*a*) high effectiveness and (*b*) low reputability. Persuasion by the former is more likely, while persuasion by the latter would be more threatening to self-esteem.

Postwarning belief change may also be derived from cognitive balance approaches (Heider, 1958; Newcomb, 1953). The forewarning informs the subject that somebody disagrees with him, thus causing a state of imbalance among cognitions and pressure to reduce this state. Belief change would then be a means of achieving better cognitive balance. This alternative derivation does not require that the subject expect actual exposure to the persuasive message; thus, a clearer test between the cognitive balance and self-esteem positions can be made if the experiment includes an additional condition in which the subject is informed of a belief contrary to his own, but is also assured that he will not be exposed to a persuasive message on that belief (cf. McGuire & Millman, 1965). The balance approach would predict belief change whether a subject expects exposure to a persuasive attack or not. Self-esteem theory, on the other hand, would predict belief change only if exposure is expected. In addition, if the balance interpretation is correct, the postwarning belief changes need not be anticipatory. The present experiment introduces a condition in which the subject is informed of a belief contrary to his own, but is also assured that no message on that belief will follow; this condition, hereafter called the "consistency control" or CC condition, in conjunction with the conditions where the subject expects a persuasive message to follow the forewarning, allows a test between the two derivations.

Method

The experiment was designed to assess the effect of forewarning on preattack beliefs under these six conditions: anticipated attack with a message attributed to a source of high effectiveness and high reputability (HH), anticipated attack by a high effectiveness and low reputability source (HL), anticipated attack by a low effectiveness and high reputability source (LH), anticipated attack by a low effectiveness and low reputability source (LL), no anticipated attack on an explicitly mentioned belief that is contrary to the subject's initial belief (CC), and no forewarning, a control condition (C).

Each subject participated in all six conditions, each condition measured by his belief on a different issue. Each issue was used with every experimental condition using different subjects. The sequence of presentation of the five issue-condition combinations that were mentioned to the subjects (one of the issues always serving as an unmentioned control) was controlled by presenting each of the combinations in every position in the sequence. The choice of obtaining data from each subject for all experimental conditions was based on several considerations, including the desire to maximize differential perception between the four source conditions. In addition, this choice made the CC manipulation both plausible in itself and comparable to the anticipated-message conditions. This design also made it economically possible to use six different issues, thus increasing the generality of the findings. The latter was also enhanced by the use of seven experimenters who, though all were males, varied in age and experimental sophistication and had formed no theoretical preferences.

Since the experiment dealt only with postwarning belief change, and not with the effect of warning on communication impact, no actual persuasive messages were presented to the subjects, though each subject was led to believe that four messages were forthcoming and was given the topic and direction of argument of a fifth message that supposedly would not be presented. Within the present experimental context, however, the forewarning itself can be considered as the persuasive communication. In these terms, the design of the experiment conforms to the "after-only" type (Hovland, Lumsdaine, & Sheffield, 1949).

The results of the experiment were evaluated by means of analysis of variance and two-tailed tests of statistical significance. Probability level for rejection of the hypothesis of no difference between means was set at .01.

Procedure

The subjects participated in small groups of from three to eight persons. Each of these groups was randomly assigned to one of the seven experimenters and to a particular sequence of one of the six issue-condition combinations. Since each issue was used in each of the six conditions (HH, HL, LH, LL, CC, and C), and since order of presentation was controlled by using five sequences of presentation (with HH, HL, LH, LL, and CC each appearing in all five positions in the sequence), 30 of these small groups were needed. The alternative of assigning individual subjects, rather than groups, to conditions would have made it impossible for the experimenter to read the materials aloud to the subjects and could also have created suspicion if the subjects discovered that the sequence and content of their materials differed.

Aside from these design variations, the experimental procedure was quite simple. After the subjects had assembled in the seminar-type room used for the experiment, the experimenter announced that he was measuring opinion change that resulted from listening to actual recorded speeches. A tape recorder, threaded with (blank) tape, was displayed prominently, and the experimenter stated that the machine would be used to play the forthcoming speeches. The instructions also indicated that information about the topics of the speeches and the speakers would be given before any of the speeches were played; in addition, the subjects were told that they were to give their opinions about the topics before and after they had heard the speeches so that the experimenter could assess any changes in their opinions. Every effort was made to convince the subjects that the speeches would be forthcoming and that the objective of the experiment was as stated.

Following the initial instructions, the subjects were given descriptions of the topics and of the direction of argument of five speeches. In addition, speaker descriptions, in terms of effectiveness and reputability, were given for four of these speeches; the instructions repeatedly stressed not only that these four speeches would be played, but also that the fifth speech, for which no speaker description was given, had not been received and, consequently, would not be played. The descriptions of the five speeches were circulated in written from, and the subjects retained them for reference during the experiment; the experimenter also read them aloud in order to make sure that the subjects paid attention.

The experimenter announced next that, before listening to the speeches, the subjects were to rate the speakers and state their opinions on the issues. The speaker ratings were used as a measure of the effectiveness of the source manipulation. The opinion measure was the dependent variable.

The experiment was complete after the administration of the opinion measure. At this point, the subjects could have been told the purpose of the experiment and could have been informed that there was never any intent to play speeches to them. Since, however, data collection was not complete, the explanation of the experimental procedures had to be postponed. Instead, the apparently distraught experimenter invoked a variety of excuses for postponing the playing of the speeches; for example, the room had been scheduled for another purpose, the tape recorder would not function, and so forth.

Subjects

Undergraduates enrolled in first psychology courses served as subjects. Participation in experiments was required, although the choice of particular experiments was open to the students. The sample contained roughly equal numbers of males and females and was likewise representative of both lower- and upper-division students. A total of 157 subjects participated, but 7 subjects were eliminated at random from those issue conditions that totaled over 25 subjects. Thus, the final number of subjects used in the experiment was 150, with 25 subjects in each of the six issue-condition variations. The subgroups within these variations that received different sequences of presentation varied in size from a low of 3 to a high of 8 subjects.

Materials

Issues. The issues were selected about two months prior to the experiment from the responses to a belief questionnaire by a sample of 191 persons similar to those subsequently used in the experiment. The questionnaire was similar to the belief questionnaire used as the dependent variable measure (see below). The items in this questionnaire included those used in the McGuire and Millman experiment, in addition to other items that were expected to satisfy the criteria for issue selection. These criteria were extremeness and homogeneity of expressed belief. All items dealt with issues that appeared to be emotional and unverifiable, rather than with technical, matter-of-fact ones, since a greater postwarning impact had been demonstrated with the former variety of issue (McGuire & Millman, 1965).

The six issues called for by the experimental design were selected on the basis of the results of the early belief survey. Eighty-five percent or more of the sample expressed beliefs that were uniformly distributed within one or the other end of the true-false belief continuum for all six issues. These were:

1. A third world war is almost certain to occur in the very near future.
2. There will soon be a serious economic depression in the United States.
3. In the near future, the United States Government will find it necessary to reduce the freedoms now constitutionally guaranteed to citizens.
4. In the near future, Americans will have very little to say in their choice of a physician.
5. Soon, college graduates will have to undertake advanced graduate study before they are considered eligible for many positions open to them today.
6. The United States will contribute very little that is new to the exploration of outer space.

With the exception of the fifth issue, initial beliefs were distributed within the false end of the continuum. To facilitate analysis and presentation of results, the fifth issue was transcribed in its mirror-image form; thus, for all six issues, low scores represent the subject's initial position, and movement toward the position advocated by the speeches is indicated by higher scores.

Forewarning. The forewarning was both general and specific to the issues. The general forewarning was effected in several ways, including the recruitment of subjects for an experiment labeled "Opinion Change," the instructions that stressed repeatedly that the objective of the experiment was to measure opinion change that would result from listening to persuasive speeches, the administration of the belief measure after the subjects were told that it was a "before" measure of their opinions, and the presence of the threaded tape recorder.

In addition to the general warning, specific warnings were given for five of the six experimental issues, the sixth issue serving as an unmentioned control. Each specific warning stated the topic of a talk and the direction of its argument. The direction of the argument was always opposite to the assumed initial stands of the majority of the subjects. Each subject was led to expect that he would hear four of these talks and was given speaker descriptions designed to create the HH, HL, LH, and LL source conditions described in the next section. The fifth was assigned to the CC condition in which the subject was repeatedly and explicitly informed that he would not hear the talk.

Source Descriptions. Descriptions designed to create perceptions of high and low speaker effectiveness were paired orthogonally with descriptions of high and low source reputability. All six issues were paired with one of the four effectiveness/reputability combinations, though any given subject served in only four different source manipulations.

High speaker effectiveness was manipulated by describing the speakers as successful and popular lecturers, award winners, and generally articulate people who were presenting prepared, organized talks. Low speaker effectiveness was created by describing the speakers as inexperienced individuals speaking under less than ideal conditions, usually extemporaneously. Speaker reputability, on the other hand, was manipulated through the speaker's occupation or affiliation with some group: thus, a federal judge, an undersecretary of defense, and a member of the President's Council of Economic Advisers were used for high reputability conditions, while an extreme right-wing free-lance author, an editorial assistant for the *Daily Worker,* and an official of the Teamster's Union represent examples of the people used for the low reputability condition. Within any given issue, the two conditions involving high reputability (HH and LH) included, to the extent that this did not interfere with the internal consistency of the source description, the same information. Thus, both sources were given the same fictitious name, the same affiliation, and the same general character. The same was true for the two low reputability conditions (HL and LL), the two high effectiveness conditions (HH and HL), and the two low effectiveness conditions (LH and LL). Space limitations do not permit a complete reproduction of the 24 source descriptions.[2] For purposes of illustration, the four descriptions used with Issue 1 (likelihood of a third world war) follow:

> HH: The Honorable James W. Bickstrup, deputy undersecretary of defense, Washington, D. C. Mr. Bickstrup is a noted spokesman for the Department of Defense; his talk has been delivered before a variety of audiences and has also been broadcast on the air with a good deal of success.
>
> HL: Joseph C. Brown, secretary of "Americans for Freedom," an organization identified with the extreme right wing of American politics. Mr. Brown is a frequent and effective spokesman for Americans for Freedom. He has spoken to many groups, and his talk was broadcast over several radio stations.
>
> LH: The Honorable James W. Bickstrup, deputy undersecretary of defense, Washington, D. C. Mr. Bickstrup is a highly regarded planner for the Department of Defense, but is not known for his public-speaking activities. His talk

[2] A complete set of the source descriptions has been deposited with the American Documentation Institute. Order Document No. 9213 from ADI Auxiliary Publications Project, Photoduplication Service, Library of Congress, Washington, D. C. 20540. Remit in advance $1.25 for microfilm or $1.25 for photocopies and make checks payable to: Chief, Photoduplication Service, Library of Congress.

is actually a series of unrehearsed, off-the-cuff comments made to a radio reporter and, consequently, may lack in organization and style of presentation.

LL: Joseph C. Brown, secretary of "Americans for Freedom," an organization identified with the extreme right wing of American politics. Mr. Brown is not a frequent speaker; his talk is actually a series of unrehearsed, off-the-cuff comments made to a radio-station reporter and, consequently, may lack in organization and style of presentation.

The effectiveness and reputability of the sources assigned to the other five issues were manipulated in a similar fashion.

Following the presentation of the issues and their sources, the subjects rated each of the four speakers that they expected to hear in terms of the kind of speaker they expected the person to be, and the kind of person they thought each of the speakers was. These ratings were made on semantic differential scales. The scales "effective-ineffective" and "persuasive-unpersuasive" were used to measure the first type of rating. The second type of rating was made on the scales "disreputable-reputable" and "trustworthy-untrustworthy." The purpose of the ratings was to check on the success of the orthogonal source manipulation.

Belief Measure. The dependent-variable belief measure consisted of a series of statements, including the six experimentally relevant items, each followed by a 15-interval graphic scale. The scale was labeled from left to right in intervals of three as "Definitely False," "Probably False," "Uncertain," "Probably True," and "Definitely True." Essentially this is the same scale that was used in several earlier studies (e.g., Papageorgis, 1963).

Results

Source Manipulation

In four of the experimental conditions, the subjects were led to anticipate communications attributed to sources that varied in effectiveness and reputability. It is necessary to show that the source descriptions did indeed create different perceptions of effectiveness and reputability. The subjects' ratings of the sources were used as indexes of their perceptions. Two semantic differential scales were used to measure perceived source effectiveness, and two similar scales were used as a measure of perceived reputability. Scores from these two scales were added, thus yielding an overall measure of each source dimension with a range from 2 to 14. The higher scores represent greater perceived effectiveness or reputability. The success of the source manipulation was evaluated by comparing mean effectiveness and reputability ratings for the high and low effectiveness and reputability conditions.

The mean comparisons showed that the source manipulations were successful. The mean for the high source reputability conditions was 11.97, while the mean for the low reputability condition was 8.44 ($p <$ .01). Similarly, the mean for high speaker effectiveness was 11.22, and

TABLE 1
Means and Standard Deviations of Postwarning Beliefs[a]

Condition	Issues 1	2	3	4	5	6
CC	6.76	5.68	6.12	6.32	7.04	3.24
	(2.86)	(3.00)	(3.58)	(3.77)	(3.47)	(3.51)
HH	7.16	6.48	6.96	5.88	6.52	2.96
	(2.99)	(2.94)	(3.74)	(3.49)	(2.98)	(2.07)
LH	5.96	6.60	6.24	6.72	6.96	3.56
	(2.20)	(3.46)	(3.93)	(4.22)	(3.15)	(2.84)
HL	7.96	5.36	7.20	6.24	6.32	2.32
	(2.88)	(2.94)	(4.16)	(4.14)	(3.08)	(1.65)
LL	6.40	5.52	6.72	5.04	5.92	2.20
	(2.29)	(2.63)	(4.34)	(2.54)	(3.31)	(1.47)
C	6.32	6.04	5.16	5.48	4.04	2.04
	(3.09)	(3.26)	(3.54)	(3.10)	(1.57)	(1.27)

[a] $N = 25$ per cell. Standard deviations appear in parentheses.

the mean for low effectiveness was 9.56, a difference also significant at the .01 level.

Belief Changes

The control mean belief for all six issues was 4.85. The means for the other conditions were: 5.99 (HH), 5.90 (HL), 6.01 (LH), 5.30 (LL), and 5.86 (CC). Except for the LL mean, all other experimental means differ significantly from the control mean ($p < .01$).

The main effect for issues was not significant. The Issue × Condition interaction was significant ($p < .01$). The interaction is primarily the result of a significant difference between LL and C on the issue dealing with constitutional freedoms, and no significant differences between HL, LL, CC, and C on the issue of a forthcoming economic depression. Table 1 presents the means and standard deviations for all conditions and issues.

Discussion

The principal conclusion suggested by the significant postwarning belief changes is that anticipation of a forthcoming persuasive message is not necessary for this kind of belief change. For five of the six experimental issues, the CC condition resulted in belief levels significantly above the control level. Moreover, the CC-induced belief levels are of the same magnitude as those induced by the anticipated message conditions that were attributed to sources with high perceived effectiveness or high perceived reputability. The results then favor a cognitive balance interpretation and suggest that postwarning belief changes may be viewed as adjustments in a person's beliefs that result from awareness that another person holds different beliefs. The present study generally replicates the McGuire and Millman (1965) findings in that (*a*) the warning causes preattack belief change, and (*b*) the source effects are negligible. At the same time the anticipatory interpretation of postwarning change given by these authors is not supported.

The finding of belief changes without anticipation of a forthcoming message and solely on the basis of information about the existence of a persuasive speech requires some comment. Two earlier attempts to induce belief change by communicating majority opinions were unsuccessful (Brock & Blackwood, 1962; Robbins, 1961). This discrepancy is most likely the result of differences in experimental procedure: the announcement of the existence of a persuasive *speech* may carry greater inconsistency-arousing potential than the knowledge of majority opinion of peers. In addition, neither of the previous studies was presented to the subjects as an opinion-change experiment. It is also possible to raise questions regarding the exact nature of the CC manipulation used in the present experiment. One objection may be that the subjects became confused as to which speeches they were scheduled to hear and which speech would not be presented. This possibility is unlikely since the instructions repeatedly indicated the specific issue-condition pairings, and the same materials were available to the subjects for reference throughout the experiment. A second possibility may be that the CC condition, because it was always presented with the anticipated speech conditions, may have acquired a status of psychological equivalence with the latter. In other words, the subjects were affected by the CC condition only because it was always paired in the design with anticipated speeches. The fact that the LL condition was not effective may argue somewhat against this interpretation, but the possibility that the CC manipulation is effective only under conditions that create a set of expectancy for other persuasive communications remains open, subject to further experimentation, and suggests caution about possibly premature generalizations of the present finding.

Although self-esteem explanations of postwarning change in belief receive little support from the present results, evidence from other studies, such as the finding of change with emotional but not with factual issues (McGuire & Millman, 1965), appears quite compatible with the self-esteem position and is not easily accounted for in terms of balance theories. A somewhat different hypothesis that would reconcile existing findings and incorporate features of both balance and self-esteem theories may be needed. Such a hypothesis may be stated as follows: A person, when asked to state his belief about an issue, may do so after assuming either of two sets or orientations toward belief expression. With the first of these sets, the person responds as an individual and expresses whatever poition he assumes he has at the time; under the second set, the person will respond only after he has weighed the significance of the item and the nature of his own position relative to a larger social context. With this second orientation, a person may, if his preresponse deliberations suggest it, express a different belief than he would under the first, individual set; he may express a belief that will be more in line with what he assumes or expects other people believe, or with his assessment of the extent of his factual knowledge about the issue, or with his feelings about how justified his belief is, and so forth.

Forewarnings, as well as many other kinds of advance information about an issue regardless of whether a person anticipates an attempt at persuasion, create tendencies that result in subsequent belief expression that includes the deliberative activity characteristic of the second, social context type of orientation. The social orientation may or may not result in modification of the individual set beliefs; if it does, the person will probably state a belief that is congruent with the advance information he has acquired, although it is conceivable that he may resist the information. The latter case amounts to an "immunization" or a "boomerang" effect of the forewarning, depending on whether forewarning is viewed as a defense-stimulating procedure or as a persuasive communication.

The term belief expression, rather than change or adoption, was used in the above analysis to suggest the need for caution in describing the effects of advance information on beliefs. The small belief change that follows warning may be no more than a fluctuation within the existing lattitude of the person's belief (Sherif & Hovland, 1961). Everyday observation suggests that, for many beliefs, people retain the privilege of varying their stand in different contexts and circumstances while still remaining on the same side of the issue.

Forewarning, of course, does not exhaust the means of altering belief-expression sets. The present hypothesis suggests effects that may result from other orientation-directed manipulations. For example, will subjects change their stand if: (*a*) They are told that their beliefs will be quoted in a publication; or (*b*) if they are led to expect that their beliefs will affect the future course of an official policy or the fate of a television show; or (*c*) if they are simply informed that their beliefs will be measured more than once? Findings from relatively simple studies of this type would allow a more proper evaluation of the present hypothesis. They may also point out the need for greater caution in the instruction procedures used in many belief- and attitude-change studies.

REFERENCES

Allyn, J., & Festinger, L. The effectiveness of unanticipated persuasive communications. *Journal of Abnormal and Social Psychology,* 1961, **62**, 35–40.

Brock, T. C., & Blackwood, J. E. Dissonance reduction, social comparison, and modification of opinion. *Journal of Abnormal and Social Psychology,* 1962, **65**, 319–324.

Deutsch, M., Krauss, R. M., & Rosenau, N. Dissonance or defensiveness? *Journal of Personality,* 1962, **30**, 16–28.

Freedman, J. L., & Sears, D. O. Warning, distraction, and resistance to influence. *Journal of Personality and Social Psychology,* 1965, **1**, 262–266.

Heider, F. *The psychology of interpersonal relations.* New York: Wiley, 1958.

Hovland, C. I., Lumsdaine, A. A., & Sheffield, F. D. *Experiments on mass communication.* Princeton: Princeton University Press, 1949.

Kiesler, C. A., & Kiesler, S. B. Role of forewarning in persuasive communications. *Journal of Abnormal and Social Psychology,* 1964, **68**, 547–549.

McGuire, W. J. Attitudes and opinions. In, *Annual review of psychology.* Vol. 17. Palo Alto, Calif.: Annual Reviews, 1966. Pp. 475–514.

McGuire, W. J., & Millman, S. Anticipatory belief lowering following forewarning of a persuasive attack. *Journal of Personality and Social Psychology,* 1965, **2**, 471–479.

McGuire, W. J., & Papageorgis, D. Effectiveness of forewarning in developing resistance to persuasion. *Public Opinion Quarterly,* 1962, **26**, 24–34.

Mills, J., & Aronson, E. Opinion change as a function of the communicator's attractiveness and desire to influence. *Journal of Personality and Social Psychology,* 1965, **1**, 173–177.

Newcomb, T. M. An approach to the study of communicative acts. *Psychological Review,* 1953, **60**, 393–404.

Papageorgis, D. Bartlett effect and the persistence of induced opinion change. *Journal of Abnormal and Social Psychology,* 1963, **67**, 61–67.

Robbins, P. R. Immediate and delayed effects of social influence upon individual opinion. *Journal of Social Psychology,* 1961, **53**, 159–167.

Sears, D. O., Freedman, J. L., & O'Connor, E. F. The effects of anticipated debate and commitment on the polarization of audience opinion. *Public Opinion Quarterly,* 1964, **28**, 617–627.

Sherif, M., & Hovland, C. I. *Social judgment.* New Haven: Yale University Press, 1961.

Discussion

Papageorgis' study had two main purposes: (1) to collect some data bearing on the source reputability and effectiveness predictions suggested by McGuire and Millman and (2) to determine if anticipation of attack on one's beliefs is a necessary condition for precommunication opinion change. These are the substantive questions, the second of which is pursued in the next article. The reasons why the Papageorgis study has not "cut off debate" on the questions are methodological. There are some interesting problems raised in the Papageorgis article and we will discuss these in ascending order of importance.

There are several rather minor problems with the procedure-problems that probably had no detectable effects on the results, but which are mentioned because one should be aware of them. Potentially, they could be disastrous.

First, subjects were run in small groups of three to eight instead of individually. This raises the question of what is the appropriate unit of analysis, group or individual. If there is any reason to suspect a lack of independence among group members, then the most appropriate unit of analysis is the group itself. In extreme cases it is easy to see why this should be. Suppose subjects had been asked to solve a series of very difficult problems, first alone and then in a group. As a group, they were able to solve all the problems, whereas alone no one could solve more than half. It would not make much sense to use individuals as the unit of analysis and attempt to argue that individual problem solving ability had improved. The appropriate unit is, of course, the group.

Often, however, the unit is not as clear. If subjects were seated around a table rating cartoons, each snickering and making comments to himself, should we use each individual's ratings or should we average the group ratings for each cartoon? If there is reason to believe that one subject may have influenced another's ratings, the group mean should be used and N would increase by 1 for each group put through the procedure.

A second problem in the Papageorgis study is that there were seven experimenters and no analysis is presented of experimenter effects. There is some evidence of a cross-sex effect in studies of experimenter bias (Rosenthal, 1966) and, since the demand characteristics were particularly salient in this procedure (e.g., opinion change was emphasized throughout), a sex of subject analysis would seem essential. Suppose Papageorgis had analyzed for experimenter effects and had found the results he does report were obtained only for female subjects who were interacting with the male experimenters. This would imply a quite different conclusion concerning the results of the study.

The issue is more general than experimenter and subject sex, however. Anytime more than one experimenter is involved in a study, it would be useful—if at all possible—to analyze for experimenter effects. Usually one hopes that none will appear, but if they do one must be very careful about generalizing the results of the study.

The third problem is more an ethical one, but it has its methodological implications also. Papageorgis (1967) notes "... the subjects could have been told the purpose of the experiment and could have been informed that there was never any intent to play speeches to them. Since, however, data collection was not complete, the explanation of the experimental procedures had to be postponed. Instead, the apparently distraught experimenter invoked a variety of excuses for postponing the playing of the speeches, etc. [p. 492]." This is a highly questionable procedure for two reasons. First, subjects had been induced to change their opinions on several issues (e.g., the probability of World War III) and were thus left with these "new" opinions. Second, there was a high likelihood of communication among subjects and future-subjects. Usually, one aspect of a debriefing is to caution subjects against revealing what goes on in the procedure. Subjects may have been suspicious upon arrival, particularly if other students had told them two different versions of why the experimenter could not play the tapes.

These are minor problems, except for the ethical question, and may have had no effect upon the results. There are other minor problems which bear on the generality of the findings such as the unexplained issue by condition interaction. The most serious flaw of the procedure is related to the within-subjects design, i.e., each subject serving in six different conditions. This means that he had to be presented and had to process and store information which "set up" five of the conditions—the sixth being the control condition for which subjects merely expressed their opinion on a previously unmentioned issue. This was a great deal of information—descriptions of five speeches and four speakers—for subjects to process and comprehend in a relatively short period of time. Papageorgis (1967) recognized what effects this might have had ". . . It is also possible to raise questions regarding the exact nature of the CC manipulation used in the present experiment. One objection may be that the subjects became confused as to which speeches they were scheduled to hear and which speech would not be presented. . . . A second possibility may be that the CC condition, because it was always presented with the anticipated speech conditions, may have acquired a status of psychological equivalence with the latter [p. 495]."

Papageorgis regards both of these possibilities as unlikely, but they seemed sufficiently compelling for the authors of the following article to carry out two experiments designed to assess the extent to which the possibilities raised by Papageorgis had influenced the results in his CC condition.

The first experiment reported in the following article was an attempt to replicate Papageorgis' procedures exactly. One condition was added to his six with the intention of evaluating the possibility that subjects had become confused about which speech they were not going to hear (CC). Many people have argued that what psychology and, particularly, social psychology, needs is more attention to exact replications of research. See what problems and ambiguities occur to you as you read this attempt at an exact replication.

Self-Esteem and Consistency as Determinants of Anticipatory Opinion Change[1]

Joel Cooper and Russell A. Jones

Recent evidence has apparently favored a consistency as opposed to a self-esteem preserving interpretation of anticipatory (i.e., precommunication) belief change. The evidence was somewhat ambiguous, however, and an extended replication (Experiment I) of earlier research indicated that the evidence favoring consistency theory had been artifactually produced. Making use of a distinction suggested by Papageorgis concerning the context of research on anticipatory belief change, a second experiment was carried out. Data from the second experiment appear to favor the self-esteem interpretation of anticipatory belief change. The data also suggest that warning of a coming influence attempt will not produce precommunication belief change when presented in a context in which self-esteem considerations are not salient.

In a series of intriguing studies, McGuire and his colleagues (McGuire & Millman, 1965; Papageorgis, 1967) have developed an originally serendipitous and statistically trivial finding into a theoretical framework. Working from an innoculation model (cf. McGuire, 1964), McGuire and Papageorgis (1962) discovered, to their surprise, that greater belief change toward agreement with anticipated persuasive attacks occurred among subjects who believed their susceptibility to persuasion was being studied than among subjects who believed the study had a more benign purpose. The finding was only a trend, but McGuire and Papageorgis (1962) offered the following suggestion:

> on occasions when we wish a person to maintain his beliefs at a high level but are unable to defend those beliefs in advance, it might be unwise to threaten that his beliefs may be attacked [p. 32].

To paraphrase McGuire (1966), seldom has so slight an effect been made to bear so heavy a burden of explanation.

[1] From the *Journal of Personality and Social Psychology* 1970, **14,** No. 4, 312–320. Received February 27, 1969. Reproduced by permission of the publisher.

Requests for reprints should be sent to Joel Cooper, Department of Psychology, Princeton University, Green Hall, Princeton, New Jersey 08540.

The authors would like to express their appreciation to Jack W. Brehm and Edward E. Jones for their helpful comments on an earlier draft of the manuscript.

At the time of writing, Dr. Jones was with Rutgers University; he is currently with The University of Kentucky. Dr. Cooper is with Princeton University.

It is beginning to appear, however, that the generalization may indeed be valid. In an attempt to understand the dynamics of the warning-anticipatory belief-change phenomenon, McGuire and Millman (1965) set out to test an elaborated version of "self-esteem" theory. Self-esteem theory assumes that people are often worried about their ability to stand up for their beliefs, and that belief change may occur after warning but before attack as a self-esteem preserving maneuver. That is, when warned of an impending attack on one of his pet beliefs, the person may change his belief toward greater agreement with the coming attack so that he can tell himself afterwards that the attack did not really have much influence on his belief. McGuire and Millman also reasoned that such a strategy would be more likely to occur with an emotional issue than with a technical one. They reasoned that a person could ascribe his change on a technical issue "to a commendable openness to evidence and ability to take in new information rather than to a socially undesirable inability to stand up for one's own opinion [p. 471]." Further, a source variable was introduced. Anticipation of persuasive attack by a highly persuasive source should make one more anxious about his ability to withstand the attack and hence more likely to make use of the anticipatory change strategy than when the anticipated attack is to come from a relatively less persuasive source.

As predicted, McGuire and Millman (1965) found that warning per se did produce an anticipatory lowering of the beliefs, and this effect appears to be due almost entirely to change on their "emotional" issues following the warning. Contrary to their prediction, there was no differential effectiveness of the warning as a function of the source of the forthcoming attack. The authors pointed out, however, that the failure to confirm the source prediction may have been due to their inadvertently pitting two components of source credibility (effectiveness and respectability) against each other in their attempt to manipulate credibility. Apart from the failure of the source manipulation to have the predicted effect, the evidence appears supportive of the self-esteem framework. As McGuire and Millman pointed out, however, it is also consistent with a dissonance framework (Festinger, 1957). Rather than leaving it at this, the authors further pointed out a method of distinguishing the two interpretations. The dissonance interpretation, according to McGuire and Millman (1965), would predict "as much belief lowering if we merely mention to the believer that the expert source holds the discrepant opinion, as if we warn him that this source is moreover about to present an attack on the belief [p. 477]." Self-esteem theory would predict less change—if any—when there is no anticipation of attack.

Papageorgis (1967) undertook to clarify the questions raised by

McGuire and Millman concerning the source's effectiveness and reputability and to obtain some evidence on the viability of the dissonance alternative to the self-esteem interpretation. Papageorgis orthogonally varied the respectability and persuasive effectiveness of the source of the anticipated communications. As McGuire and Millman pointed out, "Our revised self-esteem formulation would predict that the effect of the warning would be inversely related to the former and directly related to the latter [p. 476]." That is, self-esteem considerations should be more salient when the source is low rather than high in respectability, and high rather than low in persuasive effectiveness. In a "consistency control" condition, Papageorgis informed subjects of the existence of a persuasive communication which took a position contrary to that favored by the subjects, but told the subjects that they would not be exposed to the communication.

Papageorgis' results indicated that the manipulations of the source's effectiveness and respectability again had little effect on the amount of anticipatory belief lowering, and that significant belief lowering was obtained merely as a result of knowledge of the existence of a persuasive communication contrary to the subjects' own beliefs. Together the results appear more supportive of the consistency interpretation of anticipatory belief lowering than of the self-esteem explanation.

The present research was prompted by two factors. First, it seemed to us that Papageorgis' results were not really as supportive of a consistency interpretation as they appeared on the surface. Papageorgis presented subjects with a booklet containing descriptions of five speeches. The direction of the argument was described for each speech and was always contrary to the subjects' own belief on the issue. For four of the speeches, the source, his effectiveness, and his reputability were also described. Subjects were led to believe that they were soon to be exposed to tape recordings of the four speeches. The fifth speech, which was also described in the booklet, had "not yet arrived" and consequently was not going to be played to the subjects. No mention was made of a source for the latter speech.

As soon as subjects had read the booklet, an opinion questionnaire was administered. Subjects were asked to record their opinions on all five of the issues mentioned in the booklet, as well as on a sixth, unmentioned item. Results indicated that subjects changed their beliefs not only on the issues for which they were about to hear speeches, but also on the issue for which the speech had "not yet arrived!" The changes were all in the direction of closer agreement with the communication.

Papageorgis' results appear to argue that mere knowledge of the existence of a discrepant communication (the speech that had "not yet arrived") was sufficient to produce belief change toward closer agreement with that communication. However, it seems to us that Papageorgis (1967) placed excessive demands on the information-processing capabilities of subjects and that, as a result, subjects may have become confused as to which communications were or were not forthcoming. Subjects were confronted with a booklet describing five separate issues, and were given brief synopses of speeches on these five issues, as well as descriptions of four different speakers. If enough subjects did not pay sufficient attention to which four speeches were to be played and which one was not, then the results could simply reflect this confusion. In other words, to the extent that subjects forgot which of the five speeches was not available, the Papageorgis procedure did not provide a clear test of the "mere knowledge" hypothesis. Our first purpose, then, was to obtain clearer evidence on the "mere knowledge" hypothesis.

Before turning to our second purpose, let us look at the results of an experiment bearing on our first.

Experiment I

Method

Subjects. One hundred and thirty-nine female undergraduates at Duke University served as subjects. The subjects were volunteers from an introductory psychology course and participated in the experiment in groups of three or four. They were required to take part in a certain number of experiments, but were free to decide which studies they signed up for.

Procedure. The procedure was intended to do two things: (*a*) to replicate as closely as possible the Papageorgis (1967) study and (*b*) to assess our alternative hypothesis of his finding that mere knowledge of the existence of a discrepant persuasive communication is sufficient to cause belief lowering. To accomplish these two objectives, seven conditions were called for. Six conditions were required to replicate the design used by Papageorgis. A seventh condition was added to test our hypothesis that being told of the existence of a communication does *not* produce change when subjects are not confused by extraneous information.

In four of the conditions that were modeled after those of Papageorgis (1967), subjects anticipated having a belief attacked by communicators whose reputability as persons and effectiveness as speakers were varied. The communicator was either high in effectiveness and high in reputability (HH), high in effectiveness but low in reputability (HL), low in effectiveness but high in reputability (LH), or low in both effectiveness and reputability (LL). In a fifth condition (CC), again modeled after Papageorgis', subjects learned of the existence of a communication opposed to their belief but did not anticipate being exposed to the communication. In a sixth condition (C), no mention was made of a communication and subjects were merely asked to record their opinions on a given issue.

One hundred and four of the 139 subjects participated in the above six conditions with each subject serving in all six conditions. This was made possible by using six different issues and having each subject serve in a different condition on each issue. No actual communications were presented to the subjects. Rather, each subject was led to believe that four messages were forthcoming and was given a description of the speaker for each of the messages. As noted earlier, the effectiveness and reputability of the speakers were varied. Subjects were also told the position each of the speakers would take (always contrary to the subjects own position on each issue). In addition, subjects were given the direction of argument on a fifth communication, but were told this communication would not be presented. Following the presentation of the foregoing information in the form of a small booklet, subjects' beliefs were measured on six issues. The sixth issue served as the control condition (C) mentioned previously. Also, subjects were asked to rate the communicators in terms of their reputability and expected effectiveness.

For a detailed description of the sources, issues, sequence, and rotation of the conditions, etc., see Papageorgis (1967). The same issues, descriptions, and procedures used by Papageorgis were used in the present study, and his procedures were followed in detail.

The remaining subjects participated in a seventh condition—no anticipation (NA)—designed to assess our alternative hypothesis of Papageorgis' finding of belief change in his CC condition. The subjects in the NA condition received a booklet which described the position taken by five communications (all contrary to the subjects' own beliefs), but were told that none of the communications would be heard. The issues were the same as in the other conditions. The sixth, unmentioned issue was rotated. The communications had supposedly been damaged in shipment. After reading the booklet, subjects filled out a belief questionnaire. If our interpretation of Papageorgis' results is correct, then no opinion change should be found for any of the issues used in the NA condition.

All seven conditions were run concurrently and subjects were randomly assigned to conditions. Although several subjects took part in the experiment at the same time, they were separated from each other by large partitions and did not constitute a "group."

Results

Source Manipulations

Subjects evaluated the source of the communications they were to hear on two semantic differential scales measuring perceived source effectiveness and two scales measuring perceived reputability. As in Papageorgis' (1967) experiment, scores of each set were added, producing an overall measure of each source characteristic with a range of 2–14. Higher scores indicate greater reputability and effectiveness.

It appears that the source manipulations were effective. The mean rating for the expected effectiveness of the speaker for the high-effectiveness conditions was 11.05, compared to a mean of 9.21 for the low-effectiveness conditions ($p < .01$). It should be noted that in both high- and low-effectiveness conditions the source was seen as relatively effective. Similarly, the mean perceived reputability for the high-reputability conditions was 12 as compared to 8.14 for the low-reputability conditions ($p < .01$).

Belief Change

The results of the present experiment can best be described in relation to those of Papageorgis (1967). Both sets of results are presented in Table 1.

The result of interest from the Papageorgis study was that except for the LL mean, all other condition means (for six issues combined) differed significantly from the C mean. Thus, his CC mean of 5.86 was significantly different from the C mean of 4.84, indicating belief change in the CC condition presumably as a result of knowing that a counter-belief communication existed.

Our alternative hypothesis for the latter result was that subjects did not keep track of which one of the five communications was not to be heard and took anticipatory precautions with respect to each of the associated beliefs. The results of the present study seem to support this hypothesis (Table 1). When subjects were informed of the positions taken by the communications but did not anticipate hearing them (NA), the mean opinion score was 5.64 and was not significantly different from the control mean of 5.85. However, when we included the issue on which subjects were not to hear a communication, but knew of the position it would take, along with four issues on which they were to hear attacks (CC), the mean opinion score of 6.76 was significantly different from the control ($p < .05$). Furthermore, the CC condition of the present study produced greater anticipatory belief change than the NA condition ($p < .05$). The average belief change of the five conditions—HH, HL, LL, LH, and CC—was 6.36 and was significantly greater than the average (5.74) of the C and NA conditions ($p < .05$).

The results of Experiment I offer support for Papageorgis' finding that opinion change can be effected by anticipating a persuasive attack against one's beliefs. However, our failure to find opinion change in the NA condition supports our hypothesis that the mere knowledge of the existence of a counterbelief communication is not sufficient to induce belief lowering.

It should also be noted that the effectiveness and reputability of the source had little effect on anticipatory belief change. Analysis of variance of the 2×2 design (see Table 1) contained within the present seven conditions yielded no support for the source characteristic extension (see McGuire & Millman, 1965) of self-esteem theory (all *F*s less than 1). It is also worth noting that this is the third failure to confirm source charac-

TABLE 1
Cell Means for All Six Issues Combined[a]

Effectiveness	Reputability				
	High	Low	CC	C	
Papageorgis (1967)					
High	5.99	5.90	5.86	4.84	
Low	6.01	5.30			
	High	Low	CC	C	NA
Present results (Exp. I)					
High	6.25	6.26	6.76	5.85	5.64
Low	6.35	6.18			

[a] The higher the mean, the greater the opinion change.

teristics as a determinant of anticipatory belief change (McGuire & Millman, 1965; Papageorgis, 1967).

Even though Experiment I appears to support our notion that Papageorgis (1967) did not really have clear evidence in support of the "mere knowledge" hypothesis, we were somewhat less than satisfied with the clarity of our own results. In particular, Papageorgis (1967) obtained significant differences between each of his HH, HL, and LH conditions taken separately and the control conditions; we did not. Also, our NA condition may have appeared somewhat peculiar to subjects. That is, since none of the speeches that they were to hear arrived, it may have seemed more sensible to the subjects if they were rescheduled for a later appointment. Instead, the experimenter ushered them in and asked them to indicate their opinions on a number of issues.

The first purpose of the present research was to gather evidence on the consistency notion that mere knowledge that someone holds an opinion discrepant from one's own is sufficient to produce opinion change toward agreement with the other's opinion. The notion did not appeal to us phenomenologically, and we felt the evidence was too ambiguous. Although we were aware that it was not a question of either-or, it nevertheless appeared that self-esteem theory was a more interesting and fruitful way of looking at anticipatory change phenomena. A manipulation was needed which would make self-esteem considerations salient to subjects in one set of conditions but not in another set, and which would allow us to distinguish the consistency and self-esteem contributions without the confounding introduced in earlier studies (including our own).

Papageorgis (1968) has pointed out the value of distinguishing those studies which occur in an explicit persuasion context (i.e., emphasizing opinion change as the purpose of the experiment) from those that occur in a disguised context where subjects supposedly do not know that attempts are being made to change their opinions. (McGuire, 1969, has noted that contrary to popular belief, the former rather than the latter may be more readily generalizable to nonlaboratory situations.) In an explicit persuasion context, one would expect self-esteem considerations to be extremely salient to subjects. Hence, anticipation of persuasive attack should make subjects truly anxious about their gullibility, and anticipatory belief lowering should occur. In a disguised persuasion context, self-esteem considerations would be much less likely to enter the picture. The consistency prediction of change due to knowledge that someone else holds a discrepant opinion should apply to both the disguised and persuasion contexts. Our second purpose, then, was to bring this distinction suggested by Papageorgis (1968) to an experimental test.

It also occurred to us that any consistency effect would be more likely to exhibit itself if the holder of the discrepant opinion were highly prestigious and effective than if the holder of the discrepant opinion were anonymous. Further, this difference, according to the consistency notion, would be approximately the same in both the disguised and persuasion context. The "postinflated-deflated" version of self-esteem theory that we are working with at the moment, however, would make somewhat different predictions. As a result of several failures to confirm the "inflated" self-esteem theory's source predictions, we assume that the source is relatively irrelevant and that anticipation of persuasive attack will produce belief lowering regardless of whether the source is anonymous or described as very credible. Further, as noted earlier, self-esteem theory predicts the anticipation variable to be more effective in producing belief change in the explicit persuasion context than in the disguised context.

A second experiment was designed to investigate the effectiveness of anticipated and nonanticipated communications while taking into account the considerations described above. Subjects anticipated listening to one speech and were merely told about the existence of a second one. For half of the subjects, the experiment was described as a study in "recognition and recall" (a disguised context), and virtually no mention was made of "opinion change." The other half of the subjects, like the subjects in Papageorgis' (1967) experiment, expected to participate in an "opinion change" study (an explicit persuasion context).

In addition, for one-half of the subjects, both the anticipated and nonanticipated speeches were associated with highly prestigious and effective communicators. For the other half of the subjects, *neither* speech was associated with a communicator. This communicators described versus not described variable should also allow us to distinguish the relative contributions of consistency and self-esteem as mentioned earlier.

Experiment II

METHOD

The experimental design was a $2 \times 2 \times 2$ factorial design with an external control group. The variables were manner of describing the study to subjects (opinion change versus recognition and recall), whether or not the subjects expected to hear a communication (anticipation versus no anticipation), and whether or not the communicators were described (communicators described versus communicators not described).

Subjects. Subjects were 108 undergraduates from introductory psychology courses at Duke University. Again, subjects were required to participate in a certain number of experiments but were free to decide which studies they signed for. Three or four subjects were run simultaneously and were separated by large partitions. Subjects were randomly assigned to conditions.

Procedure. All subjects signed up for an experiment on "recall, recognition, and opinions." When subjects in the *opinion change* conditions arrived, they were told: "In this part of the experiment, we are interested in measuring opinion change that results from listening to actual recorded speeches." When subjects assigned to the *recognition* and *recall* conditions arrived, they were told: "In this part of the experiment, we are interested in finding out how well people can recall and recognize certain aspects of a communication."

The experimenter then handed out a mimeographed sheet which contained the descriptions of two speeches. The heading of the sheet was either "Recognition and recall project" or "Opinion change project," depending on the condition to which subjects had been assigned. For the *communicators described* conditions, the two paragraphs on the sheet read as follows:

1. "The Coming Economic Depression." This is a recording made by Dr. John M. Bauman. Dr. Bauman is a well known authority on economics, and a member of the President's Council of Economic Advisers, and a former Professor of Economics at Princeton University. This particular talk is a recording of Dr. Bauman's presentation over the National Educational Television Network in April of this year. At that time, the talk was acclaimed as an extremely persuasive and interesting analysis of current economic trends. The talk takes the position that a serious economic depression will affect the U. S. economy in the immediate future.

2. "Needed: Exercise of the Federal Prerogative." This is a recording made by Dr. John C. Cleveland, Deputy Director, National Institute of Health, Bethesda, Maryland. Dr. Cleveland is a distinguished sociologist whose forecasts of trends in American society influence the policies not only of the National Institute of Health but of the U. S. Government; his talk is a recording of the prepared portion of his acclaimed testimony in front of the House of Representatives Committee on Public Health. The talk takes the stand that the federal government should take more of a role in matters that have been traditionally

left to the states. Unfortunately, this recording has been damaged in shipment and cannot be used.

Consequently, subjects were led to anticipate hearing Speech 1 but were only told of the existence of Speech 2. As in Experiment I, the issues were rotated such that half of the experimental subjects anticipated hearing the economic depression speech while the other half anticipated the federal prerogative communication. These two issues were selected because the positions taken were counterattitudinal for subjects. The design was an after-only design, but data from an attitude questionnaire administered to introductory psychology students confirmed that the positions advocated were counterattitudinal for the vast majority of subjects.

Subjects assigned to the communicator not described conditions read descriptions similar to those in the communicator described conditions, except that all reference to the communicators was deleted. Only the topic and the direction of the speeches were described.

When subjects finished reading the descriptions of the communications, they were given a questionnaire containing the two opinion items and were asked to indicate their own opinions on the issues. Subjects assigned to the communicator described conditions were also given the semantic differential scales described in Experiment I, on which they were to rate the source of the communication they were to hear. Subjects assigned to the control condition merely filled out the opinion items as soon as they arrived for the experiment.

The opinion measures consisted of the following two statements: (*a*) "A serious economic depression will affect the U. S. economy in the immediate future," and (*b*) "The Federal Government should assume more of a role in matters which have been traditionally left up to the states." Each of the statements was accompanied by a 15-division scale, the same type of scale used in much of the work by McGuire (e.g., McGuire, 1964). The five labels below each scale ran from "definitely false" to "definitely true." Upon completion of the opinion items, the experiment was terminated. Subjects were told the true nature of the research and were asked not to reveal its purpose to others.

Results

The means for the two issues separately and combined are given in Table 2. Inspection of Table 2 reveals no difference as a function of issue; consequently the following results reported are for both issues combined.

The data on which Table 2 is based were analyzed by a three-way analysis of variance with repeated measures on the anticipation–no anticipation variable. The control group was compared to the experimental groups by t tests.

The analyses revealed a significant effect for the manner of introducing the study ($F = 14.1$, $df = 1/92$, $p < .05$). Subjects who were led to believe that the study was concerned with opinion change changed their opinions more than did subjects who believed that the study was concerned with recognition and recall. There was also a within-subjects inter-

TABLE 2
Opinion Means for Experiment II[a]

Condition	Communicator described: Antici- pation	Communicator described: No antici- pation	Communicator not described: Antici- pation	Communicator not described: No antici- pation	Control
Opinion change					
Federal issue	8.92	5.83	8.75	5.25	5.42
Economy issue	8.58	5.50	9.12	5.58	5.25
Combined	8.75	5.67	8.96	5.42	5.33
Recognition and recall					
Federal issue	5.83	4.92	5.75	5.75	
Economy issue	5.50	5.92	5.75	5.00	
Combined	5.67	5.42	5.75	5.38	

[a] The higher the mean, the greater the change toward agreement with the discrepant communication.

action between the manner of introducing the study and the anticipation variable ($F = 14.4$, $df = 1/92$, $p < .01$). The interaction indicates that only when subjects believed that the study was concerned with opinion change did they change their opinions in response to the expectation of being exposed to discrepant communications.

As can be seen in Table 2, the results described above appear to have been produced by the change obtained in the two anticipation–opinion change conditions. In fact, the latter two conditions were the only two to differ from the control condition (communicator described versus control: $t = 4.76$, $df = 46$, $p < .01$; communicator not described: $t = 4.79$, $df = 46$, $p < .01$).

It should be noted that in the communicator described conditions, both speakers were rated as highly effective, persuasive, reputable, and trustworthy. The two speakers were not rated differently on any dimension (all t ratios were nonsignificant).

Discussion

The results of Experiment II indicate once again that mere knowledge of the existence of a discrepant communication (the no anticipation conditions) is not sufficient to induce opinion change, at least within the given procedure. Second, it appears that forewarning of the direction of argument of a discrepant communication to which subjects anticipate exposure is sufficient to induce precommunication opinion change *only* within what Papageorgis (1968) has labeled an explicit persuasion context (our opinion change conditions).

In his recent review, Papageorgis (1968) addressed himself to the discrepancies which exist among the findings of studies on the direct effects of forewarning on opinion change. If we exclude those studies in which extraneous variables were present (such as "anticipation of debate"), there are three published studies cited by Papageorgis which obtained evidence for postwarning opinion change (McGuire & Millman, 1965; McGuire & Papageorgis, 1962; Papageorgis, 1967). The findings by McGuire and Papageorgis (1962) were really a trend, so there were two studies which obtained significant anticipatory belief change as a result of forewarning. In both the McGuire and Millman (1965) and Papageorgis (1967) studies, subjects were given advance information about the topics of the communications they were supposedly to hear. McGuire and Millman (1965) utilized what Papageorgis (1968) has characterized as a disguised persuasion context; that is, subjects were not told the true purpose of the experiment, but were led to believe that the research was a part of pretesting materials to be used in governmental personnel selection procedures. In this respect, the McGuire and Millman study is similar to the recognition and recall conditions of our second experiment—both concealed the purpose of the experiment.

Why, then, did we not obtain anticipatory change in our recognition and recall anticipation conditions? Several possibilities suggest themselves. McGuire and Millman introduced their experiment to subjects as a study of "analytic thinking ability." Such an introduction could have made self-esteem considerations more salient to subjects than our somewhat benign "recognition and recall" introduction. The result would be anticipatory change in McGuire and Millman's study, but not in the recognition and recall conditions of our Experiment II.

A second possible explanation for the discrepancy concerns the nature of the issues. It will be recalled that McGuire and Millman obtained greater anticipation belief change on emotional than on technical issues. The only definition given to these terms is that a technical issue is a "matter-of-fact" one and an emotional issue is an "unverifiable" one (McGuire & Millman, 1965, p. 471). According to this distinction, both of our issues (Experiment II) would qualify as emotional issues. In fact, the issue of a coming economic depression was one of the emotional issues used by McGuire and Millman (1965). However, McGuire[2] appears to have changed his mind about the nature of this particular issue and points out that it is really a technical one dealing with the factual ques-

[2] W. J. McGuire, personal communication, May 1969.

tion of whether or not an economic depression will occur. We would agree with the latter judgment, and, in fact, feel that subjects would view both of our issues as ones on which a great deal of technical information existed—even though there is a value judgment at the foundation of the Federal issue (whether more or less Federal control is beneficial). What we would like to suggest is, simply, that the emotional-technical dichotomy is in need of explication if it is to prove to be of heuristic value.

In contrast to McGuire and Millman (1965) and to the recognition and recall conditions of Experiment II, Papageorgis (1967) informed his subjects that he was interested in opinion change, and opinion change was emphasized throughout his procedure. Thus, the Papageorgis experiment was conceptually similar to our opinion change conditions of Experiment II. The basic finding in both was that when subjects anticipate being exposed to a persuasive communication within an explicit opinion change context they do exhibit postwarning and precommunication opinion change. However, as both of our experiments show, mere knowledge of the existence of a persuasive communication is not sufficient to induce opinion change. The only evidence for the latter appears to have been produced as an artifact of the procedure used by Papageorgis (1967).

Several other studies have appeared recently which bear on the forewarning–opinion-change question. Again, however, the discussion is limited to those studies and/or conditions within studies in which no extraneous variables were operating. In a condition in which subjects anticipated exposure to an attitude-discrepant communication but did not expect to have the opportunity to defend their position, Deaux (1968) found precommunication change did not differ significantly from zero. Since Deaux utilized a disguised persuasion context, her findings appear to coincide with our finding in the recognition and recall conditions of Experiment II, but are discrepant with the results of McGuire and Millman (1965).

Two other studies which utilized disguised persuasion contexts appear to be consistent with the results of Deaux (1968) and with those in the recognition and recall conditions of the present Experiment II. Wicklund, Cooper, and Linder (1967) found anticipatory belief change *only* when subjects had committed themselves to an unpleasant act in order to hear a communication, and not when subjects simply anticipated exposure to the discrepant communication. Linder, Cooper, and Wicklund (1968) replicated the latter finding, again confirming that anticipation of exposure to a discrepant communication was not sufficient, at least in their procedure, to produce anticipatory change.

It appears, then, that there is very little evidence for anticipatory belief change as a result of forewarning in studies which have utilized disguised persuasion contexts. In spite of the McGuire and Millman results, we feel this finding to be generally consistent with self-esteem theory, since disguised contexts do not usually make subjects concerned about their gullibility. The studies most clearly producing anticipatory belief change have utilized explicit persuasion contexts. This raises the question of demand characteristics (Orne, 1962). Are the anticipatory belief changes found in explicit persuasion contexts simply due to the generally recognized cooperativeness of the subjects? If so, the self-esteem interpretation would be superfluous.

We are inclined to doubt that the demand characteristic interpretation can account for the findings. In our Experiment II, for example, the demand characteristic interpretation would predict opinion change in the no anticipation conditions as well as in the anticipation conditions of the explicit persuasion context. Further, the demand characteristic interpretation would have predicted more opinion change in the communicator described–no anticipation condition than in the corresponding communicator not described condition. Neither of the latter predications obtained. The evidence seems to lend support to the self-esteem interpretation of anticipatory attitude change.

REFERENCES

Deaux, K. K. Variations in warning, information, preference, and anticipatory attitude change. *Journal of Personality and Social Psychology,* 1968, **9,** 157–161.

Festinger, L. *A theory of cognitive dissonance.* Stanford, Calif.: Stanford University Press, 1957.

Linder, D. E., Cooper, J., & Wicklund, R. A. Preexposure persuasion as a result of commitment to pre-exposure effort. *Journal of Experimental Social Psychology,* 1968, **4,** 470–482.

McGuire, W. J. Inducing resistance to persuasion: Some contemporary approaches. In L. Berkowitz (Ed.), *Advances in experimental social psychology.* Vol. 1. New York: Academic Press, 1964.

McGuire, W. J. Attitudes and opinions. *Annual Review of Psychology,* 1966, **17,** 475–514.

McGuire, W. J. Suspiciousness of experimenter's intent as an artifact in research. In R. Rosenthal & R. Rosnow (Eds.), *Artifact in social research.* New York: Academic Press, 1969.

McGuire, W. J., & Millman, S. Anticipatory belief lowering following forewarning of a persuasive attack. *Journal of Personality and Social Psychology,* 1965, **2,** 471–479.

McGuire, W. J., & Papageorgis, D. Effectiveness of forewarning in developing resistance to persuasion. *Public Opinion Quarterly,* 1962, **26,** 24–34.

Orne, M. T. On the social psychology of the psychological experiment: With particular

reference to the demand characteristics and their implications. *American Psychologist,* 1962, **17**, 776–783.
Papageorgis, D. Anticipation of exposure to persuasive messages and belief change. *Journal of Personality and Social Psychology,* 1967, **5**, 490–496.
Papageorgis, D. Warning and persuasion. *Psychological Bulletin,* 1968, **70**, 271–282.
Wicklund, R. A., Cooper, J., & Linder, D. E. Effects of expected effort on attitude change prior to exposure. *Journal of Experimental Social Psychology,* 1967, **3**, 416–428.

Discussion

A number of important methodological problems have been raised in this chapter. By way of summary, we provide, below, a somewhat more detailed reiteration than we have in previous chapters. Many of these problems were discussed at length in Part I. Hopefully, those earlier discussions will have become more meaningful now that you have seen at first hand how the problems can limit the value of a piece of research. There is no particular ordering in the list below, but it should be obvious that some of the problems are more serious than others.

Statistical Significance

The series of articles presented in this chapter began with a statistically trivial finding (McGuire & Papageorgis, 1962). Had the law of ".05" been adhered to rigidly, this particular version of "self-esteem" theory might never have come into existence. We do not feel that trends and tendencies should be dismissed simply because they do not reach conventional levels of significance. At the present state of the art, such an operating procedure may dispense with both babe and bath water. Nonsignificant findings should be looked at in terms of whether or not they make theoretical sense, not just in terms of their failure to reach the .05 level (Bakan, 1966).

Demand Characteristics

We encountered this difficulty in both the Papageorgis (1967) and Cooper and Jones (1970) studies. It is difficult to prescribe any general "formula" or set of procedures for circumventing this problem. Orne (1962) suggests that ". . . One procedure to determine the demand characteristics (in a particular experiment) is the systematic study of each individual subject's perception of the experimental hypothesis. If one can determine what demand characteristics are perceived by each subject, it becomes possible to determine to what extent these, rather than the experimental variables correlate with behavior. . . . The most obvious technique for determining what demand characteristics are perceived is the use of postexperimental inquiry [p. 780]."

Adequacy of Manipulations

This is one of the most serious questions, and one that has several subissues. How do we know when we have actually manipulated what we intended to manipulate? How could McGuire and Millman have known whether or not they had actually manipulated the emotionality–technicality of the issues? One way is to include some sort of check on the manipulation in a postexperimental questionnaire. Papageorgis (1967) did this. He asked subjects to rate, after reading the descriptions of the speakers they were to hear, how effective and how reputable they thought the individual speakers would be. A second way, and one that would have been more appropriate for the McGuire and Millman issue dimension, would be to have an independent group of subjects react to the manipulation—in this case rate the issues on a number of dimensions. This is essentially what Anderson (Ch. 8) and others are doing when they get ratings of adjectives from independent groups of subjects (Anderson, 1968; Rosenberg and Jones, 1971). Thus, the adjectives can be picked with prior knowledge of how subjects will view any particular adjective in isolation.

A second problem, most clearly demonstrated in the Papageorgis study, is that of making sure that subjects "understand" the manipulations. Aronson and Carlsmith (1968) provide an excellent discussion of this point. As they note ". . . The most general technique for finding out just what an independent variable manipulation is doing is to run some pretests. During the pretesting, one can conduct long, probing interviews with the subject after the experiment, or better yet, after the manipulation of the independent variable. Often the subject is capable of providing valuable hints as to where the weakness in the manipulation occurred [p. 49]." This point was also discussed earlier, in Chapter 2.

Alternative Explanations

There is not much, of a general nature, that one can say about alternative explanations. They are often quite specific to a particular experiment. There do seem to be two classes of alternative explanations which might be designated competing theoretical explanations and trivial explanations. An example of the former is presented in the discussion section of the McGuire and Millman article where they point out that dissonance theory could possibly account for some of their results—results that they explained in terms of self-esteem considerations. An example of a trivial or theoretically uninteresting explanation is the notion that the procedures used by Papageorgis (1967) confused subjects, and the obtained results in his CC condition simply reflect this confusion.

After-Only versus Before-After Measurement

The choice here depends on the particular study in question. Each alternative has its good points. McGuire and Millman say that the reason they opted for the after-only design was because the before-after "... would have had the undesirable effect of taking away some of the believer's saving ambiguity about his initial belief levels, and ambiguity is required to make psychologically feasible the use of the anticipatory lowering strategy as a self-esteem saving device [p. 476]."

Lana (1969), who has done extensive research on pretesting, points out that "... what one gains in information by utilizing a pretest he sometimes loses in increased sensitization of the subject. What he gains in purity of experimental effect by utilizing a randomization design he loses in knowledge of pretreatment conditions existing in the organism. In some cases the goals of the experiment set the risk one will take. However, in many situations one is caught between the Scylla of sensitization and the Charybdis of ignorance of pre-existing conditions. The choice of procedure may be arbitrary [p. 139]."

Within-Subject Manipulations

In all three of the preceding articles there was a within-subject manipulation, i.e., subjects served in more than one condition. It is possible that this fact influenced the results obtained. Cooper and Jones (1970) conclude "... it appears that forewarning of the direction of argument of a discrepant communication to which subjects anticipate exposure is sufficient to induce pre-communication opinion change *only* within what Papageorgis (1968) has labeled an explicit persuasion context [p. 318]." A more accurate statement of their results would be that anticipation of exposure on one message coupled with knowledge of a second communication to which one does not anticipate exposure is sufficient to induce ..., etc. It is a question for future research whether or not a between subjects manipulation of Anticipation–No Anticipation would produce the same result. It is quite conceivable that anticipatory belief change is obtained only as a contrast effect when a subject anticipates exposure to one communication but not to a second which he knows exists.

Experimenter Bias

Of the preceding three articles, only the McGuire and Millman study is immune to criticisms of experimenter bias. In both of the other articles, experimenters knew the conditions that subjects were in and could have behaved unintentionally in ways which influenced the results—especially when reading aloud the speech descriptions in the Papageorgis study and in the first experiment of Cooper and Jones. Research by Rosenthal (1966) and his colleagues, to which we have repeatedly referred, indicates the seriousness of this problem. Future research on anticipatory belief lowering must institute suitable controls for experimenter effects if any sure knowledge is to be gained.

Debriefing

There has been a growing concern among social psychologists during the last few years about the ethics of deceiving subjects in an experiment (Brown, 1962; Kelman, 1965, 1967). Most experimental social psychologists have argued that the deceptions used are innocuous (usually) and only temporary. That is, it has become standard operating procedure to explain fully all deceptions to each subject after the experiment and detail the reasons why those deceptions were necessary. This has been sufficient to soothe the consciences of most. When the debriefing is omitted, however, and subjects are left with different attitudes from those with which they arrived—as in the Papageorgis study—there is reason for concern. We advocate total disclosure of the deceptions upon completion of the experiment—a subject should never be allowed to leave the experimental setting with false information about himself or others, or with biased information about any object or issue.

One should be aware, of course, that this creates other problems. Subjects can and often do inform other subjects about the experiment, and when these others later participate in the experiment their data may be worthless. Campbell (1969) has pointed up other disadvantages of debriefing. "It provides modeling and publicity for deceit and thus serves to debase language for the respondent as well as for the experimenter. It reduces the credibility of the laboratory and undermines the utility of deceit in future experiments [p. 371]." Related to this is the fact that debriefing often informs the subject of his own gullibility and credulity. For some subjects this could be very damaging to their self-esteem. Thus, one could argue that it would be better not to debrief subjects when the deceptions are minor.

Exact Replications

Cooper and Jones attempted an exact replication of the Papageorgis study—an attempt that was only partially successful. There are many reasons for this, most of which have to do with passage of time and different subject populations. For example, Papageorgis used, as one of his HH sources, "The Honorable James W. Bickstrup, deputy undersecretary of defense." While we have no data on the question, we would guess that the perception of anyone connected with the defense department had changed drastically during the years that separated the actual running of the two experiments.

The question of exact replications is intimately related to the question of manipulating the independent variable properly. A different manipulation would be required to make a four-year-old child happy from what would be required to make a twenty two-year-old man happy. If one were interested in producing "happiness," it would be ludicrous to give a toy car and expect the same result in each.

There are conditions, of course, where exact replications are needed and would be meaningful. The important aspect, however, is that the procedures produce the same psychological states, and not that the same procedures are always followed.

Before closing this chapter it might be well to say a few words about the substantive issues. One interesting question that has received little attention is what are the conditions that produce anticipatory change away from the position to be advocated in the coming communication. As we noted earlier, there are theoretical reasons (Brehm, 1966) for expecting that such conditions do exist. A second intriguing question concerns the nature of the issue on which anticipatory change will occur. McGuire and Millman attempted to make a case for an emotional-technical dimension as being crucial. Our armchair analyses have questioned that dimension, but the problem remains. There are many other lines that subsequent research could follow.

Only one thing seems certain in this area of research, and that is that nothing is certain.

REFERENCES

Bakan, D. The test of significance in psychological research. *Psychological Bulletin,* 1966, **66,** 423–437.

Brehm, J. W., *A theory of psychological reactance.* New York: Academic Press, 1966.

Brown, R. Models of attitude change. In *New directions in psychology I.* New York: Holt, Rinehart, and Winston, 1962. Pp. 1–85.

Campbell, D. T. Prospective: artifact and control. In R. Rosenthal and R. L. Rosnow, (Eds.), *Artifact in behavioral research.* New York: Academic Press, 1969. Pp. 351–382.

Festinger, L. *A theory of cognitive dissonance.* Stanford, California: Stanford University Press, 1957.

Hovland, C. I. Reconciling conflicting results derived from experimental and survey studies of attitude change. *American Psychologist,* 1959, **14,** 8–17.

Janis, I. L. Psychological effects of warnings. In C. W. Baker and D. W. Chapman (Eds.), *Man and society in disaster.* New York: Basic Books, 1962.

Janis, I. L. Effects of fear arousal on attitude change: recent developments in theory and experimental research. In L. Berkowitz, (Ed.), *Advances in experimental social psychology.* New York: Academic Press, 1967. Pp. 166–224.

Jones, E. E. *Ingratiation: a social psychological analysis.* New York: Appleton-Century-Crofts, 1964.

Kelman, H. C. Manipulation of human behavior—an ethical dilemma for the social scientist. *Journal of Social Issues,* 1965, **21,** 31–46.

Kelman, H. C. Human use of human subjects: The problem of deception in social psychological experiments. *Psychological Bulletin,* 1967, **67,** 1–11.

Lana, R. E. Pretest sensitization. In R. Rosenthal and R. L. Rosnow (Eds.), *Artifact in behavioral research.* New York: Academic Press, 1969. Pp. 119–141.

McGuire, W. J., & Papageorgis, D. The relative efficacy of various types of prior belief-defense in producing immunity against persuasion. *Journal of Abnormal and Social Psychology,* 1961, **62,** 327–337.

McGuire, W. J., & Papageorgis, D. Effectiveness of forewarning in developing resistance to persuasion. *Public Opinion Quarterly,* 1962, **26,** 24–34.

Orne, M. T. On the social psychology of the psychological experiment: with particular reference to demand characteristics and their implications. *American Psychologist,* 1962, **17,** 776–783.

Papageorgis, D. Warning and persuasion. *Psychological Bulletin,* 1968, **70,** 271–282.

Papageorgis, D., & McGuire, W. J. The generality of immunity to persuasion produced by preexposure to weakened counter arguments. *Journal of Abnormal and Social Psychology,* 1961, **62,** 475–481.

Rosenberg, S., & Jones, R. A. Ratings of personality trait words on nine semantic properties. Unpublished manuscript, Rutgers University, 1971.

Rosenthal, R. *Experimenter effects in behavioral research.* New York: Appleton-Century-Crofts, 1966.

Chapter **10**

DEPENDENCY AND HELPING

So far we have discussed at least three starting points for research. The first involves deriving a prediction from a general theory. One of the primary advantages here is that the theory will apply to many different areas of research. For example, the "suffering leads to liking" hypothesis, and the idea that re-evaluation of alternatives occurs following a choice between two alternatives (Brehm, 1956) are both predictions derived from dissonance theory (Festinger, 1957).

The chapter on the effects of warning about the nature of a coming communication, exemplifies the second type of starting point for research. There, an unexpected finding by McGuire and Papageorgis (1962) began a series of studies, the results of which have been used to sketch the outlines of a self-esteem theory of persuasion. Much work remains before the working hypotheses become a full blown theory, but the emphasis has been using data to build a theory rather than using a theory to predict data.

The third starting point for research is more empirical than either of the others. This approach was exemplified in the article by Anderson and Barrios (1961). The idea here is to take some phenomena on which research findings are unclear and systematically manipulate any and all variables which might affect the phenomena in the hope of obtaining some order or being able to make some sense out of the seemingly contradictory and confused results. The studies presented in the present chapter come closest to this last approach. However, instead of beginning only with the results of previous studies in the literature, the attempt was made to relate that work to some norms which were assumed to exist in contemporary society. This was done by attempting to study systematically those variables and antecedent conditions which increase or decrease the probabilities of the norms being adhered to. The main thrust of the ongoing series of studies which are sampled in this chapter has been the investigation of the norm of social responsibility. This norm is presumed to be pervasive, at least among certain groups, and prescribes that one should help those who are perceived to be dependent on him. Before proceeding, however, we need to say a word about this term "dependent."

Overview of Dependency and Social Responsibility

A very common aspect of life for most people is their dependence on others and the dependence of others on them. Like many of the phenomena of interest to social psychologists, problems abound when an attempt is made to bring dependency into the lab and study its causes and effects.

The first problem is a delimitation of exactly what aspect of "dependency" is being studied. It often seems that one of the characteristics of many psychologists is a predilection for pseudo-generalization, i.e., to treat all things subsumed under the same name in everyday language as essentially the same. Clark (1969) makes clear that all dependencies are not the same. She distinguishes six varieties of dependency: (1) socio-economic, (2) developmental, (3) dependency of crisis, (4) dependency of nonreciprocal roles, (5) neurotic dependency, and (6) dependency as a culturally conditioned character trait. One could argue, for example, that the differences between neurotic dependency and the dependency of crisis are far greater than any similarity between the two.

It becomes crucial, then, to be explicit about exactly what type of dependency we are discussing. The studies discussed in this chapter use a definition derived from Berkowitz (1957). According to that definition, person A is dependent on person B: (1) to the extent that B can facilitate A's progress toward some goal and (2) to the extent to which A values the goal. This meaning of dependency, and throughout the rest of the chapter it will be the only meaning referred to by the term "dependent," is a part of everyday life for most people. Used in the above sense, we are often dependent on others. When approaching a door with our arms filled with packages, we are dependent on someone to open the door for us. We may be dependent on someone directing traffic around an accident or a taxi driver to get us rapidly to our destination. These examples do not necessarily involve emergencies, nor do they imply anything about the characteristics of the dependent person.

Working from such a definition of dependency, Berkowitz (1957) reasoned that, perhaps, interdependent group members heighten their task motivation simply because of their interdependency. One can think in terms of incentive at this point. Suppose that person A were told that he could win $5 by performing task X. We would assume that A then has some incentive for performing the task. If A were told that by performing the task not only could he win $5, but he could increase B's chances of winning $5, then, other things equal, A has an even greater incentive for performing the task. Notice that so far there is no need to posit the influence of norms, although it is possible to conceive the increase in incentive mentioned above as due to A's "motivation to conform to relevant group expectations." The assumptions then are that A and B constitute a group, and that B expects A to aid him.

To look at this relationship, Berkowitz (1957) brought subjects into a lab in pairs and, by instructions to the subjects given individually, set up four conditions.[1] The subjects were put to work on an interdependent coding task and were individually told one of the following: (1) both members of the pair were eligible for a prize, (2) only the subject himself was eligible, (3) only the subject's partner was eligible, or (4) no prize was available regardless of how well the pair performed the task. Not surprisingly, the results indicated that the subject worked harder when he himself could win a prize than when he could not. Of interest here, however, is the fact that the subjects worked significantly harder when only their partner could win a prize as compared to the situation in which neither the subject nor his partner could win.

One of the recurring problems in psychology, both human and animal, is knowing what constitutes a reward for a subject. When the subject

[1] Actually, there were five conditions, but the fifth is unimportant here.

is human, what usually happens is that the experimenter tries to imagine what he (the experimenter) would consider rewarding if he were serving as a subject in the experiment. Usually, this is a reasonably successful procedure, but it can be risky, especially if the experimenter is in some way "different" from the subjects (Jones and Gerard, 1967). The problem here is a special case of the problem of stimulus meaning as discussed by Aronson and Carlsmith (1968).

To be specific, Berkowitz (1957) argued that even when the subject in his experiment could not win a prize himself by working hard, the mere perception that his partner could win a prize was sufficient to cause the subject to exert more effort as compared to the condition in which neither the subject nor his partner could win anything. As Berkowitz and Daniels (1963) point out, however, ". . . these subjects may have anticipated some benefits . . . (since) the partner supposedly became aware of the subject's performance almost immediately. Consequently, the subject might have become relatively highly motivated to win his partner's approval [p. 430]." Social reinforcement, the approval and high regard of one's colleagues and peers, is a goal actively pursued by many people. It seems reasonable that such a factor could have been operating in the Berkowitz (1957) study. It is never sufficient, however, merely to identify a possible artifact in an experiment. Once such a confounding has been pointed at, one of two courses of action seems appropriate.

First, one can redo the experiment introducing controls for the artifact. For example, the Berkowitz study might simply have been carried out again with the addition of having the experimenter intercept communications between the subject and his partner so that the partner could not know how well or fast the subject was working at the coding task. It would have been necessary to point out this feature to the subjects, of course. Such a solution would not have been satisfactory, however, because if similar results had been obtained, one could then argue that the subject was seeking approval from the experimenter for working hard in his partner's behalf.

The second strategy, once an artifact has been identified in an experiment, is to investigate systematically the effects of that contaminant rather than simply trying to eliminate it. Such a course of action can yield an interesting and informative harvest as McGuire (1969) has pointed out in his chronology of the life of an artifact:

> A review of the progress of psychological interest in a wide variety of artifacts would, we believe, reveal a natural progression of this interest through the three stages of ignorance, coping, and exploitation. At first, the researchers

> seem unaware of the variable producing the artifact and tend even to deny it when its possibility is pointed out to them. The second stage begins as its existence and possible importance become undeniable. In this coping phase, researchers tend to recognize and even overstress the artifact's importance. They give a great deal of attention to devising procedures which will reduce its contaminating influence and its limiting of the generalizability of experimental results. The third stage, exploitation, grows out of the considerable cogitation during the coping stage to understand the artifactual variable so as to eliminate it from the experimental situation. In their attempt to cope some researchers almost inevitably become interested in the artifactual variable in its own right. It then begins to receive research attention, not as a contaminating factor to be eliminated, but as an interesting independent variable in its own right [pp. 15–16].

This is precisely what occurred with the artifact mentioned in connection with the Berkowitz (1957) study. The criticism of that study was that subjects may have anticipated winning social approval from their partners by working hard since their partners became aware almost immediately of how hard the subject had worked in their behalf. Berkowitz and Daniels (1963) carried out two experiments in which the immediacy with which the subject's partner would learn of the subject's effort in his (the partner's behalf) was an independent variable.

With the Berkowitz and Daniels (1963) studies, one can begin to see that various causal explanations are possible and various meaningful outcomes are pitted against each other. For example, if a subject worked hard for his partner only when the partner would immediately know but not when the partner would never find out about his work, then it would appear that the anticipation of social approval from his partner was what was really motivating the subject. On the other hand, if the subject had internalized a societal norm prescribing that one should aid those who are dependent on one, then the subject would work hard regardless of when the partner would find out about it.

Again, as in the Berkowitz (1957) study, subjects in the first experiment reported in Berkowitz and Daniels (1963) were signed up in pairs and upon arrival at the lab they were told that the experimenter was attempting to develop a test of supervisor ability. One of the subjects was to be a supervisor and one a worker. The subjects were put in separate rooms and both were led to believe that they had been chosen to be the worker and that the other subject was to be the supervisor. The "supervisor's" job was to instruct the worker, via a written note, about how to make paper boxes. The worker (all subjects), after reading the instructions, had a brief practice period and then a thirty minute work period. The dependent measure was the number of boxes produced by the worker.

Three independent variables were manipulated by instructions that the experimenter gave to the subject: (1) whether or not the supervisor had a chance to win a $5 prize, (2) whether or not the evaluation that the experimenter would make of the supervisor was dependent on the number of boxes the subject produced, and (3) whether the supervisor would receive periodic reports of the subject's performance or not learn of the subject's performance until after the experiment.

Results showed that only those subjects who believed the supervisor was dependent on their production of boxes for a favorable rating showed a significant increase in production after the practice period. This result did not appear to be affected by the awareness variable. Berkowitz and Daniels point out that there was some ambiguity about their awareness manipulation. They had intended that telling the subjects that their supervisor would not find out how many boxes they had produced until after the experiment would reduce their concern about winning the supervisor's approval by working hard. However, subjects in these conditions may actually have believed that the supervisor would find out about their work (or lack of it) fairly soon. "Some of the subjects could have believed the study would end in a few days, and, so, the peer might learn of their productivity relatively quickly [p. 433]." Consequently, a second experiment was conducted to overcome this difficulty.

In the second experiment all subjects were told that the supervisor might win $5. The only variables were: (1) whether or not the subject's production of boxes would affect the supervisor's chances (the supervisor either was or was not dependent on the subject for a favorable rating) and (2) whether the supervisor would get periodic reports of the subject's production.

As in the first experiment, only those subjects who had been told that their supervisor's chances of winning were dependent upon their production showed a significant rise in productivity. The awareness variable appeared to have an effect only in the low dependence conditions; that is, subjects whose supervisor was highly dependent on their production worked hard regardless of when the supervisor would learn how much they had produced. Subjects whose supervisor was not dependent on their production worked hard only when the supervisor would learn of their performance immediately.

One of the nice features of the two experiments reported by Berkowitz and Daniels (1963) is that the same experimental task was used in both. This is not too unusual when an author is reporting two experiments in one article, especially if the second experiment was designed to correct some procedural flaw in the first. It is, unfortunately, rather unusual for the same task to be used in a series of experiments, especially when that series stretches over several years. This is particularly a problem in social psychology because it makes comparability of results from different procedures so incredibly difficult—in fact, the diverse procedures used often make comparability of results impossible.

The studies by Berkowitz and his colleagues provide a refreshing contrast. In pursuing their studies of social responsibility and dependence they have stuck relatively close, as we shall see, to the experimental paradigm first reported in Berkowitz and Daniels (1963). The basic task is the box construction task in which subjects think they are working under the direction of a "supervisor" and that the supervisor's chance of winning a prize for being a good supervisor either is or is not dependent on how many boxes the subject constructs.

In the following article, Berkowitz and Daniels (1964) use the box construction task in an attempt to look more directly at the norm they have called "social responsibility." If such a norm exists, there should be some very specific types of situations that make the norm salient and more likely to be adhered to. Similarly, they reasoned that adherence to such a norm should show strong individual differences. Consequently, they were interested in both situational and personality influences on their dependent measures. In reading the three articles that follow, you should be alert to the nuances of technique and interpretation that caution against uncritical acceptance of what is reported. In addition to the specific methodological flaws in each study there are at least two general issues raised by these studies which are not dealt with.

Affecting the Salience of the Social Responsibility Norm: Effects of Past Help on the Response to Dependency Relationships[1]

Leonard Berkowitz and Louise R. Daniels

A series of experiments by the authors assumes that many people in our society are motivated to aid others who are dependent upon them because such help is prescribed by a "social responsibility norm." The present study also assumes that prior

[1] From the *Journal of Abnormal and Social Psychology*, 1964, **68**, No. 3, 275–281. Received November 13, 1962. Reproduced by permission of the publisher.

The research reported in this paper was supported in part by funds from the Graduate School of the University of Wisconsin, and in part by Grant GS-21, National Science Foundation.

Dr. Berkowitz is with the University of Wisconsin. At the time of writing, Dr. Daniels was with the University of Wisconsin; she is currently with the University of California at Los Angeles.

help can increase the salience of this norm. In a $2 \times 2 \times 2$ factorial design using 80 *S*s (college women), half of the *S*s were individually helped by a peer (*E*'s confederate) on a preliminary task, while the others were not aided. After this, the *S*s worked on another task under the supposed supervision of yet another peer, with half of the *S*s being told that the supervisor was highly dependent upon their work and the others being told that she was less dependent upon them. The first peer would supposedly learn of their work in half of the cases but not in the other half. The previously helped *S*s tended to exert the greatest effort in behalf of their dependent peer. A self-report scale assessing social responsibility tendencies was significantly correlated with the effort measure in the Prior Help-High Dependency condition.

In our society, at least, when a person learns that others are dependent upon him for their goal attainment there is a good chance that he will try to help them reach their goals. Such "socially responsible" behavior often occurs, furthermore, even when there are few, if any, social or material rewards to be gained through this effort (Berkowitz & Daniels, 1963).

The present writers account for this seemingly altruistic behavior in terms of a cultural norm prescribing that the individual should help those who are dependent upon him. A person's motivation to adhere to the social responsibility norm probably fluctuates with various situational factors. He may be relatively unwilling to work for others who are dependent upon him without return benefits if a great deal of effort is required, or if other extreme costs are anticipated. His inclination to carry out the necessary activities in behalf of the others may also weaken if he dislikes them, and conceivably may be strengthened if they are highly attractive to him (Daniels & Berkowitz, 1963). In general, then, a person is less likely to persist in responsible behavior toward others without compensatory rewards when the required effort is psychologically costly to him, and/or he holds negative attitudes toward these dependent people.

Other situational conditions probably also affect socially responsible behavior. The present research assumes that the salience of the social responsibility norm on a given occasion varies with the individual's experience in the immediately preceding situation. Since this norm involves helping others, a person should be most aware of the culturally shared prescription to aid those who are dependent upon him right after someone else had voluntarily given *him* help. The assistance he received from one person should remind him strongly that he ought to help another who is dependent upon him.

In addition to investigating the effects of prior help, the present report also inquires about the generality of the social responsibility behavior. We here regard work carried out for another's benefit as socially responsible activity but, we might ask, is this behavior in any way similar to, say, not cheating in paying one's taxes, or to keeping one's promises to others? In general, are there consistent individual differences in such responsible behavior across different kinds of situations? As a preliminary attempt to answer this question, scores on a scale presumably assessing socially responsible tendencies were related to our laboratory measures. Harris (1957) has developed a self-report scale which discriminates between elementary school children who have a reputation with their peers for acting in a socially responsible manner and those children not possessing such a reputation. Assuming the Harris scale is valid with college students, the laboratory behavior can be regarded as at least moderately representative of a variety of responsible actions if the laboratory measures are correlated with the scale scores. But remember that the saliency of the social responsibility norm is presumably greatest when the subject had just received help from one person and then is asked to aid a dependent peer. If the Harris scale reflects a motivation to conform to the responsibility norm, the scale scores should have the highest correlation with responsible behavior in the laboratory when the subjects are most aware of the norm, i.e., when the subjects work for a dependent peer after having been helped by someone else.

Method

The subjects were 80 girls enrolled in the introductory psychology course at the University of Wisconsin who volunteered in order to earn points counting toward their final grade. After signing up for the experiment the subjects were contacted individually by the experimenter and appointments for the experimental sessions were arranged.

Phase I

On arriving at the laboratory the subjects were told they would be participating in two separate experiments. The experimenter explained that the first of these experiments would involve completing a number of simple and rather mechanical paper-and-pencil tasks. Ostensibly, the experimenter merely wanted to get an idea of how long these tasks would take since the tasks were to be used in future research. It was further mentioned that these tasks were in no way measures of intelligence or personality, and that each subject would be working on a different task. The subjects were then paired off and each pair member was assigned to separate but adjacent rooms. Of the six subjects assembled at any one time, two were paid assistants posing as subjects. Two of the four experimental subjects were paired off with the paid participants, while the remaining two experimental subjects were paired off together.

Each pair was told that since the subjects had different tasks, one of the pair members might finish first. In this case, the experimenter said, the person who had completed her assignment could aid her partner if she so desired. The experimenter emphasized that helping the other subject was not mandatory. Each subject was given a letter cancellation task in which she was to cross out designated letters on a page crowded with different letters. The experimenter stated that she was interested only in how long it took to complete the assignment regardless of whether one or two people had worked on a given batch of papers. The subjects were supplied with stop watches and instructed to keep track of the time they spent.

Experimental Manipulations. The experimental subjects who had been paired with the experimenter's confederates received help in completing their tasks, while the other subjects received no such help. In the prior help condition after the subject had worked approximately 10 minutes on the highly boring task, the confederate entered the room and offered her help. To avoid making the subjects defensive, the confederate said that her task had been fairly easy. The two then worked side by side for about 7 minutes. The subjects in the no prior help condition worked alone for approximately as long as the helped subjects had taken on a shortened version of the assignment that had been given to the helped subjects.

After the subjects had finished their task, they filled out a brief questionnaire containing items which assessed their reaction to the task, their partner, and also obtained some biographic information from them.

Phase II

Upon completing the questionnaires, all six people (including the confederates) were brought together for the supposed second experiment. The procedure employed in this phase of the experiment followed closely the procedures of the previous studies in this series. The subjects were told that the purpose of this "second" experiment was to develop a measure of supervisory ability. In developing such a test, the experimenter explained, it was necessary to study supervisory behavior in a realistic work situation. The subjects were to work in pairs. One person would be the supervisor whose job it was to write instructions on how to make a paper box, while the other subject would be the worker who had to carry out these instructions. The subjects were informed that they would be working in separate rooms so that a written record of the supervisors' instructions could be obtained.

The subjects were then again assembled in pairs, but this time the "real" subjects were paired together. After each girl had seen with whom she would be working, each subject was placed in a separate room, and each was informed that she would be the worker and that her partner would be supervisor. The subjects were told that after the supervisor had finished her written instructions they would have 8 minutes to practice making boxes. During this time their work would not be counted. The subjects were given the instructions in which the experimental variables were introduced after the practice period. They then constructed boxes for 16 minutes, after which they filled out a questionnaire concerning their reactions to the experiment.

Experimental Manipulations. The experiment employed a $2 \times 2 \times 2$ factorial design. Each of the three experimental variables—prior help, dependency, and peer awareness—was introduced at two levels.

The prior help manipulation has been described above. Differences in the supervisor's supposed dependency upon the subject were created as in the previous studies. After the 8-minute practice period all subjects were informed that the supervisors would be rated on how well they had written the instructions. The supervisor with the highest rating would supposedly receive a $5.00 gift certificate at the end of the semester. Those subjects who were in the high dependency condition were told, in addition, that their partners' rating would also depend heavily on their productivity. Their production would reflect the supervisor's ability to motivate her workers. The subjects in the low dependency conditions, on the other hand, were told that since people differed so greatly in ability, their production would *not* affect their supervisors' ratings.

The peer awareness manipulation involved the paid participants. Essentially, this manipulation tested the possibility that the subject's motivation to help her supervisor might be increased if she believed the person who had helped her earlier would see her present performance. If the subject was concerned with paying back the person who had given her assistance, and viewed her work for the supervisor as an opportunity to reciprocate, she conceivably might work harder if the first person would learn of her output. It is as if she would say to the person who had helped her, "See, I'm returning your favor by working hard for someone else." In the high peer awareness conditions the subjects were informed after the practice period that the experimenter had to run an important errand and that two of the other subjects (who supposedly had been given another task) would collect their boxes after the first and second 8 minutes of the work period. The experimenter's confederates were always selected to be the collectors. If the subject had been helped earlier, the box collector in this high peer awareness treatment was the person who had given her the assistance. In the low peer awareness conditions the experimenter collected the boxes at the end of the first and second halves of the work period.

Dependent Variables

The number of boxes completed during the practice and work periods was recorded for each subject. To control for individual differences in ability, the performance for each subject was obtained by subtracting practice period from work period production, thus yielding a measure of her gain in production.

The questionnaires filled out after both Phase I and Phase II included items designed to test the effectiveness of the experimental manipulations. On most items, the subjects placed a check mark along a linear rating scale with their responses scored as the distance from one end of the scale in quarter-inch units. Included in the second questionnaire was one open-ended item and a modified form of the semantic differential on which the subjects rated their supervisors. The evaluative adjectives of the semantic differential were used to determine if the earlier help given some of the subjects in Phase I had heightened their liking for the supervisor in Phase II. Interspersed among pairs of buffer items, the evaluative adjectives were: bad-good, clean-dirty, and ugly-beautiful.

Three months after the termination of the experiment the subjects were mailed a questionnaire containing 42 items from the Harris (1957) Social Responsibility scale. Spurred on by one or two telephone calls, if such were necessary, responses were obtained from 77 of the 80 subjects.

Results

Effectiveness of Manipulations

Analysis of the questionnaire results of Phase I showed that the help manipulation had generally been successful. The girls given assistance by the experimenter's confederate tended to welcome this help and liked the confederate for giving them the aid. On an item asking whether subjects would have liked to work in the same room with the girl with whom they had been paired (actually, the confederate), the subjects who had been helped answered significantly more strongly in the affirmative than the no prior help subjects ($F = 30.89$, $p = .001$). The degree to which the subjects reported the task as boring and monotonous was not significantly affected by the help treatment. Although only the helped group answered questions assessing their appreciation for the other girls' assistance, most of these subjects indicated that they strongly appreciated the aid given them, and found the other girl pleasant to be with.

A number of items in the Phase II questionnaire attested to the effectiveness of the dependency manipulation. In comparison to the girls in the low dependency group, the subjects in the high dependency conditions reported that they felt more pressure to do a good job as workers ($F = 20.78$, $p = .001$). We assume this pressure stemmed largely from the feelings of responsibility toward their dependent partner. This felt obligation did more than create tension; it evidently made the subjects think of themselves as having a relatively important job. The high dependency subjects thus rated themselves as feeling less isolated and unimportant than the subjects in the low dependency conditions ($F = 11.02$, $p < .01$). On yet another question, while the main effect for dependency fell short of the significance at the .05 level, the subjects in the high dependency conditions were more likely to believe they were helping their partner receive a favorable rating than the low dependency subjects ($F = 3.41$, $p < .10$). Finally, on the open-ended item, "What would you say your chief motive was in making the boxes during the work period?" 25 of the 40 subjects in the high dependency conditions reported that they had wanted to help their supervisors, whereas only 5 of the 40 subjects in the low dependency condition gave this type of answer ($\chi^2 = 15.76$, $p = .001$).

The peer awareness treatment also affected some of the questionnaire responses. To the item asking how much pressure the subjects felt to do a good job, the subjects in the low peer awareness condition indicated they felt more pressure than the high peer awareness group ($F = 4.36$, $p = .05$). Although the Awareness $\times$ Prior Help interaction fell just short of the customary .05 level of significance on this item ($F = 3.36$, $p < .10$), a Duncan (1955) range test of the four means in the interaction showed that the group previously helped and whose work was seen by their helping peer felt significantly less pressure than the other three groups. (There were no reliable differences among the other conditions.) The presence of the helping peer, a person for whom the subjects had established some positive feelings, apparently had reduced the tension aroused by the experimental situation.

PERFORMANCE

As was mentioned earlier, the practice period preceding the introduction of the experimental variables yielded a measure of the subjects' baseline performance. An analysis of variance of the productivity scores for this period failed to reveal any significant differences among conditions.

The analysis of variance for the gain in the number of boxes completed during the 16-minute main work period is summarized in Table 1. The significant main effect for dependency replicates the findings of the earlier studies. The subjects who were told a peer was highly dependent on their work made significantly more boxes than the subjects in the low dependency condition.

Of central interest is the significant Dependency × Prior Help interaction ($F = 3.96$, $p = .05$). The Duncan range test of the four means involved in this interaction is given in Table 2. First, note that the difference between the high and low dependency groups is not reliable for the subjects who had not been given any help during Phase I, although the difference is in the same direction as that in our earlier studies. The absence of a significant difference here may be due primarily to the relatively brief main work period: 16 minutes instead of the 30 minutes used in our earlier research. The prior help, however, apparently heightened the task motivation of the subjects who believed a peer was dependent upon them, so that the difference between the high and low dependency groups was now reliable. As we had expected, the confederate's earlier

TABLE 1
Analysis of Variance of the Increase in Number of Boxes Completed during the 16-Minute Work Period

Source	*df*	*MS*	*F*
Dependency (A)	1	183.02	12.91[a]
Help (B)	1	1.52	—
Awareness (C)	1	.12	—
A × B	1	56.10	3.96[b]
A × C	1	1.50	—
C × B	1	17.10	—
A × B × C	1	1.03	—
Subjects within groups	72	14.181	

[a] $p = .01$.
[b] $p = .05$.

TABLE 2
Duncan Range Test of the Mean Increase in Number of Boxes Completed during the 16-Minute Work Period[a]

Condition	Dependency High	Dependency Low
Prior help	11.35_{a}	6.65_{c}
No prior help	9.40_{ab}	8.05_{bc}

[a] Cells having a subscript in common are not significantly different at the .05 level.

assistance increased their desire to aid their dependent supervisor, presumably through making them more aware of their obligation to help a dependent person.

Attitudes toward Supervisor

If the supervisor was associated in some way with the helping confederate, we reasoned, the girls in the prior help condition should have had more favorable attitudes toward their supervisor than the subjects in the no prior help treatment. Three measures of such attitudes were obtained from the final questionnaire, but significant results were found with only one of these. Thus, the helped subjects did not rate the supervisor more favorably on the evaluative scale of the semantic differential, nor did they regard her more highly as a possible roommate, than did the subjects who had not been aided by the experimenter's confederate. However, reliable differences were obtained with the third item asking, "If you were taking part in another experiment, how would you like to work with the same girl (your supervisor)?" The subjects in the prior help condition answered significantly more strongly in the "yes" direction than the nonhelped subjects ($F = 4.91$, $p < .05$). There were no other significant effects with this measure.

Correlations with Social Responsibility Scale

Since the Harris scale had not been developed with college students, an item analysis was first conducted to assess the scale's internal consistency for the present population. The sample of 77 respondents completing the mail questionnaire was divided as close to the median score for the total responsibility scale as possible. Similarly, the distribution of responses to the five alternatives ("strongly agree" to "strongly disagree") provided was also dichotomized for each item. Tetrachoric correlations were then computed between responses to the individual items and total scale scores.

Twenty-two of the items were found to have correlations of .45 or higher with the scale as a whole. These items, given in Table 3, were combined to form a revised social responsibility scale. Because the range of scores varied somewhat from condition to condition. Spearman rank-order correlations were used in testing the relationship between the scale scores and productivity gain. This analysis was confined to the four experimental conditions involved in the significant interaction of the dependency and help variables. The results are shown in Table 4.

TABLE 3
Items in Revised Social Responsibility Scale[a]

1. It is always important to finish anything that you have started. (Agree)
2. It is no use worrying about current events or public affairs; I can't do anything about them anyway. (Disagree)
3. In school my behavior has gotten me into trouble. (Disagree)
4. I have been in trouble with the law or police. (Disagree)
5. When a person does not tell all his income in order to get out of paying some of his taxes it is just as bad as stealing money from the government. (Agree)
6. When I work on a committee, I usually let other people do most of the planning. (Disagree)
7. I am often late for school. (Disagree)
8. If it is worth starting, it is worth finishing. (Agree)
9. I am the kind of person that people can count on. (Agree)
10. I do my chores the very best I know how. (Agree)
11. When you can't do a job, it is no use to try to find someone else to do it. (Disagree)
12. Why bother to vote when you can do so little with just your one vote. (Disagree)
13. Letting your friends down is not so bad because you can't do good all the time for everybody. (Disagree)
14. Our country would be a lot better off if we didn't have elections and people didn't have to vote. (Disagree)
15. It is more important to work for the good of the team than to work for your own good. (Agree)
16. I would never let a friend down when he expects something of me. (Agree)
17. People would be a lot better off if they could live far away from other people and never have anything to do for them. (Disagree)
18. Every person should give some of his time for the good of his town or city. (Agree)
19. Doing things which are important should come before things you enjoy doing. (Agree)
20. Cheating on examinations is not so bad as long as nobody ever knows. (Disagree)
21. I usually volunteer for special projects at school. (Agree)
22. When given a task I stick to it even if things I like to do better come along. (Agree)

[a] These are the items having tetrachoric correlations of .45 or higher with the original 44-item Harris (1957) scale.

TABLE 4
Rank-Order Correlations between Increase in Productivity in Work Period and Score on Social Responsibility Scale[a]

Condition	Dependency High	Dependency Low
Prior help	+.49[b] (18)	+.33 (20)
No prior help	−.12 (20)	−.10 (19)

[a] The figures in parentheses refer to the number of cases involved in the given correlation.
[b] $p \leq .05$.

As the table indicates, our original expectations were fulfilled. The only correlation with productivity reaching statistical significance was the one in the high dependency-prior help group, the condition in which the social responsibility norm presumably was most salient. It may well be, as we had assumed, that the scale scores reflect differences in motivation to conform to the responsibility norm. However, the near significant rho ($p = .10$) in the low dependency-prior help condition suggests a somewhat different interpretation. The confederate's assistance in this latter treatment may have aroused some responsibility feelings in the high scoring subjects. More aware of social responsibility as a result of the earlier help given them, these girls may have regarded high productivity as responsible behavior even though the supervisor would not benefit by such effort. If this is the case, scale differences may be indicative of differences in *awareness* of the socially prescribed obligation to act responsibly, however responsibility is defined in a given situation, as well as differences in *willingness* to act responsibly.

The near zero relationship in the high dependency group not given any help by the experimenter's confederate provides some tentative information as to the effects of the no help manipulation. The subjects not receiving assistance may have felt some resentment which decreased their motivation to conform to the responsibility norm. Or it may be that the lack of help from another in a sense gave the high scale score subjects an excuse not to act responsibly. The absence of assistance could have made relatively irresponsible behavior permissible for them.

As a test of these possibilities, the responsibility scale scores were correlated with the questionnaire responses in each of the four experimental conditions shown in Table 4. Two significant relationships emerged, both under high dependency. The first of these is consistent with the resentment interpretation of the no prior help treatment. In the case only of the girls not given any assistance by the experimenter's confederate and who then were obliged to help a dependent peer, the higher the score on the responsibility scale the *less* willing they were to work with the supervisor in another experiment (rho = .43, $p = .05$). (This is the item mentioned earlier that was significantly affected by the help-no help variable.) It is as if the felt pressures to aid the dependent supervisor experienced by the high scoring subjects had given rise to some resentment—they had not been helped earlier—and the resentment had then been generalized onto the supervisor. Obviously, however, this interpretation should be regarded with caution; the present correlation could have been the one (of the 20 relationships tested) occurring by chance.

The other significant rank-order correlation tends to support the productivity findings. In the prior help-high dependency condition only, the higher the responsibility scale score the more likely the girl was to say that the Phase I task had not made her less willing to construct boxes in Phase II (rho = .60, $p = .01$). The more responsible subjects in this group apparently did not become less motivated to help their dependent peer following their initial effort in the first part of the study.

Discussion

The present data suggest that the prior help may have heightened awareness of the responsibility norm in many of the subjects working for a dependent peer. The relatively high level of productivity in this condition, then, presumably was the result of the increased salience of the socially prescribed obligation to aid others needing help. However, there are at least two other possible explanations for this finding which cannot definitely be excluded.

One alternative explanation is based on the reciprocity principle. The girls helped by the experimenter's confederate conceivably felt some obligation to pay her back. Such feelings of obligation could have generalized to the dependent supervisor so that, in essence, by working hard for this latter person they were reciprocating for the assistance they had received. If so, the present findings can be understood by a special case of the reciprocity norm. People supposedly live up to their social obligations in order to pay back for the good turns they have received in the past and those they expect to receive in the future (cf. Gouldner, 1960). Other findings provide some tentative support for this analysis; the girls helped by the confederate tended to have a relatively high liking for the supervisor. However, this favorable attitude does not necessarily mean the helped girls associated the supervisor with the helping confederate. The assistance given them may have simply put them in a good mood. Or it may be that the girls not given help had a lower liking for their dependent peer because of resentment. Furthermore, the reciprocity explanation has some difficulty in accounting for the significant relationship between the social responsibility scale and increase in productivity in the prior help-high dependency condition.

High scores on the responsibility scale may reflect a willingness to reciprocate for past favors. But the items shown in Table 3 seem to suggest much more than this. Some of the statements (e.g., Items 5, 18, and 20) clearly imply the existence of stronger moral standards, and people agreeing with them can be assumed to have learned what is "right" and what is "wrong" ethically. In addition, however, other items appear to indicate that the high scoring person also has sufficient ego strength to conform to these moral standards. Thus, he sticks to tasks he has undertaken until they are completed (e.g., Items 1 and 8), and generally defers his pleasures until he has met his responsibilities (e.g., Items 15, 19, and 22). All in all, he describes himself as not only recognizing social standards of conduct, but also as being able and willing to live up to these ideals. He has learned, in a word, to act in a socially responsible fashion in many different situations.

The second possible alternative explanation for the condition differences reported earlier assumes that many of the girls in the prior help-high dependency treatment were conforming to the hypothesized social responsibility norm. However, this alternative contends that the no help variable served somehow to dampen this norm. Two reasons for such a weakening of the social responsibility norm have been suggested. For one, the confederate's failure to offer the subject assistance in the first phase of the study could have made it permissible for the subject not to exert effort on behalf of other people. Then too, the subjects in the high dependency-no help condition may have had negative feelings toward the supervisor. They should help her, they could have felt, but they had not been helped themselves earlier. In a sense, we might say, they resented the lack of distributive justice. While the absence of reliable productive differences between the high and low dependency groups under the no prior help treatment is consistent with either of these latter possibilities, further research is definitely needed.

REFERENCES

Berkowitz, L., & Daniels, L. R. Responsibility and dependency. *Journal of Abnormal and Social Psychology,* 1963, **66,** 429–436.

Daniels, L. R., & Berkowitz, L. Liking and response to dependency relationships. *Human Relations,* 1963, in press.

Duncan, D. Multiple range and multiple *F* tests. *Biometrics,* 1955, **11,** 1–45.

Gouldner, A. W. The norm of reciprocity: A preliminary statement. *American Sociological Review,* 1960, **25,** 161–178.

Harris, D. B. A scale for measuring attitudes of social responsibility in children. *Journal of Abnormal and Social Psychology,* 1957, **55,** 322–326.

Discussion

There are five points that we would like to alert the reader to before proceeding to the next article.

First, there appears to be room for argument concerning the reasoning behind the study. Berkowitz and Daniels state:

> The present research assumes that the salience of the social responsibility norm on a given occasion varies with the individual's experience in the immediately preceding situation. Since this norm involves helping others, a person should be most aware of the culturally shared prescription to aid those who are dependent upon him right after someone else had voluntarily given him help [p. 275].

This hypothesis is not at all certain. One could argue just the opposite, i.e., that a person would be most aware of the culturally shared prescription to aid dependent others right after someone had refused to help him. A person is most aware of his need for oxygen when he is at the bottom of a swimming pool. This is one of the hazards of working with concepts which are not precisely formulated, and it is a hazard with which social psychology is particularly well acquainted. Much of the criticism of dissonance theory, for example, has centered around the vagueness of predictions and the often exhibited ability to "explain" results no matter how they came out. It seems that the authors did not have a clear prediction to begin with.

A minor point of criticism of the Berkowitz and Daniels study concerns the use of the Harris scale. Taking a scale developed and used with elementary school children and assuming it to be valid with college students would turn most psychometricians purple with indignation. But ignoring the question of norms and cross-validation, the results with the Harris scale are not really as supportive as they appear at first glance. In the low dependency conditions, the assumption is that the norm of social responsibility is not operating. Hence, one would expect a higher correlation (Table 4) in the prior help-high dependency condition than in the prior help-low dependency condition, but +.49 is not significantly different from +.33. It is always necessary to be sure that one is making an appropriate comparison when citing things like correlations as evidence. The fact that +.49 is significantly different from a correlation of .00 is not of interest unless it is also significantly different from the correlation in the low dependency-prior help condition (.33).

The third point of interest here is that there appears to be a confounding introduced in the awareness manipulation.

> . . . in the high peer awareness conditions the subjects were informed after the practice period that the experimenter had to run an important errand and that two of the other subjects (who supposedly had been given another task) would collect their boxes, after the first and second 8 minutes of the work period. The experimenter's confederates were always selected to be the collectors. If the subject had been helped earlier, the box collector in this high peer awareness treatment was the person who had given her the assistance. In the low peer awareness conditions the experimenter collected the boxes at the end of the first and second halves of the work period [p. 277].

The confounding is evident. High peer awareness subjects had contact with another subject, and low peer awareness subjects had contact with the experimenter. Table 1 reveals that the awareness manipulation produced no effect whatever (mean square = .12) on the number of boxes completed during the work period. This result is surprising since the studies we discussed in the introduction to this chapter indicated that the awareness variable was a potent one, particularly in the low dependency conditions. What appears to have happened is that subjects worked as hard when the experimenter was going to collect their boxes as when their peer was going to collect the boxes. Given the higher status of the experimenter, this is what we would expect.

Probably the most serious flaw in the design of the Berkowitz and Daniels study is the lack of an adequate control condition. This is particularly crucial when one wants to interpret the processes occurring. For example, consider the interpretation we would place on the scores in Table 2 if there had been two control conditions in which subjects had simply been asked to make boxes after having been helped or not helped during Phase I. Suppose that with these two added conditions Table 2 had looked like this:

Mean Increase in Number of Boxes Completed during the 16-Minute Work Period

	Dependency		
	High	Low	Control
Prior help	11.35	6.65	6.50
No prior help	9.40	8.05	8.80

Such results would be clearer evidence for the social responsibility interpretation of increased help in the high dependency-prior help condition. On the other hand, if the mean in the control-prior help condition was 11.50 instead of 6.50, a quite different interpretation would be called for. Without the control conditions, one simply does not know with any assurance what interpretation is appropriate.

The final point we would like to make concerns the alternative interpretation mentioned by Berkowitz and Daniels. They point out that "The girls helped by the experimenter's confederate conceivably felt some obligation to pay her back. Such feelings of obligation could have generalized to the dependent supervisor so that, in essence, by working hard for the latter person they were reciprocating for the assistance they had received. If so, the present findings can be understood by a special case of the reciprocity norm [p. 281]."

There is no way within the Berkowitz and Daniels study of deciding whether the higher number of boxes produced in the prior help-high dependency condition was due to the operation of a norm of social responsibility or the norm of reciprocity. Partially, at least, this is due not so much to the ambiguity of results as to the ambiguity of conceptualization in setting up the design for the study. What was needed, and is always needed, is (1) an adequate "thinking through" of the conditions which should produce the phenomena of interest—here, the phenomena of interest was adherence to the norm of social responsibility—and (2) a careful consideration of whether the results obtained under these conditions will be susceptible to other interpretations. The following article by Goranson and Berkowitz presents a design which attempts to follow these two guidelines. As always, the question is how successful have they been in doing what they intended to do?

Reciprocity and Responsibility Reactions to Prior Help[1]

Richard E. Goranson and Leonard Berkowitz

The present study was conducted to clarify the findings of a previous experiment which showed that persons who had previously received help themselves were more

[1] From the *Journal of Personality and Social Psychology,* 1966, 3, No. 2, 227–232. Received August 5, 1964. Reproduced by permission of the publisher.

This research was conducted under Grant GS-21 from the National Science Foundation to Leonard Berkowitz.

Dr. Berkowitz is with the University of Wisconsin. At the time of writing, Dr. Goranson was with the University of Wisconsin; he is currently with York University.

willing to work for a dependent peer than were *S*s who had not received prior help. *S*s were 84 college women given a dull preliminary task to perform. A peer (*E*'s confederate) took the initiative in helping one third of the *S*s on this task, while she supposedly was instructed by *E* to give aid in another third of the cases, and refused to help the remaining *S*s. Following this, all *S*s were led to believe that they were to be "workers" under the guidance of a "supervisor" who was represented to half of the *S*s as being the same peer that they had encountered earlier, and to the other half as a different peer. All *S*s were further led to believe that their supervisor's chances of winning a cash prize were highly dependent on how hard *S*s worked. When the supervisor was the same person, *S*s worked harder after receiving voluntary help than did *S*s who received the compulsory help. *S*s who had been refused prior help were least willing to work for their same-person, dependent supervisor. Differences among the three help conditions for those *S*s working for the different supervisor were not significant, but the condition means were ordered in the same way.

Several authors have recently outlined models of social interaction which are essentially economic or utilitarian in nature. Thibaut and Kelley (1959) , for example, have set forth an analysis of a wide range of social behavior in terms of the rewards and costs incurred by the people involved. According to this model, each individual attempts to maximize the ratio between his own rewards and costs. The basic assumption involved here is that a person behaves or interacts in a given way because he believes that it is *to his advantage* to do so. The authors apply this analysis to simple social behavior and also to such complex social phenomena as role behavior, conformity to norms, and group leadership.

In a recent review, Gouldner (1960) has addressed himself to the area of reciprocal exchange in social relationships. His approach differs somewhat from that of the utilitarian analysts in that it lays emphasis on the normative aspects of reciprocity. Gouldner goes so far as to say that there is a *universal, moral norm* of reciprocity which makes the minimal demands that

> (1) people should help those who have helped them, and (2) people should not injure those who have helped them [p. 171].

This normative reciprocity that Gouldner proposes may violate certain economic principles. The author points out that the reciprocity norm

> engenders motives for returning benefits even when power difference might invite exploitation. The norm thus safeguards powerful people against the temptation of their own status; it motivates and regulates reciprocity as an exchange pattern, serving to inhibit the emergence of exploitative relations . . . [p. 174].

It may also be seen that in a short-term encounter it is not always economically reasonable for one person to *return* the help of another person.

Gouldner argues that if it were not for a norm of reciprocity it would be unlikely that the first person would be willing to extend his help.

> When internalized in both parties (however), the norm *obliges* the one who has first received a benefit to repay it at some time; it thus provides some realistic grounds for confidence, in the one who first parts with his valuables, that he will be repaid [p. 177].

Some writers have suggested that there may be a different kind of non-economic motive operating in some social situations. Berkowitz and Daniels (1963) have proposed that persons in our society may be motivated to help others simply because those others are dependent on them. They suggest further, that people in our society generally learn a standard of conduct prescribing that they behave in a "socially responsible" fashion. That is, among other things, they should help those who are dependent on them. Thus, people at times act on behalf of others, not for material gain or social approval, but for their own self-approval, for the self-administered rewards arising from doing what is "right."

In order to test this notion experimentally in a laboratory setting, these authors created a situation in which subjects were led to believe that they were taking part in a test of supervisory ability. The subjects were told that they were to be "workers" performing in accordance with instructions from a peer (the "supervisor"). Some subjects were told that if they performed well, their supervisor could win a prize, while the other subjects were told that their supervisor's chances did not depend on how hard they worked. The results showed that subjects worked hardest when their supervisors' ratings (and chances for a prize) were highly dependent on their performances. Subjects worked hard for their partners even when there was apparently "nothing in it" for themselves.

In a more recent study dealing with socially responsible behavior, Berkowitz and Daniels (1964) introduced the variable of *prior help*. All subjects in this experiment were required to work on a tedious preliminary task, but half of them were given help "voluntarily" from a peer (the experimenter's confederate posing as a fellow subject), while the other half was given no help. Upon completion of the preliminary task, the subjects were put through the "supervisory ability" phase of the experiment described above, with each subject believing that she was the worker and her partner the supervisor.

The results of this experiment indicated that the subjects worked hardest for the dependent supervisor when they had previously received help from the confederate. Berkowitz and Daniels (1964) suggest two possible explanations for this result. One explanation

> is based on the reciprocity principle. The girls helped by the experimenter's confederate conceivably felt some obligation to pay her back. Such feelings of obligation could have generalized to the dependent supervisor so that, in essence, by working hard for this latter person they were reciprocating for the assistance they had received. If so, the present findings can be understood as a special case of the reciprocity norm. People supposedly live up to their social obligations in order to pay back for the good turns they had received in the past and those they expect to receive in the future (cf. Gouldner, 1960) [p. 281].

The other explanation advanced involves the hypothesized social responsibility norm.

> ... prior help may have heightened awareness of the (social) responsibility norm in many of the subjects working for a dependent peer. The relatively high level of productivity in this condition, then, presumably was the result of the increased salience of the socially prescribed obligation to aid others needing help [pp. 280–281].

A further complexity in these results is pointed out by the authors; the difference in performance in the groups may have been due, not so much to heightened motivation in their *prior-help* groups, but rather to a decreased motivation in their *no-prior-help* groups. The fact that these subjects were not helped may have produced some resentment that was reflected in the lower performance. If, indeed, this was the case, this effect might also have come about in either of the two ways outlined above. The partner's failure to offer help may have prompted the subjects to "reciprocate" by *not* helping the other person, or it may have acted to "dampen" potential feelings of responsibility.

The present research is aimed at an elaboration and clarification of the findings of the Berkowitz-Daniels study. Specifically, it seeks to compare the effects of prior help as mediated by a direct reciprocity principle with the effects as mediated by an arousal or dampening of the awareness of the responsibility norm. In addition, attention will be given to the question of whether the effect of the prior-help variable is due to a heightened motivation in the case where the prior help is given, or to a decreased motivation in the case where prior help is withheld.

Method

Subjects

The subjects were 84 undergraduate women volunteers from introductory psychology, philosophy, and political science courses at the University of Wisconsin. The subjects from psychology classes were participating for experimental points to be added to their course grades. The nonpsychology subjects were recruited by the experimenter at the beginning of one of their regular class periods. These subjects were offered no inducement to sign up other than a chance to see "what psychology research is like." Subjects were each contacted by telephone to make arrangements and to insure that pairs of subjects were not previously acquainted. The subjects were assigned to the six experimental conditions as they arrived in an ABCDEFFEDCBA order.

Procedure

Experimental Conditions. Two experimental subjects and two paid participants posing as subjects were present at each session. The experimenter explained that two separate experiments would be conducted. The first experiment was represented as some necessary groundwork for a future industrial psychology study. Subjects were told that each person would be working on a different task, and that the tasks required different amounts of time to be completed. After these initial instructions, subjects were escorted to separate rooms and given three sheets, each containing 27 lines of haphazardly ordered letters. The subject's task was to circle all of the u's and to write down the time taken on each page.

Nature of Prior Help: Voluntary, Compulsory, or Refused. After five minutes, the experimenter entered the subject's room and introduced the first set of experimental manipulations. All subjects were told that the "girl next door" had finished her task. One-third of the subjects were told that the girl had voluntarily offered to help the subject with her task (*voluntary-help* treatment). In this treatment, after the experimenter left the room the confederate entered and appropriately volunteered to work on one sheet. Another third of the subjects were told that the experimenter would *instruct* the girl next door to come in and work on one of the subject's sheets (*compulsory-help* treatment). For these subjects the confederate came in and took one sheet. For the final third of the subjects, the experimenter said that the girl *might* be willing to help the subject. However, in this condition the confederate came in and pointedly refused to help the subject (*help-refused* treatment).

The voluntary-help condition and the help-refused condition were designed to establish the variable of *prior help,* analogous to that employed in the most recent Berkowitz-Daniels study. The compulsory-help condition was included as an approximation of a control group where help was in fact given, but not volunteered.

When all subjects had completed their tasks, the group was reassembled, and the second "separate experiment" was explained. As in the Berkowitz-Daniels studies, this phase was represented as a project involving the construction of a test of "supervisory ability." There were to be two "randomly selected" pairs, with a worker and a supervisor in each pair, both working on different problems. The supervisor was to write instructions as to how to construct a small paper box. The worker's job was to make boxes following the supervisor's instructions. Another problem (the construction of a paper cup) was also mentioned, but not actually used, in order to avoid possible feelings of competition between the two workers. Subjects were told to return to the rooms where they had been before, while the experimenter "randomly selected" the pairs. When the subjects were settled in their respective rooms, the experimenter informed both real subjects that they would be workers.

Working for the Same or a Different Partner. At this point the experimenter introduced the manipulation for the second variable. One half of the subjects were told that their supervisor was to be the *same* girl who had previously helped (or not helped) them. The rest of the subjects were told that their supervisor would *not* be the *same* girl, but a *different* girl.

The rest of the procedure was the same for all subjects. After six minutes the experimenter delivered the box-making instructions to the subject. These instructions were, in fact, prepared beforehand and were identical for all subjects. After receiving the instructions, the subject was given an eight-minute "practice period" in order to get a measure of the subject's natural working pace with which the work period performance could be compared.

Dependency Relation. After the eight minutes of practice, the subject was informed that her supervisor's rating would depend on the subject's output during the "work period." The subject was also informed that the supervisor was eligible for a $5 prize if she got the highest supervisory rating in the box-making experiment. In other words, it was clearly implied that the supervisor's chance of winning the prize was greatly dependent on the subject's performance.

The subject was then left alone for twenty minutes to construct paper boxes. At the end of this period the experimenter returned and gave the subject a questionnaire to fill in. Following the questionnaire, the real nature of the experiment was explained and subjects were sworn to secrecy.

Results

Effectiveness of Experimental Manipulations

The postexperimental questionnaire included several questions designed to check the effectiveness of the experimental manipulations. Analysis of responses to these questions indicated that both the prior-help and the identity-of-supervisor variables were successfully established.

Prior Help. Reponses to the question. "Were you helped at all during the first 'experiment' . . . ?" showed that all the subjects in the refused-help groups said that they *had not* received help and that all but two subjects in the voluntary-help and compulsory-help groups said that they *had* received help.

The responses to the question, "Was her help offered voluntarily?" showed that subjects in the voluntary-help conditions saw the help that they received as being offered more voluntarily than did the subjects in the compulsory-help conditions. The high correlation between being in the voluntary-help condition and reporting that the help was given voluntarily (phi = .86) clearly indicates the effectiveness of the *help* manipulation.

Identity of Supervisor. All subjects included in the analysis were able to identify their supervisor correctly as being either "the same girl that came into your room while you were working on the first experiment" or "the other girl."[2]

In summary, subjects receiving the voluntary-help treatment reported

[2] One subject in the compulsory-same condition was unable to identify her supervisor correctly and for this reason none of her scores were included in the analysis.

that the assistance that they received was given voluntarily, subjects receiving the compulsory-help treatment saw their help as much less voluntary, and those receiving the refused-help treatment reported that they were not helped at all. Subjects in the *same* supervisor conditions identified their supervisor as the same girl that they had encountered during the prior-help manipulation, and subjects in the *different* supervisor conditions identified their supervisor as someone other than the girl they had encountered in the prior-help manipulation.

Performance on the Experimental Task

The main dependent variable employed in analysis was the increase in the rate of production of boxes from the practice period to the work period. Since the work period was 2.5 times as long as the practice period, the total practice-period production was multiplied by 2.5, yielding a production rate score comparable for both periods. A correlation of .69 was obtained between these measures. The rate-of-production-increase score was then obtained by subtracting the practice-period rate from the work-period rate for each subject. The use of this rate-of-production-increase score allowed for a measure of control for the variability due to persistent individual differences in ability and motivation.

In addition to the prior-help and identity-of-supervisor variables, one additional variable was included in the analysis of the performance scores. This was the identity of the confederate who was acting as the subject's "supervisor." Since only two confederates were employed throughout the experiment, this factor was varied so that half of the subjects worked for one girl, and half for the other. The summary table for the analysis of variance of the increase-in-production-rate scores is given in Table 1.

A Duncan multiple range test of the three prior-help condition means showed that the expected relation was obtained; the mean of the voluntary conditions was greater than the mean of the compulsory conditions ($p < .05$), and the mean of the compulsory conditions was in turn larger than the mean of the refused conditions ($p < .05$).

The significant Help $\times$ Supervisor interaction, however, indicates that the effects of the prior help did not operate independently of the identity of the supervisor. In order to investigate this interaction further, a Duncan multiple range test was performed on the means of the six main experimental groups. The condition means and test results are presented in Table 2. In the three same conditions, the ordering of the means from highest to lowest is voluntary-compulsory-refused, and the differences between condition means are all significant at the .01 level. In other words, the voluntary-help treatment increased the subjects' effort in

TABLE 1

Summary Table for the Analysis of the Rate-of-Production-Increase Scores

Source	*df*	*MS*	*F*
Supervisor (same, or different) (A)	1	52.65	4.59[a]
Confederate (B)	1	.24	
Help (voluntary, compulsory, refused) (C)	2	132.94	11.60[b]
A × B	1	23.57	2.06
A × C	2	75.58	6.62[b]
B × C	2	1.39	
A × B × C	2	5.51	
Error	72	11.46	

[a] $p = .05$.
[b] $p = .01$.

working for the person who had helped them earlier, and the refused-help treatment reduced the effort put out on behalf of the person who had previously refused them help. That the prior-help manipulation had any influence at all in the three different supervisor conditions is suggested only by the fact that the means for these conditions are similarly ordered although they do not differ significantly from one another.

Questionnaire Data

A 2 × 2 × 3 (Supervisor × Confederate × Help) analysis of variance was performed on the postexperimental questionnaire items, and the significance of differences among the means of the six main experimental conditions (Supervisor × Help) was evaluated by the Duncan range test.

Social norms are most often defined in terms of the perceived expectations of others. A "social responsibility norm" would involve an individual's belief that others expect him to help those who are highly de-

TABLE 2

Means of Main Experimental Conditions for the Rate-of-Production-Increase Scores[a]

	Help		
Supervisor	Voluntary	Compulsory	Refused
Same	16.57_{a}	12.78_{b}	8.93_{c}
Different	11.70_{bc}	11.25_{bc}	10.61_{bc}

[a] Means with common subscript are not significantly different (at .05 level) by Duncan multiple range test.

pendent on him, even without the promise of any material reward. Following this reasoning, the question, "To what extent would most people have expected you to work hard to help your supervisor win the prize?" was included in the questionnaire as an index of the subjects' awareness of this kind of expectation—that is to say, as a measure of the salience of a "social responsibility norm."

In the same supervisor condition, a high score on this item probably indicates awareness of a reciprocity norm; the item here reflects the degree to which the subject believes most people would expect her to repay the individual she had encountered earlier. As Table 3 shows, the perceived expectation to work hard in the same condition is reliably stronger when the subject had received voluntary help than when the help given the subject had been required. The women felt they were particularly expected to reciprocate for favors done voluntarily for them. Interestingly, those girls who had been refused help did not seem to believe that other people would expect them to retaliate in kind. Like the subjects in the compulsory-help group, they thought there was a moderate expectation that they should aid the person who was dependent on them, even though she had refused to help them earlier.

The scores in the different supervisor conditions suggest that the responsibility norm is somewhat weaker than the norm prescribing reciprocity. More important, the subjects who had received the voluntary-help were not reliably more aware of an expectation to help this different person than were the subjects in the two other different-supervisor groups. It may be that the subjects in all of the groups were at least moderately aware of the responsibility norm because the supervisor's dependency on them was very clear and easily grasped. The differences shown in the different-supervisor condition might have been significant

TABLE 3

Means of Main Experimental Conditions for the Question, "To What Extent Would Most People Have Expected You to Work Hard to Help Your Supervisor Win the Prize?"[a]

	Help		
Supervisor	Voluntary	Compulsory	Refused
Same	10.21_a	8.14_b	8.57_b
Different	9.14_{ab}	8.86_{ab}	7.57_b

[a] Means with common subscript are not significantly different (at .05 level) by Duncan multiple range test. A high score indicates that subjects felt very much that most people would have expected them to work hard.

TABLE 4
Means of Main Experimental Conditions for the Question, "On the Basis of Whatever Impressions You Might Have, Would You Want Your Supervisor as a Roommate (Assuming You Were Looking for a Roommate)?"[a]

	Help		
Supervisor	Voluntary	Compulsory	Refused
Same	4.71_b	5.07_b	7.79_a
Different	5.86_b	4.93_b	5.36_b

[a] Means with common subscript are not significantly different (at .05 level) by Duncan multiple range test. A high score indicates a low liking.

if, for one reason or another, the situation were somewhat more ambiguous and/or the dependency relationship weaker.

That subjects in the refused conditions could have become resentful because they felt they had been treated badly in the first part of the experiment is indicated by responses to the item designed to measure the subjects' liking for their supervisors: "Would you want your supervisor as a roommate . . . ?" A comparison of the six condition means shown in Table 4 indicates that it is the refused-same condition which differs from all the others at the .05 level of significance. The refused-help treatment probably constituted a frustrating experience, producing in turn a hostility toward the supervisor when it was this person who was the source of the frustration.

Discussion

Two different, although perhaps related, normative expectations may have to be advanced to explain the present results: a norm prescribing that a dependent individual should be helped (the responsibility norm), and a social standard calling for the repayment of benefits received from others (the reciprocity norm).

As discussed earlier, the reciprocity norm has received considerable attention recently. The findings for the same supervisor groups represent a direct contribution to these formulations in that they point to one of the conditions on which an individual's feelings of obligation to make repayments may be contingent. The college women in this sample evidently regarded themselves as obligated to reciprocate for the help they had received primarily when this help had been given voluntarily. Thus, when they were working for the person who had helped them earlier they worked harder and were more definite in stating that other people would expect them to work hard when the earlier assistance had been given voluntarily rather than when it had been either required or had been refused.

The conjectured responsibility norm could well have been operating, to some extent at least, in the same-supervisor condition as well as when subjects were working for a different supervisor. This is indicated in a number of ways. For one thing, the subjects in the same-supervisor treatment who had been refused help earlier exhibited lower motivation to assist their supervisor and expressed less liking for her than did the girls in either of the other two same-supervisor groups. They were evidently annoyed at not being helped earlier. It may be that they believed the other person *should* have aided them; the societal standard had called for giving help and this norm had been violated. It is, of course, also quite possible that subjects interpreted the refusal to aid them as a personal rebuff or insult.

In the different-supervisor condition, the relatively high rate of productivity and some of the questionnaire responses point to the existence of the responsibility norm. All three groups in this treatment showed a considerable gain in productivity, perhaps largely because they believed this different person was dependent upon them. Conformity to this presumed norm could then have minimized the group differences in this condition. All three groups also reported a moderately strong expectation prescribing that they should aid their supervisor, again suggesting that most of the subjects were at least somewhat aware that they should behave in a responsible manner.

The reciprocity behavior seen in the present study probably should not be considered simply as an instance of "rational" or economic interchange. First, the work was arranged so as to minimize, for all subjects, the anticipation of any material return. Second, it was emphasized to the subjects that their "partnership" with their supervisor was to terminate with the end of the work period—in fact, subjects were led to believe they would not ever see their supervisors again. Since the relationship was not to continue, subjects had no rational motivation to repay their partners in order to "keep their credit good." Finally, as was pointed out earlier, the special influence of the perceived "voluntariness" of the prior help does not fit in well with the economic model.

REFERENCES

Berkowitz, L., & Daniels, L. R. Responsibility and dependency. *Journal of Abnormal and Social Psychology,* 1963, **66,** 427–436.

Berkowitz, L., & Daniels, L. R. Affecting the salience of the social responsibility norm: effects of past help on the response to dependency relationships. *Journal of Abnormal and Social Psychology,* 1964, **68**, 275–281.

Gouldner, A. W. The norm of reciprocity: A preliminary statement. *American Sociological Review,* 1960, **25**, 161–171.

Thibaut, J. W., & Kelley, H. H. *The social psychology of groups.* New York: Wiley, 1959.

Discussion

The Goranson and Berkowitz study is basically sound as far as procedural details go. There are some criticisms of their procedure which Greenglass (1969) mentions in the introduction to the following article, but we would like instead to call the reader's attention to some more subtle conceptual problems at this point and forego procedural criticism.

Goranson and Berkowitz state that their experiment ". . . Specifically . . . seeks to compare the effects of prior help as mediated by a direct reciprocity with the effects as mediated by an arousal or dampening of the awareness of the responsibility norm [p. 229]." The assumption was that the responsibility norm, but not the reciprocity norm, would be operative when the supervisor was a different person from the one who had helped the subjects earlier. There is some confusion here, however. In the introduction to their article the authors imply, as noted in the above quote, that they would expect reciprocity but not responsibility to be operative in those conditions in which the supervisor is the same person who earlier helped the subjects. However, in the discussion section they state that ". . . The conjectured responsibility norm could well have been operating, to some extent at least, in the same supervisor condition as well as when subjects were working for a different supervisor [p. 232]."

The study, then, has not done what it set out to do. The effects of the reciprocity norm have not been compared with the effects of the responsibility norm. Let us assume for the moment that the norm of reciprocity was not operating in the different conditions—this is a questionable assumption, as we will see in the following article, but it is one that Goranson and Berkowitz made. They also argue that the responsibility norm was operating in the different conditions. They point out that ". . . In the different-supervisor conditions the relatively high rate of productivity and some of the questionnaire responses point to the existence of the responsibility norm. All three groups in this treatment showed a considerable gain in productivity, perhaps largely because they believed this different person was dependent upon them [p. 232]." What we have, then, is one set of conditions (Different) in which the norm of responsibility was operating, and one set of conditions (Same) in which both the norm of responsibility and the norm of reciprocity were operating.

Under these circumstances it is possible, theoretically, to compare the effects of the norm of responsibility with those of the norm of reciprocity. We are still assuming reciprocity was totally uninvolved in the results in the Different conditions. Granting this assumption, the mean increase in productivity (over the practice period) for each of the three different conditions would give us the contribution of the responsibility norm. These scores are given in the last line of Table 2. In order to get the contribution of reciprocity, it would be necessary to subtract each of these scores from the corresponding increase scores for the Same conditions. Following this procedure, we can construct a new Table, say Table 2′ based on Table 2.

This leaves one with quite a different impression of the relative contributions of the two norms. Contrary to the impression left by Goranson and Berkowitz, responsibility appears to be the more powerful of the two norms. We have devoted some space to this analysis in the hope of serving two related purposes. First, of course, is the goal of sensitizing the reader to the necessity of careful thinking about exactly what an article has done in relation to what it set out to do.

Second, we think this interpretation of the Goranson and Berkowitz article provides an excellent starting point for a topic we would like to discuss in the final chapter—the question of "crucial" experiments as opposed to multiple working hypotheses. We defer that topic here in order to present the following article by Greenglass. The Greenglass paper clarifies several aspects of the previous studies and broadens the concept of reciprocity as defined by Gouldner (1960). Perhaps it is symptomatic of social psychological research, but the Greenglass paper is an excellent example of a study that both advances and retards our understanding.

TABLE 2′
Contribution of Reciprocity and Responsibility In Terms of Increased Production Over the Practice Period

	Prior help		
	Voluntary	Compulsory	Refused
Reciprocity	4.87	1.53	−1.78
Responsibility	11.70	11.25	10.61

Effects of Prior Help and Hindrance on Willingness to Help Another: Reciprocity or Social Responsibility[1]

Esther R. Greenglass

An experiment using 72 young female undergraduates examined the effects of prior help on subsequent help giving. An ostensible peer (*P1*) gave a third of the subjects help in winning a prize. Another third of the subjects received no help, and the remaining subjects were hindered. Another person (*P2*), needing the subject's help, was represented to half of the subjects as similar to *P1*, and to the remaining subjects as dissimilar to *P1*. Prior help led to high help for *P2* regardless of *P1-P2* similarity. Prior hindrance resulted in hindrance for a similar *P2* and help for a dissimilar *P2*. It was concluded that while a subject's help for *P2* in the prior help condition was a function of a new norm of social responsibility, a subject's hindrance of a similar *P2* in the prior hindrance condition was due to either the negative norm of reciprocity or to a generalization of resentment. The relatively high amount of help that the subject gave to a dissimilar *P2* after receiving hindrance was attributed to the subject's exaggerated awareness of the normative requirements of the situation prescribing help.

Recent research suggests that behavior in certain situations is governed by a norm of social responsibility which prescribes that people should help those needing it even though the beneficiaries (or their surrogates) had not helped them earlier and may not provide repayment in the future (Berkowitz & Daniels, 1963; Berkowitz, Klanderman, & Harris, 1964; Daniels & Berkowitz, 1963; Goranson & Berkowitz, 1966). Further research has demonstrated that after prior help, subjects gave greater help to a dependent person than did subjects who received no prior help (Berkowitz & Daniels, 1964; Goranson & Berkowitz, 1966). Berkowitz and Daniels (1964) suggested that prior help from one person may have increased help for another person because it increased the salience of the social responsibility norm, thereby reminding the subject to help a dependent person.

One explanation for the results reported by Berkowitz and Daniels (1964) involves the norm of reciprocity which prescribes that people should give benefits to those from whom benefits have been received previously, as well as to those from whom benefits are expected (Gould-

[1] From the *Journal of Personality and Social Psychology*, 1969, **11**, No. 3, 224–231. Received August 1, 1968. Reproduced by permission of the publisher.

This article is based upon a dissertation submitted to the University of Toronto. The author is indebted for the encouragement and direction of her thesis supervisor, Harry Kaufmann. Appreciation is also expressed to A. John Arrowood and A. Martin Wall for their helpful advice.

Requests for reprints should be sent to E. R. Greenglass, Department of Psychology, York University, 4700 Keele Street, Downsview, Ontario, Canada.

The author is with York University.

ner, 1960). In the Berkowitz-Daniels (1964) experiment, the norm of reciprocity may have contributed to the relatively high help extended by the subject after receiving prior help from the experimenter's confederate. Feelings of obligation arising from prior help may have generalized to the dependent person so that by working hard for her, the subject thought she was reciprocating for the assistance received earlier from the experimenter's confederate.

Goranson and Berkowitz (1966) attempted to separate the effects of the norm of social responsibility from those of reciprocity on helping behavior. They found that when subjects were required to work for the *same* person who had helped them, they worked hardest for that person (i.e., reciprocated most strongly) when his prior assistance had been given them voluntarily, less hard when assistance had been required, and least hard when it had been refused. They concluded that an individual feels obligated to reciprocate prior help when this help is given voluntarily. However, the hypothesized social responsibility norm could also have been operative to some extent.

In addition to conjectured norms, there are other factors which may produce helping behavior. Individuals often behave in a way that they perceive is expected by others in order to achieve their approval. Kelman (1958) calls this process *compliance,* as opposed to *internalization* where the individual behaves in a certain way because the content of the behavior is intrinsically rewarding to him. According to Crowne and Marlowe (1964), people describe themselves in a socially desirable way in order to obtain approval from others. Extending this line of thought to Goranson and Berkowitz (1966), the subject's help for the same person who helped her previously may have been influenced by considerations of social desirability—the subject may have helped the dependent person in order to win hers or the experimenter's approval by giving the same person the help the subject perceived was expected.

Another possible determinant of helping in an experiment may be seen as the "demand characteristics" which Orne (1962) described as cues in the procedure and instructions which convey the experimenter's true hypothesis. For example, in the Goranson-Berkowitz experiment, although subjects were misled as to the experimenter's hypothesis, the experimental situation may have become relatively transparent to the subject. She might have perceived that helping was the behavior expected by the experimenter since she was required to help the same person who helped her. Assuming that the subject is motivated to be a *good* subject by validating the experimenter's hypothesis (Orne, 1965), her help for the same person who helped her may have been a function of the demand characteristics rather than the independent variables.

The present experiment will examine the relative contributions of the norms of social responsibility and reciprocity while controlling for other possible determinants of helping behavior.[2] In Phase I, the subject was led to believe that she was highly dependent on one person's help, *P1*, for attainment of a prize. In Phase II, the subject was told that a second person, *P2*, was highly dependent on the subject's help for attainment of a different prize. Thus, in both phases of the study, the subject, theoretically, was aware of the general social responsibility norm which prescribes that it is appropriate to aid those needing help. By making *P1* different from *P2*, in all experimental conditions, the effects of social desirability are presumably equalized throughout. Since *P1* and *P2* are different persons, the experimental situation should not, theoretically, be transparent to the subject, thereby diminishing the chances that the subject guesses the true hypothesis.

The response elicited by the reciprocity norm, the repayment response, is conceptualized here as operating according to the principle of stimulus generalization. That is, the repayment response is regarded as capable of generalizing from the initial source of helping, *P1*, to other similar persons, *P2*, with greater strength of the helping response the greater the similarity. If the effects of prior help are mediated by the reciprocity norm, there should be a generalization of the repayment response and thereby high help to *P2* only when *P1* and *P2* are similar, with little help given to *P2* when *P1* and *P2* are dissimilar. If, however, prior help heightens the salience of the norm of social responsibility which prescribes that it is appropriate to extend high help to others, then high help should be given to *P2* regardless of *P2*'s similarity to *P1*. If both reciprocity and social responsibility are operative, more help should be given to *P2* when *P2* is similar to *P1* than when *P2* is dissimilar to *P1*. If the subject's help for *P2* (when *P1* and *P2* are similar) is a function of both norms, there is, as yet, no way of assessing the relative contributions of the two norms. In order to separate further the effects of the two norms, the present experiment also investigates the effect of *hindrance* from *P1* on the subject's subsequent behavior towards *P2*. After prior hindrance, reciprocity should produce hindrance for *P2* only when *P1* and *P2* are similar. Emphasis is placed here not on the repayment of help but on the return of injuries, and is found in the *negative* norms of reciprocity (Gouldner, 1960). Social responsibility should not be a major determinant here since the social responsibility norm prescribes help

[2] One of the variables which was controlled was the salience of the social responsibility norm. In order to eliminate its differential effects on helping among experimental conditions, the salience of the social responsibility norm was maximized throughout by means of experimental instructions.

rather than hindrance. After prior hindrance, the existing norm of social responsibility should produce help for *P2* when *P1* and *P2* are dissimilar. If, however, prior hindrance establishes a new norm of hindrance which prescribes hindrance as appropriate behavior in this situation, then hindrance should be expressed towards *P2* regardless of *P2*'s similarity to *P1*.

Method

SUBJECTS

The subjects were 72 young women between the ages of 17 and 21 who were enrolled in the introductory course at the University of Toronto. They were required to serve four hours as psychological subjects.

PHASE I

The subject was individually told the ostensible purpose of the study, which was to find out how well people evaluate how hard someone has worked on a job. Subjects were told that they would have to work for a period of time after which their work would be rated according to two criteria, and that they stood to win points according to each. One criterion, an objective one, was "productivity": 5 points for every article made. Another criterion was "motivation to work" as judged by another person. The experimenter explained that every subject would be required to perform two tasks: She would be asked to work on a job after which another subject would evaluate her motivation to work. Each subject would also be required to evaluate someone else's motivation to work on a different task. Presumably, subjects were called together in groups of three, none of whom would ever know who the others were. Actually, there was only one subject present during each session. Using an (ostensible) randomization procedure, the subject was to be evaluated *first* by another girl, *P1*, then the subject was to assess a different girl, *P2*.

The subject was asked to fill in the first eight items on an attitude and value questionnaire consisting of 11 items. This questionnaire is a modified version of one devised by Kaufmann and Zener (1966). The subject was asked to check the alternative response on a 7-point scale which best expressed her degree of agreement or disagreement with each item. The items consisted of general statements in the areas of politics, morality, and religion. *P1* would see the subject's questionnaire before she rated her motivation, presumably to get some idea of what the subject was like.[3] The subject's job was to make paper boxes for 8 minutes and she was to receive a productivity score consisting of 5 points for every box she made, as well as a motivation score from *P1*. The assignment of a motivation score was the pretext for the introduction of the help

[3] The real reason for asking the subject to fill in this questionnaire was to make the later similarity manipulation believable. The similarity manipulation involved showing the subject two copies of the same questionnaire which were ostensibly filled in by *P1* and *P2*. In some preliminary work in which the subject was not asked to fill in this questionnaire, some subjects had become suspicious and asked why the other two girls had filled in the questionnaire while they (subjects) did not.

and hindrance manipulations to be explained below. If, on the basis of her examination of the boxes, *P1* thought that the subject had high motivation, she could add points. *P1* could add no points if she thought the subject had average motivation, and she could deduct points for low motivation. The subject's overall score consisted of the algebraic sum of points assigned according to the two criteria.

The experimenter explained that of all the subjects in the study who had made boxes, the one with the highest overall score would win a gift certificate. It was emphasized that the subject was not competing with either *P1* or *P2* for the same gift certificate—they were ostensibly in different contests. If the subject were to perceive that she was competing with *P2*, she might be reluctant to help her (Deutsch, 1949). All subjects received a productivity score of 65 since they were asked to stop working after they had completed 13 boxes. The experimenter then took the subject's boxes to *P1* who allegedly assigned the subject a motivation score.

Experimental Manipulations. The experiment employed a 2×3 factorial design. Similarity between *P1* and *P2* was introduced on two levels, and nature of prior help was introduced on three levels. Subjects were randomly assigned to each of the six experimental treatment conditions.

Differences in *similarity* between *P1* and *P2* were created using the same questionnaire filled in earlier by the subject. The subject received two copies of the same questionnaire partially filled in supposedly by *P1* and *P2*. In the *P1-P2* similarity condition, *P1* and *P2* held similar attitudes and values; in the *P1-P2* dissimilarity condition, they showed opposite views. The results of a pilot study showed that the subject tended to see herself as more similar to *P1* and *P2* when she had checked a certain set of alternatives than when *P1* and *P2* had checked the opposite set of alternatives. Moreover, when the subject perceived herself as similar to *P1* and *P2*, she saw them as "liberal." She saw the opposite personality as "conservative." In order to control simultaneously for the effects of *P2*'s personality, as well as similarity between the subject and *P1*, and between *P2* and the subject, the personalities that *P1* and *P2* ostensibly had were counterbalanced in the similarity and dissimilarity conditions.

The subject received the questionnaire presumably to get some idea of what the other two girls were like. She was to fill in the last three items on each questionnaire the way *P1* and *P2* would have responded if they had been allowed to complete them. The experimenter explained that the subject's responses would be studied to determine the accuracy of her impression of *P1* and *P2*. The real reason for asking the subject to fill in the questionnaires was to check on the effectiveness of the similarity (dissimilarity) manipulation.

The *nature of prior help* manipulation involved the number of points that *P1* assigned to the subject for "motivation to work." The experimenter brought back the subject's boxes with *P1*'s numerical assessment of the subject's motivation written on the rating sheet, which was sealed in an envelope. *P1* had also written the subject a brief message telling her why she had given her that particular motivation score. The subject was asked not to reveal the score she received in order to make more believable the experimenter's later assurance that she would not be seeing the motivation score that the subject assigned to *P2*. These anonymous evaluations should have minimized the effects of social desirability as well as implicit and situational cues.

For the subjects in the prior help condition, *P1* added 38 points, which she stated in her message she felt the subject deserved for high motivation to work. In the no prior help condition, *P1* gave the subject no points, and she commented that the subject's motivation was about average. In the prior hindrance condition, *P1* deducted 38 points from the subject's productivity score, stating that in her opinion the subject had low motivation. The subject then filled in a brief questionnaire consisting of items which assessed the effectiveness of the help manipulation as well as the subject's liking for *P1*. For most items, the subject's responses were scored on a 7-point scale.

Phase II

The subject's task was to evaluate *P2*'s motivation to work on the basis of her examination of nine paper cups ostensibly made by *P2*. The subject was instructed to write *P2* a brief message telling her why she gave her the numerical score. *P2* was supposedly competing with subjects who had made paper cups for a different gift certificate from the one for which the subject was eligible. Both the subject and *P2* had approximately the same productivity score.

Main Dependent Variable. The measure of the amount of help or hindrance extended was the number of points for motivation that the subject either added to or deducted from *P2*'s productivity score.

Checks on the Similarity Manipulation. The second check on the similarity manipulation ascertained how well the subject could recall *P1-P2* similarity approximately one half hour after the original manipulation. The subject was to fill in three blank items the way she recalled that *P1* and *P2* had done so on the original questionnaire. Also, she was to indicate the extent to which she agreed with the statement that *P1* and *P2* would have a great deal in common if they knew each other. This question was designed to find out the degree to which the subject's perceptions of similarity in attitude and values between *P1* and *P2* had generalized to their total personality.

The subject then filled in a brief questionnaire consisting of items which assessed the degree to which she thought she had helped or hindered *P2*, as well as her liking for *P2*. In the postexperimental inquiry, the subject was asked (*a*) a series of questions designed to check on the effectiveness of the experimental instructions and (*b*) a series of questions designed to ascertain if the subject perceived the true purpose of the experiment. In the debriefing session, the experimenter told the subject that she had misled her and the true purpose of the experiment was explained.

Results

Amount of Help (Number of Points) Given to *P2*

Table 1 presents the mean number of points given to *P2* in each of the Help × Similarity conditions. The analysis of variance results are

TABLE 1

Mean Amount of Help (Number of Points) Given to *P2* in Each of the Help × Similarity Conditions[a]

Similarity	Prior hindrance	No prior help	Prior help
P1 similar to *P2*	−12.3	6.2	34.7
P1 dissimilar to *P2*	18.8	7.4	30.4

[a] $n = 12$ per cell.

TABLE 2
Analysis of Variance of the Amount of Help (Number of Points) Given to $P2$ for Motivation to Work

Source	*df*	*MS*	*F*
Nature of prior help (N)	2	6,127.1	111.6[a]
Similarity between $P1$ and $P2$ (S)	1	1,577.4	28.7[a]
Personality of $P2$ (P)	1	.2	<1
$N \times S$	2	2,183.7	39.8[a]
$N \times P$	2	1.6	<1
$S \times P$	1	.2	<1
$N \times S \times P$	2	2.2	<1
Error	60	54.9	

[a] $p < .01$.

summarized in Table 2. As predicted earlier, there was a significant effect due to the helping variable ($p < .01$): the subject gave *P2* more points after prior help than after no prior help was received. The similarity variable did not significantly affect the number of points given in either the prior help ($t = 1.82$, $df = 22$, *ns*)[4] or the no prior help conditions ($t < 1$, $df = 22$, *ns*). There was a significant interaction between the helping and similarity variables ($p < .01$), which was due solely to the difference between the similarity and dissimilarity conditions after prior hindrance was received ($t = 9.97$, $df = 22$, $p < .01$): after prior hindrance, the subject gave *P2* points when *P1* and *P2* were dissimilar, and she deducted points when *P1* and *P2* were similar. In the dissimilarity condition, there were significant differences in the number of points *P2* received as a function of the helping variable: *P2* received more points in the prior help than in the prior hindrance condition ($t = 4.50$, $df = 22$, $p < .01$), and she received more points in the prior hindrance condition than in the no prior help condition ($t = 4.19$, $df = 22$, $p < .01$).

Tests of the Effectiveness of the Experimental Manipulations

Similarity Manipulation. The first check on the similarity (dissimilarity) manipulation was the degree of similarity between the preferences the subject checked for *P1* and *P2* on the last three items of the attitude and value questionnaire. The results of Tukey's (1959) test showed that the distance scores over the last three items were significantly smaller in the similarity than in the dissimilarity condition (total > 13, $p < .001$). (The smaller the distance score, the higher the perceived similarity be-

[4] All tests of significance reported are two-tailed.

tween *P1* and *P2*.) Further evidence for the success of the similarity manipulation was found in the differences in degree of similarity between the girls in their responses, as the subject remembered them, to three of the questions that had been filled out earlier ostensibly by *P1* and *P2*. Distance scores were significantly smaller in the similarity than in the dissimilarity condition (total > 13, $p < .001$). Third, while subjects in the similarity condition agreed with the statement that *P1* and *P2* would have a great deal in common, subjects in the dissimilarity condition disagreed.

Help Manipulation. Questionnaire I, administered at the end of Phase I, included items to test the effectiveness of the help manipulation, a measure of the subject's liking for *P1*, and a question which asked the subject the criteria *P1* used in assessing the subject's motivation. One of the items asked the subject the extent to which *P1* had helped her win the gift certificate. An analysis of variance of these data showed a significant main effect for the helping variable ($F = 339.5$, $df = 2/66$, $p < .01$) and a significant linear trend for the three "help" conditions ($F = 677.1$, $df = 1/66$, $p < .01$). In the prior help condition, the subject tended to state that she had been helped, while in the no prior help condition the subject stated that she was "neither helped nor hindered." In the prior hindrance condition, the subject tended to state that she had been hindered.

Other questionnaire results point to the differential degree of satisfaction engendered by the "help" manipulation. There was a significant effect due to the help manipulation ($F = 68.3$, $df = 2/66$, $p < .01$), and a significant linear trend for the three "help" conditions ($F = 135.5$, $df = 1/66$, $p < .01$). A subject who received prior help from *P1* indicated greater satisfaction with her rating than a subject who received no prior help, while a subject who was hindered was relatively dissatisfied with *P1*'s rating.

The helping variable had a significant effect on the subject's liking for *P1* ($F = 10.1$, $df = 2/66$, $p < .01$). *P1* was liked significantly more in the prior help condition than in the no prior help and prior hindrance conditions combined.

Subjects in each of the six experimental conditions stated that they thought *P1* had used the following five types of criteria in assessing their motivation to work: quantity and/or quality, difficulty of the task, the subject's attitude and value questionnaire, criticisms of the boxes, and other criteria which include intuition, etc. There appeared to be no difference in the frequency with which each of the different criteria was used among conditions.

TEST OF THE SUBJECT'S AWARENESS OF AMOUNT OF HELP OR HINDRANCE EXTENDED TO *P2*

Questionnaire II, administered at the end of Phase II, included items which assessed the degree to which the subject thought she had helped or hindered *P2*, a measure of the subject's liking for *P2*, and a question which asked the subject which criteria she used in assessing *P2*'s motivation. One of these items asked the subject to what extent she had helped *P2*. There was a significant difference between the responses of subjects in the prior hindrance condition (when *P1* and *P2* were similar) and the responses of subjects in the other five treatment conditions. When *P1* and *P2* were similar, and the subject deducted points, the subject stated that she had hindered *P2*; subjects in the other conditions who gave points tended to state that they had helped *P2* to some extent. The subject's liking for *P2* was not related to the differential help treatments ($F < 1$, $df = 2/66$, *ns*); subjects who hindered *P2* did not like her less than did subjects who helped *P2* (see Table 3).

Subjects in each of the six experimental conditions stated that they had used the following five types of criteria in assessing *P2*'s motivation to work: quantity and/or quality, difficulty of the task, *P2*'s attitude and value questionnaire, criticisms of the cups, and other criteria such as intuition, etc. There appeared to be no difference in the frequency with which each of the different criteria was used among conditions.

ANALYSIS OF THE SUBJECT'S MESSAGE TO *P2*

The subject's message was analyzed by computing the frequency with which a number of criteria were mentioned, such as quantity and/or quality of the cups, difficulty with the task, faults with the cups, etc. Although subjects in all conditions found fault with the cups, subjects in the prior hindrance condition (when *P1* and *P2* were similar) mentioned faults most frequently and used them as their sole basis for their

TABLE 3
Mean Scores: Item 4, Questionnaire II: "If You Met Number 23, How Much Do You Think You Would Like Her?"[a]

Similarity	Prior hindrance	No prior help	Prior help
P1 similar to *P2*	5.2[b]	5.3	5.6
P1 dissimilar to *P2*	5.5	5.3	4.8

[a] Number 23 refers to *P2*.
[b] High scores indicate high liking.

minus ratings of *P2*'s motivation. It appears that subjects who deducted points were able to substantiate their minus ratings by referring to the faults with the cups. While subjects in the other conditions noticed the faults, generally, they made it clear to *P2* that they were not penalizing her for them, and in some cases these faults were taken as further evidence of "high motivation" since they were signs of *P2*'s haste. There appeared to be no difference in the frequency with which the other criteria were used among the conditions.

Results of the Postexperimental Inquiry

1. The subject was asked questions concerning some of the deceptions. All subjects stated that their work period was 8 minutes. When asked when the experimenter would see the motivation score they gave to *P2*, all subjects replied that the experimenter would not see it. They stated that they would never meet or know who the other two girls were.
2. When asked about the purpose of the experiment, subjects repeated, for the most part, what the experimenter had told them in the instructions. None of the subjects guessed the true purpose of the experiment or the questionnaires.

Discussion

The results supported the hypothesis that prior help increases the salience of the norm of social responsibility which prescribes that it is appropriate, in this situation, to extend high help to dependent others—in the prior help condition, the subject was extending high help to *P2* regardless of her similarity or dissimilarity to *P1*. Further, evidence for the operation of the social responsibility norm in the no prior help condition is found in subjects' responses to the question of how much they thought they had helped (or hindered) *P2*. Most subjects stated that they had helped *P2* to some extent.

There are two, perhaps related, alternative explanations for the subject's behavior toward *P2* after prior hindrance. The subject's hindrance of a similar *P2* may have been a function of the negative norm of reciprocity (or the talion law of "an eye for an eye") which prescribes that it is appropriate to return an injury after receiving hindrance. *P2*'s similarity to *P1* presumably functioned as a cue which activated the negative norm of reciprocity and thereby resulted in the subject's reciprocating *P1*'s hindrance by hindering *P2*. Since all subjects stated that they had hindered *P2*, there is evidence that subjects were *not* behaving according to the general prescription that one does not hinder a dependent person. Because all subjects in the prior hindrance condition deducted fewer points from *P2* than *P1* had deducted, it may be that the subject was aware of the social responsibility norm which prescribes help.

Another explanation for the subject's behavior in the prior hindrance condition is based on a model proposed by Berkowitz (1964), which states that prior frustration induces a tendency to aggress, and the strength of the aggressive response is a direct function of the degree of association or similarity between the object of the potential aggression and the anger instigator. Presumably, *P2*'s similarity to *P1* influenced the strength of *P2*'s "aggressive cue" value which elicited hindrance towards *P2*. In other words, hostility was displaced from *P1* to *P2* according to the principle of stimulus generalization. The subject's resentment towards *P1* was expressed in her responses to Questionnaire I, that she was dissatisfied with *P1*'s assessment of her, and in her responses in the post-experimental inquiry, that she was annoyed by *P1*'s "capricious" behavior. The subject, however, did not extend the total amount of hostility that she might have because of the normative requirements of the situation which prescribed help to *P2*. Thus, when *P1* and *P2* were dissimilar, neither aggressive cues nor conditions necessary for the operation of the reciprocity norm were present, and the social responsibility norm became a major determinant of the subject's relatively high help for *P2*.

The subject's behavior in this study was probably not a function of the demand characteristics since the results of a "nonexperiment"[5] suggested that the true purpose of the study was not readily apparent to the subject.

An alternative explanation for the results is that the differential help conditions produced a judgmental effect. That is, subjects in the three help conditions learned to employ different criteria in judging *P2* on the basis of the criteria they perceived were employed by *P1*. However, there were no differences among conditions in the criteria subjects used to judge *P2*.

Conceivably, subjects in the prior help condition might have been put in a good mood as a result of their gain, and their good will generalized to *P2*. On the other hand, there was evidence that subjects in the prior

[5] The nonexperiment is used to ascertain whether or not the true experimental hypotheses are conveyed to the subject by the demand characteristics (Riecken, 1962). The procedure involved giving the subject the instructions that were destined for an actual experimental subject and asking her to imagine how she would behave *if* she were a subject in the experiment. The experimenter then asked the subject a series of questions concerning what she thought was the true purpose of the experiment (Orne, 1959).

hindrance condition were resentful. If the subject's hindrance of *P2* was due to a generalization of resentment from *P1* to *P2*, there should also have been a generalization of dislike from *P1* to *P2*. There was no evidence, however, that *P2* was liked any less when she was hindered than when she was helped. These findings are consistent with the reciprocity hypothesis whose origins are perceived in social norms while asserting nothing about affective responses.

REFERENCES

Berkowitz, L. Aggressive cues in aggressive behavior and hostility catharsis. *Psychological Review,* 1964, **71**, 104–122.

Berkowitz, L., & Daniels, L. R. Responsibility and dependency. *Journal of Abnormal and Social Psychology,* 1963, **66**, 429–436.

Berkowitz, L., & Daniels, L. R. Affecting the salience of the social responsibility norm: effects of past help on the response to dependency relationships. *Journal of Abnormal and Social Psychology,* 1964, **68**, 275–281.

Berkowitz, L., Klanderman, S., & Harris, R. Effects of experimenter awareness and sex of subject and experimenter on reactions to dependency relationships. *Sociometry,* 1964, **27**, 327–337.

Crowne, D. P., & Marlowe, D. *The approval motive.* New York: Wiley, 1964.

Daniels, L. R., & Berkowitz, L. Liking and response to dependency relationships. *Human Relations,* 1963, **16**, 141–148.

Deutsch, M. The effects of cooperation and competition upon group process. *Human Relations,* 1949, **2**, 199–231.

Goranson, R. E., & Berkowitz, L. Reciprocity and responsibility reactions to prior help. *Journal of Personality and Social Psychology,* 1966, **3**, 227–232.

Gouldner, A. W. The norm of reciprocity: A preliminary statement. *American Sociological Review,* 1960, **25**, 161–171.

Kaufmann, H., & Zener, L. Perceived similarity and liking as functions of manipulated similarity and subjective favorability. Unpublished manuscript, University of Toronto, 1966.

Kelman, H. C. Compliance, identification and internalization: Three processes of attitude change. *Journal of Conflict Resolution,* 1958, **2**, 51–60.

Orne, M. T. The demand characteristics of an experimental design and their implications. Paper presented at the meeting of the American Psychological Association, Cincinnati, September 1959.

Orne, M. T. On the social psychology of the psychological experiment: With particular reference to demand characteristics and their implications. *American Psychologist,* 1962, **17**, 776–783.

Orne, M. T. Demand characteristics and their implications for real life: The importance of quasi-controls. Paper presented at the meeting of the American Psychological Association, Chicago, September 1965.

Riecken, H. W. A program for research on experiments in social psychology. In N. F. Washburne (Ed.) , *Decisions, values, and groups.* New York: Pergamon Press, 1962.

Tukey, J. W. A quick, compact, two-sample test to Duckworth's specifications. *Technometrics,* 1959, **1**, 31–48.

Discussion

One of the dangers inherent in the use of concepts like "experimenter bias" and "demand characteristics" is that they will be thrown about too loosely. If such concepts degenerate to the level of explaining away previous results as the sole justification for further research, they become useless. One of the criticisms that Greenglass makes of the Goranson-Berkowitz study is that the results may have been due to the subjects' perceiving certain demand characteristics in the procedure:

> ". . . in the Goranson-Berkowitz experiment, although subjects were misled as to the experimenter's hypothesis, the experimental situation *may have* become relatively transparent to the subject. She *might have* perceived that helping was the behavior expected by the experimenter since she was required to help the same person who helped her . . . (emphasis added; Greenglass, 1969, p. 225).

If someone feels that the results of a particular study are not due to the manipulated independent variables, but to some confounding or demand characteristic or experimenter bias, he incurs a twofold obligation. First, he should provide a logical, plausible explanation about how he thinks the results were produced and not simply dismiss the results as "probably" or "maybe" due to demand characteristics. Second, the critic should make explicit the limitations of the explanation he is proposing. If, for example, demand characteristics, and not reciprocity, explain the results in the Same-Voluntary condition of the Goranson-Berkowitz study, is reciprocity still an adequate explanation for the difference in results between the Same-Compulsory condition and the Same-Refused condition? Do demand characteristics explain this difference also? Vague criticism is useless. The critic should formulate his criticism well and make it to the point so that it, in turn, can be evaluated and criticized.

In Part I we discussed several ways of assessing the manner in which subjects perceive the experimental manipulations. Greenglass adds one to that list. She concludes, as the result of a "nonexperiment," that ". . . the subjects' behavior in this study was probably not a function of the demand characteristics (p. 230)." As described in a footnote, her "nonexperiment . . . involved giving the subject the instructions that were destined for an actual experimental subject and asking her to imagine how she would behave *if* she were a subject in the experiment." Concluding from the remarks of "subjects" in this "nonexperiment" that results with subjects in the real experiment were not a function of demand characteristics is obviously a non sequitar. As Orne (1962) suggests, ". . . one procedure to determine the demand characteristics (in a particular experiment) is the systematic study of each individual subject's perception of the experimental hypothesis [p. 780]." Studying the perceptions of "as if" subjects is not an adequate substitute. The results of many studies (e.g., Willis and Willis, 1970) have shown that responses of "as if" subjects do not correspond with those of involved subjects except in certain limited types of situations.

Neither Greenglass nor Goranson and Berkowitz included a straight control condition in which subjects were not put through Phase I of the experiment. There are some obvious complications in setting up such a control condition in order to make the other conditions comparable, but the enhanced understanding possible would appear to make it worth the effort. Such a condition would have enabled us to discover, for example, whether the results in the no prior help conditions resulted from a suppression of aid or whether the results in the prior help condition indicated an increase in aid. Without the additional control condition, there is no way of knowing.

It is somewhat disappointing that Greenglass decided to use a different experimental task from that used by Berkowitz and his associates. Had she stuck to the same procedure of having subjects construct boxes, instead of awarding points, the results would have been easier to compare to the Berkowitz results.

One could argue, of course, that one should change the procedure as much as possible if one is interested in the conceptual relations. As E. E. Jones (1966) puts it "... The notion of conceptual generality (in contrast to empirical generality) implies that our interest should transcend our particular operations. . . . The question is whether the same *conceptual* relation that is reflected in one set of results can be shown to obtain elsewhere—with procedures adapted to the changed setting or sample [p. 3]." The issue of exact versus conceptual replications is an important one and we will discuss it at greater length in the final chapter.

Earlier we alluded to a general problem characteristic of all the studies in this area. The problem is related to the discussion of the preceding paragraph and centers on the low external validity for most of the studies of dependence and responsibility. As Campbell and Stanley (1963) define it ". . . *External Validity* asks the question of *generalizability:* to what populations, settings, treatment variables, and measurement variables can this effect be generalized? [p. 5]" After reading these three articles and their associated problems, we fear that the verdict is "very few, if any."

This area of research does not seem to have caught on as well as some of the others we have discussed. This may be due to the haziness of the concepts involved, although this is hardly sufficient reason given the haziness of many social psychological concepts. What appears to have held back progress as much as anything is the difficulty of devising suitable procedures which would allow one to partial out the effects of, for example, responsibility, reciprocity, and equity. In spite of these and other difficulties, interest in the area has continued. Berkowitz and his associates have found social class differences (Berkowitz, 1968; Berkowitz and Friedman, 1967) in socially responsible behavior using the same laboratory task that Goranson and Berkowitz used. Other studies (Daniels and Berkowitz, 1963) have found that liking for the dependent other is a powerful determinant of the amount of aid given, but only under some conditions. Another line of research has investigated the effects of the perceived source of the other's dependence (Horowitz, 1968). Thus, the research is continuing. What appears called for is a theoretical integration of the various findings and the development of a more sophisticated methodology for sorting out the various influences on socially responsible behavior.

REFERENCES

Anderson, N. H., & Barrios, A. A. Primacy effects in personality impression formation. *Journal of Abnormal and Social Psychology,* 1961, **63,** 346–350.

Aronson, E., & Carlsmith, J. M. Experimentation in social psychology. In G. Lindzey and E. Aronson (Eds.), *Handbook of social psychology.* Vol. 2. Reading, Massachusetts: Addison-Wesley, 1968. Pp. 1–79.

Berkowitz, L. Effects of perceived dependency relationships upon conformity to group expectations. *Journal of Abnormal and Social Psychology,* 1957, **55,** 350–354.

Berkowitz, L. Responsibility, reciprocity, and social distance in help giving: An experimental investigation of English social class differences. *Journal of Experimental Social Psychology,* 1968, **4,** 46–63.

Berkowitz, L., & Daniels, L. R. Responsibility and dependency. *Journal of Abnormal and Social Psychology,* 1963, **66,** 429–436.

Berkowitz, L., & Friedman, P. Some social class differences in helping behavior. *Journal of Personality and Social Psychology,* 1967, **5,** 217–225.

Brehm, J. W. Postdecision changes in the desirability of alternatives. *Journal of Abnormal and Social Psychology,* 1956, **52,** 384–389.

Campbell, D. T., & Stanley, J. C. *Experimental and quasi-experimental designs for research.* Chicago: Rand-McNally, 1963.

Clark, M. Cultural values and dependency in later life. In R. A. Kalish (Ed.), *The dependencies of old people.* Ann Arbor, Michigan: Institute of Gerontology, 1969. Pp. 59–72.

Daniels, L. R., & Berkowitz, L. Liking and response to dependency relationships. *Human Relations,* 1963, **16,** 141–148.

Festinger, L. *A theory of cognitive dissonance.* Stanford, California: Stanford University Press, 1957.

Gouldner, A. W. The norm of reciprocity: a preliminary statement. *American Sociological Review,* 1960, **25,** 161–178.

Horowitz, I. A. Effect of choice and locus of dependence on helping behavior. *Journal of Personality and Social Psychology,* 1968, **8,** 373–376.

Jones, E. E. Conceptual generality and experimental strategy in social psychology. Paper read at the International Congress of Psychology, Moscow, 1966.

Jones, E. E., & Gerard, H. B. *Foundations of Social Psychology.* New York: Wiley, 1967.

McGuire, W. J. Suspiciousness of experimenter's intent. In R. Rosenthal and R. L. Rosnow (Eds.), *Artifact in behavioral research.* New York: Academic Press, 1969. Pp. 13–57.

McGuire, W. J., & Papageorgis, D. Effectiveness of forewarning in developing resistance to persuasion. *Public Opinion Quarterly,* 1962, **26,** 24–34.

Orne, M. T. On the social psychology of the psychological experiment: with particular reference to demand characteristics and their implications. *American Psychologist,* 1962, **17,** 776–783.

Willis, R. H., & Willis, Y. A. Role playing versus deception: An experimental comparison. *Journal of Personality and Social Psychology,* 1970, **16,** 472–477.

Chapter 11

POSTSCRIPT

> . . . the goal of the social scientist is always to achieve interpretable comparisons, and . . . the goal of methodology is to rule out those plausible rival hypotheses which make comparisons ambiguous and tentative (Webb, Campbell, Schwartz, and Sechrest, 1966, page 5) .

The quotation from Webb *et al.* (1966) raises the issue that we would like to discuss briefly in this chapter. It is a very complex issue and one that has many subcategories ranging from the questions of exact replications to education of researchers. Such could and have filled volumes. Here we would simply like to make explicit our positions on a couple of the subcategories—positions which have evolved partly from close readings of the literature in the five content areas sampled in the preceding chapters.

Replications

Exact replications of research are routine for most of the "hard" sciences. In chemistry, for example, at temperature *X*, pressure *Y*, etc., hydrogen and oxygen are expected to combine in the same manner in Israel as they are in Egypt. In social psychological research, however, Israelis are not necessarily expected to react in the same manner to a given stimulus as Egyptians. One could argue, of course, that if we pick a stimulus which has the same "meaning" to both Israelis and Egyptians we would get the same reaction. Or, more likely, if we picked a stimulus A which has the same meaning to Israelis as stimulus B has to Egyptians, we would get equivalent reactions when we presented A and B to Israelis and Egyptians, respectively. This would not be an exact replication since A and B are different. Assuming there were other differences in setting such as time of day, experimenters, etc., our Israeli-Egyptian study would qualify as a conceptual replication because it illustrates ". . . two features of a replication which focuses on conceptual generality: (a) tailoring an independent variable to fit the outlook of subjects in a particular locale, and (b) making arbitrary changes in procedure that should not affect the basic result . . . (Jones, 1966, p. 4) ."

There is a danger involved, however. If our conceptual replication fails to reproduce the original result we are left with an empirical puzzle. Was it the change in the independent variable which caused the failure or was it the change in the supposedly "extraneous" aspects of the setting? If a conceptual replication (or "Heteromethod replication"; Campbell, 1969) fails, it might then be worthwhile to retrace our steps and try an exact replication.

It should be apparent, however, that replications are often simply unfeasible and unreasonable. Suppose next year some researcher at the University of Oregon decides he wants to try to replicate Rosenberg's (1965) study of evaluation apprehension. In Rosenberg's study, Ohio State University students were the subjects and the experiment was on attitude change. The issue involved was Ohio State's participation in the Rose Bowl and was a very "hot" issue at the time the study was carried out. An exact replication of this study would be impossible. The same issue could not be used, settings would of necessity be different, experimenters would have to be different, and the campus atmosphere surrounding the original study could not be duplicated.

The best time and place for a replication to occur is in the lab of the initial investigator before he publishes his results. One could argue that this is unnecessary if the first result is statistically significant, but such an argument misses the point of replications. If a result significant at the .05 level was artifactually produced, then a replication with a different experimenter, setting, subjects, etc., would be unlikely to reproduce the same result. There are ways of carrying out this recommendation without the added time and expense of a complete second study; for example, having two experimenters each run half the subjects in every cell of a design and then analyzing the results for an experimenter effect. If none appears, one could place more faith in the results than if only one experimenter had been used.

Another possibility, suggested by one of our colleagues, is that perhaps all masters theses should be exact replications of previous research. It is true that in some areas of social psychology exact replications are possible and should be carried out routinely. This is particularly the case in those areas which are somewhat more precise: impression formation, computer simulation, game behavior, risky shift, etc. It does appear, however, that conceptual replications are not only more "natural" for social psychology, but promise a more rapid advancement of the field.

Multiple Working Hypotheses

Many years ago T. C. Chamberlain (1890) proposed a method which, if followed, would provide one kind of self check which often appears called for in social psychology. We have been advocating Chamberlain's method throughout this book. The method of multiple working hypotheses endeavors ". . . to bring up into view every rational explanation of new phenomena, and to develop every tenable hypothesis respecting their cause and history. The investigator then becomes the parent of a family of hypotheses: and, by his parental relation to all, he is forbidden to fasten his affections unduly upon any one (p. 756)." A "pet" theory or hypothesis can be, and often is, a disaster. It seems to act as a blinder, causing the investigator to see only what he wants to see. The method of multiple working hypotheses assumes that one is interested in an accurate explanation of phenomena and not in "proving" one's pet theory.

Aside from the nearsightedness which appears to be characteristic of pet theory holders in general, there are at least two subtle assumptions which they all seem to be working under. Simply put, these assumptions are that phenomena are determined by single causes and that there are a few basic principles of human behavior which—when discovered—should suffice to explain all the phenomena currently of interest to social psychologists. Both of these are dangerous assumptions which could cripple any scientific endeavor concerned with explaining and understanding human behavior.

Chamberlain was aware of the dangers of the first assumption when he formulated the method of multiple working hypotheses. "In following a single hypothesis, the mind is presumably led to a single explanatory conception. But an adequate explanation often involves the coordination of several agencies, which enter into the combined result in varying proportions. The true explanation is therefore necessarily complex (p. 756)." To take an example from social psychology (Chapter 8), why should we expect primacy in impression formation to be due either to a discounting of inconsistent information or the directed interpretation hypothesis? Why not both? Similarly (Chapter 9), why should we expect anticipatory belief lowering to be due to McGuire and Millman's (1965) self-esteem interpretation or the consistency hypothesis? Why not both?

Such a concern for the multiple causes of phenomena gives research a different slant. The investigator becomes less concerned with isolating the cause and more interested in specifying the conditions under which cause *A* predominates, and how those conditions differ from the conditions under which cause *B* is primary in producing the effect in question. An ideal, probably unattainable at present for most of social psychology, would be the ability to specify the proportions of variance in one's dependent variable which were due to *A*, *B*, . . . , *N* independent variables. A somewhat analogous situation exists in medicine. Is a germ the cause of a disease? Suppose the organism is not susceptible to that disease? Why do we hesitate to call susceptibility a cause?

The second assumption under which pet theorists seem to be operating is that human behavior is basically explainable by one or, at most, a few simple principles. Social psychologists often seem not to know their own history and appear hell-bent upon repeating its mistakes. Allport (1968) was, in our opinion, overly optimistic in saying that the age of "simple and sovereign" theories was past. During the 18th and 19th centuries, social philosophers tended to select one "simple and sovereign" principle that seemed to hold the key to all social behavior. An example is hedonism, the idea that all of man's actions are designed to gain pleasure. The pull of such unitary principles is still strong.

Strong Inference

J. R. Platt (1964) has argued that those disciplines of science which are progressing most rapidly have in common a method of doing scientific research for which he has proposed the name *strong inference.*

> Strong inference consists of applying the following steps to every problem in science, formally and explicitly and regularly:
>
> 1. Deriving alternative hypotheses
> 2. Devising a crucial experiment (or several of them), with alternative possible outcomes, each of which will, as nearly as possible, exclude one or more of the hypotheses
> 3. Carrying out the experiment so as to get a clean result
>
> 1′. Recycling the procedure, making subhypotheses or sequential hypotheses to refine the possibilities that remain; and so on (p. 347).

There is nothing particularly new or startling about Platt's proposal. Many of the articles we have reprinted in the preceding chapters were the results of just such a procedure.

Platt, however, is advocating the systematic use of strong inference—the self conscious, explicit, and habitual listing out of all plausible rival alternative explanations for each and every experimental result. How does one go about it?

> The most important thing is to keep in mind that this kind of thinking is not a lucky knack but a system that *can* be taught and learned. The molecular biologists today are living proof of it. The second thing is to be explicit and formal and regular about it, to devote a half hour or an hour to analytical thinking every day, writing out the logical tree and the alternatives and crucial experiments explicitly in a permanent notebook [Platt, 1964, p. 352].

Within social psychology, D. T. Campbell (1969) has recently advanced essentially the same argument. "Thus the only process available for establishing a scientific theory is one of 'eliminating plausible rival hypotheses (p. 354).' " Campbell addresses himself primarily to elimination of artifactual explanations as opposed to sorting out rival theoretical hypotheses. The real task of understanding behavior, of course, involves both. Not only must the good researcher be technically competent enough to produce "clean" results, he must be intellectually capable of designing conditions which will allow him to distinguish competing theoretical explanations.

> Social psychologists are not apologetic for their fragments because they assume that omniscience is a collective rather than a solitary product . . . and they know that rather than the discovery of truth, it is more accurate to portray their work as the gradual emancipation of knowledge from errors. Thus fragments are inevitable, but they indirectly attest to the fact that relevance to the human condition is being maintained [Weick, 1969, p. 993].

REFERENCES

Allport, G. W. The historical background of modern social psychology. In G. Lindzey and E. Aronson (Eds.), *Handbook of social psychology*. Reading, Massachusetts: Addison-Wesley, 1968, Volume I.

Campbell, D. T. Prospective: artifact and control. In R. Rosenthal and R. L. Rosnow (Eds.), *Artifact in behavioral research*. New York: Academic Press, 1969. Pp. 351–382.

Chamberlain, T. C. The method of multiple working hypotheses. *Science,* 1890, **15,** 92. (Reprinted in *Science,* 1965, **148,** 754–759.)

Jones, E. E. Conceptual generality and experimental strategy in social psychology. Paper presented at the International Congress of Psychology, Moscow, U.S.S.R., August 1–7, 1966.

McGuire, W. J., & Millman, S. Anticipatory belief lowering following fore-warning of a persuasive attack. *Journal of Personality and Social Psychology,* 1965, **2,** 471–479.

Platt, J. R. Strong inference. *Science,* 1964, **146,** 347–352.

Rosenberg, M. J. When dissonance fails: on eliminating evaluation apprehension from attitude measurement. *Journal of Personality and Social Psychology,* 1965, **1,** 28–42.

Webb, E. J., Campbell, D. T., Schwartz, R. D., & Sechrest, L. *Unobtrusive measures: Nonreactive research in the social sciences.* Chicago: Rand-McNally, 1966.

Weick, K. E. Social psychology in an era of social change. *American Psychologist,* 1969, **24,** 990–998.

SUBJECT INDEX

I

L

M

N

O

P

R

S

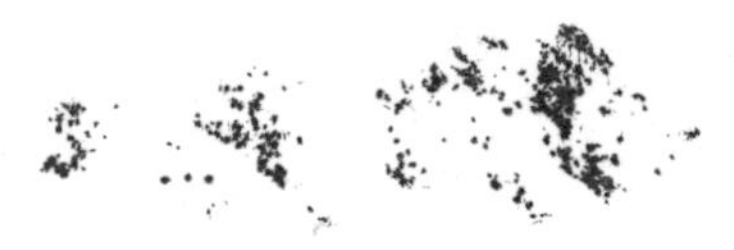

DATE DUE

JUN 2 7 '76			
MAR 5 1980			
FEB 1 7 '83			
FEB 1 6 84			
MAR 1 6 '84			
APR 1 7 1986			
APR 28 '87			
APR 30 '89			
MAY 11 '90			
MAR 18 '96			
APR 15 '96			
MAY 1 3 1996			

GAYLORD PRINTED IN U.S.A.